S0-BJA-662

The Ecocriticism Reader

The Ecocriticism Reader

LANDMARKS IN LITERARY ECOLOGY

Edited by Cheryll Glotfelty and Harold Fromm

■ THE UNIVERSITY OF GEORGIA PRESS ■ ATHENS AND LONDON ■

Athens, Georgia 30602

Designed by Kathi Dailey Morgan
Set in Sabon and Gills Sans by Tseng Information Systems, Inc.
Printed and bound by Thomson-Shore, Inc.
This book is printed on recycled paper that meets the guidelines for permanence and durability of the Committee on Production Guidelines for Book Longevity of the Council on Library Resources.

Printed in the United States of America

00 99 98 97 96 C 5 4 3 2 1

00 99 98 97 96 P 5 4 3 2 1

Library of Congress Cataloging in Publication Data

The ecocriticism reader : landmarks in literary ecology /
Cheryll Glotfelty, ed., Harold Fromm, ed.
p. cm.
Includes bibliographical references and index.
ISBN 0-8203-1780-2 (alk. paper). — ISBN 0-8203-1781-0
(pbk. : alk. paper)
1. Criticism. 2. Ecology in literature. 3. Nature in literature.
I. Glotfelty, Cheryll. II. Fromm, Harold.
PN81.E24 1996
801'95—dc20 95-32150

British Library Cataloging in Publication Data available

CONTENTS

■■■

PREFACE

■ ■ ■

One day late in the 1980s an unsolicited packet arrived in the mail that was radically to alter my professional life as a literary scholar-critic and to have repercussions in my private life as well. The contents consisted of a form letter and bibliography from a Cornell graduate student in English named Cheryll Burgess. She was finishing up a dissertation on three American women writers, but her most intense interest seemed to be the anything-but-apparent connection between literature and the environment. Her plans were ambitious, not to say grandiose: to pursue an interest in ecology while remaining a literary professional, to promulgate the conception of "ecocriticism" while producing an anthology of ecocritical essays, and formally to become the first American professor of literature and the environment.

The bibliography contained more than two hundred essays and books that bore some relation to the idea of ecocriticism, but even more useful was the potential mailing list it provided of authors who might be of some assistance in producing the ecocritical anthology. Writing to most of them, Cheryll Burgess described her aims, included a copy of the bibliography, and waited for replies—which soon began to pour in. One result of this large-scale operation was that I found myself agreeing to serve as chief assistant, although not without some unease that with most of the hard and creative work already done I would emerge in the role of an unearned beneficiary of someone else's groundbreaking labors. Although I have helped to make some decisions and discovered a number of essays to include, this preface gives me the opportunity to disclaim major status.

As things turned out, much more than Cheryll Burgess Glotfelty's original aims have been realized. She has in fact promulgated an awareness of ecocriticism (a term often credited to the essay we have included by William H. Rueckert), she has produced her anthology, and (believe it or not) she has indeed become, as far as we know, the first academic whose appointment includes "literature and the environment" in its title. Furthermore, my own ecological consciousness, which was very great to start with, has been raised beyond anything I could have imagined, because the present enterprise changed the direction of my personal and professional lives by fusing together what had previously been disparate and unrelated activities in literature and in ecology. Professor Glotfelty's substantial influence in the ecological/nature-writing wing of American Studies has touched a large number of other people as well—through her many conference papers, networking activities, and the original bibliography. Fired by her dedication, I organized and chaired the first session on ecocriticism to be offered at the Modern Language Association convention (in 1991), a remarkably well-attended event, at which we discovered the large number of practicing ecocritics that we knew nothing about, many of them starved for colleagues.

In all, I am happy to own up to my pleasure and my debt in having been a part of this fertile enterprise.

Harold Fromm

ACKNOWLEDGMENTS

■ ■ ■

A researcher friend in physics once said that if you want to know how long it will take to complete a project, you must multiply the time you think it will take by two and then raise the answer to the next higher order of magnitude. One indication that the so-called gap between the sciences and the humanities is indeed bridgeable is that the formula that describes experimental physics also obtained in editing this anthology, which has taken not three months but six years to produce.

As the years have stretched on, the number of people who have offered help and encouragement has increased exponentially. It is a privilege to thank them here and to acknowledge our indebtedness for their friendship, advice, and support. For early belief in this book and for their steadfast backing, we owe a great deal to Jean Frantz Blackall, William Howarth, and Glen Love. A four-year Jacob Javits fellowship allowed Cheryll to begin this book while still in graduate school. For their enthusiasm and generosity we would like to thank each of the contributing authors and, in addition, James Applewhite, Lawrence Buell, Del Ivan Janik, Leo Marx, James C. McKusick, Patrick D. Murphy, Val Plumwood, Ann Ronald, Peter Schwenger, Patricia Clark Smith, Denys Trussell, and Frederick Waage.

For their assistance in compiling the list of recommended reading, "virtual" thanks goes to members of the e-mail network for the Association for the Study of Literature and Environment, most especially to Stephen Adams, Karla Armbruster, Jonathan Bate, Ruth Blair, Michael Branch, Lawrence Buell, SueEllen Campbell, Tom Dean, Jim Dwyer, Sara Farris, Jhan Hochman, Mary Jenkins, Michael Kowalewski, Glen Love, Ralph Lutts, Dan Noland, Sean O'Grady, Daniel Patterson, Steve Phelan, Daniel Philippon, Diane Quantic, Elizabeth Raymond, Stephanie Sarver, Tom

Scanlan, Jim Stebbings, Philip Terrie, Paul Tidwell, H. Lewis Ulman, Kathleen Wallace, Louise Westling, and David Williams.

The members of the Association for the Study of Literature and Environment have given us a welcome sense of community, leavening the work with a good deal of fun. Best wishes to Lorraine Anderson, Ralph Black, Paul Bryant, Lawrence Buell, SueEllen Campbell, Carol Cantrell, John Calderazzo, Michael P. and Valerie Cohen, Chris Cokinos, Nancy Cook, Terrell Dixon, Elizabeth Dodd, Jim Dwyer, John Elder, Greta Gaard, Michael Hood, William Howarth, Mark Hoyer, Verne Huser, Zita Ingham, Rochelle Johnson, Glen Love, Tom Lyon, Ian Marshall, Thomas Meyers, David Morris, Michael Munley, Molly Murfee, Patrick Murphy, Alicia Nitecki, Daniel Patterson, Daniel Philippon, Anne Phillips, Michele Potter, Laurie Ricou, David Robertson, Ann Ronald, Susan Rosowski, Suzanne Ross, Kent Ryden, Don Scheese, Mark Schlenz, Matthias Schubnell, Julie Seton, Gary Snyder, Lisa Spaulding, Ron Steffens, Tom Stuckert, Stan Tag, David Taylor, David Teague, Mikel Vause, Allison Wallace, and Louise Westling. Special praise and affection go to Mike Branch, Sean O'Grady, and Scott Slovic.

At the University of Nevada, Reno, Cheryll would like to thank her colleagues for their friendship and support. Stacy Burton and Mary Webb have been particularly wonderful. Sincere thanks are due to Dean of Arts and Sciences Ann Ronald for bold vision and for making things happen, to Robert Merrill for his editorial acumen and dedication to the English Department he chairs, and to secretaries Linda Gorelangton and Geri McVeigh, who make our academic lives not only possible but pleasant. Cheryll would like to acknowledge the students in her Spring 1991 graduate seminar, "Ecocriticism: Literary Criticism and Ecological Consciousness," as well as the graduate students she currently advises, all of whom bring her great intellectual treasures.

Finally, we send love to our family and friends, who make life a joy. Loren, Evelyn, and Stan Acton, Eileen Pape, Laura Koeninger, Gretchen Diether, and Elizabeth Doherty—warmest thanks to you all. Gloria Fromm and Steve Glotfelty, you are always in our hearts and in our lives.

▪ ▪ ▪ The authors and the Press gratefully acknowledge permission to reprint the following pieces:

Paula Gunn Allen, "The Sacred Hoop: A Contemporary Perspective." From *The Sacred Hoop: Recovering the Feminine in American Indian Traditions* by Paula

Gunn Allen. © 1986, 1992 by Paula Gunn Allen. Reprinted by permission of Beacon Press.

SueEllen Campbell, "The Land and Language of Desire: Where Deep Ecology and Post-Structuralism Meet." From *Western American Literature* 24.3 (November 1989): 199–211. Reprinted by permission of *Western American Literature* and the author.

Cynthia Deitering, "The Postnatural Novel: Toxic Consciousness in Fiction of the 1980s." From *Praxis* 4 (1992): 29–36. Reprinted by permission of *Praxis* and the author.

Neil Evernden, "Beyond Ecology: Self, Place, and the Pathetic Fallacy." From *North American Review* 263.4 (Winter 1978): 16–20. Reprinted by permission of *North American Review* and the author.

Harold Fromm, "From Transcendence to Obsolescence: A Route Map." From the *Georgia Review* 32 (Fall 1978): 543–52. Reprinted by permission of the *Georgia Review* and the author.

Annette Kolodny, "Unearthing Herstory: An Introduction" and excerpts from "Making it with Paradise: The Twentieth Century, Some Thoughts for Our Bicentennial." From *The Lay of the Land: Metaphor as Experience and History in American Life and Letters* by Annette Kolodny. © 1984 by the University of North Carolina Press. Reprinted by permission of the University of North Carolina Press and the author.

Ursula K. Le Guin, "The Carrier Bag Theory of Fiction." From *Dancing at the Edge of the World: Thoughts on Words, Women, Places*. © 1986 by Ursula K. Le Guin. Reprinted by permission of Grove/Atlantic, Inc.

Glen A. Love, "Revaluing Nature: Toward an Ecological Criticism." From *Western American Literature* 25.3 (November 1990): 201–15. Reprinted by permission of *Western American Literature* and the author.

Thomas J. Lyon, "A Taxonomy of Nature Writing." From *This Incomperable Lande: A Book of American Nature Writing* edited by Thomas J. Lyon. © 1989 by Thomas J. Lyon. Reprinted by permission of Houghton Mifflin Company.

Christopher Manes, "Nature and Silence." From *Environmental Ethics* 14 (Winter 1992): 339–50. Reprinted by permission of *Environmental Ethics* and the author.

Joseph W. Meeker, "The Comic Mode." From *The Comedy of Survival: Studies in Literary Ecology* by Joseph W. Meeker. New York: Scribner's, 1972. © 1972, 1973, 1974 by Joseph W. Meeker. Reprinted by permission of the author.

Vera L. Norwood, "Heroines of Nature: Four Women Respond to the American Landscape." From *Environmental Review* 8.1 (Spring 1984): 34–56. © 1984 by The American Society for Environmental History. Reprinted by permission of *Environmental Review*.

Dana Phillips, "Is Nature Necessary?" From *Raritan* 13.3 (Winter 1993). © 1993 by *Raritan*, 31 Mine St., New Brunswick, New Jersey, 08903. Reprinted by permission of *Raritan*.

William Rueckert, "Literature and Ecology: An Experiment in Ecocriticism." From the *Iowa Review* 9.1 (Winter 1978): 71–86. Reprinted by permission of the *Iowa Review* and the author.

Scott Russell Sanders, "Speaking a Word for Nature." From *Secrets of the Universe* by Scott Russell Sanders. © 1991 by Scott Russell Sanders. Reprinted by permission of Beacon Press.

Don Scheese, "*Desert Solitaire:* Counter-Friction to the Machine in the Garden." From *North Dakota Quarterly* 59.2 (Spring 1991): 211–27. Reprinted by permission of *North Dakota Quarterly* and the author.

Leslie Marmon Silko, "Landscape, History, and the Pueblo Imagination." From *Antaeus* 57 (Autumn 1986): 83–94. © 1986 by Leslie Marmon Silko. Reprinted by permission of the author, her agent Sara Chalsant, and Wylie, Aitken and Stone Incorporated.

Scott Slovic, "Nature Writing and Environmental Psychology: The Interiority of Outdoor Experience." Adapted from the introduction to *Seeking Awareness in American Nature Writing: Henry Thoreau, Annie Dillard, Edward Abbey, Wendell Berry, and Barry Lopez.* © 1992 by the University of Utah Press. Used by permission of the University of Utah Press.

Frederick Turner, "Cultivating the American Garden." From *Rebirth of Value: Meditations on Beauty, Ecology, Religion, and Education* by Frederick Turner. © 1991 by the State University of New York. Reprinted by permission of the State University of New York Press.

Lynn White, Jr., "The Historical Roots of Our Ecologic Crisis." From *Science* 155.3767 (10 March 1967): 1203–7. © AAAS. Reprinted by permission of the American Association for the Advancement of Science.

CHERYLL GLOTFELTY

Introduction

■ ■ ■

LITERARY STUDIES IN AN AGE OF ENVIRONMENTAL CRISIS

Literary studies in our postmodern age exist in a state of constant flux. Every few years, it seems, the profession of English must "redraw the boundaries" to "remap" the rapidly changing contours of the field. One recent, authoritative guide to contemporary literary studies contains a full twenty-one essays on different methodological or theoretical approaches to criticism. Its introduction observes:

> Literary studies in English are in a period of rapid and sometimes disorienting change. . . . Just as none of the critical approaches that antedate this period, from psychological and Marxist criticism to reader-response theory and cultural criticism, has remained stable, so none of the historical fields and subfields that constitute English and American literary studies has been left untouched by revisionist energies. . . . [The essays in this volume] disclose some of those places where scholarship has responded to contemporary pressures.[1]

Curiously enough, in this putatively comprehensive volume on the state of the profession, there is no essay on an ecological approach to literature. Although scholarship claims to have "responded to contemporary pressures," it has apparently ignored the most pressing contemporary issue of all, namely, the global environmental crisis. The absence of any sign of an environmental perspective in contemporary literary studies would seem to suggest that despite its "revisionist energies," scholarship remains *academic* in the sense of "scholarly to the point of being unaware of the outside world" (*American Heritage Dictionary*).

If your knowledge of the outside world were limited to what you could infer from the major publications of the literary profession, you would quickly discern that race, class, and gender were the hot topics of the late twentieth century, but you would never suspect that the earth's life support systems were under stress. Indeed, you might never know that there was an earth at all. In contrast, if you were to scan the newspaper headlines of the same period, you would learn of oil spills, lead and asbestos poisoning, toxic waste contamination, extinction of species at an unprecedented rate, battles over public land use, protests over nuclear waste dumps, a growing hole in the ozone layer, predictions of global warming, acid rain, loss of topsoil, destruction of the tropical rain forest, controversy over the Spotted Owl in the Pacific Northwest, a wildfire in Yellowstone Park, medical syringes washing onto the shores of Atlantic beaches, boycotts on tuna, overtapped aquifers in the West, illegal dumping in the East, a nuclear reactor disaster in Chernobyl, new auto emissions standards, famines, droughts, floods, hurricanes, a United Nations special conference on environment and development, a U.S. president declaring the 1990s "the decade of the environment," and a world population that topped five billion. Browsing through periodicals, you would discover that in 1989 *Time* magazine's person of the year award went to "The Endangered Earth."

In view of the discrepancy between current events and the preoccupations of the literary profession, the claim that literary scholarship has responded to contemporary pressures becomes difficult to defend. Until very recently there has been no sign that the institution of literary studies has even been aware of the environmental crisis. For instance, there have been no journals, no jargon, no jobs, no professional societies or discussion groups, and no conferences on literature and the environment. While related humanities disciplines, like history, philosophy, law, sociology, and religion have been "greening" since the 1970s, literary studies have apparently remained untinted by environmental concerns. And while social movements, like the civil rights and women's liberation movements of the sixties and seventies, have transformed literary studies, it would appear that the environmental movement of the same era has had little impact.

But appearances can be deceiving. In actual fact, as the publication dates for some of the essays in this anthology substantiate, individual literary and cultural scholars have been developing ecologically informed criticism and theory since the seventies; however, unlike their disciplinary cousins mentioned previously, they did not organize themselves into an identifiable group; hence, their various efforts were not recognized as belonging to a distinct critical school or movement. Individual studies appeared in a wide variety of places and were categorized under a miscellany of subject headings, such as American Studies, regionalism, pastoralism, the frontier, human ecology, science and literature, nature in literature, landscape in literature, or the names of the authors treated. One indication of the disunity of the early efforts is that these critics rarely cited one another's work; they didn't know that it existed. In a sense, each critic was inventing an environmental approach to literature in isolation. Each was a single voice howling in the wilderness. As a consequence, ecocriticism did not become a presence in the major institutions of power in the profession, such as the Modern Language Association (MLA). Graduate students interested in environmental approaches to literature felt like misfits, having no community of scholars to join and finding no job announcements in their area of expertise.

BIRTH OF ENVIRONMENTAL LITERARY STUDIES

Finally, in the mid-eighties, as scholars began to undertake collaborative projects, the field of environmental literary studies was planted, and in the early nineties it grew. In 1985 Frederick O. Waage edited *Teaching Environmental Literature: Materials, Methods, Resources,* which included course descriptions from nineteen different scholars and sought to foster "a greater presence of environmental concern and awareness in literary disciplines."[2] In 1989 Alicia Nitecki founded *The American Nature Writing Newsletter,* whose purpose was to publish brief essays, book reviews, classroom notes, and information pertaining to the study of writing on nature and the environment. Others have been responsible for special environmental issues of established literary journals.[3] Some universities began to include literature courses in their environmental studies curricula, a few inaugurated new institutes or programs in nature and culture, and some English departments began to offer a minor in environmental literature. In 1990 the University of Nevada, Reno, created the first academic position in Literature and the Environment.

Also during these years several special sessions on nature writing or environmental literature began to appear on the programs of annual literary conferences, perhaps most notably the 1991 MLA special session organized by Harold Fromm, entitled "Ecocriticism: The Greening of Literary Studies," and the 1992 American Literature Association symposium chaired by Glen Love, entitled "American Nature Writing: New Contexts, New Approaches." In 1992, at the annual meeting of the Western Literature Association, a new Association for the Study of Literature and Environment (ASLE) was formed, with Scott Slovic elected first president. ASLE's mission: "to promote the exchange of ideas and information pertaining to literature that considers the relationship between human beings and the natural world" and to encourage "new nature writing, traditional and innovative scholarly approaches to environmental literature, and interdisciplinary environmental research." In its first year, ASLE's membership swelled to more than 300; in its second year that number doubled, and the group created an electronic-mail computer network to facilitate communication among members; in its third year, 1995, ASLE's membership had topped 750 and the group hosted its first conference, in Fort Collins, Colorado. In 1993 Patrick Murphy established a new journal, *ISLE: Interdisciplinary Studies in Literature and Environment,* to "provide a forum for critical studies of the literary and performing arts proceeding from or addressing environmental considerations. These would include ecological theory, environmentalism, conceptions of nature and their depictions, the human/nature dichotomy and related concerns."[4]

By 1993, then, ecological literary study had emerged as a recognizable critical school. The formerly disconnected scattering of lone scholars had joined forces with younger scholars and graduate students to become a strong interest group with aspirations to change the profession. The origin of ecocriticism as a critical approach thus predates its recent consolidation by more than twenty years.

DEFINITION OF ECOCRITICISM

What then *is* ecocriticism? Simply put, ecocriticism is the study of the relationship between literature and the physical environment. Just as feminist criticism examines language and literature from a gender-conscious perspective, and Marxist criticism brings an awareness of modes of production and economic class to its reading of texts, ecocriticism takes an earth-centered approach to literary studies.

Ecocritics and theorists ask questions like the following: How is nature represented in this sonnet? What role does the physical setting play in the plot of this novel? Are the values expressed in this play consistent with ecological wisdom? How do our metaphors of the land influence the way we treat it? How can we characterize nature writing as a genre? In addition to race, class, and gender, should *place* become a new critical category? Do men write about nature differently than women do? In what ways has literacy itself affected humankind's relationship to the natural world? How has the concept of wilderness changed over time? In what ways and to what effect is the environmental crisis seeping into contemporary literature and popular culture? What view of nature informs U.S. Government reports, corporate advertising, and televised nature documentaries, and to what rhetorical effect? What bearing might the science of ecology have on literary studies? How is science itself open to literary analysis? What cross-fertilization is possible between literary studies and environmental discourse in related disciplines such as history, philosophy, psychology, art history, and ethics?

Despite the broad scope of inquiry and disparate levels of sophistication, all ecological criticism shares the fundamental premise that human culture is connected to the physical world, affecting it and affected by it. Ecocriticism takes as its subject the interconnections between nature and culture, specifically the cultural artifacts of language and literature. As a critical stance, it has one foot in literature and the other on land; as a theoretical discourse, it negotiates between the human and the nonhuman.

Ecocriticism can be further characterized by distinguishing it from other critical approaches. Literary theory, in general, examines the relations between writers, texts, and the world. In most literary theory "the world" is synonymous with society—the social sphere. Ecocriticism expands the notion of "the world" to include the entire ecosphere. If we agree with Barry Commoner's first law of ecology, "Everything is connected to everything else," we must conclude that literature does not float above the material world in some aesthetic ether, but, rather, plays a part in an immensely complex global system, in which energy, matter, *and ideas* interact.

But the taxonomic name of this green branch of literary study is still being negotiated. In *The Comedy of Survival: Studies in Literary Ecology* (1972) Joseph W. Meeker introduced the term *literary ecology* to refer to "the study of biological themes and relationships which appear in literary works. It is simultaneously an attempt to discover what roles have been played by literature in the ecology of the human species."[5] The term *eco-*

criticism was possibly first coined in 1978 by William Rueckert in his essay "Literature and Ecology: An Experiment in Ecocriticism" (reprinted in this anthology). By ecocriticism Rueckert meant "the application of ecology and ecological concepts to the study of literature." Rueckert's definition, concerned specifically with the science of ecology, is thus more restrictive than the one proposed in this anthology, which includes all possible relations between literature and the physical world.[6] Other terms currently in circulation include *ecopoetics, environmental literary criticism,* and *green cultural studies.*

Many critics write environmentally conscious criticism without needing or wanting a specific name for it. Others argue that a name is important. It was precisely because the early studies lacked a common subject heading that they were dispersed so widely, failed to build on one another, and became both difficult to access and negligible in their impact on the profession. Some scholars like the term *ecocriticism* because it is short and can easily be made into other forms like *ecocritical* and *ecocritic.* Additionally, they favor *eco-* over *enviro-* because, analogous to the science of ecology, ecocriticism studies relationships between things, in this case, between human culture and the physical world. Furthermore, in its connotations, *enviro-* is anthropocentric and dualistic, implying that we humans are at the center, surrounded by everything that is not us, the environment. *Eco-,* in contrast, implies interdependent communities, integrated systems, and strong connections among constituent parts. Ultimately, of course, usage will dictate which term or whether any term is adopted. But think of how convenient it would be to sit down at a computerized database and have a single term to enter for your subject search. . . .

THE HUMANITIES AND THE ENVIRONMENTAL CRISIS

Regardless of what name it goes by, most ecocritical work shares a common motivation: the troubling awareness that we have reached the age of environmental limits, a time when the consequences of human actions are damaging the planet's basic life support systems. We are there. Either we change our ways or we face global catastrophe, destroying much beauty and exterminating countless fellow species in our headlong race to apocalypse. Many of us in colleges and universities worldwide find ourselves in a dilemma. Our temperaments and talents have deposited us in literature departments, but, as environmental problems compound, work as usual seems unconscionably frivolous. If we're not part of the solution, we're part of the problem.

How then can we contribute to environmental restoration, not just in our spare time, but from within our capacity as professors of literature?[7] The answer lies in recognizing that current environmental problems are largely of our own making, are, in other words, a by-product of culture. As historian Donald Worster explains,

> We are facing a global crisis today, not because of how ecosystems function but rather because of how our ethical systems function. Getting through the crisis requires understanding our impact on nature as precisely as possible, but even more, it requires understanding those ethical systems and using that understanding to reform them. Historians, along with literary scholars, anthropologists, and philosophers, cannot do the reforming, of course, but they can help with the understanding.[8]

Answering the call to understanding, scholars throughout the humanities are finding ways to add an environmental dimension to their respective disciplines. Worster and other historians are writing environmental histories, studying the reciprocal relationships between humans and land, considering nature not just as the stage upon which the human story is acted out, but as an actor in the drama. They trace the connections among environmental conditions, economic modes of production, and cultural ideas through time.

Anthropologists have long been interested in the connection between culture and geography. Their work on primal cultures in particular may help the rest of us not only to respect such people's right to survive, but also to think about the value systems and rituals that have helped these cultures live sustainably.

Psychology has long ignored nature in its theories of the human mind. A handful of contemporary psychologists, however, are exploring the linkages between environmental conditions and mental health, some regarding the modern estrangement from nature as the basis of our social and psychological ills.

In philosophy, various subfields like environmental ethics, deep ecology, ecofeminism, and social ecology have emerged in an effort to understand and critique the root causes of environmental degradation and to formulate an alternative view of existence that will provide an ethical and conceptual foundation for right relations with the earth.

Theologians, too, are recognizing that, as one book is subtitled, "The Environment Is a Religious Issue." While some Judeo-Christian theologians attempt to elucidate biblical precedents for good stewardship of the earth, others re-envision God as immanent in creation and view the earth itself as sacred. Still other theologians turn to ancient Earth Goddess worship, Eastern religious traditions, and Native American teachings, belief systems that contain much wisdom about nature and spirituality.[9]

Literary scholars specialize in questions of value, meaning, tradition, point of view, and language, and it is in these areas that they are making a substantial contribution to environmental thinking. Believing that the environmental crisis has been exacerbated by our fragmented, compartmentalized, and overly specialized way of knowing the world, humanities scholars are increasingly making an effort to educate themselves in the sciences and to adopt interdisciplinary approaches.

SURVEY OF ECOCRITICISM IN AMERICA

Many kinds of studies huddle under the spreading tree of ecological literary criticism, for literature and the environment is a big topic, and should remain that way. Several years ago, when I was attempting to devise a branding system that would make sense of this mixed herd, Wallace Stegner—novelist, historian, and literary critic—offered some wise counsel, saying that if he were doing it, he would be inclined to let the topic remain "large and loose and suggestive and open, simply literature and the environment and all the ways they interact and have interacted, without trying to codify and systematize. Systems are like wet rawhide," he warned; "when they dry they strangle what they bind."[10] Suggestive and open is exactly what ecocriticism ought to be, but in order to avoid confusion in the following brief survey of ecocritical work to date, I am going to do some codifying. Let us hereby agree that the system is not to be binding. Nonetheless, Elaine Showalter's model of the three developmental stages of feminist criticism provides a useful scheme for describing three analogous phases in ecocriticism.[11]

The first stage in feminist criticism, the "images of women" stage, is concerned with representations, concentrating on how women are portrayed in canonical literature. These studies contribute to the vital process of consciousness raising by exposing sexist stereotypes—witches, bitches, broads, and spinsters—and by locating absences, questioning the purported universality and even the aesthetic value of literature that distorts or ignores altogether the experience of half of the human race. Analogous efforts in ecocriticism study how nature is represented in literature. Again, consciousness raising results when stereotypes are identified—Eden, Arcadia, virgin land, miasmal swamp, savage wilderness—and when absences are noticed: where *is* the natural world in this text? But nature per se is not the only focus of ecocritical studies of representation. Other topics include the frontier, animals, cities, specific geographical regions, rivers, mountains, deserts, Indians, technology, garbage, and the body.

Showalter's second stage in feminist criticism, the women's literary tradition stage, likewise serves the important function of consciousness raising as it rediscovers, reissues, and reconsiders literature by women. In ecocriticism, similar efforts are being made to recuperate the hitherto neglected genre of nature writing, a tradition of nature-oriented nonfiction that originates in England with Gilbert White's *A Natural History of Selbourne* (1789) and extends to America through Henry Thoreau, John Burroughs, John Muir, Mary Austin, Aldo Leopold, Rachel Carson, Edward Abbey, Annie Dillard, Barry Lopez, Terry Tempest Williams, and many others. Nature writing boasts a rich past, a vibrant present, and a promising future, and ecocritics draw from any number of existing critical theories—psychoanalytic, new critical, feminist, Bakhtinian, deconstructive—in the interests of understanding and promoting this body of literature. As evidence that nature writing is gaining ground in the literary marketplace, witness the staggering number of anthologies that have been published in recent years.[12] In an increasingly urban society, nature writing plays a vital role in teaching us to value the natural world.

Another effort to promulgate environmentally enlightened works examines mainstream genres, identifying fiction and poetry writers whose work manifests ecological awareness. Figures like Willa Cather, Robinson Jeffers, W. S. Merwin, Adrienne Rich, Wallace Stegner, Gary Snyder, Mary Oliver, Ursula Le Guin, and Alice Walker have received much attention, as have Native American authors, but the horizon of possibilities remains suggestively open. Corresponding to the feminist interest in the lives of women authors, ecocritics have studied the environmental conditions of an author's life—the influence of place on the imagination—demonstrating that where an author grew up, traveled, and wrote is pertinent to an understanding of his or her work. Some critics find it worthwhile to visit the places an author lived and wrote about, literally retracing the footsteps of John Muir in the Sierra, for example, to experience his mountain raptures personally, or paddling down the Merrimac River to apprehend better the physical context of Thoreau's meandering prose.

The third stage that Showalter identifies in feminist criticism is the theoretical phase, which is far reaching and complex, drawing on a wide range of theories to raise fundamental questions about the symbolic construction of gender and sexuality within literary discourse. Analogous work in ecocriticism includes examining the symbolic construction of species. How has literary discourse defined the human? Such a critique questions the dualisms prevalent in Western thought, dualisms that separate meaning from matter, sever mind from body, divide men from women, and wrench humanity from nature. A related endeavor is being carried out under the hybrid label "ecofeminism," a theoretical discourse whose theme is the link between the oppression of women and the domination of nature. Yet another theoretical project attempts to develop an ecological poetics, taking the science of ecology, with its concept of the ecosystem and its emphasis on interconnections and energy flow, as a metaphor for the way poetry functions in society. Ecocritics are also considering the philosophy currently known as deep ecology, exploring the implications that its radical critique of anthropocentrism might have for literary study.

THE FUTURE OF ECOCRITICISM

An ecologically focused criticism is a worthy enterprise primarily because it directs our attention to matters about which we need to be thinking. Consciousness raising is its most important task. For how can we solve environmental problems unless we start thinking about them?

I noted above that ecocritics have aspirations to change the profession. Perhaps I should have written that I have such aspirations for ecocriticism. I would like to see ecocriticism become a chapter of the next book that redraws the boundaries of literary studies. I would like to see a position in every literature department for a specialist in literature and the environment. I would like to see candidates running on a green platform elected to the highest offices in our professional organizations. We have witnessed the feminist and multi-ethnic critical movements radically transform the profession, the job market, and the canon. And because they have transformed the profession, they are helping to transform the world.

A strong voice in the profession will enable ecocritics to be influential in mandating important changes in the canon, the curriculum, and university policy. We will see books like Aldo Leopold's *A Sand County Almanac* and Edward Abbey's *Desert Solitaire* become standard texts for courses in American literature. Students taking literature and composition courses will be encouraged to think seriously about the relationship of humans to nature, about the ethical and aesthetic dilemmas posed by the environmental crisis, and about how language and literature transmit values with profound ecological implications. Colleges and universities of the twenty-first century will require that all students complete at least one interdisciplinary course in environmental studies. Institutions of higher learning will one day do business on recycled-content paper—some institutions already do.

In the future we can expect to see ecocritical scholarship becoming ever more interdisciplinary, multicultural, and international. The interdisciplinary work is well underway and could be further facilitated by inviting experts from a wide range of disciplines to be guest speakers at literary conferences and by hosting more interdisciplinary conferences on environmental topics. Ecocriticism has been predominantly a white movement. It will become a multi-ethnic movement when stronger connections are made between the environment and issues of social justice, and when a diversity of voices are encouraged to contribute to the discussion. This volume focuses on ecocritical work in the United States. The next collection may well be an international one, for environmental problems are now global in scale and their solutions will require worldwide collaboration.[13]

In 1985, Loren Acton, a Montana ranch boy turned solar astronomer, flew on the Challenger Eight space shuttle as payload specialist. His observations may serve to remind us of the global context of ecocritical work:

> Looking outward to the blackness of space, sprinkled with the glory of a universe of lights, I saw majesty—but no welcome. Below was a welcoming planet. There, contained in the thin, moving, incredibly fragile shell of the biosphere is everything that is dear to you, all the human drama and comedy. That's where life is; that's where all the good stuff is.[14]

ESSAYS IN THIS COLLECTION

This book is intended to serve as a port of entry to the field of ecocriticism. As ecocriticism gains visibility and influence within the profession, increasing numbers of people have been asking the question, "What *is* ecocriticism?" Many others who are developing an interest in ecocriticism want to know what to read to learn more about this approach to literary studies. Professors who are familiar with ecocriticism and its history nevertheless have had difficulty teaching the subject because until now there has been no general introductory text.

Together, the essays in this anthology provide an answer to the question, "What is ecocriticism?" These essays will help people new to this field to gain a sense of its history and scope, and to become acquainted with its leading scholars. These are the essays with which anyone wishing to undertake ecocritical scholarship ought to be familiar. In addition, this anthology of seminal and representative essays will facilitate teaching; no longer will professors have to rely on the dog-eared photocopies that have been circulating in the ecocritical underground, nor will they need to worry about violating copyright laws.

This sourcebook, consisting of both reprinted and original essays, looks backward to origins and forward to trends. Many of the seminal works of ecocriticism—works of the 1970s by Joseph Meeker, William Rueckert, and Neil Evernden, for example—received little notice when first published, and have since become difficult to obtain. One of the purposes of this anthology is to make available those early gems, thereby acknowledging the roots of modern ecocriticism and giving credit where credit is due. Another purpose of the anthology is to present exemplary recent essays, fairly general in nature, representing a wide range of contemporary ecocritical approaches.

In selecting essays for this volume, then, we have sought to include not only the classics but pieces on the cutting edge. In our coverage of theory, we have avoided essays choked with technical jargon in favor of accessible pieces written in lucid prose. In addition, we have chosen what we consider to be works of brilliance, those pieces that open doors of understanding, that switch on a light bulb in the mind, that help the reader to see the world in a new way. In our coverage of criticism, we have avoided essays that treat a single author or a single work in favor of general essays, discussing a variety of texts and representing a range of critical approaches. While some of the critical essays are argumentative, others are instructional in nature, designed to introduce the reader to a body of literature (such as Native American literature), a genre (such as American nature writing), or a critical approach (such as Bakhtinian dialogics). In short, we sincerely believe that every selection herein is a "must read" essay.

The book is divided into three sections, reflecting the three major phases of ecocritical work. We begin with theory in order to raise some fundamental questions about the relationship between nature and culture and to provide a theoretical foundation upon which to build the subsequent discussions of literary works. The second section studies representations of nature in fiction and drama, including reflections on the ecological significance of literary modes and narrative structures, from Paleolithic hunting stories to postmodern mystery novels. The final section focuses on environmental literature in America, encompassing both Native American stories and the Thoreauvian nature-writing tradition.

I. Ecotheory: Reflections on Nature and Culture

Section one opens with a famous essay by historian Lynn White, Jr., entitled "The Historical Roots of Our Ecologic Crisis." White argues that the environmental crisis is fundamentally a matter of the beliefs and values that direct science and technology; he censures the Judeo-Christian religion for its anthropocentric arrogance and dominating attitude toward nature. White's article sparked heated debate and led to increased environmental consciousness within the Christian church. Christopher Manes in "Nature and Silence" uses the theories of Michel Foucault to consider how both literacy and Christian exegesis have rendered nature silent in Western discourse. He contends that nature has shifted from an animistic to a symbolic presence and from a voluble subject to a mute object, such that in our culture only humans have status as speaking subjects. Harold Fromm in "From Transcendence to Obsolescence: a Route Map" speculates on how the Industrial Revolution affected humanity's conception of its relationship to nature, warning that technology has created the false illusion that we control nature, allowing us to forget that our "unconquerable minds" are vitally dependent upon natural support systems.

While the first three essays discuss versions of alienation from nature, the next two essays analyze how linguistic and aesthetic categories condition the ways that we interact with nature. In "Cultivating the American Garden," Frederick Turner directs our attention to the problem of defining nature. Is the natural opposed to the human? Is the natural opposed to the social and cultural? If everything is natural, then of what use is the term? He discusses cooking, music, landscape painting, and gardening, as healthy mediators between culture and nature. In "The Uses of Landscape:

the Picturesque Aesthetic and the National Park System" Alison Byerly reveals the way that European aesthetics of the picturesque inform management of America's public lands; park administrators are like publishers, she suggests, whose job it is "to produce and market an interpretation of nature's text."

The next three essays of the ecotheory section turn to the science of ecology to consider how this discipline applies to the literary arts. William Howarth's "Some Principles of Ecocriticism" traces the development of the science of ecology, analyzes traditional points of hostility between the sciences and the humanities, and anticipates the ways that ecocriticism will help to forge a partnership between these historic enemy cultures. After outlining a theory and history of ecocritical principles, he describes a basic library of thirty books, distilled from years of interdisciplinary reading. In "Beyond Ecology: Self, Place, and the Pathetic Fallacy" Neil Evernden argues that discoveries in ecology and cellular biology revolutionize our sense of self, teaching us that "there is no such thing as an individual, only an individual-in-context," no such thing as self, only "self-in-place." Accordingly, literature, via metaphor, should help us to *feel* the relatedness of self with place. Writing in 1978, William Rueckert ("Literature and Ecology: An Experiment in Ecocriticism") coins a new term—*ecocriticism*—to describe his endeavor, proposing to "discover something about the ecology of literature," that is, about the way that literature functions in the biosphere. Describing a poem as stored energy, Rueckert explains that reading is an energy transfer and that critics and teachers act as mediators between poetry and the biosphere, releasing the energy and information stored in poetry so that it may flow through the human community and be translated into social action.

The final essays of this section posit environmentalist versions of poststructuralist theory. Whereas some ecocritics condemn poststructuralism for its seeming denial of a physical ground to meaning, SueEllen Campbell ("The Land and Language of Desire: Where Deep Ecology and Post-Structuralism Meet") finds striking parallels in the fundamental premises, critical stance, and basic tactics of poststructuralism and ecological philosophy. David Mazel's "American Literary Environmentalism as Domestic Orientalism" draws upon the theories of Jurij Lotman, Michel Foucault, and, most suggestively, Edward Said, to argue that "the construction of the environment is itself an exercise of cultural power." After demonstrating that "the environment" is a social and linguistic construct, Mazel argues that ecocritics ought to be asking questions on the order of "What has counted as the environment, and what *may* count? Who marks off the conceptual boundaries, and under what authority, and for what reasons?"

II. Ecocritical Considerations of Fiction and Drama

Section two opens with a meditation on narrative by novelist Ursula K. Le Guin entitled "The Carrier Bag Theory of Fiction." Le Guin observes that the (male) activity of hunting has produced a tradition of "death" stories having a linear plot, a larger-than-life hero, and inevitable conflict. She urges that an alternative (female) tradition of "life" stories develop, which might look to seed gathering as its model, conveying a cyclical sense of time, describing a community of diverse individuals, and embracing an ethic of continuity. The next essay, "The Comic Mode," is a chapter from Joseph W. Meeker's pioneering work *The Comedy of Survival* (1972). Speaking as both an ethologist and a scholar of comparative literature, Meeker in this book regards literary production as an important characteristic of the human species—analogous to flight in birds or radar in bats—and he asserts that literature

> should be examined carefully and honestly to discover its influence upon human behavior and the natural environment—to determine what role, if any, it plays in the welfare and survival of mankind and what insight it offers into human relationships with other species and with the world around us. (3–4)

He coins the term *literary ecology* for this enterprise. In the chapter reprinted here, Meeker considers the literary modes of comedy and tragedy, finding that, from an ecological standpoint, comedy promotes healthy, "survival" values, while tragedy is maladaptive.

While Le Guin and Meeker consider literary modes, the remaining essays in this section turn their attention to specific literary works in America from the colonial period to the postmodern. Annette Kolodny's *The Lay of the Land: Metaphor as Experience and History in American Life and Letters* (1975) is by now a classic critique of male-authored American literature, exposing the pervasive metaphor of land-as-woman, both mother and mistress, as lying at the root of our aggressive and exploitive practices. The excerpts reprinted here present the kernel of Kolodny's thesis, concluding that although the land-as-woman metaphor may once have been adaptive, it now must be replaced with a new one. In "Speaking a Word for Nature" Scott Russell Sanders surveys much of the same literary terrain Kolodny does in her book, progressing from Bradford, to Bartram, to Emerson, to Thoreau, to Faulkner, and praising these authors for their strong sense of nature. Sanders finds, however, that contemporary, critically acclaimed fiction lacks an awareness of the natural world that exists outside the "charmed circle" of "the little human morality play," a myopia that mirrors the blindness of our culture at large.

The final two essays in this section consider postmodern and "postnatural" literature, discovering that this literature offers clues to a basic shift in American consciousness. In "The Postnatural Novel: Toxic Consciousness in Fiction of the 1980s" Cynthia Deitering finds contemporary novels to be littered with references to garbage, signaling a fundamental shift in historical consciousness, a shift from a culture defined by its production to a postindustrial culture defined by its waste. In "Is Nature Necessary?" Dana Phillips maintains that the difference between Hemingway and Hiaasen is the difference between modernism and postmodernism. In modernism the roots of culture lie in nature, whereas in postmodernism nature is replaced by commodified representation.

III. Critical Studies of Environmental Literature

Section three serves as a refreshing tonic after the pessimistic accounts of postmodern literature that concluded section two. The lead essay of this section is Glen A. Love's "Revaluing Nature: Toward an Ecological Criticism," one of the most influential essays of the current ecocritical movement. Love first speculates that literary studies have remained indifferent to the environmental crisis in part because our discipline's limited humanistic vision has led to a narrowly anthropocentric view of what is consequential in life. He then recommends that revaluing nature-oriented literature can help redirect us from ego-consciousness to "eco-consciousness."

The willingness to "revalue" nature-oriented literature has led many readers to seek wisdom in Native American texts. These well-meaning readers are often ignorant of the cultural and historical background necessary to understand this literature. In "The Sacred Hoop: A Contemporary Perspective," Paula Gunn Allen characterizes some distinctive ways of perceiving reality and some fundamental assumptions about the universe that inform American Indian literature, making it qualitatively different from Western literary traditions. Leslie Marmon Silko, herself a Laguna Pueblo storyteller, writes in "Landscape, History, and the Pueblo Imagination" about the Pueblo people, describing their relationship to the land of the American Southwest. Pueblo oral narratives function to explain the world, to help people survive in it, and to transmit culture. Specific features of the landscape help people remember the stories, and the stories help them to live in the land; traveling through the storied landscape corresponds to an interior journey of awareness and imagination in which the traveler grasps his or her cultural identity.

One flourishing form of environmental literature in America is the previously undervalued genre of nature writing. Nature writing appears as an "untrampled snowfield," in the words of one scholar, simply inviting critical exploration. The remaining essays in this section provide a general introduction to the genre and represent a broad spectrum of critical approaches to it.

In "A Taxonomy of Nature Writing" Thomas J. Lyon, a leading nature-writing scholar, describes the genre in quasi-taxonomic terms, based on the relative prominence of three important dimensions: natural history information, personal responses to nature, and philosophical interpretation of nature. Michael Branch's "Indexing American Possibilities: The Natural History Writing of Bartram, Wilson, and Audubon" reviews the work of botanist William Bartram, ornithologist Alexander Wilson, and painter John James Audubon to suggest that it is inaccurate to consider Henry David Thoreau the progenitor of American nature writing, that, in fact, Thoreau is a direct heir of the early romantic natural historians, whose contributions deserve recognition. Don Scheese's "*Desert Solitaire:* Counter-Friction to the Machine in the Garden" considers one of Thoreau's most colorful followers, Edward Abbey. Scheese insists that although Abbey resisted the label "nature writer," he nevertheless falls squarely in the tradition of nature writing established by Thoreau and carried on by John Muir and Aldo Leopold, all of whom sought to instill a land ethic in the American public.

In order to convey a sense of the tradition of women's nature writing and to explore the difference between masculine and feminine environmental ethics, Vera L. Norwood ("Heroines of Nature: Four Women Respond to the American Landscape") reviews the work of Isabella Bird, Mary Austin, Rachel Carson, and Annie Dillard, finding that even as these women defend wild nature, their attitude toward it is ambivalent, part of them preferring the safe and the tame. Counterbalancing the many critics of nature writing who appreciate its careful attentiveness to the nonhuman, Scott Slovic ("Nature Writing and Environmental Psychology: The Interiority of Outdoor Experience") claims that the eye of the nature writer is most often turned inward. Nature writers such as Annie Dillard, Edward Abbey, Wendell Berry, and Barry Lopez go to nature in order to induce elevated states of consciousness within themselves, he suspects, and in their accounts of the phenomenon of awareness they are as much literary psychologists as they are natural historians.

The collection concludes with Michael J. McDowell's consideration of what critical approach seems most promising for an ecological analysis of landscape writing. In "The Bakhtinian Road to Ecological Insight" McDowell argues that because the Russian philosopher and literary critic Mikhail Bakhtin incorporates much of the thinking about systems and relationships embraced by the hard sciences, his literary theories provide an ideal perspective for ecocritics, particularly Bakhtin's notions of dialogics, including the "chronotope" and the "carnivalesque." After reviewing Bakhtinian dialogics, McDowell offers several suggestions for undertaking "practical ecocriticism." The end of his essay sounds a perfect final note for this book as a whole, and, indeed, for the ecocritical project in general: "Every text, as Bakhtin unfailingly tells us, is a dialogue open for further comments from other points of view. There is no conclusion."

To enable the reader to pursue further study, we have included some reference material at the back of the book. In order to keep this volume affordably priced and easy to use, we have resisted the temptation to include a comprehensive bibliography on literature and the environment, which would be a book in itself.[15] Instead, we have compiled an annotated bibliography of the most important books in ecocriticism. Selections for the bibliography are based on responses to an electronic-mail survey of 150 ecocritics. Reading these books will provide an excellent grounding in the field. The list of periodicals and professional organizations should help interested readers stay abreast of ecocritical scholarship and will show the lone scholar who howls in the wilderness how to become a member of a growing community of scholars active in ecological literary studies. We trust that this book, like a good map, will inspire intellectual adventurers to explore the ecocritical terrain.

NOTES

1. Stephen Greenblatt and Giles Gunn, eds., *Redrawing the Boundaries: The Transformation of English and American Literary Studies* (New York: MLA, 1992) 1–3.

2. Frederick O. Waage, ed., *Teaching Environmental Literature: Materials, Methods, Resources* (New York: MLA, 1985) viii.

3. Special environmental issues of humanities journals include *Antaeus* 57 (Autumn 1986), ed. Daniel Halpern, reprint, as *On Nature* (San Francisco: North Point Press, 1987); *Studies in the Humanities* 15.2 (December 1988), "Feminism, Ecology and the Future of the Humanities," ed. Patrick Murphy; *Witness* 3.4 (Winter 1989), "New Nature Writing," ed. Thomas J. Lyon; *Hypatia* 6.1 (Spring 1991), "Ecological Feminism," ed. Karen J. Warren; *North Dakota Quarterly* 59.2 (Spring 1991), "Nature Writers/Writing," ed. Sherman Paul and Don Scheese; *CEA Critic* 54.1 (Fall 1991), "The Literature of Nature," ed. Betsy Hilbert; *West Virginia University Philological Papers* 37 (1991), "Special Issue Devoted to the Relationship Between Man and the Environment," ed. Armand E. Singer; *Weber Studies* 9.1 (Winter 1992), "A Meditation on the Environment," ed. Neila C. Seshachari; *Praxis* 4 (1993), "Denatured Environments," ed. Tom Crochunis and Michael Ross; *Georgia Review* 47.1 (Spring 1993), "Focus on Nature Writing," ed. Stanley W. Lindberg and Douglas Carlson; *Indiana Review* 16.1 (Spring 1993), a special issue devoted to writing on nature and the environment, ed. Dorian Gossy; *Ohio Review* 49 (1993), "Art and Nature: Essays by Contemporary Writers," ed. Wayne Dodd; *Theater* 25.1 (Spring/Summer 1994), special section on "Theater and Ecology," ed. Una Chaudhuri; *Weber Studies* 11.3 (Fall 1994), special wilderness issue, ed. Neila C. Seshachari and Scott Slovic.

4. Information on *The American Nature Writing Newsletter,* the Association for the Study of Literature and Environment (ASLE), and *ISLE* can be found in the Periodicals and Professional Organizations section at the back of this book.

5. Joseph W. Meeker, *The Comedy of Survival: Studies in Literary Ecology* (New York: Scribner's, 1972) 9. A chapter of Meeker's seminal work is reprinted in this anthology.

6. Wendell V. Harris in "Toward an Ecological Criticism: Contextual versus Unconditioned Literary Theory" (*College English* 48.2 [February 1986]: 116–31) draws upon Saussure's distinction between *langue* and *parole,* defining "ecological" theories (he includes speech-act theory, the sociology of knowledge, argumentation theory, and discourse analysis) as those that investigate the individual *parole* and the interactive contexts—the "interpretive ecologies" (129)—that make communication possible.

Marilyn M. Cooper in "The Ecology of Writing" (*College English* 48.4 [April

1986]: 364–75) proposes an "ecological model of writing, whose fundamental tenet is that writing is an activity through which a person is continually engaged with a variety of socially constituted systems" (367).

Harris and Cooper use the science of ecology (specifically its concepts of webs, habitat, and community) as an explanatory metaphor to develop a model of human communication, but they do not explore how this human activity interacts with the physical world, and so their studies are not ecocritical as I am proposing that the term be used.

7. Although this book focuses on scholarship, it is through teaching that professors may ultimately make the greatest impact in the world. For ideas on teaching, see Waage, *Teaching Environmental Literature; CEA Critic* 54.1 (Fall 1991), which includes a section entitled "Practicum," 43–77; Cheryll Glotfelty, "Teaching Green: Ideas, Sample Syllabi, and Resources," and William Howarth, "Literature of Place, Environmental Writers," both in *ISLE* 1.1 (Spring 1993): 151–78; Cheryll Glotfelty, "Western, Yes, But Is It Literature?: Teaching Ronald Lanner's *The Pinon Pine*," *Western American Literature* 27.4 (February 1993): 303–10. The Association for the Study of Literature and Environment (ASLE) maintains a syllabus exchange available to its members. For a provocative discussion of the role of higher education in general, see David W. Orr, *Ecological Literacy: Education and the Transition to a Postmodern World* (Albany: State University of New York Press, 1992).

8. Donald Worster, *The Wealth of Nature: Environmental History and the Ecological Imagination* (New York: Oxford University Press, 1993) 27.

9. I do not presume to have full command of the range of environmental work in these and other related fields, but I can direct the reader to some good introductory books and key journals.

In environmental history, see the journal *Environmental History Review*. In addition, see Donald Worster, ed., *The Ends of the Earth: Perspectives on Modern Environmental History* (New York: Cambridge University Press, 1988); Worster, *The Wealth of Nature;* Richard White, "American Environmental History: The Development of a New Historical Field," *Pacific Historical Review* 54.3 (August 1985): 297–335; "A Round Table: Environmental History," *Journal of American History* 76.4 (March 1990), which includes a lead essay by Donald Worster and responding statements by Alfred W. Crosby, Richard White, Carolyn Merchant, William Cronon, and Stephen J. Pyne.

In anthropology, see Marvin Harris, *Cannibals and Kings: The Origins of Cultures* (New York: Vintage, 1991); Mark Nathan Cohen, *Health and the Rise of Civilization* (New Haven: Yale University Press, 1989).

In psychology, see Irwin Altman and Joachim F. Wohlwill, eds., *Behavior and the Natural Environment* (New York: Plenum Press, 1983); Rachel Kaplan and Stephen Kaplan, *The Experience of Nature: A Psychological Perspective* (New York: Cambridge University Press, 1989); Theodore Roszak, *The Voice of the Earth* (New

York: Simon and Schuster, 1992); Morris Berman, *Coming to Our Senses: Body and Spirit in the Hidden History of the West* (New York: Bantam, 1989); Paul Shepard, *Nature and Madness* (San Francisco: Sierra Club, 1982); Theodore Roszak, Mary E. Gomes, and Allen D. Kanner, eds., *Ecopsychology: Restoring the Earth, Healing the Mind* (San Francisco: Sierra Club, 1995).

In philosophy, see the journal *Environmental Ethics*. An excellent introductory anthology is Michael E. Zimmerman et al., eds., *Environmental Philosophy: From Animal Rights to Radical Ecology* (Englewood Cliffs, N.J.: Prentice Hall, 1993). Also good are Carolyn Merchant, *Radical Ecology: The Search for a Livable World* (New York: Routledge, 1992); Max Oelschlaeger, ed., *The Wilderness Condition: Essays on Environment and Civilization* (Washington, D.C.: Island Press, 1992).

In theology, a fine introduction to the current environmental thinking of a variety of the world's major religions is Steven C. Rockefeller and John C. Elder, eds., *Spirit and Nature: Why the Environment Is a Religious Issue* (Boston: Beacon, 1992). See also Charles Birch et al., eds., *Liberating Life: Contemporary Approaches to Ecological Theology* (Maryknoll, N.Y.: Orbis Books, 1990); Eugene C. Hargrove, ed., *Religion and Environmental Crisis* (Athens: University of Georgia Press, 1986).

10. Wallace Stegner, letter to the author, 28 May 1989.

11. See Elaine Showalter, "Introduction: The Feminist Critical Revolution," *The New Feminist Criticism: Essays on Women, Literature, and Theory,* ed. Elaine Showalter (New York: Pantheon, 1985) 3–17. I first presented these ideas in a conference paper: Cheryll Burgess [Glotfelty], "Toward an Ecological Literary Criticism," annual conference of the Western Literature Association, Coeur d'Alene, Idaho, October 1989.

12. The following are only some of the most recent nature writing and nature poetry anthologies:

Adkins, Jan, ed. *Ragged Mountain Portable Wilderness Anthology.* Camden, Maine: International Marine Publishing, 1993.

Anderson, Lorraine, ed. *Sisters of the Earth: Women's Prose and Poetry about Nature*. New York: Vintage, 1991.

Begiebing, Robert J., and Owen Grumbling, eds. *The Literature of Nature: The British and American Traditions*. Medford, N.J.: Plexus, 1990.

Finch, Robert, and John Elder, eds. *The Norton Book of Nature Writing*. New York: Norton, 1990.

Halpern, Daniel, ed. *On Nature*. San Francisco: North Point Press, 1987.

Knowles, Karen, ed. *Celebrating the Land: Women's Nature Writings, 1850–1991*. Flagstaff, Ariz.: Northland, 1992.

Lyon, Thomas J., ed. *This Incomperable Lande: A Book of American Nature Writing*. Boston: Houghton Mifflin, 1989.

Lyon, Thomas J., and Peter Stine, eds. *On Nature's Terms: Contemporary Voices*. College Station: Texas A&M University Press, 1992.

Merrill, Christopher, ed. *The Forgotten Language: Contemporary Poets and Nature*. Salt Lake City: Gibbs M. Smith, 1991.

Morgan, Sarah, and Dennis Okerstrom, eds. *The Endangered Earth: Readings for Writers*. Boston: Allyn and Bacon, 1992.

Murray, John A., ed. *American Nature Writing 1994*. San Francisco: Sierra Club, 1994.

———. *Nature's New Voices*. Golden, Colo.: Fulcrum, 1992.

Pack, Robert, and Jay Parini, eds. *Poems for a Small Planet: Contemporary American Nature Poetry*. Hanover: University Press of New England, 1993.

Ronald, Ann, ed. *Words for the Wild: The Sierra Club Trailside Reader*. San Francisco: Sierra Club, 1987.

Sauer, Peter, ed. *Finding Home: Writing on Nature and Culture from Orion Magazine*. Boston: Beacon, 1992.

Slovic, Scott H., and Terrell F. Dixon, eds. *Being in the World: An Environmental Reader for Writers*. New York: Macmillan, 1993.

Swann, Brian, and Peter Borrelli, eds. *Poetry from the Amicus Journal*. Palo Alto, Calif.: Tioga, 1990.

Walker, Melissa. *Reading the Environment*. New York: Norton, 1994.

Wild, Peter, ed. *The Desert Reader*. Salt Lake City: University of Utah Press, 1991.

13. For a promising first step in international collaboration, see *The Culture of Nature: Approaches to the Study of Literature and Environment*, ed. Scott Slovic and Ken-ichi Noda (Kyoto: Minerva Press, 1995).

14. This quote, and many others from astronauts and cosmonauts around the world, is printed in *The Home Planet*, ed. Kevin W. Kelley (New York: Addison-Wesley, 1988) 21. I am proud to say that Loren Acton is my father.

15. For a reasonably comprehensive bibliography of critical studies of literature and the environment, see Alicia Nitecki and Cheryll Burgess [Glotfelty], eds., "Literature and the Environment: References," *The American Nature Writing Newsletter* 3.1 (Spring 1991): 6–22. An excellent annotated bibliography of nature writing and scholarship appears in Lyon, *This Incomperable Lande* 399–476. The Association for the Study of Literature and Environment (ASLE) publishes an annual bibliography, available to ASLE members; see *Association for the Study of Literature and Environment, ASLE Bibliography 1990–1993*, ed. Zita Ingham and Ron Steffens, which is 120 pages in length, describing 700 works, with annotations and subject divisions.

WORKS CITED

Greenblatt, Stephen, and Giles Gunn, eds. *Redrawing the Boundaries: The Transformation of English and American Literary Studies*. New York: MLA, 1992.

Kelley, Kevin W., ed. *The Home Planet*. New York: Addison-Wesley, 1988.
Meeker, Joseph. *The Comedy of Survival: Studies in Literary Ecology*. New York: Scribner's, 1972.
Rueckert, William. "Literature and Ecology: An Experiment in Ecocriticism." *Iowa Review* 9.1 (Winter 1978): 71–86.
Showalter, Elaine, ed. *The New Feminist Criticism: Essays on Women, Literature, and Theory*. New York: Pantheon, 1985.
Waage, Frederick O., ed. *Teaching Environmental Literature: Materials, Methods, Resources*. New York: MLA, 1985.
Worster, Donald. *The Wealth of Nature: Environmental History and the Ecological Imagination*. New York: Oxford University Press, 1993.

PART ONE

Ecotheory: Reflections on Nature and Culture

LYNN WHITE, JR.

The Historical Roots of Our Ecologic Crisis

■ ■ ■

A conversation with Aldous Huxley not infrequently put one at the receiving end of an unforgettable monologue. About a year before his lamented death he was discoursing on a favorite topic: Man's unnatural treatment of nature and its sad results. To illustrate his point he told how, during the previous summer, he had returned to a little valley in England where he had spent many happy months as a child. Once it had been composed of delightful grassy glades; now it was becoming overgrown with unsightly brush because the rabbits that formerly kept such growth under control had largely succumbed to a disease, myxomatosis, that was deliberately introduced by the local farmers to reduce the rabbits' destruction of crops. Being something of a Philistine, I could be silent no longer, even in the interests of great rhetoric. I interrupted to point out that the rabbit itself had been brought as a domestic animal to England in 1176, presumably to improve the protein diet of the peasantry.

All forms of life modify their contexts. The most spectacular and benign instance is doubtless the coral polyp. By serving its own ends, it has created a vast undersea world favorable to thousands of other kinds of animals and plants. Ever since man became a numerous species he has affected his environment notably. The hypothesis that his fire-drive method of hunting created the world's great grasslands and helped to exterminate the monster mammals of the Pleistocene from much of the globe is plausible, if not proved. For 6 millennia at least, the banks of the lower Nile have been a human artifact rather than the swampy African jungle which nature, apart from man, would have made it. The Aswan Dam, flooding 5000 square miles, is only the latest stage in a long process. In many regions terracing or irrigation, overgrazing, the cutting of forests by Romans to build ships to fight Carthaginians or by Crusaders to solve the logistics problems of their expeditions, have profoundly changed some ecologies. Observation that the French landscape falls into two basic types, the open fields of the north and the *bocage* of the south and west, inspired Marc Bloch to undertake his classic study of medieval agricultural methods. Quite unintentionally, changes in human ways often affect nonhuman nature. It has been noted, for example, that the advent of the automobile eliminated huge flocks of sparrows that once fed on the horse manure littering every street.

The history of ecologic change is still so rudimentary that we know little about what really happened, or what the results were. The extinction of the European aurochs as late as 1627 would seem to have been a simple case of overenthusiastic hunting. On more intricate matters it often is impossible to find solid information. For a thousand years or more the Frisians and Hollanders have been pushing back the North Sea, and the process is culminating in our own time in the reclamation of the Zuider Zee. What, if any, species of animals, birds, fish, shore life, or plants have died out in the process? In their epic combat with Neptune have the Netherlanders overlooked ecological values in such a way that the quality of human life in the Netherlands has suffered? I cannot discover that the questions have ever been asked, much less answered.

People, then, have often been a dynamic element in their own environment, but in the present state of historical scholarship we usually do not know exactly when, where, or with what effects man-induced changes came. As we enter the last third of the twentieth century, however, concern for the problem of ecologic backlash is mounting feverishly. Natural science, conceived as the effort to understand the nature of things, had flourished in several eras and among several peoples. Similarly there had been an age-old accumulation of technological skills, sometimes growing rapidly, sometimes slowly. But it was not until about four generations ago that Western Europe and North America arranged a marriage between science and technology, a union of the theoretical and the empirical approaches to our natural environment. The emergence in widespread practice of the Baconian creed that scientific knowledge means technological power over nature can scarcely be dated before about 1850, save in the chemical industries, where it is anticipated in the eighteenth century. Its acceptance as a normal pattern of action may mark the greatest event in human history since the invention of agriculture, and perhaps in nonhuman terrestrial history as well.

Almost at once the new situation forced the crystallization of the novel concept of ecology; indeed, the word *ecology* first appeared in the English language in 1873. Today, less than a century later, the impact of our race upon the environment has so increased in force that it has changed in essence. When the first cannons were fired, in the early fourteenth century, they affected ecology by sending workers scrambling to the forests and mountains for more potash, sulfur, iron ore, and charcoal, with some resulting erosion and deforestation. Hydrogen bombs are of a different order: a war fought with them might alter the genetics of all life on this planet. By 1285 London had a smog problem arising from the burning of soft coal, but our present combustion of fossil fuels threatens to change the chemistry of the globe's atmosphere as a whole, with consequences which we are only beginning to guess. With the population explosion, the carcinoma of planless urbanism, the now geological deposits of sewage and garbage, surely no creature other than man has ever managed to foul its nest in such short order.

There are many calls to action, but specific proposals, however worthy as individual items, seem too partial, palliative, negative: ban the bomb, tear down the billboards, give the Hindus contraceptives and tell them to eat their sacred cows. The simplest solution to any suspect change is, of course, to stop it, or, better yet, to revert to a romanticized past: make those ugly gasoline stations look like Anne Hathaway's cottage or (in the Far West) like ghost-town saloons. The "wilderness area" mentality invariably advocates deep-freezing an ecology, whether San Gimignano or the High Sierra, as it was before the first Kleenex was dropped. But neither atavism nor prettification will cope with the ecologic crisis of our time.

What shall we do? No one yet knows. Unless we think about fundamentals, our specific measures may produce new backlashes more serious than those they are designed to remedy.

As a beginning we should try to clarify our thinking by looking, in some historical depth, at the presuppositions that underlie modern technology and science. Science was traditionally aristocratic, speculative, intellectual in intent; technology was lower-class, empirical, action-oriented. The quite sudden fusion of these two, towards the middle of the nineteenth century, is surely related to the slightly prior and contemporary democratic revolutions which, by reducing social barriers, tended to assert a functional unity of brain and hand. Our ecologic crisis is the product of an emerging, entirely novel, democratic culture. The issue is whether a democratized world can survive its own implications. Presumably we cannot unless we rethink our axioms.

THE WESTERN TRADITIONS OF TECHNOLOGY AND SCIENCE

One thing is so certain that it seems stupid to verbalize it: both modern technology and modern science are distinctively *Occidental*. Our technology has absorbed elements from all over the world, notably from China; yet everywhere today, whether in Japan or in Nigeria, successful technology is Western. Our science is the heir to all the sciences of the past, especially perhaps to the work of the great Islamic scientists of the Middle Ages, who so often outdid the ancient Greeks in skill and perspicacity: al-Rāzī in medicine, for example; or ibn-al-Haytham in optics; or Omar Khayyám in mathematics. Indeed, not a few works of such geniuses seem to have vanished in the original Arabic and to survive only in medieval Latin translations that helped to lay the foundations for later Western developments. Today, around the globe, all significant science is Western in style and method, whatever the pigmentation or language of the scientists.

A second pair of facts is less well recognized because they result from quite recent historical scholarship. The leadership of the West, both in technology and in science, is far older than the so-called Scientific Revolution of the seventeenth century or the so-called Industrial Revolution of the eighteenth century. These terms are in fact outmoded and obscure the true nature of what they try to describe—significant stages in two long and separate developments. By A.D. 1000 at the latest—and perhaps, feebly, as much as 200 years earlier—the West began to apply water power to industrial processes other than milling grain. This was followed in the late twelfth century by the harnessing of wind power. From simple beginnings, but with remarkable consistency of style, the West rapidly expanded its skills in the development of power machinery, labor-saving devices, and automation. Those who doubt should contemplate that most monumental achievement in the history of automation: the weight-driven mechanical clock, which appeared in two forms in the early fourteenth century. Not in craftsmanship but in basic technological capacity, the Latin West of the later Middle Ages far outstripped its elaborate, sophisticated, and esthetically magnificent sister cultures, Byzantium and Islam. In 1444 a great Greek ecclesiastic, Bessarion, who had gone to Italy, wrote a letter to a prince in Greece. He is amazed by the superiority of Western ships, arms, textiles, glass. But above all he is astonished by the spectacle of waterwheels sawing timbers and pumping the bellows of blast furnaces. Clearly, he had seen nothing of the sort in the Near East.

By the end of the fifteenth century the technological superiority of Europe was such that its small, mutually hostile nations could spill out over all the rest of the world, conquering, looting, and colonizing. The symbol of this technological superiority is the fact that Portugal, one of the weakest states of the Occident, was able to become, and to remain for a century, mistress of the East Indies. And we must remember that the technology of Vasco da Gama and Albuquerque was built by pure empiricism, drawing remarkably little support or inspiration from science.

In the present-day vernacular understanding, modern science is supposed to have begun in 1543, when both Copernicus and Vesalius published their great works. It is no derogation of their accomplishments, however, to point out that such structures as the *Fabrica* and the *De revolutionibus* do not appear overnight. The distinctive Western tradition of science, in fact, began in the late eleventh century with a massive movement of translation of Arabic and Greek scientific works into Latin. A few notable books—Theophrastus, for example—escaped the West's avid new appetite for science, but within less than 200 years effectively the entire corpus of Greek and Muslim science was available in Latin, and was being eagerly read and criticized in the new European universities. Out of criticism arose new observation, speculation, and increasing distrust of ancient authorities. By the late thirteenth century Europe had seized global scientific leadership from the faltering hands of Islam. It would be as absurd to deny the profound originality of Newton, Galileo, or Copernicus as to deny that of the fourteenth century scholastic scientists like Buridan or Oresme on whose work they built. Before the eleventh century, science scarcely existed in the Latin West, even in Roman times. From the eleventh century onward, the scientific sector of Occidental culture has increased in a steady crescendo.

Since both our technological and our scientific movements got their start, acquired their character, and achieved world dominance in the Middle Ages, it would seem that we cannot understand their nature or their present impact upon ecology without examining fundamental medieval assumptions and developments.

MEDIEVAL VIEW OF MAN AND NATURE

Until recently, agriculture has been the chief occupation even in "advanced" societies; hence, any change in methods of tillage has much importance. Early plows, drawn by two oxen, did not normally turn the sod but merely scratched it. Thus, cross-plowing was needed and fields tended to be squarish. In the fairly light soils and semiarid climates of the Near East and Mediterranean, this worked well. But such a plow was inappropriate to the wet climate and often sticky soils of northern Europe. By the latter part of the seventh century after Christ, however, following obscure beginnings, certain northern peasants were using an entirely new kind of plow, equipped with a vertical knife to cut the line of the furrow, a horizontal share to slice under the sod, and a moldboard to turn it over. The friction of this plow with the soil was so great that it normally required not two but eight oxen. It attacked the land with such violence that cross-plowing was not needed, and fields tended to be shaped in long strips.

In the days of the scratch-plow, fields were distributed generally in units capable of supporting a single family. Subsistence farming was the presupposition. But no peasant owned eight oxen: to use the new and more efficient plow, peasants pooled their oxen to form large plow-teams, originally receiving (it would appear) plowed strips in proportion to their contribution. Thus, distribution of land was based no longer on the needs of a family but, rather, on the capacity of a power machine to till the earth. Man's relation to the soil was profoundly changed. Formerly man had been part of nature; now he was the exploiter of nature. Nowhere else in the world did farmers develop any analogous agricultural implement. Is it coincidence that modern technology, with its ruthlessness toward nature, has so largely been produced by descendants of these peasants of northern Europe?

This same exploitive attitude appears slightly before A.D. 830 in Western illustrated calendars. In older calendars the months were shown as passive personifications. The new Frankish calendars, which set the style for the Middle Ages, are very different: they show men coercing the world around them—plowing, harvesting, chopping trees, butchering pigs. Man and nature are two things, and man is master.

These novelties seem to be in harmony with larger intellectual patterns. What people do about their ecology depends on what they think about themselves in relation to things around them. Human ecology is deeply conditioned by beliefs about our nature and destiny—that is, by religion. To Western eyes this is very evident in, say, India or Ceylon. It is equally true of ourselves and of our medieval ancestors.

The victory of Christianity over paganism was the greatest psychic revolution in the history of our culture. It has become fashionable today to say that, for better or worse, we live in "the post-Christian age." Certainly the forms of our thinking and language have largely ceased to be Christian, but to my eye the substance often remains amazingly akin to that of the past. Our daily habits of action, for example, are dominated by an implicit faith in perpetual progress which was unknown either to Greco-Roman antiquity or to the Orient. It is rooted in, and is indefensible apart from, Judeo-Christian teleology. The fact that Communists share it merely helps to show what can be demonstrated on many other grounds: that Marxism, like Islam, is a Judeo-Christian heresy. We continue today to live, as we have lived for about 1700 years, very largely in a context of Christian axioms.

What did Christianity tell people about their relations with the environment?

While many of the world's mythologies provide stories of creation, Greco-Roman mythology was singularly incoherent in this respect. Like Aristotle, the intellectuals of the ancient West denied that the visible world had had a beginning. Indeed, the idea of a beginning was impossible in the framework of their cyclical notion of time. In sharp contrast, Christianity inherited from Judaism not only a concept of time as nonrepetitive and linear but also a striking story of creation. By gradual stages a loving and all-powerful God had created light and darkness, the heavenly bodies, the earth and all its plants, animals, birds, and fishes. Finally, God had created Adam and, as an afterthought, Eve to keep man from being lonely. Man named all the animals, thus establishing his dominance over them. God planned all of this explicitly for man's benefit and rule: no item in the physical creation had any purpose save to serve man's purposes. And, although man's body is made of clay, he is not simply part of nature: he is made in God's image.

Especially in its Western form, Christianity is the most anthropocentric religion the world has seen. As early as the second century both Tertullian and Saint Irenaeus of Lyons were insisting that when God shaped

Adam he was foreshadowing the image of the incarnate Christ, the Second Adam. Man shares, in great measure, God's transcendence of nature. Christianity, in absolute contrast to ancient paganism and Asia's religions (except, perhaps, Zoroastrianism), not only established a dualism of man and nature but also insisted that it is God's will that man exploit nature for his proper ends.

At the level of the common people this worked out in an interesting way. In Antiquity every tree, every spring, every stream, every hill had its own *genius loci,* its guardian spirit. These spirits were accessible to men, but were very unlike men; centaurs, fauns, and mermaids show their ambivalence. Before one cut a tree, mined a mountain, or dammed a brook, it was important to placate the spirit in charge of that particular situation, and to keep it placated. By destroying pagan animism, Christianity made it possible to exploit nature in a mood of indifference to the feelings of natural objects.

It is often said that for animism the Church substituted the cult of saints. True; but the cult of saints is functionally quite different from animism. The saint is not *in* natural objects; he may have special shrines, but his citizenship is in heaven. Moreover, a saint is entirely a man; he can be approached in human terms. In addition to saints, Christianity of course also had angels and demons inherited from Judaism and perhaps, at one remove, from Zoroastrianism. But these were all as mobile as the saints themselves. The spirits *in* natural objects, which formerly had protected nature from man, evaporated. Man's effective monopoly on spirit in this world was confirmed, and the old inhibitions to the exploitation of nature crumbled.

When one speaks in such sweeping terms, a note of caution is in order. Christianity is a complex faith, and its consequences differ in differing contexts. What I have said may well apply to the medieval West, where in fact technology made spectacular advances. But the Greek East, a highly civilized realm of equal Christian devotion, seems to have produced no marked technological innovation after the late seventh century, when Greek fire was invented. The key to the contrast may perhaps be found in a difference in the tonality of piety and thought which students of comparative theology find between the Greek and the Latin Churches. The Greeks believed that sin was intellectual blindness, and that salvation was found in illumination, orthodoxy—that is, clear thinking. The Latins, on the other hand, felt that sin was moral evil, and that salvation was to be found in right conduct. Eastern theology has been intellectualist. Western theology has been voluntarist. The Greek saint contemplates; the Western saint acts. The implications of Christianity for the conquest of nature would emerge more easily in the Western atmosphere.

The Christian dogma of creation, which is found in the first clause of all the Creeds, has another meaning for our comprehension of today's ecologic crisis. By revelation, God had given man the Bible, the Book of Scripture. But since God had made nature, nature also must reveal the divine mentality. The religious study of nature for the better understanding of God was known as natural theology. In the early Church, and always in the Greek East, nature was conceived primarily as a symbolic system through which God speaks to men: the ant is a sermon to sluggards; rising flames are the symbol of the soul's aspiration. This view of nature was essentially artistic rather than scientific. While Byzantium preserved and copied great numbers of ancient Greek scientific texts, science as we conceive it could scarcely flourish in such an ambience.

However, in the Latin West by the early thirteenth century natural theology was following a very different bent. It was ceasing to be the decoding of the physical symbols of God's communication with man and was becoming the effort to understand God's mind by discovering how his creation operates. The rainbow was no longer simply a symbol of hope first sent to Noah after the Deluge: Robert Grosseteste, Friar Roger Bacon, and Theodoric of Freiberg produced startlingly sophisticated work on the optics of the rainbow, but they did it as a venture in religious understanding. From the thirteenth century onward, up to and including Leibnitz and Newton, every major scientist, in effect, explained his motivations in religious terms. Indeed, if Galileo had not been so expert an amateur theologian he would have got into far less trouble: the professionals resented his intrusion. And Newton seems to have regarded himself more as a theologian than as a scientist. It was not until the late eighteenth century that the hypothesis of God became unnecessary to many scientists.

It is often hard for the historian to judge, when men explain why they are doing what they want to do, whether they are offering real reasons or merely culturally acceptable reasons. The consistency with which scientists during the long formative centuries of Western science said that the task and the reward of the scientist was "to think God's thoughts after him" leads one to believe that this was their real motivation. If so, then modern Western science was cast in a matrix of Christian theology. The dynamism of religious devotion, shaped by the Judeo-Christian dogma of creation, gave it impetus.

AN ALTERNATIVE CHRISTIAN VIEW

We would seem to be headed toward conclusions unpalatable to many Christians. Since both *science* and *technology* are blessed words in our contemporary vocabulary, some may be happy at the notions, first, that, viewed historically, modern science is an extrapolation of natural theology and, second, that modern technology is at least partly to be explained as an Occidental, voluntarist realization of the Christian dogma of man's transcendence of, and rightful mastery over, nature. But, as we now recognize, somewhat over a century ago science and technology—hitherto quite separate activities—joined to give mankind powers which, to judge by many of the ecologic effects, are out of control. If so, Christianity bears a huge burden of guilt.

I personally doubt that disastrous ecologic backlash can be avoided simply by applying to our problems more science and more technology. Our science and technology have grown out of Christian attitudes toward man's relation to nature which are almost universally held not only by Christians and neo-Christians but also by those who fondly regard themselves as post-Christians. Despite Copernicus, all the cosmos rotates around our little globe. Despite Darwin, we are *not,* in our hearts, part of the natural process. We are superior to nature, contemptuous of it, willing to use it for our slightest whim. The newly elected Governor of California, like myself a churchman but less troubled than I, spoke for the Christian tradition when he said (as is alleged), "when you've seen one redwood tree, you've seen them all." To a Christian a tree can be no more than a physical fact. The whole concept of the sacred grove is alien to Christianity and to the ethos of the West. For nearly 2 millennia Christian missionaries have been chopping down sacred groves, which are idolatrous because they assume spirit in nature.

What we do about ecology depends on our ideas of the man-nature relationship. More science and more technology are not going to get us out of the present ecologic crisis until we find a new religion, or rethink our old one. The beatniks, who are the basic revolutionaries of our time, show a sound instinct in their affinity for Zen Buddhism, which conceives of the man-nature relationship as very nearly the mirror image of the Christian view. Zen, however, is as deeply conditioned by Asian history as Christianity is by the experience of the West, and I am dubious of its viability among us.

Possibly we should ponder the greatest radical in Christian history since Christ: Saint Francis of Assisi. The prime miracle of Saint Francis is the fact that he did not end at the stake, as many of his left-wing followers did. He was so clearly heretical that a General of the Franciscan Order, Saint Bonaventura, a great and perceptive Christian, tried to suppress the early accounts of Franciscanism. The key to an understanding of Francis is his belief in the virtue of humility—not merely for the individual but for man as a species. Francis tried to depose man from his monarchy over creation and set up a democracy of all God's creatures. With him the ant is no longer simply a homily for the lazy, flames a sign of the thrust of the soul toward union with God; now they are Brother Ant and Sister Fire, praising the Creator in their own ways as Brother Man does in his.

Later commentators have said that Francis preached to the birds as a rebuke to men who would not listen. The records do not read so: he urged the little birds to praise God, and in spiritual ecstasy they flapped their wings and chirped rejoicing. Legends of saints, especially the Irish saints, had long told of their dealings with animals but always, I believe, to show their human dominance over creatures. With Francis it is different. The land around Gubbio in the Apennines was being ravaged by a fierce wolf. Saint Francis, says the legend, talked to the wolf and persuaded him of the error of his ways. The wolf repented, died in the odor of sanctity, and was buried in consecrated ground.

What Sir Steven Ruciman calls "the Franciscan doctrine of the animal soul" was quickly stamped out. Quite possibly it was in part inspired, consciously or unconsciously, by the belief in reincarnation held by the Cathar heretics who at that time teemed in Italy and southern France, and who presumably had got it originally from India. It is significant that at just the same moment, about 1200, traces of metempsychosis are found also in western Judaism, in the Provençal *Cabbala*. But Francis held neither to transmigration of souls nor to pantheism. His view of nature and of man rested on a unique sort of pan-psychism of all things animate and inanimate, designed for the glorification of their transcendent Creator, who, in the ultimate gesture of cosmic humility, assumed flesh, lay helpless in a manger, and hung dying on a scaffold.

I am not suggesting that many contemporary Americans who are concerned about our ecologic crisis will be either able or willing to counsel with wolves or exhort birds. However, the present increasing disruption of the global environment is the product of a dynamic technology and science which were originating in the Western medieval world against which Saint Francis was rebelling in so original a way. Their growth cannot be understood historically apart from distinctive attitudes toward nature which are deeply grounded in Christian dogma. The fact that most people do not think of these attitudes as Christian is irrelevant. No new set of basic values has been accepted in our society to displace those of Christianity. Hence we shall continue to have a worsening ecologic crisis until we reject the Christian axiom that nature has no reason for existence save to serve man.

The greatest spiritual revolutionary in Western history, Saint Francis, proposed what he thought was an alternative Christian view of nature and man's relation to it: he tried to substitute the idea of the equality of all creatures, including man, for the idea of man's limitless rule of creation. He failed. Both our present science and our present technology are so tinctured with orthodox Christian arrogance toward nature that no solution for our ecologic crisis can be expected from them alone. Since the roots of our trouble are so largely religious, the remedy must also be essentially religious, whether we call it that or not. We must rethink and refeel our nature and destiny. The profoundly religious, but heretical, sense of the primitive Franciscans for the spiritual autonomy of all parts of nature may point a direction. I propose Francis as a patron saint for ecologists.

CHRISTOPHER MANES

Nature and Silence

■ ■ ■

A Tuscarora Indian once remarked that, unlike his people's experience of the world, for Westerners, "the uncounted voices of nature . . . are dumb."[1] The distinction, which is borne out by anthropological studies of animistic cultures, throws into stark relief an aspect of our society's relationship with the nonhuman world that has only recently become an express theme in the environmental debate. Nature *is* silent in our culture (and in literate societies generally) in the sense that the status of being a speaking subject is jealously guarded as an exclusively human prerogative.

The language we speak today, the idiom of Renaissance and Enlightenment humanism, veils the processes of nature with its own cultural obsessions, directionalities, and motifs that have no analogues in the natural world. As Max Oelschlaeger puts it, ". . . we are people who presumably must think of the world in terms of the learned categorical scheme of Modernism."[2] It is as if we had compressed the entire buzzing, howling, gurgling biosphere into the narrow vocabulary of epistemology, to the point that someone like Georg Lukács could say, "nature is a societal category"—and actually be understood.[3]

In contrast, for animistic cultures, those that see the natural world as inspirited, not just people, but also animals, plants, and even "inert" entities such as stones and rivers are perceived as being articulate and at times intelligible subjects, able to communicate and interact with humans for good or ill. In addition to human language, there is also the language of birds, the wind, earthworms, wolves, and waterfalls—a world of autonomous speakers whose intents (especially for hunter-gatherer peoples) one ignores at one's peril.

To regard nature as alive and articulate has consequences in the realm of social practices. It conditions what passes for knowledge about nature and how institutions put that knowledge to use.[4] Michel Foucault has amply demonstrated that social power operates through a regime of privileged speakers, having historical embodiments as priests and kings, authors, intellectuals, and celebrities.[5] The words of these speakers are taken seriously (as opposed to the discourse of "meaningless" and often silenced speakers such as women, minorities, children, prisoners, and the insane). For human societies of all kinds, moral consideration seems to fall only within a circle of speakers in communication with one another. We can, thus, safely agree with Hans Peter Duerr when he says that "people do not exploit a nature that speaks to them."[6] Regrettably, our culture has gone a long way to demonstrate that the converse of this statement is also true.

As a consequence, we require a viable environmental ethics to confront the silence of nature in our contemporary regime of thought, for it is within this vast, eerie silence that surrounds our garrulous human subjectivity that an ethics of exploitation regarding nature has taken shape and flourished, producing the ecological crisis that now requires the search for an environmental counterethics.

Recognizing this need, some strains of deep ecology have stressed the link between listening to the nonhuman world (i.e., treating it as a silenced subject) and reversing the environmentally destructive practices modern society pursues.[7] While also underscoring the need to establish communication between human subjects and the natural world, John Dryzek has recently taken exception with this "anti-rationalist" approach of deep ecology, which he suspects is tainted by latent totalitarianism.[8] As an alternative, he proposes to expand Habermas's notion of a discursively rational community to include aspects of the nonhuman, to break the silence of nature, but to retain the language of humanism that suffuses the texts, institutions, and values we commonly celebrate as the flowers of the Enlightenment. Others, such as Murray Bookchin, have in like fashion also attempted to rescue reason from its own successes at quieting the messy "irrationality" of nature, to have their *ratio* and ecology too.[9]

It is a dubious task. By neglecting the origin of this silence in the breakdown of animism, the humanist critics of deep ecology reiterate a discourse that by its very logocentrism marginalizes nature, mutes it, pushes it into a hazy backdrop against which the rational human subject struts upon the epistemological stage. It has become almost a platitude in modern philosophy since Kant that reason (as an institutional motif, not a cognitive faculty) is intimately related to the excesses of political power and self-interest. As Foucault puts it, "we should not need to wait for bureaucracy or concentration camps to recognize the existence of such relations." [10] The easy alliance of power and reason that sustains those institutions involved in environmental destruction also sustains their discourses. Thus, at the very least, we should look askance at the emancipatory claims humanists like Dryzek and Bookchin are still making for reason in the field of environmental philosophy.

In this paper, I want to avoid the jaded polemic between rationality and the irrational, and enter the issue "perpendicularly," so to speak, by taking the silence of nature itself (not the desire to rescue reason, the human subject, or some other privileged motif) as a cue for recovering a language appropriate to an environmental ethics. In particular, this approach requires that I consider how nature has grown silent in our discourse, shifting from an animistic to a symbolic presence, from a voluble subject to a mute object. My aim is neither a critique of reason nor a history of Western representations of nature, both of which have been made happily redundant by a century of scholarship. Rather, I offer a brief genealogy of a discourse, including reason, that has submerged nature into the depths of silence and instrumentality.

Heidegger is surely correct when he argues that all language both reveals and conceals.[11] However, our particular idiom, a pastiche of medieval hermeneutics and Renaissance humanism, with its faith in reason, intellect and progress, has created an immense realm of silences, a world of "not saids" called nature, obscured in global claims of eternal truths about human difference, rationality, and transcendence.[12] If the domination of nature with all its social anxieties rests upon this void, then we must contemplate not only learning a new ethics, but a new language free from the directionalities of humanism, a language that incorporates a decentered, postmodern, post-humanist perspective. In short, we require the language of ecological humility that deep ecology, however gropingly, is attempting to express.

In his comprehensive study of shamanism, Mircea Eliade writes: "All over the world learning the language of animals, especially of birds, is equivalent to knowing the secrets of nature. . . ." [13] We tend to relegate such ideas to the realm of superstition and irrationality, where they can easily be dismissed. However, Eliade is describing the perspective of animism, a sophisticated and long-lived phenomenology of nature. Among its characteristics is the belief (1) that all the phenomenal world is alive in the sense of being inspirited—including humans, cultural artifacts, and natural entities, both biological and "inert," and (2) that not only is the nonhuman world alive, but it is filled with articulate subjects, able to communicate with humans.[14]

Animism undergirds many contemporary tribal societies, just as it did our own during pre-Christian times. Indeed, the overwhelming evidence suggests the universality of animism in human history.[15] Even in modern technological society, animistic reflexes linger on in attenuated form. Cars and sports teams are named after animals (as if to capture sympathetically their power). Children talk to dolls and animals without being considered mentally ill, and are, in fact, read fairy tales, most of which involve talking animals. Respectable people shout at machines that do not operate properly. While modern scholarship tends to focus on "explaining" this kind of thinking in psychological or sociological terms, my interest lies in the sense it gives us of what might be called the "animistic subject," a shifting, autonomous, articulate identity that cuts across the human/nonhuman distinction. Here, human speech is not understood as some unique faculty, but as a subset of the speaking of the world.

Significantly, animistic societies have almost without exception avoided the kind of environmental destruction that makes environmental ethics an explicit social theme with us.[16] Many primal groups have no word for wilderness and do not make a clear distinction between wild and domesticated life, since the tension between nature and culture never becomes acute enough to raise the problem.[17] This fact should strike a cautionary note for those, such as Bookchin and Robert Gardiner, who illegitimately use modern technological societies to stand for all humanity throughout history in global claims about culture compelling humans to "consciously *change* [nature] by means of a highly institutionalized form of community we call 'society.'"[18] Our distracted and probably transitory culture may have this giddy compulsion; culture per se does not.

In the medieval period, animism as a coherent system broke down in our culture, for a variety of reasons.[19] Not the least of these was the introduction of two powerful institutional technologies: literacy and Christian exegesis.

Jack Goody argues that alphabetic writing "changes the nature of the representations of the world," because it allows humans to lay out discourse and "examine it in a more abstract, generalised and 'rational' way."[20] This scrutiny encouraged the epistemological inference, apparently impossible in oral cultures where language exists only as evanescent utterances, that meaning somehow resides in human speech (more particularly in those aspects of it susceptible to rational analysis), not in the phenomenal world. Down this road lies the counterintuitive conclusion that only humans can act as speaking subjects.

Taking Goody's analysis a step farther, David Abram maintains that our relationship with texts is "wholly animistic," since the articulate subjectivity that was once experienced in nature shifted to the written word.[21] At one time nature spoke; now texts do ("it says . . ." is how we describe writing). As cultural artifacts, texts embody human (or ostensibly divine) subjects, but stand conspicuously outside nature, whose status as subject therefore becomes problematical in ways unknown to nonliterate, animistic societies.

The animistic view of nature was further eroded by medieval Christianity's particular mode for interpreting texts, exegesis. Christian theology was clear, if uneasy, on this point: all things—including classical literature, the devil, Viking invasions, sex, and nature—existed by virtue of God's indulgence and for his own, usually inscrutable, purposes.[22] With this point in mind, exegesis, the branch of religious studies dedicated to interpreting the Bible, concluded that behind the *littera,* the literal (often mundane) meaning of a biblical passage, lay some *moralis,* a moral truth established by God. And beyond that lurked some divine purpose, the *anagogue,* almost certainly beyond the ken of human intellect, unless divine revelation obligingly made it evident.

The cognitive practice of exegesis overflowed the pages of the Bible onto other texts and ultimately onto the phenomenal world itself. By the twelfth century, the German philosopher Hugh of St. Victor could talk about "the Book of nature"—a formulation that would have puzzled a Greek or Roman intellectual of the classic period, not to mention Hugh's own tribal ancestors just a few centuries earlier.[23] Like the leaven or mustard seeds in Christ's parables, the things in nature could thus be seen as mere *littera*—signs that served as an occasion for discovering deeper realms of meaning underlying the forms of the physical world. According to medieval commentators, eagles soared higher than any other bird and could gaze upon the sun, undazzled, because they were put on Earth to be a symbol of St. John and his apocalyptic vision, not the other way round. From this hermeneutical perspective, it was inconceivable that eagles should be autonomous, self-willed subjects, flying high for their own purposes without reference to some celestial intention, which generally had to do with man's redemption. Exegesis swept all things into the net of divine meaning.

Such, at least, was the theory (and although it appears alien to modern thought, we should consider that our relationship with nature, despite its outward empiricism, is not that different; we have replaced the search for divine meanings with other "transcendental" concerns such as discerning the evolutionary *telos* of humanity[24]). Exegesis established God as a transcendental subject speaking through natural entities, which, like words on a page, had a symbolic meaning, but no autonomous voice. It distilled the veneration of word and reason into a discourse that we still speak today.

It is, of course, a simplification to suggest that a period as intellectually and institutionally diverse as the Middle Ages experienced nature in one way only.[25] Nevertheless, in broadest terms, for the institutions that dominated discourse during the Middle Ages (i.e., the Church and aristocracy), nature was a symbol for the glory and orderliness of God. This idea found its cosmological model in the so-called *scala naturae* or "Great Chain of Being," a depiction of the world as a vast filigree of lower and higher forms, from zoophytes to Godhead, with humankind's place higher than beasts and a little less than angels, as the Psalm puts it. Curiously, for the medieval exegete, the Great Chain of Being at times acted as a theological restraint against abusing the natural world, at least within the hushed, abstracted cells of the cloister. Thomas Aquinas invoked the *scala naturae* in an argument that—*mutatis mutandis*—could have been made by a conservation biologist condemning monoculture:

> [T]he goodness of the species transcends the goodness of the individual, as form transcends matter; therefore the multiplication of species is a greater addition to the good of the universe than the multiplication of individuals of a single species. The perfection of the universe therefore requires not only a multitude of individuals, but also diverse kinds, and therefore diverse grades of things.[26]

When the Renaissance inherited the *scala naturae,* however, a new configuration of thought that would eventually be called humanism converted it from a symbol of human restraint in the face of a perfect order to an emblem of human superiority over the natural world. Originally a curriculum emphasizing classical learning, humanism came to emphasize a faith in reason, progress, and intellect that would become the cornerstone of modern technological culture.[27] Drawing on humanity's position in the Great Chain between "dumb beasts" and articulate angels, humanism insisted there was an ontological difference between *Homo sapiens* and the rest of the biosphere, infusing a new and portentous meaning to the ancient observation that humans had rational discourse while animals did not. "Man" became, to quote Hamlet, "the beauty of the world! the paragon of animals!" (though Shakespeare, as if aware of the absurdity of the claim, follows this statement with an obscene joke at Hamlet's expense).[28] The tragic soliloquist might have added: the sole subject of the phenomenal world. About the same time *Hamlet* was written, Francis Bacon expressed this teleological craze more bluntly: "Man, if we look to final causes, may be regarded as the centre of the world; inasmuch that if man were taken away from the world, the rest would seem to be all astray, without aim or purpose. . . ."[29]

Strained by the scientific revolution, the celestial links to this chain may have grudgingly come undone in our time (conveniently leaving our species at the apex of the order), but its cultural residue still haunts the human and physical sciences. It is the source of the modern notion that *Homo sapiens* stands highest in a natural order of "lower life forms"—a directionality that comes straight out of the *scala naturae,* which seems to hover translucently before our eyes, distorting our representations of the natural world into hierarchical modes, while itself remaining all but invisible.[30]

The Great Chain of Being, exegesis, literacy, and a complex skein of institutional and intellectual developments have, in effect, created a fictionalized, or more accurately put, fraudulent version of the species *Homo sapiens:* the character "Man," what Muir calls "Lord Man." And this "Man" has become the sole subject, speaker, and rational sovereign of the natural order in the story told by humanism since the Renaissance.[31]

Our representations of nature may have undergone a variety of important permutations since the Middle Ages, molding and conditioning our discourse about respecting or abusing the natural world. But the character of "Man" as the only creature with anything to say cuts across these developments and persists, even in the realm of environmental ethics. It is the fiction reiterated by Bookchin in his teleological description of evolution as "a cumulative thrust toward ever-greater complexity, ever-greater subjectivity, and finally, ever-greater mind with a capacity for conceptual thought, symbolic communication of the most sophisticated kind, and self-consciousness in which natural evolution knows itself purposively and willfully."[32] Through humanism, the boisterous, meandering parade of organic forms is transfigured into a forced march led by the human subject.

It is hardly surprising that this subject should demand such an overbearing role in environmental philosophy. Post-Enlightenment emancipatory thought, from idealism to Marxism to Freud, has made the human subject the expectant ground of all possible knowledge. Empiricism may have initiated an "interrogation" of nature unknown to medieval symbolic thought, but in this questioning no one really expects nature to answer. Rather, the inquiry only offers an occasion to find meanings and purposes that must by default reside in us. As the self-proclaimed soliloquist of the world, "Man" is obliged to use *his* language as the point of intersection between the human subject and what is to be known about nature, and therefore the messy involvement of observer with the observed becomes an obsessive theme of modern philosophy.[33] In the form of the Heisenberg Principle, it has even entered the serene positivism of scientific thought.

Postmodern philosophy has rudely challenged this transcendental narcissism, viewing the subject as fragmented and decentered in the social realm, a product of institutional technologies of control rather than the unmoved mover of all possible knowledge.[34] This challenge has set the stage for the reevaluation of the silence of nature imposed by the human subject. In environmental ethics, however, resistance to the tendentious rhetoric of "Man" has come almost exclusively from the camp of deep ecology.

From one perspective, the biocentric stance of deep ecology may be understood as focusing evolutionary theory and the science of ecology onto the idiom of humanism to expose and overcome the unwarranted claim that humans are unique subjects and speakers. Although regrettably silent on the issue, biologists qua biologists recognize that humans are not the "goal" of evolution any more than tyrannosaurs were during their sojourn on Earth. As far as scientific inquiry can tell, evolution has no goal, or if it does we cannot discern it, and at the very least it does not seem to be us. The most that can be said is that during the last 350 million years natural selection has shown an inordinate fondness for beetles—and before that trilobites.

This observation directly contradicts the *scala naturae* and its use in humanist discourse. From the perspective of biological adaptation, elephants are no "higher" than earwigs; salamanders are no less "advanced" than sparrows; cabbages have as much evolutionary status as kings. Darwin invited our culture to face the fact that in the observation of nature there exists not one scrap of evidence that humans are superior to or even more interesting than, say, lichen.

Predictably, we declined the invitation. Not everyone likes being likened to lichen, and traditional humanists in the environmental debate, explicitly or implicitly, continue to affirm the special subject status of "Man." Bookchin, for instance, insists that humans have a "second nature" (culture) which gives them not only the right but the duty to alter, shape and control "first nature" (the nonhuman world).[35] Henryk Skolimowski sounds a similar trumpet of ecological manifest destiny, proclaiming: "We are here . . . to maintain, to creatively transform, and to carry on the torch of evolution."[36] While refreshingly more restrained, Dryzek seems to accept Habermas's position that the essence of communication is reason—which is not coincidently the kind of discourse favored by human subjects, or more precisely by that small portion of them who are heirs of the Enlightenment. Almost all of us, including biologists, refer to "lower" and "higher" animals, with the tacit understanding that *Homo sapiens* stands as the uppermost point of reference in this chimerical taxonomy. (Contrast this system of arrangement with the decentered and hence more accurate taxonomy of many American Indian tribes who use locutions such as "four-legged," "two-legged," and "feathered.")

It is no exaggeration to say that as a cultural phenomenon, as opposed to a scientific discourse, evolutionary theory has been absorbed by the *scala naturae* and strategically used to justify humanity's domination of nature. Evolution is often represented graphically as a procession of life forms moving left to right, starting with single-celled organisms, then invertebrates, fish, amphibians, and so on up to "Man," the apparent zenith of evolution by virtue of his brain size, self-consciousness, or some other privileged quality. Strictly speaking this tableau, which we have all seen in high school textbooks, only describes *human* evolution, not evolution in general. Nevertheless, for a technological culture transfixed by the presumed supremacy of intellect over nature, human evolution *is* evolution for all intents and purposes. The emergence of *Homo sapiens* stands for the entire saga of biological adaptation on the planet, so that everything that came before takes its meaning, in Baconian fashion, from this one form.[37]

None of this directionality has any corroboration in the natural world. Rather, it belongs to the rhetoric of Renaissance humanism, even though it has also found its way into environmental ethics. Bookchin, for example, has proudly proclaimed that his philosophy is "avowedly humanistic in the high Renaissance meaning of the term," which he associates with "a shift in vision . . . from superstition to reason."[38] It cannot be emphasized enough, however, that, the velleities of humanist philosophers notwithstanding, in nature there simply is no higher or lower, first or second, better or worse.

There is only the unfolding of life form after life form, more or less genealogically related, each with a mix of characteristics. To privilege intellect or self-consciousness, as opposed to photosynthesis, poisoned fangs, or sporogenesis, may soothe ancient insecurities about humanity's place in the cosmos, but it has nothing to do with evolutionary theory and does not correspond to observable nature.

In similar fashion, biocentrism brings to bear the science of ecology upon the exclusionary claims about the human subject. From the language of humanism one could easily get the impression that *Homo sapiens* is the only species on the planet worthy of being a topic of discourse. Ecology paints quite a different, humbling, picture. If fungus, one of the "lowliest" of forms on a humanistic scale of values, were to go extinct tomorrow, the effect on the rest of the biosphere would be catastrophic, since the health of forests depends on *Mycorrhyzal* fungus, and the disappearance of forests would upset the hydrology, atmosphere, and temperature of the entire globe. In contrast, if *Homo sapiens* disappeared, the event would go virtually unnoticed by the vast majority of Earth's life forms. As hominids, we dwell at the outermost fringes of important ecological processes such as photosynthesis and the conversion of biomass into usable nutrients. No lofty language about being the paragon of animals or the torchbearer of evolution can change this ecological fact—which is reason enough to reiterate it as often as possible.

Mercifully, perhaps, there exist other touchstones for appraising human worth besides ecology and evolutionary theory—philosophy, literature, art, ethics, the legacy of the Renaissance and Enlightenment, for the most part, that Dryzek, Bookchin, and other humanist environmentalists clamor to preserve. When, however, the issue is the silencing of nature by the rhetoric of "Man," we need to find new ways to talk about human freedom, worth, and purpose, without eclipsing, depreciating, and objectifying the nonhuman world. Infused with the language of humanism, these traditional fields of knowledge are ill-equipped to do so, wedded as they are to the monologue of the human subject.

Bill Devall, coauthor of *Deep Ecology,* once suggested that deep ecology involves learning a new language.[39] Indeed, environmental ethics must aspire to be more than just an explicit schema of values proclaimed as "true," for ethics are implicated in the way we talk about the world, the way we perceive it. In an attempt to reanimate nature, we must have the courage to learn that new language, even if it puts at risk the privileged discourse of reason—and without a doubt, it does.

A language free from an obsession with human preeminence and reflecting the ontological humility implicit in evolutionary theory, ecological science, and postmodern thought, must leap away from the rhetoric of humanism we speak today. Perhaps it will draw on the ontological egalitarianism of native American or other primal cultures, with their attentiveness to place and local processes. Attending to ecological knowledge means metaphorically relearning "the language of birds"—the passions, pains, and cryptic intents of the other biological communities that surround us and silently interpenetrate our existence. Oelschlaeger has convincingly argued that such relearning is precisely what "wilderness thinkers" such as Thoreau and Snyder are attempting to do.[40]

Dryzek suggests that rational discourse can make an agenda of this listening to place, its requirements and ways. But, as he himself points out, the discourse of reason is not a private attribute, but a communal endeavor. As such, it is enmeshed in the institutions that have silenced nature through the production of various kinds of knowledge—psychological, ethical, political—about "Man."

I am not advocating here a global attack on reason, as if the irrational were the key to the essence of the human being the way humanists claim reason is. I am suggesting the need to dismantle a particular historical use of reason, a use that has produced a certain kind of human subject that only speaks soliloquies in a world of irrational silences. Unmasking the universalist claims of "Man" must be the starting point in our attempt to reestablish communication with nature, not out of some nostalgia for an animistic past, but because the human subject that pervades institutional knowledge since the Renaissance already embodies a relationship with nature that precludes a speaking world. As scholars, bureaucrats, citizens, and writers, we participate in a grid of institutional knowledge that constitutes "Man" and his speaking into the void left by the retreat of animism. Therefore, we have to ask not only how to communicate with nature, as Dryzek does, but *who* should be doing the communicating. "Man," the prime fiction of the Renaissance, will not do.

Perhaps the new language we require can draw upon an earlier practice from our own culture: the medieval contemplative tradition with its sparseness, sobriety, and modesty of speech. Alan Drengson, editor of the deep ecology journal, *The Trumpeter,* has established the Ecostery Project, which hopes to revive a medieval social form: monasteries whose purpose is to promote an understanding of, reverence for, and dialogue with nature. Medieval discourse, for all its absurdities, at times revealed a refined sense of human limitation and respect for otherness, virtues much needed today. The contemplative tradition, too, was a communicating without the agenda of reason.

For half a millennium, "Man" has been the center of conversation in the West. This fictional character has occluded the natural world, leaving it voiceless and subjectless. Nevertheless, "Man" is not an inevitability. He came into being at a specific time due to a complex series of intellectual and institutional mutations, among them the sudden centrality of reason. He could just as inexplicably vanish. To that end, a viable environmental ethics must challenge the humanistic backdrop that makes "Man" possible, restoring us to the humbler status of *Homo sapiens:* one species among millions of other beautiful, terrible, fascinating—and signifying—forms.

As we contemplate the *fin de siècle* environmental ruins that stretch out before us, we can at least be clear about one thing: the time has come for our culture to politely change the subject.

NOTES

A viable environmental ethics must confront "the silence of nature"—the fact that in our culture only humans have status as speaking subjects. Deep ecology has attempted to do so by challenging the idiom of humanism that has silenced the natural world. This approach has been criticized by those who wish to rescue the discourse of reason in environmental ethics. I give a genealogy of nature's silence to show how various motifs of medieval and Renaissance origins have worked together historically to create the fiction of "Man," a character portrayed as sole subject, speaker, and *telos* of the world. I conclude that the discourse of reason, as a guide to social practice, is implicated in this fiction and, therefore, cannot break the silence of nature. Instead, environmental ethics must learn a language that leaps away from the motifs of humanism, perhaps by drawing on the discourse of ontological humility found in primal cultures, postmodern philosophy, and medieval contemplative tradition.

1. Quoted in Hans Peter Duerr, *Dreamtime: Concerning the Boundary Between Wilderness and Civilization,* trans. Felicitas Goodman (Oxford: Basil Blackwell, 1985), p. 90.

2. Max Oelschlaeger, "Wilderness, Civilization, and Language," ed. Max Oelschlaeger, *The Wilderness Condition: Essays on Environment and Civilization* (San Francisco: Sierra Club Books, 1992), p. 273.

3. George Lukács, *History and Class Consciousness,* trans. Rodney Livingstone (Cambridge, Mass.: MIT Press, 1968), p. 234.

4. Surely one reason laws against the inhumane treatment of pets have entered our rigorously anthropocentric jurisprudence must be the sense that domesticated animals communicate with us (presumably in ways wild animals do not) and therefore acquire a vague status as quasi-subjects.

5. See, especially, Michel Foucault, *Madness and Civilization,* trans. Richard Howard (New York: Vintage, 1973), pp. i–x; "What Is an Author?" *Language, Counter-Memory, Practice: Selected Essays and Interviews by Michel Foucault,* ed. Donald F. Bouchard, trans. Donald F. Bouchard and Sherry Simon (Ithaca, N.Y.: Cornell University Press, 1977), pp. 113–38.

6. Duerr, *Dreamtime,* p. 92.

7. See, especially, John Seed, Joanna Macy, Pat Fleming, Arne Naess, *Thinking like a Mountain: Toward a Council of All Beings* (Philadelphia: New Society Publishers, 1988). For an original and enlightening discussion of the interrelationship between language and wilderness, see Oelschlaeger, "Wilderness, Civilization, and Language," pp. 271–308.

8. John S. Dryzek, "Green Reason: Communicative Ethics for the Biosphere," *Environmental Ethics* 12 (1990): 200.

9. Murray Bookchin, *The Ecology of Freedom* (Palo Alto, Calif.: Cheshire Books, 1982).

10. Michel Foucault, *Politics, Philosophy, Culture: Interviews and Other Writings, 1977–1984,* trans. Alan Sheridan (New York: Routledge, 1988), p. 59.

11. Martin Heidegger, *An Introduction to Metaphysics,* trans. Ralph Mannheim (New Haven, Conn.: Yale University Press, 1959), pp. 93–206.

12. I use the term "Renaissance humanism" broadly to include a pastiche of the cultural obsessions mentioned, which have continued through the Enlightenment. The "meaning" of these motifs may change as different institutions use them strategically for different purposes. Nevertheless, they have been consistently deployed in the domination of nature, the issue at hand here.

13. Mircea Eliade, *Shamanism: Archaic Techniques of Ecstacy* (Princeton: Princeton University Press, 1972), p. 98.

14. See Robert H. Lowie, *Primitive Religion* (New York: Boni and Liveright, 1924), pp. 99–135. Like humanism, animism may have many "meanings" depending on how institutions use it, but the institutions in animistic societies tend to wield power in a manner too discontinuous and inefficient to dominate discourse the way ours do. See Stanley Diamond, *In Search of the Primitive: A Critique of Civilization* (New Brunswick, N.J.: Transaction, 1974).

15. See Edward B. Tyler, *Primitive Culture* (New York: Holt and Co., 1889), p. 425; Louise Bàckman and Àke Hultkranz, *Shamanism in Lapp Society* (Stockholm: Alquist and Wiksell, 1978), p. 27. Although Bàckman and Hultkranz only discuss shamanism, it is well-attested that shamanistic practices depend on an animistic world view.

16. The Easter Islanders, whose culture was apparently animistic, are the only

exception I know of, and their problems probably tell us more about the fragility of island ecosystems than social structures.

17. See Darrell Addison Posey, "The Science of the Mebêngôkre," *Orion* (Summer 1990): 16–23; Jon Christopher Crocker, *Vital Souls: Bororo Cosmology, Natural Symbolism, and Shamanism* (Tucson: University of Arizona Press, 1988).

18. Murray Bookchin, "Social Ecology versus 'Deep Ecology': A Challenge for the Ecology Movement," *Green Perspectives, Newsletter of the Green Program Project* 4–5 (Summer 1987): 27; Robert W. Gardiner, "Between Two Worlds: Humans in Nature and Culture," *Environmental Ethics* 12 (1990): 339–52.

19. Animism had already collapsed in classical Mediterranean cultures with the earlier introduction of literacy and humanism. See Morris Berman, *The Reenchantment of the World* (New York: Bantam, 1984), p. 57.

20. Jack Goody, *The Domestication of the Savage Mind* (Cambridge: Cambridge University Press, 1977), p. 37.

21. David Abram, "On the Ecological Consequences of Alphabet Literacy: Reflections in the Shadow of Plato's *Phaedrus*," unpublished essay, 1989.

22. See Arthur O. Lovejoy, *The Great Chain of Being: A Study of the History of an Idea* (Cambridge: Harvard University Press, 1950), pp. 67–98. For a contrast between the exegetical and non-exegetical traditions in the Middle Ages, see Cecil Wood, "The Viking Universe," *Studies for Einar Haugen* (The Hague, Paris: Mouton, 1972), pp. 568–73.

23. Hugh of St. Victor, *The Didascalicon of Hugh of St. Victor: A Medieval Guide to the Arts,* trans. Jerome Taylor (New York: Columbia University Press, 1961), p. 64. The metaphor of the world as a book appeared as early as Augustine's *Confessions,* but it did not begin to mold discourse about nature until the later Middle Ages.

24. For a discussion of the "return of exegesis," see Michel Foucault, *The Order of Things: An Archaeology of the Human Sciences* (New York: Vintage Press, 1973), pp. 297–99.

25. As early as the thirteenth century, Albertus Magnus, mentor of Thomas Aquinas, was already writing "natural histories" that were extra-, if not anti-exegetical. Albertus Magnus, *Man and Beast,* trans. James J. Scanlan (Binghamton, N.Y.: Medieval and Renaissance Texts and Studies, 1987).

26. Thomas Aquinas, *Summa contra gentiles,* bk. 3, chap. 71. Quoted in Lovejoy, *The Great Chain of Being,* p. 77. Aquinas, of course, meant species in the philosophical, not the biological sense, but the principle is strikingly similar.

27. See David Ehrenfeld, *The Arrogance of Humanism* (Oxford: Oxford University Press, 1978).

28. William Shakespeare, *Hamlet,* act 2, sc. 2, lines 306–10.

29. *The Philosophical Works of Francis Bacon,* ed. Robert Leslie Ellis and James Spedding (1905; reprint ed., Freeport, N.Y.: Books for Libraries Press, 1970), 6:747.

30. For a discussion of this "translucent" quality of representations, see Roland Barthes, *Mythologies,* trans. Annette Lavers (New York: Hill and Wang, 1972), pp. 109–59.

31. The concept of "Man" as a fiction is taken from Foucault, *The Order of Things,* though I have shifted his usage to accommodate the theme of nature's silence.

32. Bookchin, "Social Ecology," p. 20.

33. For a comprehensive discussion of the problematic use of the human subject as the ground of knowledge since the Enlightenment, see Foucault, *The Order of Things,* pp. 303–43.

34. See, for instance, Foucault, "Critical Theory/Intellectual History," *Politics, Philosophy, Culture,* pp. 17–46.

35. Bookchin, "Social Ecology," p. 21. In a recent article, Bookchin truculently denies that he endorses the domination of nature, but then goes on to suggest with a straight face that perhaps humans should someday terraform the Canadian barrens (presumably after removing the polar bears) into something more to our liking (or to the liking of whatever institution is powerful enough to carry out such a bizarre scheme). "Recovering Evolution: A Reply to Eckersley and Fox," *Environmental Ethics* 12 (1990): 253–74.

36. Henryk Skolimowski, *Eco-Philosophy* (Boston: Marion Boyers, 1981), p. 68.

37. Although scientists, of course, are well aware of the difference, and do represent evolution in a more genealogically correct manner, the scientific representation lacks the cultural resonance of the humanized tableau.

38. Bookchin, "Social Ecology," p. 20.

39. Bill Devall, personal correspondence, 17 October 1988.

40. Oelschlaeger, "Wilderness, Civilization, and Language."

HAROLD FROMM

From Transcendence to Obsolescence

■ ■ ■

A ROUTE MAP

Although the age-old problem of the conflict between body and mind that has tortured philosophers from Plato to Kant and obsessed the Church from Augustine to Pope Paul has been resolved in modern philosophical thinking by the elimination of "mind" as an autonomous entity, the conflict would appear to have returned again to haunt us in a new guise. The idealized emphasis on "rational" in the concept of man as the rational animal which characterized Platonic-Christian thought for two millennia had generally been the product of man's sense of his own physical weakness, his knowledge that Nature could not be tamed or bent to his own will. In lieu of the ability to mold Nature to serve his own ends, man had chosen to extol and mythify that side of his being that seemed to transcend Nature by inhabiting universes of thought that Nature could not naysay. The triumphs of intellect and imagination by thinkers and artists, and the heroic transcending of the body by saints and martyrs who said "No" to their earthborn limitations, provided for centuries the consolations of a victory that could be obtained not by winning the battle but by changing the battlegrounds.

In the course of human history until the twentieth century there was never any serious likelihood that man could win the body-mind battle on the field of the body. If one found that it was necessary to produce ten children in order to insure the survival of five, if one could be swept away by plagues that killed hundreds of thousands, if one lost one's teeth by thirty, could not be certain of a food supply for more than a few days, carted one's own excrements out to the fields or emptied chamberpots out the window, one could hardly come to believe (despite man's fantastic ability to believe almost anything) that one's ideal self would ever stand forth on the field of the body, in the natural world. Nature was indeed the enemy, whom one propitiated in the forms of gods and goddesses or saints and martyrs, but who would finally do one in en route to one's *true* home, Abraham's bosom. Good sense taught that it was pointless to waste what little life one did have in a quarrel with the cruelty of Nature when the rational solution could only have been to accept a final repose in the kindness of God. If man was indeed made in the image of God, then it was reasonable to assume that only God could fully appreciate "man's unconquerable mind," while a just assessment of reality required that the field of the body be given up—as how could one do otherwise?—to Nature.

The exaltation of religious figures during all of Hebrew-Christian history prior to modern times was an acknowledgement that saints, prophets, priests, and nuns more fully embodied man's spiritual ideals than most people and that an approximation to spiritual perfection, however difficult, was a more realistic goal than that of bodily self-sufficiency or domination over Nature. The fascination with the fall of heroes in history and fiction involved a painful recognition that nothing physical could endure, not merely in the obvious sense that everything created must inevitably die but that everything created can barely stay alive. The philosophy of *carpe diem*—make your sun run fast if you can't make it stand still, to echo Marvell—was never a prevailing one. For most people, the fear of human fragility and a lack of substantial power against the material world made profound self-confidence a luxury only for kings, who themselves derived their power from God. For others, realism required an acceptance of the Divine will: existence was a gift and the creature had no rights. All was grace.

But by the eighteenth century, the rise of industrialism in the West was accompanied by a decline of religion that cannot be seen as an accidental concurrence. And from then on the trend accelerates. As the average man becomes more enabled to live in comfortable houses that resist the elements, to escape most of the childhood diseases that had made fecundity a virtue, to preserve his teeth into middle or old age, to store food for weeks, months, or years ahead, to communicate rapidly through time and space, to move long distances with ease, to dispose of his excrements through indoor plumbing that makes them all magically vanish in a trice, his perception of Nature undergoes a startling alteration. No longer does

Nature seem quite so red in tooth and claw; for a man is much less likely now to perish from the heat or cold, to starve for want of food; his formerly intolerable dependency on the caprices of Nature is no longer so gross; his relation to the other animals and to the vegetable creation appears thickly veiled—by air conditioning, frozen foods, washing machines, detergents, automobiles, electric blankets, and power lawnmowers. And most startling of all, his need for transcendence seems to fade away. For what, after all, is so dreadfully unpleasant about contemporary Western middle-class life that it needs to be transcended? Yes, of course, traffic jams on the freeways are a strain and suburban life can be parodied, but on the scale of things, in relation to man's historical life on earth, the ills of suburbia are not so drastic as to encourage an unduly hasty shuffling off of this mortal coil.

It has been said again and again that modern Western man's comfortable life amidst the conveniences of technology has caused him to suffer a spiritual death, to feel alienated, empty, without purpose and direction. And that may very well be the case. But nevertheless a radical distinction must be made: the need for transcendence experienced by most human beings prior to modern times was a very different one from that which is claimed to exist today. It is not likely that the human race before our time, despite its life dominated by religions and churches and yearnings for transcendence, was a jot more spiritualized than it is today. For if the connection between the growth of industry and the decline of religion is a real one, the earlier spiritual longings appear as an escape from man's vulnerable position in his battle with Nature. It was not that man's aesthetic sensitivities to the Idea of the Good and the Idea of the Beautiful were any more developed in past history; rather, man's need to escape from an intolerable physical life was infinitely greater than ours, for our physical lives are not very oppressive. That "other," "better" world offered by religion could not have been *worse* than the "real" one, even in the duties that it required on earth, and as a mere fantasy it offered extreme gratification. When I speak of man's previous need for transcendence over the insupportable conditions of physical life, I do not refer to the needs of great creative people—artists, thinkers, craftsmen—who by their very temperaments can never be satisfied with any status quo. I speak of the masses of people whose spiritual lives were necessary to make their physical lives endurable and who, had choice been possible, would certainly have preferred physical comforts over spirituality. This situation does not for the most part now exist: television and toilets have made the need for God supererogatory. Western man does not generally live in fear of Nature, except when earthquakes or cancer strike, for he is mostly unaware of a connection with Nature that has been artfully concealed by modern technology. Almost every deprivation has its accessible remedy, whether hunger, cold, illness, or mere distance; and there is rarely a need, except at a few moments during one's lifetime, to go crying either to papa or to God the Father.

If a need for transcendence does exist today, a question that I am not here pursuing, it is in any case not the same need that formerly was so widespread. It is a need based on satiety and not on deprivation, and it does not seek a haven in another world but rather a more beautiful version of this one. What I *am* concerned to examine here is what has happened as a result of the Industrial Revolution to man's conception of his relationship with Nature and what has become the present form of the old mind-body duality.

To the average child of the United States in the present day Nature is indeed a great mystery, not insofar as it is incomprehensible but insofar as it is virtually nonexistent to his perceptions. Not only do most children obtain without delay the nurturing commodities for a satisfied bodily life, but they are rarely in a position to experience a connection between the commodity that fills their need and its natural source. "Meat" consists of red geometrical shapes obtained in plastic packages at the supermarket, whose relationship to animals is obscure if not wholly invisible. Houses are heated by moving a thermostat and clothes are washed by putting them into a washing machine. Even the child's most primitive natural functions are minimally in evidence and it is not surprising that various psychological problems turn up later on in life when man's sensual nature has in some way been concealed at every point by technology. (I recall a student who once remarked that she had no desire to venture out into the country to "enjoy Nature" when she could see all the trees she wanted on color TV.)

The reader should be assured that I am not engaged in presenting these observations in an effort to make the familiar attack on "technology." I have no personal objections to meat in plastic containers or flush toilets and air conditioning. In fact, I like them very much. I have no desire to hunt animals, to chop down trees for firewood, to use an outhouse, or to have smallpox. I have no interest in a "return to Nature," which strikes me as an especially decadent form of aestheticism, like an adult of forty pretending to have the innocence of a child. My consciousness as a person living at a particular stage of history cannot be wiped away by a decision to perform a Marie Antoinette. I would much prefer to listen to music or work in the garden than to struggle for survival. I have presented a picture of a hypothetical child who sees no relation between the red glob in the plastic carton and the animal from which it came, not to attack either technology or modern techniques of child raising. What I am trying to do is to present a picture of man's current relation to Nature.

With Nature barely in evidence and man's physical needs satisfied beyond what could have been imagined one hundred years ago, man's mind would appear to have arrived at a state of altogether new autonomy and independence—not this time the independence of a mind that has given up all hope of dominating Nature and satisfying the flesh and therefore seeking in desperation a haven in Abraham's bosom; rather, this time, a mind so assured of its domination of Nature and its capacity to satisfy the flesh that it seems to be borne up on its own engine of Will, cut off from any nurturing roots in the earth. Mind, now soaring not on wings of fear but on sturdy pinions of volition, can say to Nature, "*Retro Sathanas!*" Do not presume, it would say, to interfere with my self-determination, for if you do, I will flip on the air conditioning, switch on the electronic air cleaner, swallow down the antibiotics, spread on the weed killer, inject the flu vaccine, fill up the gas tank.

But while all of this newfound mental assurance has been building up, when man has finally found a home in the world, when he feels he is lord of all he surveys, when he no longer needs to have his spirit stroked by the right hand of God—a new "trouble" (which I put in quotation marks because it is thought by some to be purely imaginary) rears its ugly head: man's nurturing environment threatens to stop nurturing and to start killing.

One opens the newspaper each day to find four or five articles whose burden is that pesticides contaminate the food of farm animals in Michigan; Kepone is being dumped in waterways, asbestos fibers in Lake Superior; poison gases render uninhabitable a village in Italy; the Parthenon is decaying faster in ten years than in the previous thousand because of automobile exhausts; ozone and sulfur dioxide increase mortality rates in Chicago and Los Angeles.

Although we had been taught in our high-school science classes for decades that neither matter nor energy could be created or destroyed, suddenly it dawns upon someone that the refuse being dumped into the oceans and atmosphere for years and years in ever-increasing quantities does not "go away." Where was it supposed to go? Suddenly, the human race has been put into the position of affluent teen-agers who dump beer cans from their moving sportscar and then drive off. The cans appear to have vanished, but no, there they are, astoundingly enough, rolling around the neighborhood where they had been dumped. And when the teen-agers arrive home, they find other beer cans dumped by other teen-agers. The neighborhood is a place of beer cans; the ocean a place of toxic effluents; the sky is vaporized garbage. And to add insult to injury, man's unconquerable mind turns out to have a mouth, through which it is fed; and worse still, it is being fed garbage. Its own!

Before continuing, let us stop for a moment to see where we have been: in the early days, man had no power over Nature and turned, instead, to his mind and its gods for consolation. Meanwhile, his mind produces a technology that enables his body to be as strong as the gods, rendering the gods superfluous and putting Nature in a cage. Then it appears that there is no Nature and that man has produced virtually everything out of his own ingenuity and it can be bought in a supermarket or a discount store, wrapped in plastic. By now, man is scarcely aware that he is eating animals and producing wastes or that the animals come from somewhere and the wastes are headed somewhere. This "somewhere" turns out to be, practically speaking, a finite world whose basic components cannot be created or destroyed although (and here is the shocker) they can be turned into forms that are unusable by man. As more and more of these basic materials are rendered unusable by man, it becomes apparent that man has failed to see that now, as in the past, the roots of his being are in the earth; and he has failed to see this because Nature, whose effects on man were formerly *immediate,* is now *mediated* by technology so that it appears that technology and not Nature is actually responsible for everything. This has given to man a sense that he mentally and voluntarily determines the ground of his own existence and that his body is almost a dispensable adjunct of his being. This is modern man's own peculiar mythology: The Myth of Voluntary Omnipotence. It is the contemporary form of the Faust legend, a legend which in all of its variants ends the same way.

Nowhere is this modern version of the Faust myth so apparent as in the words of industrial corporations who attack the basic conception of environmental protection. If the classic flaw of the tragic hero is overweening pride and a refusal to acknowledge his own finitude, the contemporary Faustian attitude is archetypically struck in the advertisements of steel and oil companies protesting that "stagnation is the worst form of pollution." The current terminology of doublespeak can be seen in the modish word "trade-offs," a concept which would admirably serve as the basis for present-day tragic drama. One would suppose from such talk that modern industrial corporations, with their fears of economic stagnation and their estimate of clean air as an unaffordable economic luxury, were Shelleyan Prometheuses, defending man's sublime aspirations in the face of a tyrannical and boorish Zeus. *Sic itur ad astra,* indeed!

The continual appearance of the concept of "trade-offs," in which one sacrifices the "luxury" of an uncontaminated environment in order to permit economic "progress," brings to my mind a cartoon that I saw years ago, before anybody ever heard of the environment: two emaciated and threadbare prisoners are bound with manacles and pedicles to the middle of a wall about four stories high in an immense featureless white room. Flailing upon the wall, about two stories above the ground, one enfeebled prisoner says to the other, "Now here's my plan. . . ." Is this not an emblem of modern man? Oblivious of his roots in the earth or unwilling to acknowledge them, intent only upon the desires of his unconquerable mind, he refuses to see that his well-nurtured body and Faustian will are connected by fine tubes—a "life-support system," if you wish—to the earth. Can those Faustian thoughts continue without a narrowly prescribed nutriment for the body, a nutriment prescribed not by that Faustian mind itself but by a biological determination that has been *given* rather than *chosen?* Are not the limitations once described as the will of God and as "grace" as much limitations now as they have ever been in the past? Unless man can create himself, unless he can determine his own existential nature, how can he talk—absurdly, madly, derangedly—about "trade-offs" with the environment or "negotiations" with Nature? Can one negotiate with the *données* of human existence? Even a Promethean Sisyphus needs food to push his rock.

I recently had occasion to publish two essays describing the traumatic effects which polluted air has had upon my wife and me during the past six years, one of my major points being that we are not "cardiac and respiratory patients" but normally healthy people whose lives have been radically altered by industrial emissions since we came to live in the Chicago area. One of these essays, a brief account of our experiences that appeared in the *New York Times* and was subsequently reprinted in other newspapers, brought me a number of interesting and varied responses from readers. A letter that particularly struck me read as follows:

> Dear Sir:
> Since all of the environmentalists who worry about pollution are also consumers of the products of these belching plants (the automobile for instance by which you reach your farm), what IS the answer? Do we cut off our noses to spite our faces? Do we destroy our economy: eliminate many necessities of life; go back to living in tents for the sake of clean air? The answers are complex.

This was a profoundly disturbing letter. The writer was by no means insensitive to the problems of our time; she saw that a complex dilemma is involved; and she was obviously very concerned about the entire affair. Yet her expression "for the sake of clean air" is a familiar one and reveals that the heart of the problem has not been grasped. For when she asks, "Do we eliminate many of the necessities of life for the sake of clean air?" one wants to know: what are the necessities of life in comparison with which clean air cannot be regarded as a necessity? But to ask this is to raise a purely rhetorical question, for the problem is really an ontological and not an ecological one.

When the writer refers to the "necessities of life" one must ask what it is that she means by *life,* and I am proposing that by "life" she means her desires and her will; by the "economy" and "necessities" she means those things which support her mind's conception of itself. There is not a body in sight. She sees steps taken to preserve the environment as actions "for the sake of" clean air. She does not see them as "for the sake of" her own biological existence. *Somehow,* she is alive: she eats food, drinks water, breathes air, but she does not see these actions as *grounds of life;* rather, they are acts that *coincide* with her life, her life being her thoughts and wishes. The purity of the elements that make her life possible is not seen as a condition of existence. Instead, the economy, the "necessities" and not "living in tents" are what matter. *That* is life. Her existence on earth somehow takes care of itself and if it does take care of itself, then why sacrifice the "necessities" of life "for the sake of" the superfluities, like "clean air"?

The pattern of thought which this letter reflects becomes clearer if we make some substitutions: "Do we eliminate necessities of life for the sake of clean air?" could equally well be presented as "Do we give up smoking for the sake of avoiding lung cancer?" since smoking occupies the role (for those who feel they must smoke) of a necessity of life and "avoiding lung cancer" occupies the position of "for the sake of clean air." However, "avoiding lung cancer" can be more clearly stated as "remaining alive," which would then yield the question: "Do we give up smoking for the sake of remaining alive?" And in a final transformation we may obtain: "Do we give up the necessities of life for the sake of remaining alive?" I offer that as the paradigmatic question behind all of the similar ones that people ask. On the surface, we are faced with a paradox: how can someone ask whether it is necessary to give up a condition of life in order to remain alive? But the paradox evaporates when we realize that the "necessity" is no necessity at all, from the viewpoint of our biological existence. Rather, the "necessity" (smoking, the present economy, etc.) is a mental stance, a wish, that in fact is inimical to the survival of the body that would make it possible to continue to fulfill the wish.

We are able to see that this is a variant of the traditional mind-body problem, the view here being that man is his mind, that man is his thoughts and wishes. But man's sublime mind (not to mention the very unsublime wishes described above), while it may wander at will through the universe and be connected to the heavens at one end, is connected at the other to the earth. As free as that mind may appear in its wanderings, thoughts rely on calories, because they are fueled by the same metabolic processes that make all other human activities possible. A thought may have no weight and take up no space, but it exists as part of a stream of consciousness that is made possible by food, air, and water. Every moment of man's existence as a human being is dependent upon a continuous burning up of energy, his classical tragic conflict consisting of a mind that is capable of envisioning modes of existence that are not supportable by a human engine thusly fueled. The confidence of Oedipus that he could outwit causation provides the model for the present environmental dilemma. But there is little that is new about this dilemma besides its peculiarly contemporary terms. The struggle between the "necessities of modern life" and the "environment" is the age-old struggle between the individual will and the universe, the substance, in other words, of classical tragedy.

Thus "the problem of the environment," which many people persist in viewing as a peripheral arabesque drawn around the "important" concerns of human life, must ultimately be seen as a central philosophic and ontological question about the self-definition of contemporary man. For all one's admiration of man's unconquerable mind and its Faustian aspirations, that mind would seem to be eminently conquerable, particularly by itself. It is, after all, a very frail vessel, floating upon a bloodstream that is easily contaminated by every passing impurity: alcohol, nicotine, sulfur dioxide, ozone, Kepone, DDT, sodium nitrite, red dye #2—the list appears endless. As much as at any time in the past, however, man's relationship with Nature is nonnegotiable. Perhaps within a certain narrow range man's constitution is susceptible to adaptation, but in the light of the innumerable and arbitrary concurrences that make human life possible, man's adaptability seems very limited indeed. In the past, man's Faustian aspirations were seen against the background of his terrifying weakness in the face of Nature. Today, man's Faustian posturings take place against a background of arrogant, shocking, and suicidal disregard of his roots in the earth.

FREDERICK TURNER

Cultivating the American Garden

■ ■ ■

Suppose the Grand Canyon were man-made. It could have been formed (though it wasn't) by agricultural or industrial erosion; the results of poor farming methods can look very similar—artificial badlands—if on a smaller scale. Would this hideous scar on the fair face of the earth still be a national park? Would anyone visit it other than groups of awed schoolchildren studying Environmental Destruction, absorbing the dreadful lesson of what can happen to a desert raped by human exploiters? Strip mining can produce spectacular and dramatic landscapes. W. H. Auden loved the lead-mining landscape of Cornwall above all others; the evocative and aromatic hillsides of the Mediterranean, with their olives, sages, thyme, and dwarf conifers, are a result of centuries of deforestation, goat herding, and the building of navies, roads, and cities. The Niagara Falls may one day have to be shored up to make them look "natural"; for they are eating their way back an inch a year and will "naturally" dwindle into ordinary rapids. To an ecologist unschooled in American myth, the most astonishingly unnatural places on earth would be certain regions of the American continent from which the presence of the dominant species—us—had been meticulously removed, as if a million acres had been cleared of earthworms. I mean, of course, the wilderness areas.

The cognitive dissonances that many Americans may have experienced while reading this first paragraph suggest a problem in our use of the words "nature" and "natural." If we define natural as that which is opposed to human, then we must face the fact that we are "scientific" creationists and should be on the side of those who would have the school boards ban even the mention of evolution. If we define natural as that which is opposed to social and cultural, while insisting that humans are natural, then we will have revealed our adherence to a theory of human nature (Rousseau's, actually) asserting that humankind is naturally solitary and unsocial, a theory that all of the human sciences—anthropology, psychology, paleoanthropology, linguistics, ethology—emphatically deny. But if everything that happens is natural, including Love Canal and Alamogordo, then what becomes of our tendency to value the natural and revere nature? And if the word refers to everything, is it of any use at all?

All societies, Lévi-Strauss tells us, distinguish between culture and nature. But the philosophical, moral, and esthetic dimensions of the distinction differ profoundly from one society to another. Indeed, one might almost categorize societies, in a way that would nicely cut across the usual economic, technological, and historical distinctions, solely by the content of their nature/culture distinction. Is nature "good" and culture "bad," or vice versa? Is nature dynamic and culture static, or the other way around? Is nature self-aware and culture innocent? Is nature personal, culture collective? Is it important for a society to emphasize the distinction in some of these categories, while denying it in others? Do not the factional, ideological, and political conflicts within all cultures consist to a large extent in a struggle over the strategic definition of these words and their exclusive possession?

Each of us surely has a pretty good idea of the "correct" answers to these questions of definition; where and how do we learn them? Are we prepared to argue for them? If someone else's answers are different from mine, is she wrong? Tasteless? Wicked?

There is a wonderful exchange on this problem of definition in Shakespeare's *The Winter's Tale*. Perdita has just declared that she won't have carnations or "streak'd gillyvors" in her garden because, like an American nature freak, she disapproves of the fact that they have been bred and hybridized by genetic technology.

> PERDITA . . . There is an art, which in their piedness shares
> With great creating Nature.
>
> POLIXENES Say there be;
> Yet Nature is made better by no mean
> But Nature makes that mean; so, o'er that art,
> Which you say adds to Nature, is an art
> That Nature makes. You see, sweet maid, we marry
> A gentler scion to the wildest stock,
> And make conceive a bark of baser kind
> By bud of nobler race. This is an art
> Which does mend Nature, change it rather; but
> The art itself is Nature.

As usual, Shakespeare says it all: the subtext here is that Perdita is a base shepherdess who wants to marry the prince, Polixenes' son; but of course, she is really a princess herself, though she doesn't know it. Without going into the complexities of lineage, breeding, and social convention that are at work here, let us look at what this passage tells us about gardening. First of all, Shakespeare has clearly grasped the distinction between mere growth and what came to be called evolution. Aristotle amended Plato's system, in which all change was essentially pathological and incoherent, by proposing the notion of a foreordained and meaningful growth proper to each individual species. However, the idea of that radical evolutionary change by which one species turns into another would have been nauseating to him. Shakespeare's Perdita has already observed what Darwin noticed 200 years later, that changes in species can be brought about by selective breeding and hybridization—those primitive forms of recombinant DNA bioengineering. She doesn't like it, but Shakespeare gives Polixenes a remarkable argument in favor of human tampering with the essence of life itself. He takes up Perdita's snide use of the word "art" and turns it around to include perhaps even the very dramatic medium in which he has his being. He insists that human art is not only a product of nature, but one of the creative instruments of nature in doing what it does. *We* are *natura naturans,* nature naturing.

Most of us, asked what nature is, would probably make a vague gesture toward the nearest patch of green vegetation and say, to begin with, something like "Well, it's what's out there, not what's in here." A little prompting would elicit any number of other imaginary characteristics; one can go out into nature, but even when one is in it, it is still "out there." Nature was here before we (the colonists and immigrants) came, and in fact was here before the Indians. Nature bears the weight of our activities, but in the long run renews itself and remains just as it was. Left to itself, nature settles into a balance, a rhythm, that is eternal and unchanging. (Do we not recognize the phrases from countless Walt Disney wildlife movies?) Nature is dangerous but purifying, innocent yet wise, the only real touchstone of what is good and right and beautiful.

It should be clear that this nature has very little in common with natural reality as it is illuminated for us by science. Nature, according to science, is as much "in here" as it is "out there." Our bodies and brains are a result of evolution, which is a natural process so paradigmatic that it could almost be said to be synonymous with nature itself. Moreover, we are by nature social, having been naturally selected, through millions of years of overlapping genetic and cultural evolution, to live in a cooperative cultural matrix. The most powerful selective pressure on our genes since our line broke away from those of the other primates has prompted us toward cities; thus we are by nature hairless, brainy, infantile, gregarious, oversexed, long-lived, artistic, talkative, and religious.

If we want to fall back on saying that the natural is what has not been interfered with, as opposed, say, to the artificial, science will give us little comfort. For a scientist who must take observable and measurable evidence as the only warrant for the reality of being, the universe is exactly and only the interference of everything with everything else. Quantum theory shows that nothing can be observed or measured without being interfered with; if nature is what has not been interfered with, nature does not exist.

Nature, as revealed by evolutionary biology, paleobiology, and geology, is violent, unbalanced, improvisatory, dynamic. The new paradigm in paleobiology, as it is expounded in the symposium, *Earth's Earliest Biosphere: Its Origin and Evolution,* under the editorship of J. William Schopf, holds that the first living inhabitants of the planet, whose metabolisms were anaerobic, so thoroughly poisoned their own ecosphere that they were forced to develop protective mechanisms or to retreat to marginal ecological niches. Indeed, the poison gas with which they polluted the atmosphere was the corrosive element oxygen. Luckily, new life-forms evolved that were able to use the explosive powers of oxygen as a source of energy, and they went on to develop eukaryotic cell structure, multicellular organization, sex, and eventually us.

It is worth quoting the sober prose of some of the contributors to the symposium. J. M. Hayes: "An environment without oxygen, the earth was then a different planet . . . the paleobiological record shows, nevertheless, that life existed on that different planet, and it is widely held that the advent of oxygenic photosynthesis [the release of oxygen as a byproduct of living metabolism using light as an energy source, as modern plants do] was the singular event that led eventually to our modern environment." David J. Chapman and J. William Schopf: "The toxicity of uncombined oxygen is well-established. . . . Obviously, therefore the appearance of oxygen-producing photosynthesis and a resulting oxygenic environment necessitated the development of a series of intracellular protective devices and scavengers, particularly in those organisms producing oxygen and in those nonmobile organisms that were unable to use behavioral mechanisms to escape the effects of this newly abundant reactive gas."

Our precious oxygen, then, is the toxic waste of the first polluters. Imagine the cataclysm this must have been for those early life-forms: for millions of years, the poison advanced and retreated, leaving an extraordinary record of its vicissitudes in iron-banded rock formations, which show alternate layers of rusted (oxidized) and unrusted (unoxidized) iron ore. But the pollution won in the end; and the "natural" species of the time were replaced by what our authors call "a new, highly successful mode of evolutionary advance, one based chiefly on the development of new morphologies and innovative body plans among megascopic, multicellular, sexually reproducing eukaryotes."

It does not get us off the hook to define nature as the unreflexive, the unpremeditated, and thus distinguish it from human cultural activity. Obviously, it would be foolish to impute human values and motives to natural phenomena other than ourselves. But it would be even more foolish to assert uniqueness in the possession of motives and values. It would clearly be wrong to deny that a raccoon can see because it doesn't have the same sort of brain as we do. It would be just as wrong to deny to the raccoon the calculating, and in some sense self-aware, intentions that its every move with relation to the garbage can announces. And when one studies the responses of a whole species' gene pool to environmental change—responses which seem powerfully to imply anticipation and preparation for future changes—one comes to feel that the rest of nature is no more innocent than we. Our cunning and reflexiveness are simply faster than anything else's. Nature's specialty is reflexiveness, and we are better at it than the rest of nature. The DNA molecule is the reflexiveness of matter; the animal mind is the reflexiveness of instinct; the human mind is the reflexiveness of the animal mind.

Nature is the process of increasing self-reference and self-measurement. Evolution is how nature finds out what it is. In the first moment of the Big Bang it didn't have the faintest idea. It didn't even have laws to obey. It lucked into the first ones, and has been improvising in the direction of greater definiteness and concreteness ever since. We human beings are what nature has provisionally defined itself as being, given the richest field of permutations (terrestrial chemistry) and the longest period of unhindered research; indeed, there may well be a scientific sense in which "the proper study of mankind is man."

But if nature is not innocent, perhaps it can still be wise. Alas, no again. Those of us who have seen an incompetent squirrel miss the easy branch he was aiming at, or have reflected more gloomily on the idiotic and improvident proliferation of relatively simple and inflexible biomes (climax forests, for instance), must suspect that nature in general is at least as capable of making mistakes as the representative of it that is most embarrassed by its own mistakes: ourselves.

On the other hand, nature is pathetically willing, as it were. The flowers growing in the desolation of Mount St. Helens testify to what in human beings we would call a lunatic hopefulness, the optimism of the amateur. Or consider the courtship ritual of the blue satin bowerbird, which, convinced that its own color is the most beautiful in the world, builds the bluest nest it can to attract its mate, painting it with chewed-up blueberries and decorating it with blue flowers, bits of blue paper, and its own feathers; a nest which, since it is on the ground and vulnerable to predators, is never used by the lucky bride. (She later builds a sensible little nest in a tree.) This charming unwisdom is more attractive, perhaps, than wisdom. Wisdom sits still and doesn't make a fool of itself. Nature sends in the clowns.

If our prejudices about nature can be so wrong, perhaps we are just as wrong about its antonym, culture. For Americans, culture means to a large extent technology; indeed, the latter might well be named more frequently as the opposite of nature. If nature, in our myth, is eternal, unchanging, pure, gentle, wise, innocent, balanced, harmonious, and good, then culture (*qua* technology) must be temporary, progressive, polluting, violent, blind, sophisticated, distorted, destructive, and evil. At its best, technology is for us an euphoric escape from nature; at its worst, a diabolical destruction of it. Our "gut" meaning for technology is machines of metal, oil, and electricity; we often forget that technology, strictly speaking, also includes the violins of Stradivarius, horsebreeding, handwriting, yeast baking, orchards, cheesemaking, and villanelles.

This ideological opposition of culture and nature—with no mediating term—has had real consequences. More often than need be, Americans confronted with a natural landscape have either exploited it or designated it a wilderness area. The polluter and the ecology freak are two faces of the same coin; they both perpetuate a theory about nature that allows no alternative to raping it or tying it up in a plastic bag to protect it from contamination.

How did we come to this peculiar view of nature and culture? The two great historical givens in American culture are Puritanism and the frontier. The defining characteristic of Puritanism is its denial of the validity and permissibility of mediating terms. Puritanism abhors the corruptions of ritual and mystery. It insists upon an absolute sincerity untainted by practical or esthetic considerations; it has promoted a view of marriage in which any compromise with family and property interests is a base betrayal of the spiritual absolute of love; and, as is clear in the works of Nathaniel Hawthorne, it has a horror of any spiritual miscegenation between the human and the natural. Like the small boy who will eat only food whose living origin has been utterly pummeled out of it, the Puritan likes his nature as spiritually dead as a doornail.

The frontier experience both confirmed and profoundly modified this predisposition. In the first place, the frontier seemed to be the embodiment of the boundary between matter and spirit. Matter was "out there" beyond the frontier; spirit was "in here" among the brethren; and the witch-hunt preserved the distinction. But the Puritan distrust of the means of expression and of the accommodations and compromises that make society possible led to a revulsion of feeling that we find raised to noble eloquence and genuine insight in the works of Thoreau. The true assertion of the purity of the spirit was to "go back to nature," to build a cabin in the woods, to ship aboard a whaler, to be a mountain man, to "light out for the Territory," as Huck Finn puts it, and leave behind the soft, corrupting, and emasculating sophistications of "sivilization." In nature one could discover for oneself the real meaning of America's political liberation: our natural solitude, our natural equality, our natural selfishness. From this myth has come great good and great evil: the realized ideal of huge populations living in freedom from the ancient and degrading limitations of conservative technologies, as well as the heroic glory of the space program—but also the daily abandonment of wives by their husbands and the odd ethics of defaulting on child support.

If nature is the opposite of society, then the natural man is essentially asocial, or even antisocial. So Rousseau argued, at any rate, and though the idea has done more damage in France than in America, it has been very influential on this side of the Atlantic. To its credit, it has been used to justify the sturdy individualism enshrined in the Constitution; we vote one by one in the privacy of a booth, and this solitary act is at the core of our political system. Likewise, we vote by our choice of purchase in the free market, and our instinctual bias for the individual helps defend the market against the pressures of monopoly capitalism, paternalistic government, restrictive trade unions, and puritanical consumer groups. If the most important human unit is the individual, then the courts should rule in favor of the individual in every case where he or she comes into conflict with other human units (the family, the neighborhood, the corporate body).

As an empirical fact, our natural solitude has little scientific foundation. We evolved as social beings; our ancestors were tribal; our babies cannot grow up without the company of their kind, and so an *enfant sauvage*, that ancient human dream of innocence, would be impossible; our closest relatives, the chimpanzees and gorillas, are so social that it has been said that "one chimpanzee is no chimpanzees." The notion of natural solitude has thus introduced distortions into what might otherwise have been a more harmonious balance of constitutional guarantees. Those distortions include the neglect and isolation of persons, especially the young and old; we regard privacy as a natural right, but not community, which may well be a more important human need. As the Talking Heads have said of "people like us," we don't want freedom, we don't want justice, we just want someone to love.

The notion of natural equality has been brought to the rescue of that grand old phrase in the Declaration of Independence: "We hold these truths to be self-evident; that all men are created equal." This phrase appears to be an empirical statement about human nature and as such is buttressed by the authority of Plato, Hobbes, and Rousseau. But suppose it were simply wrong? There is virtual unanimity among the human sciences that great variations in natural abilities exist among human beings. Indeed, a social species based on the cooperative division of labor cannot survive without variation in natural capacities. Is it not therefore unwise to hold the Constitution hostage to an erroneous claim that equality is an empirical fact? The wording of this phrase (we "hold" these truths to be truths) suggests a wiser alternative: that equality is something we stipulate as a ground rule, perhaps as a corrective to our natural inequality.

Other distortions have been created by the notion of natural self-interest. Modern sociobiology, anthropology, and psychology show that self-interest is not the fundamental human drive but only one of several, which include deeply instinctive impulses toward altruism, sacrifice, agonistic behavior, gregariousness, and loyalty. The entirely self-interested individual is clearly a grotesque pathological aberration produced by extraordinary circumstances, the exception that proves the rule. Perhaps those circumstances might be reproduced if the impersonal state or corporation were totally to supplant the community (which is what Pol Pot, no doubt a devoted student of Rousseau during his years in Paris, was trying to do in Cambodia), but the last few years have shown how durable, indeed how unexpectedly flourishing, are the ethnic, religious, and microcultural communities in the heart of the modern world.

Do the Europeans handle the nature/culture distinction any better than we? In some sense, yes. The greatest moments of European cultural brilliance have overcome the falseness and the sterility of the distinction: the gardens of Hadrian, of the Medicis, of the Bourbons, of the great English gardeners. Perhaps the Republic itself. The Renaissance city. The lovers in Shakespeare and Mozart. French and Italian cuisine. The bourgeois family, that vitally creative—if flawed—institution. Claude Lorrain and Nicholas Poussin and Claude Monet. Baroque music. Gardens, music, landscape painting, cooking: each mediates between culture and nature in a fertile and inventive way.

But the Europeans have run up against the limits of their own ideas. For Europe, freedom is a choice between alternatives that are finally limited. Culture and nature may be in greater harmony, but they are both constrained by a system that is entropically running down. For Americans, true freedom is not the choice at the ballot box but the opportunity to create a new world out of nothing: a Beverly Hills, a Disneyland, a Dallas, a Tranquility Base. Growth can still happen in Europe, but evolution will happen in America, if its academic discouragers do not prevail—and it will take place in the personal as well as the cosmic sphere.

The European model of kinship is parental: we are defined by where and whom we came from, and the cause, the parent, is more full of that quality that characterizes the effect than is the effect itself. Only if the child can transcend the parent, and if the parent measures her own success solely by the transcendence, can evolution take place in the cultural realm. Americans model kinship not on parenthood but on marriage; not on the relationship we are given but on the relationship we create. So the child can be greater than the parent, the effect more essential than the cause, the creation more creative than the creator; even eternity, as Blake (a natural American) put it, is in love with the productions of time. The European past is a prison; the American past is the most wonderful raw material. The European future is "held in store," as they say; but the American futures are to be created.

We do not need to accept our myth of nature and culture. The state of America is the state of being able to change our myths. We can forge in the smithies of our souls the conscience of our race, a project James Joyce gave up as impossible for Ireland. Thoreau rejoiced in the indubitable capacity to change himself by conscious endeavor; the wood of Melville's ship of human destiny "could only be American."

But Thoreau and Melville still bear the marks of damage by the American myth; both needed to escape the complications of heterosexual relationships and go back to nature, to achieve what they achieved. Henry James and T. S. Eliot had to move to England to begin to garden their impressions. Contemporary women writers must likewise dismiss the male culture to find a space to breathe, and must likewise suffer an impoverishment of that "radiant and porous" creativity which Virginia Woolf rightly located in androgyny. So, then: How do we change our myth? What model do we use to heal the breach in our ideas and to release the enormous cultural energies of a new American renaissance?

I believe that we must trust human intention more than human instinct, because intention evolved out of and as an improvement upon instinct. But if intention is to be thus trusted, it must be fully instructed in the instincts that are its springboard and raw material; otherwise, intention may do more harm than good. For this instruction, we must turn not only to the human sciences but also to the species' ancient wisdom as it is preserved in myths, rituals, fairy tales, and the traditions of the performing arts. Perhaps our soundest model will be the art of gardening.

We know that we can ruin things, especially complex and subtle things, by that domineering overconsciousness that Coleridge saw in himself as "the intellect that kills" and that Keats diagnosed in him as an "irritable grasping after fact and reason." Shakespeare implies in *The Winter's Tale* that the human power of transformation need not be like that at all. To create, to use our technology—our "art," as he calls it—is as natural to us as breathing, if we do it the right way. Let us accept our self-consciousness as appropriate to us, and rejoice in its occasional absurdity, rather than attempt to escape into a kind of prelapsarian spontaneity. Our spontaneity must be found at the heart of our self-awareness, and nowhere else. It is not enough to be, as Coleridge put it, "wisely passive" before nature; we know from quantum theory that reality reveals itself only to the active questioner. And if acting is natural to us, then we may achieve in action a contemplative absorption that is as wise as any meditative trance.

Any gardener will instantly recognize the state of mind I have just described. As one moves about the flower beds, weeding, propagating, pruning the apple tree, shifting the rock in the rock garden an inch or two to make room for the roots of a healthy erica, one becomes a subtle and powerful force of natural selection in that place, placing one's stamp on the future of the biosphere; but it feels like pottering, like a waking dream. "Meantime the mind, from pleasure less/Withdraws into its happiness," says Marvell.

The creation and use of other technologies, even those of steel and glass and oil and electricity, need be no different. It is all gardening, if we see it right. If we distrust our technology, we distrust our own nature, and nature itself. And this distrust inevitably makes us helpless and passive before the technical powers of others, and resentful, and disenfranchised. Let us seize our powers to ourselves: our artistic and esthetic capacities, which make use of the whole brain, not just the anxious calculations of the linguistic centers in the left temporal lobe.

We must take responsibility for nature. That ecological modesty which asserts that we are only one species among many, with no special rights, we may now see as the abdication of a trust. We are, whether we like it or not, the lords of creation; true humility consists not in pretending that we aren't, but in living up to the trust that it implies by service to the greater glory and beauty of the world we have been given to look after. It is a bad shepherd who, on democratic principles, deserts his sheep.

The time is ripe to begin planting the American garden. This demands an assessment of such cultural resources as already exist. America has access not only to the great European traditions of gardening but also to the glorious legacies of the Chinese, the Japanese, and the Indians. One large and unique role that the American garden can fulfill is that of synthesis, the harmonious and fertile juxtaposition of past and foreign cultures. But is there not something of its own that America can contribute to the tradition?

On the face of it, the project of an American garden may not look promising. In the vernacular, the word "garden" has come to mean little better than a vegetable patch; its substitutes, "yard" and "lawn," seem explicitly to deny an artistic or decorative intent. Nevertheless, our garden can draw on the unique promise of American developments in the great mediators between nature and culture: cookery, music, and the family. Cookery transforms raw nature into the substance of human communion, routinely and without fuss transubstantiating matter into mind; in the past twenty years, American cuisine has been transformed from something resembling British or German provincial cooking into a serious and sophisticated art with virtuoso practitioners and a solid literature. Music, as Bosch knew, is at once the most sensual of pleasures and the loftiest and most divine exercise of the spirit; because it doesn't seem to depend on ideas, music has never embarrassed the American genius, and our domestic amalgam of jazz, bluegrass, European folk and art music, and the blues is now the classical idiom of the entire world. As for the American family, its special promise has already been pointed out: our emphasis on the elective aspects of the family puts the human intention of the spouses themselves in charge of family life in a way that is unprecedented among human societies. If the gardening of a marriage becomes imaginatively feasible, we will have a chance at a remarkable psychic enfranchisement for parents and children alike.

The American garden will not just be what George Steiner calls an "archive of Eden": a collection of good ideas from elsewhere. Such a vision of America derives from the suicidal European notion that we are at the end of history, with nothing left to us but a cataloguing of the past or a suitably tasteful self-annihilation. But if we are to avoid being merely derivative, we must be bold in our assessment of the raw materials of the American garden, and reject nothing until it has fully proved its uselessness—not even Disneyland, the shopping malls of the Sunbelt, the atriums of Hyatt hotels, the imaginary Ringworld gardens of the High Frontier, their lakes and forests vertiginously slathered over the inner surface of a gigantic aluminum band spinning in the cloudless dazzle of the naked sun. Let us consider the sheer scale of America, and the perspective of it as seen from the freeway, the Ferris wheel, the skyscraper, the jet plane. There is enough room to plant gardens for all the citizens of the republic, not just a wealthy aristocracy. Let us make a virtue of the colossal earthworks we have dug for our industrial purposes, and of our capacity for truly heroic alterations of the landscape.

This American garden will not only grow, but evolve; and that means it must encompass change and death and self-awareness (which is the awareness of death). This is why water, which flows, shatters itself, and reflects, is so important in a garden. The true artists of Eden have always built into it a sort of shiver, the possibility of a cloud passing over the sun and transforming the glowing landscape into a tragic or heroic mode. Coleridge's Xanadu has its terrifying chasm, its caverns measureless to man, its sunless sea. "Is there no change of death in paradise?" asks Wallace Stevens, and answers: "Death is the mother of beauty." He is echoing that artist who painted a skull in his pastoral landscape and inscribed next to it, in a mossy stone, the words *et in Arcadia ego:* yes, I too am in Arcadia.

ALISON BYERLY

The Uses of Landscape

■ ■ ■

THE PICTURESQUE AESTHETIC AND THE NATIONAL PARK SYSTEM

A national park should represent a vignette of primitive America.
—Report, Advisory Board on Wildlife Management, March 1963

Those who wish to preserve our country's remaining wilderness areas are faced with many of the same questions that literary critics have learned to ask themselves: what constitutes a proper understanding of this "text"? Does it have an inherent value, or is its value contingent on the use to which it is put? At what point does the act of appreciation become an act of appropriation in which its intrinsic qualities are sacrificed to the agenda of its audience? Environmentalists, like literary theorists, differ sharply in their responses to these problems. Their attitudes range from the New Critical stance of the Nature Conservancy, whose stated mission is to identify and maintain the world's most valuable ecosystems; to the reader-response flexibility of the Sierra Club, which advocates informed use by members of a select interpretive community; to the Marxist vigilance of groups like Greenpeace and Earth First!, which expose the political and economic structures that form the basis for many decisions about an area's potential value. Developing an appropriate attitude toward nature is even more problematic for the government agencies that control most of the nation's public lands. If we imagine environmentalists to be like literary critics, then park administrators are publishers: their job is to produce and market an interpretation of nature's text that renders it accessible to the public.

The affinity I am suggesting between the interpretation of texts and the interpretation of nature presupposes that what we call nature or wilderness is a fiction, a cultural myth. I will concentrate in this essay on the aesthetic dimension of the wilderness myth and how it has affected our management of public lands, primarily by focusing on a specific comparison, between the aesthetic of the "picturesque" as it was developed in England and America in the eighteenth and nineteenth centuries and the aesthetic of "wilderness" as it is manifested in the controversies surrounding the National Park Service's management of Yellowstone National Park. Although the complex questions of wilderness management cannot be adequately addressed here,[1] I hope that the juxtaposition of these two contexts for viewing landscape will illustrate the usefulness of practicing self-conscious criticism of our reading of nature.

▪ ▪ ▪ The American idea of the wilderness might seem closer to the aesthetic category of the sublime than to the picturesque. In fact, the American wilderness has gradually been transformed from a sublime landscape into a series of picturesque scenes. The sublime vistas that staggered the imaginations of early settlers in a sense no longer exist. The feeling of awe that is inspired by a "sublime" scene depends on the spectator's sense of its dominant power and its ability to call forth a visionary grasp of infinity. The American wilderness, however, has been gradually reduced and circumscribed until it no longer seems to stretch into infinity, but is contained and controlled within established boundaries. The conscious aesthetic framing of the landscape that typified the picturesque movement is, I will argue, replicated in the carefully delineated borders of our national parks.[2]

Although the picturesque movement constructed itself as a form of disinterested artistic appreciation of nature, it in fact represented an elitist appropriation of the environment. The specific qualities the picturesque aesthetic required from a scene were based on principles derived from painting, not from nature, and hence many parks and gardens needed tasteful "improvement" in order to conform. This aestheticization of landscape removed it from the realm of nature and designated it a legitimate object of artistic consumption.

The aesthetic view of the wilderness that is part of the picturesque legacy has had a crucial effect on public land management policies. It has taught us to value nature, but the criterion for evaluation is the quality of aesthetic experience a landscape provides. The aestheticization of landscape permits the viewer to define and control the scene, yet fosters the illusion that the scene is part of self-regulating nature. The viewer seems to be an incidental spectator of the beauties of nature when in fact man has created the "view" himself by announcing and promoting it as "scenic." The idea of wilderness refers to the absence of humanity, yet "wilderness" has no meaning outside the context of the civilization that defines it. This paradox requires that we experience the wilderness without changing its status *as* wilderness. This can only be done by constructing an aesthetic image of the wilderness that allows us to avoid confronting its reality.

An artwork remains fixed, presenting the same face to succeeding generations, though interpretations of it may differ; a living ecosystem, however, cannot achieve that stasis. Pete Gunther has pointed out that man and nature bear different relations to time: "Man lives in a progressive, expressive, non-repetitive time; ecology is the science of cyclical repetition" (112). One way to reconcile these two opposing movements, the arrow and the circle, is to freeze them both. They intersect in a static image of a harmonious relation between man and nature—an image that, as we will see, is best illustrated by the American conception of the National Park.

Because the American idea of the picturesque is rooted in British aesthetic theory, I will focus on its development in Europe before discussing its influence in the New World.

Toward the end of the eighteenth century, the word *picturesque*—which had once referred to things that were graphic, visually particular, capable of being represented in a picture—came to designate a specific mode of pictorialism. The British cult of the picturesque originated with Salvator Rosa and Claude Lorrain, whose landscape paintings were seen and occasionally brought back to England by the travelers who flooded Italy after the Treaty of Utrecht in 1713. English travelers who had seen Italy and the Alps while on the Grand Tour wanted to recapture their experience in Britain, and suddenly the Lake District, the Wye Valley, the West Country, and parts of Scotland became fashionable destinations (Watson 13). Such tourists were aided in finding picturesque views by guidebooks and landscape poems; they sometimes carried "Claude glasses," tinted convex mirrors, usually oval or circular, which the viewer could use to create a "picture" by standing with his or her back to the landscape and looking at the scene framed in the mirror. Thus, these early tourists' enjoyment of landscape was based less on an appreciation of nature itself than on the secondary image of nature that they themselves constructed—either literally, through their amateur sketches, or imaginatively, simply in the way that they viewed the scenery.

The picturesque sensibility had an immediate effect on English landscape gardening. Formally arranged flower beds gave way to irregularly designed spaces characterized by "the judicious placing of artificial ruins . . . the sudden opening of 'prospects,' and . . . the juxtaposition of different effects" (Watson 17). Picturesque landscape gardening took the aestheticization of landscape to extremes: instead of merely seeking out appropriate views, the viewer altered the landscape in order to create them for himself. Mario Praz points out that "counterfeit neglect" was the effect these gardens strove for; they were deliberately designed to appear ravaged by time (21).[3] Reference to the passage of time was artificially introduced and carefully controlled, giving the scene itself a timeless, mythic quality.

The picturesque scene is able to obscure the boundary between nature and human art because the origin of its "artistry" is unfixed. Although the actual implementation of picturesque aesthetic principles often involved ludicrous contrivance, in theory the picturesque is accidental. The viewer stumbles upon a scene or a prospect in which the elements are arranged "as if" in a picture; he or she mentally frames the scene through a process that is part recognition, part creation. The apparently "accidental" manifestation of the picturesque implies that the scene's properties are inherent, ready to be discovered. The presence of the spectator, however, is no accident. It is the spectator who engages the machinery of the picturesque aesthetic, mentally manufacturing a work of art where before there had been a work of nature. The defining feature of the picturesque scene is not chance but its opposite: pure intentionality. The picturesque scene is an early example of "found art": an artwork that exists only in the viewer's determination to label it "art."

The popularity of the picturesque movement was perhaps due to the fact that it rendered the landscape accessible and comprehensible in a way that was, paradoxically, both democratic and elite. It was aesthetically democratic because it permitted anyone to become an artist: those who could not sketch picturesque scenes could "create" them by an act of vision. A picturesque scene does not have to be painted on a canvas—it need only be "framed" by an appreciative spectator. But it was socioeconomically elite, because while artistic talent and original judgment were not required to participate in the picturesque, money was. Scenic tours abroad or in the Lake District required leisure time as well as money, and picturesque landscaping at home required an estate with gardens large enough to accommodate mazes and prospects. Raymond Williams has suggested that the landscaping of parks and the eighteenth-century enclosure of land are "related parts of the same process . . . in the one case the land is being organized for production . . . while in the other it is being organized for consumption—the view, the ordered proprietary repose, the prospect" (124). The picturesque appreciation of landscape was in fact an appropriation of landscape that had more to do with the attitude of the viewer than the inherent qualities of the scene, which was valued only to the degree that it could be made to conform to preconceived aesthetic principles.

The picturesque aesthetic as it was developed in English painting and poetry was eventually imported to America, exerting considerable influence on poetry and art here long after it ceased to be in vogue in England. The descriptive writing of Alexander Wilson and Washington Irving, and popular books such as Joshua Shaw's *Picturesque Views of American Scenery* (1820–21) and William Guy Wall's *Hudson River Portfolio* (1821–25), made it a part of American culture (Nygren 52–56). British visitors to America helped popularize tourism here, too, so that by the early 1800s the Schuylkill River, the White Mountains, the Hudson River, and the Catskill Mountains were among the picturesque spots enjoyed by foreign and native travelers (Robertson 193–204). Clearly, the American wilderness differed greatly from the English landscapes that determined the specific aesthetic elements of an ideally "picturesque" scene. But the self-conscious aesthetic mastery that characterized the picturesque was reflected in American attitudes toward nature.

▪▪▪ As I suggested earlier, the various government agencies that are entrusted with our public lands embody a bewildering diversity of purposes. In fact, many individual agencies operate under the burden of internal contradictions within their stated objectives. The Bureau of Land Management and the U.S. Forest Service, for example, control the disposition of their lands for "resource activities" that include wilderness preservation, but also timber production, domestic livestock grazing, minerals development, and other commercial uses (*Preserving Our Natural Heritage* 89). The National Park Service, too, espouses goals that are potentially incompatible. Its job is "to provide for the highest quality of use and enjoyment of the National Park System by increased millions of visitors in the years to come," as well as "to conserve and manage for their highest purpose the natural, historical, and recreational resources of the National Park System" (*Natural Heritage* 24). "Conservation" in this context means management rather than protection, and the "highest purpose" of these resources is necessarily defined as their availability for "use and enjoyment."

In addition, the National Park Service has acquired a symbolic role in the public mind that goes beyond its stated objectives. As natural areas in the United States have diminished, the public has come to perceive the National Park Service as its primary provider of the wilderness experience. And yet, as the number of park visitors has grown, the parks have moved farther and farther away from a state that could be described as "wild." In fact, they were not originally intended to be wilderness preserves at all. When Yellowstone National Park was created in 1872, it was described as "a public park or pleasuring ground"; as Roderick Nash points out, its establishment involved "no *intentional* preservation of wild country" (Nash 112).[4] The passage of the 1964 Wilderness Act established a system whereby parts of the national parks, as well as other federal lands, could be designated "wilderness areas," but these, too, were to be "administered for the use and enjoyment of the American people," though "in such manner as will leave them unimpaired for future use and enjoyment as wilderness" (Allin 277).

The Wilderness Act's own definition of wilderness reveals the paradox involved. The visitor to a wilderness area should find a place that has not been visited. A wilderness is "an area where the earth and its community of life are untrammelled by man . . . which generally appears to have been affected primarily by the forces of nature, with the imprint of man's work substantially unnoticeable; [which] has outstanding opportunities for solitude" (Allin 278). It is difficult to see how such an area could remain untrammeled while being used by even a small percentage of the American people, or how it could provide opportunities for solitude to numerous visitors. This description applies only to specified "wilderness areas," but large sections of some parks are so designated: in Yellowstone, for example, 61 percent of the land is managed as "wilderness" (Mealey 208). Furthermore, it does in many ways represent a popular mandate for what a national park *ought* to be. Fortunately, an escape route is encoded in its language: it designates an area that "appears" to be affected primarily by nature, one in which man's imprint is present but "substantially unnoticeable." It describes an image, not a reality.

This image of the wilderness is as much of an aesthetic construct as picturesque views of the Lake District, and, some would argue, equally elitist. William Tucker suggests, for example, that there is a class dimension to the insistence of many wilderness enthusiasts on excluding motorized vehicles, which represent "different tastes in recreation," from wilderness areas. In a kind of reverse chic, upper-middle-class environmentalists hike, canoe, or ride on horseback, claiming that the motorboats and snowmobiles often preferred by less wealthy visitors profane the "authentic" wilderness experience. Tucker concludes that "wildernesses . . . are essentially parks for the upper middle class" (18,17).[5]

But although true wildernesses may be accessible only to a privileged few, national parks can approximate the wilderness experience for a larger audience by presenting a landscape that reproduces a scenic *facsimile* of wilderness, a mythologized image of what we would like the wilderness to be. Evidence of human activity is carefully erased, but humans themselves are not excluded. On the contrary, their spectatorial presence is essential to the idea of wilderness. The old question of whether a tree falling in the forest makes a sound if no one is there to hear it encapsulates the paradox: a tree standing in the forest is not a part of the "wilderness" unless a civilized observer is there to see it. Gary Snyder points out that the word *wild* is defined in dictionaries "by what—from a human standpoint—it is not" (Snyder 9). The framing of the wilderness area by contrast to the civilization that surrounds it is a process analogous to the picturesque framing of landscape described earlier. While the specific characteristics of the two aesthetics differ, the mechanism of appropriation is the same.

The extent to which public land is considered a specifically aesthetic resource is apparent in the rhetoric of its staunchest defenders. An article in *Parks and Recreation* insists that we must "understand our cultural as well as economical ties to the land," illustrating its point by listing some of the many writers, artists, and composers whose work was influenced by their love of nature (LaPage and Ranney 5). An activist promoting the idea of reintroducing wolves into the park points to their "symbolic" importance to our culture: "How do you say what it means to have lost the wolf in a place like Yellowstone? How do you say what a Mozart symphony is? How do you say what it's like to lose the *Mona Lisa?*" (Fugate 18). The wolves' value is authenticated by comparison to humankind's greatest artistic achievements.

The Sierra Club exploited this conception of nature as akin to art in its famous 1966 print ads protesting dams in the Grand Canyon. Congressional proposals introduced in 1963 sought authorization to build dams in the Grand Canyon in order to create a deeper river, destroying the canyon's value as a fossil record but making it easier for casual visitors to view the canyon walls, since they could use large powerboats instead of rafts or canoes. The Sierra Club ran full-page ads in major newspapers with the headline: "SHOULD WE ALSO FLOOD THE SISTINE CHAPEL SO TOURISTS CAN GET NEARER THE CEILING?" (*Sierra Club* 30). The idea that altering nature constitutes a kind of desecration could only be established, it seems, by comparing it to art. In a sense, the Grand Canyon is a piece of "found art" that we have framed as a proper object of aesthetic contemplation, and to destroy "The Grand Canyon" is to destroy something we ourselves have made. It must therefore be protected for the same reasons that we protect all parts of our cultural heritage.

The term *outdoor museums,* introduced in 1923 by Robert Sterling Yard of the National Parks Association, and still widely used to describe the national parks (Brockman 140), embodies a conception of conservation that treats the national park's contents as art objects to be valued for their appearance and preserved in their existing state. A recent article on politics and ecological reform suggests that "environmentalists could learn a good deal about park management from those who run museums." A museum "typically needs more space and additional art objects, but it has a limited endowment . . . Trades are commonly made of one kind of painting for another." The author proposes that individual parks be placed under the control of a board of directors who would have "a fiduciary duty to a narrow set of goals, such as the preservation of wilderness," but would be empowered to generate revenue by selectively exploiting "intensive recreation possibilities, scientific research, or even the potential mineral values of park lands" (Stroup 178). Interestingly, one of the most common areas of expertise in the educational backgrounds of park superintendents is landscape architecture—it is second only to law enforcement (Chase, "What Washington Doesn't Know" 143). Park superintendents are not scientists; they are curators and policemen, protectors of valuable commodities.

This sense of nature as a picturesque commodity is reflected in the design and management of the national parks. The access highways that traverse them are filled with Scenic Overlooks, roadside pulloffs that designate ideal picture-taking locations. The virtually identical photographs that many visitors bring back from Rocky Mountain, Yosemite, or Yellowstone are in a sense replicas of the watercolor scenes that early British tourists brought back from Italy or the Lake District.

The importance of maintaining the aesthetic illusion of wilderness is reflected in numerous controversies that have surrounded Yellowstone Park (often called "the crown jewel" of the national park system) in recent years. In the 1960s, for example, the park adopted a policy of shooting elk in order to reduce a herd that had become far too large for the park to sustain. The oversized herd had developed in response to an earlier policy of killing the elk's predators in order to protect this popular animal. As Alston Chase points out, "Yellowstone needed more animals for the tourists to see." In 1967, Park Superintendent Anderson suggested that management should work to increase the availability of "wildlife shows for visitors" (quoted in Chase, *Playing God* 51). In response to public protest at the elk herd reduction, the secretary of the interior established a committee to evaluate the park service game management program. Chaired by zoologist A. Starker Leopold (son of Aldo Leopold), the committee issued a report outlining an influential philosophy of wildlife management that sought to maintain the parks as independent ecosystems. The Leopold report insisted that "observable artificiality in any form must be minimized and obscured in every possible way." By using "the utmost in skill, judgment, and ecological sensitivity," the report claimed, "a reasonable illusion of primitive America could be re-created" (Chase 33–34). The essential goal was that the park *appear* to be a natural wilderness. Artificiality could not be "observable"; instead, the park must sustain the illusion of a natural, primeval state. Like the ruins in a picturesque garden, it would emblematize a vanished past, presenting a perfect picture of the lost American wilderness.[6]

The policy outlined in the Leopold report affected every aspect of Yellowstone's management. When the park's bear policy was questioned in the early 1970s, a study of its bear population was undertaken but then quietly suppressed and discontinued by the Park Service. The collars that the scientists used to track the bears were considered "unsightly" and had to be removed before the park's upcoming centennial celebration (Chase 157). As early as 1868, John Muir had recognized the necessity of catering to the picturesque tastes of park visitors. "Even the scenery habit in its most artificial forms . . . mixed with spectacles, silliness and kodaks . . . may well be regarded as a hopeful sign of the times," he wrote (Runte 172).

A *Newsweek* article about the Yellowstone fires noted that "Yellowstone remains an enduring symbol of the American wilderness" ("Fighting for Yellowstone" 18). It is not an *example,* but a *symbol* of wilderness; it functions as a representation or illustration of the concept. But the Park Service's insistence on treating Yellowstone as if it were in fact a naturally regulated, self-enclosed ecosystem has, Alston Chase has argued, resulted in contradictory and damaging policies. Even as a public relations gesture, "natural control" often backfired. When bears were deprived of access to the garbage they had grown dependent on, and forced to feed themselves "naturally," they became aggressive and attacked park visitors, causing a public outcry. In one highly publicized incident, spectators became infuriated when park rangers allowed a bison to drown when they could easily have rescued him. Tourists wanted an image of wilderness, not a realistically dangerous wilderness experience.

The impossibility of this "illusion" sustaining itself without help became dramatically visible in the summer of 1988 as wildfires swept through the park, eventually reaching almost a million acres of land and destroying some 40 percent of the park's territory. The park's "let it burn" policy dictated that all naturally occurring fires be permitted to run their course unless they posed an imminent threat to life or property. Although environmentalists were quick to defend the policy, which was intended to allow, in the words of the park's chief scientist John Varley, the natural cycle of "rebirth and renewal of the park's ecosystem" ("Yellowstone: Up in Smoke" 36), the public was outraged at the spectacle of the nation's first national park consumed by flames.[7] President Reagan expressed the confusion of the average American at this counterintuitive approach to "conservation" when he called the policy "a cockamamie idea" ("Burn Baby Burn" 14). The static image of the wilderness lodged in the collective consciousness did not readily accommodate the idea of change. Pictures, after all, do not change; they merely hang on the walls of the museum.

As we saw earlier, the picturesque scene, though mentally constructed by the spectator, presents itself as a fortuitous accident; the public reaction to a genuine "accident" at Yellowstone exposed this apparent autonomy as an illusion. There was far more discussion about the Park Service's refusal to assert control over the fires than about the actual effect on the park. Although the media duly reported the scientific reasoning that lay behind the "let it burn" policy, their coverage of the fires reflected the popular perception that the park service had been negligent. The headlines from the major newsmagazine stories on the fire emphasize the Park Service's lack of control: "Burn Baby Burn! Stop Baby Stop!" (*U.S. News and World Report*); "Did the Park Service Fiddle While Rome Burned?" (*Business Week*); "Yellowstone: Up in Smoke" (*Newsweek*); " 'We Could Have Stopped This' " (*Time*). Many of these stories focused on the massive efforts that were finally mounted to halt the fires (some ten thousand fire fighters, including two thousand army troops, eventually participated) and on the question of whether it would have been possible to succeed if the fire fighting had started sooner.[8] Louisa Wilcox, of the Greater Yellowstone Coalition, pointed out that the destruction is "part of living in an ecosystem that is wild and uncontrollable" ("We Could Have Stopped This" 19), but clearly the public did not want its park to be genuinely beyond its control.

The intensity of public concern about the Yellowstone fires was connected, as many people noted at the time, to the widespread environmental fears roused by the abnormally hot summer of 1988. The sight of Yellowstone's parched forests feeding an unstoppable inferno became the ultimate symbol of the vulnerability of nature to the forces unleashed by technology. In his book *Strange Weather,* Andrew Ross points out that extreme weather events are often linked in the public consciousness with contemporaneous political and social events: "Instances of prolonged meteorological abnormality expose popular and official anxieties about the economy of change and constancy that regulates our everyday lives" (233). The hot summer of 1988, he suggests, focused our fears of global warming, and our anxiety about America's place within a global economy, by providing a premonitory image of the future (232–33). Our apparent inability to control the natural processes at work within the boundaries of Yellowstone, then, became the most telling sign of the environmental apocalypse we had brought upon ourselves.

Ironically, a main reason for the fires' rapid spread may have been the dead trees and underbrush that had accumulated during the many years in which park policy had been to suppress all fires. Therefore, some have argued, it was unreasonable to treat the fires as part of a natural cycle when previous interference had already rendered the park an artificial environment (Chase, "Neither Fire Suppression nor Natural Burn a Sound Scientific Option" 24). Recognizing the illusoriness of the aesthetic image that constituted "Yellowstone National Park" would perhaps have allowed for a more accurate approximation of "natural" development. But the whole concept of *natural control,* as the oxymoronic term implies, rests on the paradoxical assumption that only human interference can guarantee a natural state of affairs.

▪ ▪ ▪ It is of course easier to criticize the aesthetic view of landscape than to define alternative criteria of "value" in nature. Even committed environmentalists disagree about the reasons for protecting wilderness areas. Land that has been preserved from commercial exploitation may serve scientific, recreational, spiritual, or aesthetic purposes, or some combination of these. Since Aldo Leopold first called for a "land ethic" that would extend the community regulated by social conduct to include "soils, waters, plants, and animals" (204), philosophers have developed theories of environmental ethics that attribute to nature an inherent value independent of any such uses. So-called "deep ecologists" argue that nature possesses the same moral standing and natural rights as human beings.[9] The most radical proponents of this view, the members of Earth First!, see "The Defense of Mother Nature" as a task that merits the same human risk and civil disobedience as the antislavery and civil rights movements. But most independent environmental organizations attempt to formulate policy based on a specific sense of why nature is useful to humankind.

The stated mission of the Nature Conservancy, for example, is "to preserve plants, animals, and natural communities that represent the diversity of life on Earth by protecting the lands and water they need to survive" (*Nature Conservancy Annual Report 1990* 5). Its ideal is to preserve land for scientific, rather than recreational, uses. Unlike most other environmental groups, it does not choose the land it deems worthy of protection on the basis of visual beauty. A recent article on its work notes that "ironically, the Conservancy often performs its mission best when the property in question has no particular scenic value" (Selcraig 52).

The Sierra Club, on the other hand, lists as its primary interest "to explore, enjoy and protect the wild places of the earth," and indeed its first goal after its founding in 1892 was to " 'render accessible' the Sierra Nevada and other West Coast mountain ranges" (McCloskey and Carr 4,5). Known to many people primarily for the stunning nature photography displayed in its popular calendars, it seeks to increase public awareness and enjoyment of the environment. But while the Nature Conservancy emphasizes scientific, and the Sierra Club recreational, uses of land, they both rely on picturesque appreciation of the landscape to further their goals.

In fact, all of the major environmental groups depend on selling an attractive vision of nature, as is evident in the competition between the glossy magazines each one produces for its members. *National Geographic* is, of course, the standard by which these vicarious forays into nature are judged. *Sierra* and *Wilderness* are both substantial magazines, complete with lengthy feature articles and advertising, while *Nature Conservancy* recently expanded from an undersized format into a full-sized magazine with more sophisticated graphics and layout. All are structured around large reproductions of scenic photographs. The Wilderness Society entices prospective members with the offer of a free book of Ansel Adams photographs, while the Audubon Society's most recent membership appeals emphasize the benefits of "enjoying the spectacle of nature through *Audubon* magazine," which, they assure us, is "the most beautiful published anywhere." The experience of this "fine art book" is an armchair substitute for the experience of nature itself: "Reading it makes you feel the same way you do after a walk in the deep woods, or a swim in a crystal lake. You are rewarded. Enriched. Uplifted" (Berle, n.p.). Clearly, environmental groups do agree on one thing: the way to promote nature is to illustrate its picturesque beauty. Our insistence that the natural world should not merely exist but also satisfy our aesthetic sensibilities is, it seems, difficult to overcome.

In the aftermath of the Yellowstone fires, considerable political pressure was brought to bear on the agriculture and interior secretaries and on National Parks Director William Penn Mott, Jr., forcing reconsideration of the "natural control" policy. In 1991 a review team composed of representatives from public land agencies issued a new set of recommendations that honored the theory of "natural control" but imposed numerous restrictions that prevent implementation of the policy except under specific conditions (Lowry 83). Many of the issues raised by the fire policy have recently resurfaced in the controversy surrounding the decision to reintroduce wolves to Yellowstone. There, too, the problem is that a "more natural" ecosystem can only be attained through deliberate human effort—and now that wolves are an "optional" part of Yellowstone, many people choose to reject that option.

The National Park Service's immediate strategy for countering public criticism and forestalling damage to Yellowstone Park's tourist trade after the fires was, not surprisingly, to redefine the park's image. By September 1988 it had begun a "campaign to sell the charred forest parkland as 'nature's laboratory,' a place to watch the world remake itself" (Egan 6). The park still provided a spectacle, but now it was a test tube rather than a museum. Aesthetic appreciation was to be replaced by scientific curiosity. While this change in attitude was perhaps forced upon park administrators, it does provide a model for a more flexible and responsible use of the parks. Recognition that we do not in fact create the wilderness, but that it makes and remakes itself, is the first step toward learning to read nature's text as something other than fiction.

NOTES

1. For a useful introduction to some of the issues involved, see John C. Hendee et al., *Wilderness Management,* 2d ed., rev. (Golden, Colo.: North American Press, 1990).

2. In his essay, "Towards a Poetics of Culture" (in *The New Historicism,* ed. H. Aram Veeser [New York: Routledge, 1989]) Stephen Greenblatt meditates briefly on the significance of the signs and railings on the Nevada Falls Trail at Yosemite National Park, noting that "the wilderness is at once secured and obliterated by the official gestures that establish its boundaries" (9).

3. For a comprehensive history of the picturesque movement, see, in addition to Praz and Watson, Christopher Hussey, *The Picturesque: Studies in a Point of View* (New York: G. P. Putnam, 1927); Walter J. Hipple, *The Beautiful, the Sublime, and the Picturesque in Eighteenth-Century British Aesthetic Theory* (Carbondale: Southern Illinois University Press, 1957); Elizabeth Wheeler Manwaring, *Italian Landscape in Eighteenth-Century England* (New York: Oxford University Press, 1925). A succinct discussion of the picturesque, and reproductions of some picturesque paintings, can be found in *William Wordsworth and the Age of English Romanticism,* ed. Jonathan Wordsworth et al., the catalogue of the 1988 Rutgers University/Wordsworth Trust exhibition.

4. For an excellent overview of the establishment of Yellowstone and the development of the National Park System as a whole, see Runte.

5. The problems posed by the various recreations and amenities sought by vacationers are explored in detail by Sax. The classic example of the "elitist" attitude is, of course, Edward Abbey's attack on industrial tourism. He suggests that each visitor to a park be told: "PARK YOUR CAR, JEEP, TRUCK, TANK, MOTORBIKE, SNOWMOBILE, MOTORBOAT, JETBOAT, AIRBOAT, SUBMARINE, AIRPLANE, JETPLANE, HELICOPTER, HOVERCRAFT, WINGED MOTORCYCLE, ROCKETSHIP, OR ANY OTHER CONCEIVABLE TYPE OF MOTORIZED VEHICLE . . . GET ON YOUR HORSE, MULE, BICYCLE, OR FEET, AND COME ON IN" (*Desert Solitaire* [New York: Ballantine, 1968] 65–66).

6. Paul Shepard notes that early visitors to Yellowstone appreciated the "architectural qualities" of its unusual rock formations, which seemed like "natural ruins" (*Man in the Landscape* [New York: Knopf, 1967] 253).

7. John D. Varley himself almost predicted such a response in a paper he presented at a 1987 National Park Service Ecosystem Management Workshop. He noted that the public regards Yellowstone as a kind of "aquarium," and fails to recognize that it is a "dynamic and interactive" ecosystem ("Managing Yellowstone National Park into the Twenty-First Century" in *Ecosystem Management,* ed. Agee and Johnson 218).

8. Forest Service fire use specialist Walt Thomascak said later: "'When conditions get as bad as it was in the summer of 1988, you're wasting your money trying to suppress fires. But the public would never accept the fact that any federal agency merely stood around and watched a forest as it was consumed by flames, so the federal agencies have to put on a good show'" (quoted in George Wuerthner, "The Flames of '88," *Wilderness* 52.185 [Summer 1989]: 50).

9. A survey of the development of environmental ethics in the fields of religion and philosophy is presented by Roderick Nash in *The Rights of Nature* (Madison: University of Wisconsin Press, 1989). See also *Reweaving the World: The Emergence of Ecofeminism,* ed. Irene Diamond and Gloria Feman Orenstein (San Francisco: Sierra Club, 1990). For a general philosophical overview of the idea of wilderness from prehistory through deep ecology, see Max Oelschlaeger, *The Idea of Wilderness* (New Haven: Yale University Press, 1991).

WORKS CITED

Abbey, Edward. *Desert Solitaire: A Season in the Wilderness*. New York: Ballantine, 1968.

Agee, James K., and Darryll R. Johnson, eds. *Ecosystem Management for Parks and Wilderness*. Seattle: University of Washington Press, 1988.

Allin, Craig W. *The Politics of Wilderness Preservation*. Westport, Conn.: Greenwood, 1982.

Berle, Peter A. A. National Audubon Society Letter 90–92, n.d.

Brockman, C. Frank, et al. *Recreational Use of Wild Lands*. 3d ed. New York: McGraw-Hill, 1979.

"Burn Baby Burn! Stop Baby Stop!" *U.S. News and World Report* 19 September 1988: 14–16.

Chase, Alston. "Neither Fire Suppression nor Natural Burn Is a Sound Scientific Option." *New York Times* 18 September 1988: 4, 24.

———. *Playing God in Yellowstone: The Destruction of America's First National Park*. Boston: Atlantic Monthly, 1986.

———. "What Washington Doesn't Know About the National Park System." In *The Yellowstone Primer: Land and Resource Management in the Greater Yellowstone Ecosystem,* ed. John A. Baden and Donald Leal. San Francisco: Pacific Research Institute for Public Policy, 1990.

"Did the Park Service Fiddle While Rome Burned?" *Business Week* 26 September 1988: 48.

Egan, Timothy. "Yellowstone, and Its Sales Pitch, Undergo Rebirth." *New York Times* 24 September 1988: A6.

"Fighting for Yellowstone." *Newsweek* 19 September 1988: 18–20.

Fugate, Sandy. "Making Room for Wildness in Yellowstone." *Kalamazoo College Quarterly* 52.2 (Spring/Summer 1990): 17–19.

Greenblatt, Stephen. "Towards a Poetics of Culture." In *The New Historicism,* ed. H. Aram Veeser. New York: Routledge, 1989. 1–14.

Gunther, Pete A. Y. "Creativity and Ecology." In *Creativity in Art, Religion, and Culture,* ed. Michael H. Mitias. Wurzburg: Konighausen Neumann, 1985. 107–16.

Hendee, John C., et al. *Wilderness Management.* 2d ed., rev. Issued by the International Wilderness Leadership Foundation in cooperation with the USDA Forest Service. Golden, Colo.: North American Press, 1990.

LaPage, Wilbur F., and Salley Ranney. Excerpt from "The Heart and Soul of Culture," *Parks and Recreation* July 1988. Reprint, in *Taking Sides: Clashing Views on Controversial Environmental Issues.* 3d ed. Ed. Theodore D. Goldfarb. Guilford, Conn.: Dushkin Publishing Group, 1989. 4–10.

Leopold, Aldo. *A Sand County Almanac and Sketches Here and There.* Ed. Robert Finch. 1949. Reprint, New York: Oxford University Press, 1987.

Little, Charles E. "The Old Wild Life: Wolves and Bears and a Vision for the Greater Yellowstone Ecosystem." *Wilderness* 54. 193 (Summer 1991): 10–25.

Lowry, William C. *The Capacity for Wonder: Preserving National Parks.* Washington, D.C.: The Brookings Institution, 1994.

McCloskey, Michael, and Patrick Carr. "Why the Sierra Club? Our Purposes, Beliefs and Goals." *The Sierra Club: A Guide.* Sierra Club, 1989.

Mealey, Stephen P. "U.S. Forest Service Wilderness Management: Challenge and Opportunity." In *Ecosystem Management,* ed. Agee and Johnson. 193–216.

Nash, Roderick. *The Rights of Nature: A History of Environmental Ethics.* Madison: University of Wisconsin Press, 1989.

———. *Wilderness and the American Mind.* 3d ed. New Haven: Yale University Press, 1967; rpt. 1982.

Nature Conservancy 1990 Annual Report. November/December 1990.

Nygren, Edward J. "From View to Vision." In *Views and Visions: American Landscape before 1830,* ed. Edward J. Nygren. Washington: Corcoran Gallery of Art, 1986. 3–82.

Oelschlaeger, Max. *The Idea of Wilderness: From Prehistory to the Age of Ecology.* New Haven: Yale University Press, 1991.

Ounsby, Ian. *The Englishman's England: Taste, Travel, and the Rise of Tourism.* Cambridge: Cambridge University Press, 1990.

Praz, Mario. *The Romantic Agony.* Trans. Angus Davidson. Oxford: Oxford University Press, 1970; rpt. 1979.

Preserving Our Natural Heritage. Vol. I: *Federal Activities.* Prepared for the U.S. Department of the Interior, National Park Service, Office of the Chief Scientist by the Nature Conservancy. Washington: U.S. Government Printing Office, 1975.

Robertson, Bruce. "The Picturesque Traveler in America." In *Views and Visions: American Landscape before 1830,* ed. Nygren. 187–210.

Ross, Andrew. *Strange Weather: Culture, Science and Technology in the Age of Limits.* New York: Verso, 1991.

Runte, Alfred. *National Parks: The American Experience.* 2d ed., rev. Lincoln: University of Nebraska Press, 1987.

Sax, Joseph L. *Mountains without Handrails: Reflections on the National Parks.* Ann Arbor: University of Michigan Press, 1980.

Scott, Douglas. "Conservation and the Sierra Club." *The Sierra Club: A Guide.* Sierra Club, 1989.

Selcraig, Bruce. "The Secrets of Gray Ranch." *New York Times Magazine* 3 June 1990: 28–68.

Shepard, Paul. *Man in the Landscape: A Historic View of the Esthetic of Nature.* New York: Knopf, 1967.

Sholly, Dan R., with Steven M. Newman. *Guardians of Yellowstone: An Intimate Look at the Challenges of Protecting America's Foremost Wilderness Park.* New York: Morrow, 1991.

Snyder, Gary. "Good, Wild, Sacred." *The Practice of the Wild.* San Francisco: North Point Press, 1990. 78–96.

Stroup, Richard L. "Rescuing Yellowstone from Politics: Expanding Parks While Reducing Conflict." In *The Yellowstone Primer: Land and Resource Management in the Greater Yellowstone Ecosystem,* ed. John A. Baden and Donald Leal. San Francisco: Pacific Research Institute for Public Policy, 1990.

Tucker, William. "Is Nature Too Good for Us?" Excerpt from *Progress and Privilege: America in the Age of Environmentalism,* 1982. Reprint, in *Taking Sides: Clashing Views on Controversial Environmental Issues.* 3d ed. Ed. Theodore D. Goldfarb. Guilford, Conn.: Dushkin Publishing Group, 1989. 11–22.

Varley, John D. "Managing Yellowstone National Park into the Twenty-First Century: The Park as an Aquarium." In *Ecosystem Management* ed. Agee and Johnson. 216–25.

Watson, J. R. *Picturesque Landscape and English Romantic Poetry.* London: Hutchinson, 1970.

"We Could Have Stopped This." *Time* 5 September 1988: 19.

Williams, Raymond. *The Country and the City.* New York: Oxford University Press, 1973.

Wuerthner, George. "The Flames of '88." *Wilderness* 52.185 (Summer 1989): 41–54.

"Yellowstone: Up in Smoke." *Newsweek* 5 September 1988: 36.

WILLIAM HOWARTH

Some Principles of Ecocriticism

■ ■ ■

Ecocriticism is a name that implies more ecological literacy than its advocates now possess, unless they know what an embattled course ecology has run during its history. *Eco* and *critic* both derive from Greek, *oikos* and *kritis,* and in tandem they mean "house judge," which may surprise many lovers of green, outdoor writing. A long-winded gloss on *ecocritic* might run as follows: "a person who judges the merits and faults of writings that depict the effects of culture upon nature, with a view toward celebrating nature, berating its despoilers, and reversing their harm through political action." So the *oikos* is nature, a place Edward Hoagland calls "our widest home," and the *kritos* is an arbiter of taste who wants the house kept in good order, no boots or dishes strewn about to ruin the original decor.

I am toying with words, in the hope they will raise some questions about ecocriticism and its future. If its political agenda insists on an Us-Them dichotomy, then ecocriticism cannot be self-scrutinizing, only adversarial. Since ecology studies the relations between species and habitats, ecocriticism must see its complicity in what it attacks. All writers and their critics are stuck with language, and although we cast *nature* and *culture* as opposites, in fact they constantly mingle, like water and soil in a flowing stream. Living in an era of environmental crisis, we respond to the call of vatic, strident voices: Abbey, Berry, Dillard, Williams. If against nature's enemies our favorite authors take righteous stands, who are we to question their ideas or ask if they produce good writing?

Consider a story by Barry Lopez, a writer I much admire as an artist and thinker. "Landscape and Narrative," from *Crossing Open Ground* (1989), recounts a Nunamiut hunting tale about a man on a snowmobile who tracks a wolverine over rolling tundra. The animal now and then pauses to look back at its pursuer. As the hunter tops a rise, suddenly his prey bounds straight at *him,* over the windshield and onto his chest, a nose tackle that overturns both hunter and vehicle. The wolverine does not bite or scratch, just fixes "the man with a stare" and then walks away. Lopez says the story is typical, "not so much making a point as evoking something about contact with wild animals that would never be completely understood."

I find that statement misleading, since the story makes a point—not about the enigma of wildlife, but about the folly of human pursuit, especially on snowmobiles. A hunter on foot would be another story, and also with a different point. Earlier Lopez offers his own thoughts on wolverines, who "are seldom observed . . . easily excite the imagination . . . loom suddenly in the landscape with authority . . . have a deserved reputation for resoluteness." Those dry abstractions echo the author's training in scholastic philosophy, loading his essay with a didactic freight. Since the native story is paraphrased, it's hard not to feel something got lost in translation. At the end Lopez says he passed the wolverine story to a friend, apparently a wildlife biologist who lives with Cree, to get their thoughts: " 'You know,' he told me, 'how they are. They said, 'That could happen.' "

Lopez faithfully enters double quotes, which I should triple to indicate that I am citing what Lopez says his friend said about the Cree response to a Nunamiut story. The four levels of narration do not just repeat a tradition, but screen and filter it through layers of learning and bias about time, places, animals, and people. Yet Lopez's essay is not about narrational complexity, or the fact that observers alter the conditions they are studying, but about his theory that we dwell always in two landscapes, internal and external, and that stories bring those two together. That's not a bad theory, but the wolverine story fails to prove it. We'll never know what the Cree thought, but let's say "That could happen" expresses their confidence and agreement: yes, such an incident is possible. Why? Perhaps they know more about wolverines than Lopez does—or at least more than he chooses to tell us.

When I turn for assistance to Hartley H. T. Jackson and his *Mammals of Wisconsin* (1961), a wealth of meaning emerges. Common names for the wolverine are American glutton, devil bear, and skunk bear, owing to two factors: wolverines eat everything and they stink. They relish decayed, festering carrion and give off a sulfuric musk, secreted from anal glands. Solitary animals, they possess few social skills: they make rude dens, mate briefly and sullenly, push the kits out at five months to fend for themselves. Their ruthless ferocity is widely feared: bear and puma will retreat from wolverines, and with good reason, for they can kill large animals, taking down deer and even moose. How? With efficient dispatch, they leap upon a fleeing victim and tear off its head. When the Cree say "That could happen," they may mean that the Nunamiut on his roaring, stinking, gassified sled was lucky to get off with a warning. And the point is well taken: unlike hunters or writers, nature makes direct statements, without implication or analysis.

In reading Lopez or any other nature writer, I try to work within a set of informed, responsible principles, derived from four disciplines: ecology, ethics, language, and criticism. To me they offer combinations of theory and method that explore environmental literature. As an interdisciplinary science, ecology describes the relations between nature and culture. The applied philosophy of ethics offers ways to mediate historic social conflicts. Language theory examines how words represent human and nonhuman life. Criticism judges the quality and integrity of works and promotes their dissemination. Each discipline stresses the relations of nature and literature as shifting, moving shapes—a house in progress, perhaps, unfinished and standing in a field. In the following speculative account of these principles, I am looking for ways to help ecocritics sustain their role as *kritos* while assessing the literary *oikos* before them.

ECOLOGY AND ETHICS

Ecology is a science strongly connected to a history of verbal expression. In the medicine rites of early people, shamans sang, chanted, and danced stories to heal disease or prevent disaster, which they saw as states of disharmony or imbalance in nature. Classical scholars sustained that equity by reading or mapping the body and earth as analogous realms, using *theoria* and *investigium* (speculating and tracking), to define the limits of *scientia* (knowledge). Ancient science was dyadic because it portrayed nature as a composite, formed of opposite elements. Lucretius reasoned that matter and process are inseparable, with all substance—rocks, water, grain—made by actions that either join or sunder. This holism declined as knowledge grew in the Middle Ages, through the Islamic refinement of mathematics and the dividing of Christian universities into separate science-language curricula. Descartes's rationalism further exaggerated that split, yet for centuries the natural, descriptive sciences remained bound to words of local, vernacular origin. The biological names of species were quite haphazard until Carolus Linnaeus compiled his *Systema Naturae* (1734), a treatise that used Latin inflections to classify organisms into a categorical taxonomy, or naming system. This dead language was static and hierarchical, imposing on nature the fixed ranks of kingdom, phylum, class, order, family, genus, species.

After 1750 global exploration and colonization by Western powers promoted dynamic new ideas in the natural sciences, as major discoveries enlarged known space and time. Within a century, scientists charted ocean currents, traced the ice ages, found the site of Troy and the remains of Neanderthal and Cro-Magnon people. These events prompted new ways to read the earth, peering into "prehistory," the time before writing existed. Books about the travels of Humboldt, Lyell, Agassiz, and Darwin spread the recognition that time is deep and change constant. Their vision of the past as a linear, progressive advancement paralleled the work of philology, then seeking the prehistoric origins of Western and Eastern language (Aarsleff). The tendency to see words as organic, with branching roots and stems, coincided with the biological quest for naming species by form and function.

Darwin's theory of evolution took Linnaean taxonomy, the nouns of nature, and attached them to verbs, the actions that shape change. His key discoveries occurred on South Pacific islands, where he observed finches with variant beaks, according to whether they fed on seeds or insects (Weiner). This evidence of a relationship between habit and form led Darwin to plot evolution as three concurrent phases: heredity, what parents pass to offspring; mutation, what offspring may alter; and natural selection, what all generations must do to survive, adapt to circumstance. In this continual exchange of information nature functioned like a language, and in 1866 Gregor Mendel charted its syntax with genetics, the code of reproduction.

By this time Western nations were experiencing both rapid industrial growth and environmental loss. One historian sees that shift as dialectical, from Arcadian to imperialist phases of culture (Worster 1993), for ecology appeared when naturalists began to write about the detrimental impact of mass societies. Henry D. Thoreau traced the effect of woodlots on forest succession in 1860 (Howarth), and in 1864 George Perkins Marsh published *Man and Nature,* a study of erosion produced by land clearance and overgrazing. Credit for coining *ecology* in 1869 goes to Ernst Haeckel, a

German zoologist who taught at Jena. Haeckel wrote popular essays that earned his peers' disfavor, but today he is admired as a founder of biogenetics and author of the theorem, "ontogeny recapitulates phylogeny" (one organism's life repeats a species' history).

That concern for relating individual to mass echoed Haeckel's reading of Comte and Marx. *Ecology* inflected the Linnaean term natural *economy* (Worster 1985) from *oikonomia* to *oikologia*, house mastery to house study, a shift that changed species from resources into partners of a shared domain. Haeckel's science reflected his socialist convictions. In an era torn by violent nationalist strife, from civil war in America to clashes throughout Europe, Haeckel considered how organisms sustain complex social alliances that shape their number and distribution. Comparing data on the birth, death, and migration of species, he found that organisms replicate their native form in widening gyres, from organism to population to community. Each level of these surroundings, or "environments," creates complex, interrelated networks. Using statistical models, he traced patterns of flow and exchange between food and energy, the signs of an ecosystem's carrying capacity. Ecology thus absorbed Linnean taxonomy, quantified Darwinian evolution, and revolutionized Mendelian genetics, creating what amounts to a vernacular and democratic science. Open to the common, everyday discourse of species, ecology ranged freely across many fields, dipping into evolution, behavior, and physiology—and earning the hostility of classical science.

Ecology became an accepted lingua franca not in Europe but on the fertile, level plains of mid-America. Passage of the Morrill Land Grant Act (1862) gave large tracts to Midwestern states for endowing agricultural and mechanical colleges. The schools had two goals, low-cost education and research as a public service, which encouraged the growth of applied, interdisciplinary study. Land Grant science was frankly bipartisan, supporting agricultural industry that converted prairie grassland into corn-wheat monocultures, but also recovering evidence of the region's lost biodiversity. The founding papers in modern ecology (1887–99) were by scientists from Illinois, Wisconsin, and Michigan who studied glacial lakes and dunes, those recovering zones where plants and animals rapidly form successional communities (Real). Where land had lain fallow for eons, the ecologists found a myriad of interactive species, a principle later dramatized in Aldo Leopold's popular celebration of Wisconsin marsh and prairie, *A Sand County Almanac* (1949).

As a vernacular science, ecology was widely adopted by many disciplines to read, interpret, and narrate land history. Rapid settlement and spoilage of American land after 1900 spurred the rise of resource conservation in forestry and fishery, as ecological concepts of association, climax, and niche arose to describe the biomes of eastern forest and western grasslands. Several ecologists wrote histories of regional land-use, linking biogeography to agronomy and sociology to examine natural and cultural interaction (Malin). This work enlarged the research community, leading to the founding of the Ecological Society of America in 1920 (Egerton). Not all scientists greeted the new trend warmly. Marston Bates objected to "ecology" replacing natural history because ecologists were too literary, using rhetoric and symbols instead of precise data. Behind these complaints lay a century of lexical growth, as the early languages of biology generated the broader discourse of ecological story.

The years of Depression and World War II turned ecology even more strongly toward public narrative, for in crossing boundaries it resisted the managerial aspect of conservation and challenged its support of resource-extractive industries. Many preservationists invoked ecological principles to save wilderness or protest military-industrial research, so by the 1960s some observers saw ecology as subversive, a vital component of leftist politics (Shepard). To radical ecofeminists, science became an oppressive, male-authored enemy that insisted on the biological necessity of sexual reproduction (Daly). These voices reflected how much ecology had become a medicine sung by modern shamans to heal a sick world.

Through social discourse ecology also defined ethical principles, as in Rachel Carson's landmark work, *Silent Spring* (1962), which aroused a sense of conscience about pesticides that poison ground water and destroy biodiversity. Eco-patriots in the 1970s attacked their enemies—military, political, technological, commercial—as greedy, anthropocentric forces that defamed the true course of evolution (Disch). The perceived decline of public ethics in the 1980s, when commerce began to profit from "green" policies, inspired Deep Ecology, a concept that spurned destructive ideology and called for recovering the "earth wisdom" of native American cultures (Devall). While some observers criticized the logic and biocentrism of Deep Ecology (Luke, Wright), at century's end ecology remained a popular model for understanding nature, and for relating places through biogeography and land history.

Over its long course of coming to power, ecology became a narrative mode because natural science never fully rejected vernacular language.

In geology today, the English names of land forms often reflect human sources:

foot, head, vein, arm, mouth	bodies
divide, joint, shelf, sill, column, vent	buildings
shield, spit, dike, fork, lock	tools
basin, pan, kettle, bowl, sink, trough	utensils
cap, mantle, belt, girdle	clothes

This persistent attachment to cultural memory is why words in science have variable meanings. Ecology found its voice by studying the properties of species, their distribution across space, and their adaptive course in time. In tracing those relations, ecology often used metaphors: water is the sculptor of landscape, life is patchy, ecosystems build linking chains or webs (Tudge). This verbal felicity has attracted some writers who sentimentalize ecology, exaggerating its holism with mythic and romantic imagery (Oates). Such notions seem naive to modern ecologists, who find less evidence in nature of wholeness or stability than of nonlinear, discontinuous order (Hayles).

Ecology advanced from description to advocacy after 1960, as its stories presented ethical choices that affect land and people. Just as telescopes and satellite photographs provided new maps of the earth (Kepes, Hall), so did ecological study shape a new ethics in landscape history. This altered vision of land-use also revised histories of American culture, since most of its early myths (frontier, virgin land, garden) derived from the imperious natural science that drove European exploration and settlement across the New World. Once described as the conquest or "winning" of a continent (Goetzmann) the American experience is now increasingly seen as a series of questionable readings, their rhetoric of relentless progress emulating the investigative methods of early natural history (Regis).

Eco-historians of America thus regard the scenes of contact between natives and explorers as a clash of land and sea-based values (Hendrickson), or they see the early settlers as coastal dwellers who undertook to clear forests and so extend the frontier margin of civil order (Cronon, Harrison). Another view of the clearances: they repeat the settling of the Old World, once also called virgin land. Forests tutored the American colonials by promoting migration and development while teaching them to observe limits and sustain resources, the beginnings of earth management (Bechmann, Perlin).

In the early national years, settlers breached the eastern ranges and spilled into open grasslands, creating on the prairie a settlement of northern Europeans (Looney). Upon this empty and enigmatic "blank page" men and women wrote lives that revised social traditions and adapted their homes and towns to regional resources (Hurt, Fairbanks, Eaton). Later on, sectional strife between North and South over slavery became a struggle between two bioregions, once economic partners but now devolved into deadly enemies (Cowdrey). The far West seemed to offer respite, for on the plains people could build frontier settlements, or cross the mountains in pursuit of silver and gold—all dreams that later failed, exhausting and emptying the region (Huseboe, Limerick, Matthews).

In the twentieth century, the American story is of limits reached and strained, a time of sobering recognition that human growth can destroy natural resources; but those losses also awoke a new sense of land and the intricate relations it supports. Remote and unpopulated places, from desert Southwest to the tundra of northern Alaska, aroused the passions of environmentalist defenders, who sought what Thoreau called "the tonic of wildness." Open, unsettled land continues to raise ethical choices, testing the ability of human beings to learn from land. In the darker moments of history, ecology offers to culture an ethic for survival: land has a story of its own that cannot be effaced, but must be read and retold by honest writers (Murray).

A future source of cultural history may be landscape ecology, which avoids distinctions between natural and disturbed regions and uses a new spatial language to describe land by shape, function, and change. This dynamic view accepts chaos theory and its emphasis on diverse complexity. Landscape ecologists ask new questions about regions: where are they, what do they give or take, alter and influence? They also provide metaphors for land—such as mosaic, patch, corridor, matrix—that use a situational ethics, arguing that disturbance is inevitable, whether it comes from natural or cultural causes, and that landscape is a continuous history, never quite completed (Forman).

LANGUAGE AND CRITICISM

This account of ecology and ethics may explain why ecocriticism has won advocates but faces resistance in current literary studies. Connecting science and literature is difficult, for their cultures have grown widely apart.

As we have seen, classic disciplines are suspicious of new approaches and will dismiss them as flimsy. Perhaps the greatest obstacle to acceptance is that much-privileged species, *Professores literati,* who praise innovation but tend to preserve the status quo. Literary theorists will regard ecocritics as "insufficiently problematic" if their interests do not clearly match current ideological fashion. An ethical politics is welcome, yet not if it focuses on such nonhuman topics as scenery, animals, or landfill dumps.

Those problems seem to lie far afield from literary study, yet in fact texts do reflect how a civilization regards its natural heritage. We know nature through images and words, a process that makes the question of truth in science or literature inescapable, and whether we find validity through data or metaphor, the two modes of analysis are parallel. Ecocriticism observes in nature and culture the ubiquity of signs, indicators of value that shape form and meaning. Ecology leads us to recognize that life speaks, communing through encoded streams of information that have direction and purpose, if we learn to translate the messages with fidelity.

To see how far these values dwell from current humanism, we may turn to a Modern Language Association guide, *Redrawing the Boundaries: The Transformation of Literary Studies* (1992). As its title implies, this survey proposes a sweeping act of land reform in all literary *fields,* medieval to postcolonial, by using bold spatial imagery: ideas *intersect at odd angles,* disciplinary *maps* raise questions of *boundaries* (national, racial, sexual, political), *frontiers* project beliefs that shape imagined *spaces.* Yet this geography is only rhetorical, according to its mappers, because literature dwells Nowhere: "The odd thing, in fact, about literature as an imagined territory is that there are apparently no natural limits—and hence, it would seem, there are apparently no natural limits to the field of literary criticism" (Greenblatt and Gunn 6).

The dogma that culture will always master nature has long directed Western progress, inspiring the wars, invasions, and other forms of conquest that have crowded the earth and strained its carrying capacity. Humanists still bristle with tribal aggression, warring for dominion even though they spurn all forms of hegemony. The boldest new scholars have focused on 1500–1900, four centuries of global dominion, with such revisionist ferocity as to sustain what Leah S. Marcus astutely calls "a set of geographic metaphors . . . that suggest our continuing engagement on one level with a cast of mind we have rejected on another" (Greenblatt and Gunn 61). Many recent works of critical theory chart *borders, boundaries, frontiers, horizons, margins,* but these tropes also have no natural or geographical reference (Marshall). Yet if current literary maps are devoid of content, postmodern geographers are not: several have used contemporary theory to re-examine the spatial, perceptual, and textual conventions of maps and land (Entrikin, Monmonier, Wood).

Ecocriticism seeks to redirect humanistic ideology, not spurning the natural sciences but using their ideas to sustain viable readings. Literature and science trace their roots to the hermeneutics of religion and law, the sources for early ideas of time and space, or history and property. Concepts of property and authority are central directives in science; hence its long service to Western expansion (Bowler). Today science is evolving beyond Cartesian dualism toward quantum mechanics and chaos theory, where volatile, ceaseless exchange is the norm. While some forms of postmodern criticism are following this lead, many humanists still cling to a rationalist bias that ignores recent science.

Postmodern critics now describe science as a culture, one with social and political impact, and as a language that possesses rare powers of definition (Beer, Hayles, Jordanova, Levine, Williams). Others have traced literary borrowings of science, as in Thoreau's use of botany or Twain's studies of evolution (Boudreau, Cummings); and readers of science fiction–fantasy recognize how literature raids science for utopic or dystopic imagery (Erlich). Science fiction views technology as either alien or brethren; it blazes trails into the frontier of outer space; it forecasts ecological collapse (Barter, Mogen, Rabkin). These narratives emulate the theories and experiments of science yet challenge its inherent faith in progress. Such an ironic, relativistic mode is comic and corrective, providing a rhetorical proxy for the ethics of ecology (Elgin, Wendlen).

Despite these interests, many humanists distort the nature of scientific inquiry. One literary historian describes changing canons in the mid-1980s as "competing verbal worlds" that evolve toward greater complexity and diversity (Elliott). That view misstates the Darwinian theory of natural selection, which holds that variance results not from competition but adaptation to crisis. Darwin's phrase, "survival of the fittest," means not strongest but most fit, best suited to change. Such misreadings suggest why today's cultural and biological ideas of diversity are at odds: minorities demand a right to their survival, while science fears a coming extinction. Ironically, that late phase in evolution generates the greatest cooperation among species (Wilson, *Diversity of Life*).

The humanistic critique of science advances on many fronts, attacking its narrow cultural superiority (Gehlen) or its wide reach and willful obscurity (Medawar). A source of both hope and fear, science presents solutions that only generate new problems, as in the bioethical riddles spawned by genetic engineering: should we destroy all "defective" genes? To some critics, such questions suggest that scientists too often ignore the policy implications of their discoveries (Weissmann). Science also remains stubbornly male-dominant, excluding women from its "hard" disciplines and justifying the practice with specious logic (Hubbard). These discriminatory conditions offend humanistic values of distribution and integration, which ecocritics assume in principle.

Throughout the twentieth century, literary theory has often challenged the scale and verity of science. The "human sciences" of Dilthey asserted differences between scientific knowledge and human understanding, laying emphasis on consciousness and sympathetic insight as traits cultivated by civilization. War and genocide dimmed this optimism, yet among humanists the conviction endures that experience is mind-centered and free of reference to actualities of space and time. Literary critics still place an expansive trust in poetry and dreams, states they see as providing alternative relations to material substance. Hence the persistence of psychoanalytic criticism, despite recent advances in medicine that provide chemical aids for mental disease. As philosophers of mood and ego, humanists are inclined to trust "the talking cure" above pharmacology, finding lithium or Prozac less reliable than Freud and Kristeva.

Cultural critics share an attachment to ideology and a distrust of physical experience. Marxist theory has influenced environmental history, often by ignoring natural science. In Marxist readings, economics determines social history; hence capitalism becomes the source for all conflict, oppression, and environmental abuse (Crosby). Such views ignore many inconvenient facts: that disturbance is commonplace in nature; that aborigines and socialists often commit ecocide. Revolutionary theories tend to ignore natural constraints on production: as farmers have long known, floods and locusts can destroy years of rational planning. A more consistent approach examines how social systems change as rural agrarian life evolves toward urban industry (Benjamin, Williams). This emphasis on the interaction of place and work agrees with ecology, which charts how physical conditions may affect beliefs. Historians who accept such a teleology are anticipating ecocriticism, which shares the hope that flawed social conditions may be improved.

In the poststructuralist wave of discourse analysis, references to the natural sciences are almost entirely missing. Phenomena instead become cultural constructs, void of physical content and subject to cryptic readings. One cultural theorist describes climate and landscape as little more than political conspiracies (Ross, *Strange Weather*), a bias echoed in New Historical readings of culture as shaped entirely by race, gender, class, money, and other factors of material social life. While their political emphasis is welcome, these approaches foreground social conditions and minimize the natural forces that affect history (Thomas, *New Historicism*). For deconstruction, on the other hand, all notions of order and structure become anathema, since language is assumed to have no stable meaning. This view is seen as mainly hostile to authoritarian rule, not as a new idea about nature or culture (Argyros).

Ecocriticism, instead of taxing science for its use of language to represent (mimesis), examines its ability to point (deixis). More developed in Asian than European languages (Liu), deixis locates entities in space, time, and social context. Through deixis, meaning develops from what is said or signed relative to physical space: I-you, here-there, this-that. Common as air or water, deixis expresses relative direction and orientation, the cognitive basis for description (Jarvella). In learning to read land, one can't just name objects but point to what they do: pines live in sandy soil, oaks in clay, and thus their rates of water absorption differ. As one scholar of place notes, the landscape contains many names and stories, so that learning and writing them becomes a way of mapping cultural terrain (Ryden). A biogeographer works in similar ways, reading regional life and land forms, then using ecology to map their interactions (Brown).

In their autobiographical writings, biologists often assert that language helps them develop powers of assimilation and expression. For Lewis Thomas, the core of life is language, which he sees as both mechanical and organic, "and the principal way we transform energy" (Thomas, *Lives of a Cell*). Edward O. Wilson, firmly committed to science writing, also holds that poetry makes science "convergent in what they might eventually disclose about human nature" (Wilson, *Biophilia*). These are not nostalgic concessions to metaphor, but revelations drawn from lives of fieldwork, reading natural signs and finding ways to write them for readers. The earth sciences are "descriptive" because they explain natural forms through verbal composition. In the view of one scholar, Darwin achieved his synthesis of evolutionary theory through the act of composing, by writing out narrative and exposition that spurred larger inferences (Tallmadge). Geologists often describe tectonic processes as "writing in stone," for that analogy recounts their task of learning natural history (Raymo).

The habit of description has made earth scientists conscious of how words shape their disciplines. An example is *Keywords in Evolutionary Biology* (1992), in which scholars of science, philosophy, and history explicate influential terms that have changed their meaning across time. The keywords, a noun coined by cultural historian Raymond Williams (1976), range from *adaptation to teleology,* and their evolving significance has shaped theory and politics in many fields. As the editors note, keywords reflect not just semantic debates but "a rough map of some of the territory of dispute and change" (Keller 6). That terrain is rugged, for scientific terms are affected by social and lexical change. Such instability opens science at least partially to metaphor, which enlarges meaning, just as ecocriticism seeks to examine how metaphors of nature and land are used and abused.

Ecocritics may detect more parity between literary and scientific writing than other postmodernists, but that view is not eccentric or unprecedented. The early formalists present systematic studies of language, so regular in Jakobson as to resemble genetic code. New Critics used close readings to explore the intricate diversity of words, insisting that they share an organic coherence (Krieger). Structuralism and semiotics focused on descriptive language, offering precise descriptions of the signs and signifying that form culture (Blanchard). Reader-response theory stressed the social, transactive nature of reading in "interpretive communities" (Fish). Studies of orality and literacy examined the evolution of language from internal to external forms, as writing objectified ideas but also conquered pre-literate cultures (Burns, Goody).

Also anticipating ecocriticism were structuralist critics of myth and anthropology who examined symbols, often from agricultural fertility rites, that explain natural conditions or try to prevent disasters, such as famine and flood (Blumenberg). Ethnic and postcolonial studies have a strong regional emphasis, but they dwell on political or cultural spaces rather than their physical environs. In time, ecocriticism may provide critics of race and ethnicity with a view of how those social constructions relate to larger histories of land use and abuse. As land is traded, people are degraded, moved to and from regions as mere chattel in an invidious property system (Dixon).

Ecocriticism finds its strongest advocates today in feminist and gender critics, who focus on the idea of place as defining social status. Of particular interest is "a woman's place," often described as an attic or closet, that contains yet sustains individuals until they locate a congenial environs (Gilbert and Gubar, *Madwoman in the Attic;* Sedgwick). Some feminists equate anatomy with geography, envisioning the female body/text as a "no man's land" aligned against a hostile masculine world, the patriarchal settlement (Gilbert and Gubar, *No Man's Land;* Pagano, Kolodny). But in this work most ideas of sexual difference still derive from Freudian theory, rather than recent biogenetics. Ecocriticism urges the study of gender to examine evolutionary biology, where communities are not just cultural spaces.

ECOCRITICISM: A BASIC LIBRARY

Having outlined a theory and history of ecocritical principles, I want in closing to describe some basic texts and the areas of culture they treat. After years of reading across several disciplines, from evolutionary biology and landscape architecture to environmental history and ethics, I've come to see that ecocriticism is evolving loosely because its authors share no sense of canon. Often they use similar rubrics, such as Landscape, Place, Region, Urban, Rural, Nature, and Environment, but since disciplinary biases remain strong, these studies rarely cross-fertilize. What follows is a brief account of thirty books I have found useful, grouped by fields. I have omitted essay collections and works cited above, focusing on major texts and examples of strong interdisciplinary analysis. All are readable, teachable, and practical examples of ecocriticism at work, reflecting the issues and genres that have attracted leading thinkers.

Natural Sciences

A fine guide to natural history is Peter Farb, *Face of North America: The Natural History of a Continent* (New York: Harper & Row, 1963), which describes the diversity of landscapes, from coasts to deserts, and how they are shaped by land-water, plant-animal processes. A good collection of natural history ideas and writings is William Beebe, *The Book of Naturalists: An Anthology of the Best Natural History* (Princeton: Princeton University Press, 1988). Pro-Darwin and anti-ecology, Beebe includes naturalist writers from Aristotle to Rachel Carson. For a history of ideas in modern biology, see Ernest Mayr, *The Growth of Biological Thought* (Cambridge, Mass.: Harvard University Press, 1982), who focuses on the concepts of diversity, evolution, variation, and inheritance. The best introduction to ecology is Edward O. Wilson, *The Diversity of Life* (Cambridge, Mass.: Harvard University Press, 1992), an overview of biodiversity and why environmental stewardship is urgently needed. Wilson traces how new species appear and vanish, explaining that five previous extinctions were natural but the sixth and perhaps last is human-caused and potentially most destructive. Finally, Peter J. Bowler, *The Norton History of the Environmental Sciences* (New York: W. W. Norton, 1994), offers a comprehensive history and cultural critique of Western natural science, from antiquity to modern environmentalism.

Geography

Geography has emerged in recent years as a dynamic field that spans the natural and social sciences. A leading college text is James H. Brown and Arthur C. Gibson, *Biogeography* (St. Louis: C. V. Mosby, 1983), which explains how geological and ecological processes create the geographical distribution of plants and animals. William Norton, *Explorations in the Understanding of Landscape* (New York: Greenwood Press, 1989), examines how sociology, geography, and ecology study landscape by defining the physical and ideological structures that create patterns of human land-use and settlement. The geographical psychology of landscape is the concern of J. Douglas Porteous, *Landscapes of the Mind: Worlds of Sense and Metaphor* (Toronto: University of Toronto Press, 1990), which attacks the banality of modern urban life as a surface "landscape-only" view of the world, devoid of the sensuous freedom and playful exploration of childhood.

Social Sciences

An important early work on the sociopolitical aspects of place is Emma Bell Miles, *Spirit of the Mountains* (Knoxville: University of Tennessee Press, 1975), a "bicultural" study, first published in 1905, that offers a sensible, intuitive view of Appalachia and the importance of matriarchy in mountain cultures. The best account of land politics and economics is Peter M. Wolf, *Land in America: Its Value, Use, and Control* (New York: Pantheon Books, 1981), which studies land as means of wealth for public and private owners. Wolf explains the history of land sales and profits, plus the arcana of taxes, valuations, zoning, development, and other forms of land regulation, including wilderness preservation. In his study of ecopolitics, Bryan Norton, *Toward Unity among Environmentalists* (New York: Oxford University Press, 1991), argues that the conservation-preservation split stems from two different languages, utilitarian and biocentric, that arose during the Hetch Hetchy controversy between Gifford Pinchot and John Muir. For ethics and policy studies, see Donald Van DeVeer, *The Environmental Ethics and Policy Book: Philosophy, Ecology, Economics* (Belmont, Calif.: Wadsworth Publishing, 1993), a reader that indicates how scientific beliefs often guide the moral assumptions behind economic and environmental policy. Key topics include preservation of biodiversity, relations with species, ecosystems and biospheres, decision making and conflict resolution.

History

Intellectual history maps the progress of ideas, often independent of natural or social evidence. An early example is Clarence J. Glacken, *Traces on the Rhodian Shore: Nature and Culture in Western Thought from Ancient Times to the End of the 18th Century* (Berkeley: University of California Press, 1967), which examines three major concepts, the designed earth, its influence on man, and man's effect on it. A more focused intellectual history is Donald Worster, *Nature's Economy: A History of Ecological Ideas* (Cambridge: Cambridge University Press, 1985), which argues that the historic progress from taxonomy to ecology arose from personal and cultural needs.

Landscape history, an aspect of architectural design, examines the relations between built and natural environments. Central to this approach is the idea of landscape as "shaped land," perceived and molded by the human presence. A fine survey of early history is John R. Stilgoe, *Common Landscape of America, 1580–1845* (New Haven: Yale University Press, 1982), which traces common or shared landscapes as they evolve from local into national forms. In Stilgoe's account, rural places strongly influence urban until the industrial revolution, when the old synthesis of land and design collapses. He has also written important studies of railroads, suburbs, and shorelines as historical landscapes. A work of major theoretical influence is John Brinkerhoff Jackson, *Discovering the Vernacular Land-*

scape (New Haven: Yale University Press, 1984), in which the vernacular, or everyday, materials form a "system of man-made spaces" on the earth, always artificial, synthetic, and subject to sudden, unpredictable change.

Social history has been dominated by Marxist economics, notably in the work of Raymond Williams, whose *The Country and the City* (New York: Oxford University Press, 1973) shaped a generation of scholars in environmental history. Williams argues that the relation between country and city evolved from pressures exerted by capitalism, and that images of those environs must be attached to a material continuum, in which they interact. The most comprehensive application of this theory to American history is William Cronon, *Nature's Metropolis: Chicago and the Great West* (New York: W. W. Norton, 1991), an account of how a city shaped the mid-continent landscape and economy through building commodity markets. Hence the frontier is an urban phenomenon, sustained by Swift, Armour, and Sears.

Postmodern history has adopted other cultural constructs as sources of revision. Paul Carter, *The Road to Botany Bay: An Essay in Spatial History* (Chicago: University of Chicago Press, 1987), defines the Australian past as not temporal but spatial; less a manifest destiny than a nonlinear, random filling of space, according to cultural priorities. Neil Evernden, *The Social Creation of Nature* (Baltimore: Johns Hopkins University Press, 1992) argues that nature is a social entity, evolving steadily and thus not a stable frame for environmental discussion. An outstanding reader that summarizes these and many other lines of historical inquiry is Carolyn Merchant, *Major Problems in American Environmental History* (Lexington, Va.: D. C. Heath, 1993). Using excerpts from historical documents and scholarly essays, plus maps, charts, and glossaries, Merchant presents a feminist and Marxist perspective but also attends to scientific and economic evidence.

American Studies

American Studies scholars work "between" disciplines and so often examine issues of placement as they affect regions and peoples. A significant work on native space is David Murray, *Forked Tongues: Speech, Writing and Representation in North American Indian Texts* (London: Pinter Publishers, 1991), which studies the ideology of translation in many documents, from early treaties to recent ethnography. Allen W. Batteau, *The Invention of*

Appalachia (Tempe: University of Arizona Press, 1990), argues that urban elites, mainly journalists and novelists, created romantic imagery that effaced the region's actual history and geography. Places affect both sides of a controversy, as in Ralph H. Lutts, *The Nature Fakers: Wildlife, Science and Sentiment* (Golden, Colo.: Fulcrum, 1990), which reviews the 1903–8 clash between sentimental and scientific nature writers to pose a larger discussion about the cultural rhetoric of wildlife ethics. In the same manner, Belden C. Lane, *Landscapes of the Sacred: Geography and Narrative in American Spirituality* (New York: Paulist Press, 1988), uses a background in theology to reflect on a hermeneutics of landscape; the sacramentalizing of mountains, deserts, and other locales.

Literature and Media

Work in literature has been quite mixed, often owing to its lack of interdisciplinary content. An example is Gillian Tindall, *Countries of the Mind: The Meaning of Place to Writers* (London: Hogarth Press, 1991), which is concerned not with actual but imagined landscapes, on the grounds that readers may thus see their own places without reference to the originals. On the other hand, Leonard Lutwack, *The Role of Place in Literature* (Syracuse: Syracuse University Press, 1984) preserves a sense of both actual and psychological realms in reviewing two opposed ideas about the earth: it is a hostile, alien place; and yet also man's true home, a schism that creates strong tensions between literal geography and its symbolic purposes. New forms of media promise to complicate that certainty; Joshua Meyrowitz, *No Sense of Place: The Impact of Electronic Media on Social Behavior* (New York: Oxford University Press, 1985), argues that television and computers have created cultures no longer shaped by physical location.

Other literary studies have compared genres to scientific paradigms of nature. A pioneering work, Joseph W. Meeker, *The Comedy of Survival: Studies in Literary Ecology* (New York: Charles Scribner's Sons, 1974) uses ecology to examine human-environment relations in various genres and how they may integrate, allowing us to live in a "comic mode" that is detached, ironic, forgiving about human frailty and dedicated to aligning with the natural order. Gillian Beer, *Darwin's Plots: Evolutionary Narrative in Darwin, George Eliot, and Nineteenth-Century Fiction* (Boston: Routledge & Kegan Paul, 1983) explores how novelists assimilated and resisted evolutionary theory, often to create "a determining fiction."

Only recently have scholars begun to define environmental texts, as in Frederick O. Waage, *Teaching Environmental Literature: Materials, Methods, Resources* (New York: MLA, 1985), which introduces the genre in its historic and pedagogic contexts, with practical examples of classes, field projects, and reading lists. The most ambitious effort yet to offer a critical history is Lawrence Buell, *The Environmental Imagination: Thoreau, Nature Writing, and the Formation of American Culture* (Cambridge, Mass.: Harvard University Press, 1995), which uses the figure of Thoreau as a prophetic center from whom radiate essays on such contexts as pastoralism, nature, seasons, place, and pilgrimage. Thoreau brings my account to an end, for he is the author who wrote, "Shall I not have intelligence with the earth? Am I not part leaves and vegetable mould myself?"

NOTE

My thanks to Harold Fromm, Cheryll Glotfelty, Anne Matthews, and Dana Phillips for helpful readings; to Sarah Churchwell, Kelly Flynn, McKay Jenkins, and Patrick O'Kelley for research assistance; and to Princeton University for funding support.

WORKS CITED

Aarsleff, Hans C. *The Study of Language in England, 1780–1860*. Minneapolis: University of Minnesota Press, 1983.

Argyros, Alexander J. *A Blessed Rage for Order: Deconstruction, Evolution, and Chaos*. Ann Arbor: University of Michigan Press, 1992.

Bartter, Martha A. *The Way to Ground Zero: The Atomic Bomb in American Science Fiction*. Westport, Conn.: Greenwood, 1988.

Bates, Marston. *The Nature of Natural History*. Princeton: Princeton University Press, 1990.

Bechmann, Ronald. *Trees and Man: The Forest in the Middle Ages*. New York: Paragon House, 1990.

Beer, Gillian. *Darwin's Plots: Evolutionary Narrative in Darwin, George Eliot, and Nineteenth-Century Fiction*. Boston: Routledge & Kegan Paul, 1983.

Benjamin, Walter. *Illuminations*. New York: Harcourt, 1968.

Blanchard, Marc E. *Description: Sign, Self, Desire: Critical Theory in the Wake of Semiotics*. The Hague: Mouton, 1979.

Blumenberg, Hans. *Work on Myth*. Cambridge, Mass.: MIT Press, 1985.

Boudreau, Gordon V. *The Roots of Walden and the Tree of Life*. Nashville: Vanderbilt University Press, 1990.

Bowler, Peter J. *The Norton History of the Environmental Sciences*. New York: Norton, 1993.

Brown, James H., and Arthur C. Gibson. *Biogeography*. St. Louis: C. V. Mosby, 1983.

Burns, Alfred. *The Power of the Written Word: The Role of Literacy in the History of Western Civilization*. New York: Lang, 1989.

Cowdrey, Albert E. *This Land, This South: An Environmental History*. Lexington: University Press of Kentucky, 1983.

Crosby, Alfred. "Ecological Imperialism." In *Major Problems in American Environmental History*. Ed. Carolyn Merchant. Lexington, Mass.: D. C. Heath, 1993.

Cummings, Sherwood. *Mark Twain and Science: Adventures of a Mind*. Baton Rouge: Louisiana State University Press, 1988.

Daly, Mary. *Gyn/Ecology: The Metaethics of Radical Feminism*. Boston: Beacon, 1978.

Devall, Bill, and George Sessions. *Deep Ecology: Living as if Nature Mattered*. Salt Lake City, Utah: Gibbs M. Smith, 1985.

Disch, Robert. *The Ecology of Conscience: Values for Survival*. Englewood Cliffs, N.J.: Prentice-Hall, 1970.

Dixon, Melvin. *Ride Out the Wilderness: Geography and Identity in Afro-American Literature*. Urbana: University of Illinois Press, 1987.

Eaton, Leonard K. *Landscape Artist in America: The Life and Work of Jens Jensen*. Chicago: University of Chicago Press, 1964.

Egerton, Frank, et al. *History of American Ecology*. New York: Arno Press, 1977.

Elgin, Don D. *The Comedy of the Fantastic: Ecological Perspectives on the Fantasy Novel*. Westport, Conn.: Greenwood, 1985.

Elliott, Emory. *Columbia Literary History of the United States*. New York: Columbia University Press, 1988.

Entrikin, Nicholas. *The Betweenness of Place: Towards a Geography of Modernity*. Baltimore: Johns Hopkins University Press, 1991.

Erlich, Richard. *Clockwork Worlds: Mechanized Environments in Science Fiction*. Westport, Conn.: Greenwood, 1983.

Fairbanks, Carol. *Prairie Women: Images in American and Canadian Fiction*. New Haven: Yale University Press, 1986.

Fish, Stanley. *Is There a Text in this Class? The Authority of Interpretive Communities*. Cambridge, Mass.: Harvard University Press, 1980.

Forman, Richard, and Michel Godron. *Landscape Ecology*. New York: John Wiley & Sons, 1986.

Gehlen, Arnold. *Man, His Nature and Place in This World*. New York: Columbia University Press, 1988

Gilbert, Sandra, and Susan Gubar. *The Madwoman in the Attic: The Woman Writer and the Nineteenth-Century Literary Imagination.* New Haven: Yale University Press, 1979.

Gilbert, Sandra, and Susan Gubar. *No Man's Land: The Place of the Woman Writer in the Twentieth Century.* New Haven: Yale University Press, 1988.

Gleick, James. *Chaos: Making a New Science.* New York: Viking, 1987.

Goetzmann, William. *Exploration and Empire: The Explorer and Scientist in the Winning of the American West.* New York: Norton, 1966.

Goody, Jack R. *The Logic of Writing and the Organization of Society.* Cambridge: Cambridge University Press, 1986.

Greenblatt, Stephen, and Giles Gunn. *Redrawing the Boundaries: The Transformation of English and American Literary Studies.* New York: MLA, 1992.

Hall, Stephen S. *Mapping the Next Millennium: The Discovery of New Geographies.* New York: Random House, 1992.

Harrison, Robert Pogue. *Forests: The Shadow of Civilization.* Chicago: University of Chicago Press, 1992.

Hayles, N. Katherine. *Chaos Bound: Orderly Disorder in Contemporary Literature and Science.* Ithaca: Cornell University Press, 1990.

Hendrickson, Robert. *The Ocean Almanac.* New York: Doubleday, 1984.

Hoagland, Edward. Preface to Penguin Nature Library volumes.

Howarth, William. *The Book of Concord: Thoreau's Life as a Writer.* New York: Viking, 1982.

Hubbard, Ruth. *Biological Woman: The Convenient Myth.* Cambridge, Mass.: Shenckman, 1982.

Hurt, James. *Writing Illinois: The Prairie, Lincoln, and Chicago.* Urbana: University of Illinois Press, 1992.

Huseboe, Arthur R., and William Geyer. *Where the West Begins: Essays on the Middle West and Siouxland Writing.* Sioux Falls: Center for Western Studies, 1978.

Jackson, Hartley H. T. *Mammals of Wisconsin.* Madison: University of Wisconsin Press, 1961.

Jarvella, Robert J., and Wolfgang Klein. *Speech, Place, and Action: Studies of Deixis and Related Topics.* New York: John Wiley & Sons, 1982.

Jordanova, Ludmilla. *Languages of Nature: Critical Essays on Science and Literature.* London: Free Association Books, 1986.

Keller, Evelyn Fox, and Elisabeth A. Lloyd, *Keywords in Evolutionary Biology.* Cambridge, Mass.: Harvard University Press, 1992.

Kepes, Gyorgy. *The New Landscape in Art and Science.* Chicago: Paul Theobald, 1956.

Kolodny, Annette. *The Lay of the Land: Metaphor as Experience and History in American Life and Letters.* Chapel Hill: University of North Carolina Press, 1979.

Krieger, Murray. *A Reopening of Closure: Organicism against Itself.* New York: Columbia University Press, 1989.

Kuhn, Thomas S. *The Structure of Scientific Revolutions.* Chicago: University of Chicago Press, 1970.

Levine, George, and Alan Rauch. *One Culture: Essays in Science and Literature.* Madison: University of Wisconsin Press, 1987.

Limerick, Patricia Nelson. *Desert Passages: Encounters with the American Deserts.* Albuquerque: University of New Mexico Press, 1985.

Liu, James J. *Language—Paradox—Poetics: A Chinese Perspective.* Ed. Richard John Lynn. Princeton: Princeton University Press, 1988.

Looney, Sandra, et al. *The Prairie Frontier.* Sioux Falls: Nordland Heritage Foundation, 1984.

Lopez, Barry. *Crossing Native Ground.* New York: Vintage, 1989.

Luke, Timothy. "The Dreams of Deep Ecology," *Telos* (Summer 1988).

Malin, James C. *History and Ecology: Studies of the Grassland.* Lincoln: University of Nebraska Press, 1984.

Marshall, Donald. *Contemporary Critical Theory: A Selected Bibliography.* New York: MLA, 1993.

Matthews, Anne. *Where the Buffalo Roam.* New York: Grove Weidenfeld, 1992.

Medawar, Peter. *The Threat and the Glory: Reflections on Science and Scientists.* New York: Oxford University Press, 1991.

Mogen, David. *Wilderness Visions: Science Fiction Westerns.* San Bernadino: Borgo Press, 1982.

Monmonier, Mark. *Mapping It Out: Expository Cartography for the Humanities and Social Sciences.* Chicago: University of Chicago Press, 1993.

Murray, David. *Forked Tongues: Speech, Writing, and Representation in North American Indian Texts.* London: Pinter Publishers, 1991.

Oates, David. *Earth Rising: Ecological Belief in an Age of Science.* Corvallis: Oregon State University Press, 1989.

Pagano, Jo Anne. *Exiles and Communities: Teaching in the Patriarchal Wilderness.* Albany: State University of New York Press, 1990.

Perlin, John. *A Forest Journey: The Role of Wood in the Development of Civilization.* New York: Norton, 1989.

Rabkin, Erik, et al. *The End of the World.* Carbondale: Southern Illinois University Press, 1983.

Raymo, Chet. *Written in Stone: A Geological and Natural History of the Northeastern United States.* Chester, Conn.: Globe Pequot Press, 1989.

Real, Leslie A., and James H. Brown. *Foundations of Ecology: Classic Papers with Commentaries.* Chicago: University of Chicago Press, 1991.

Regis, Pamela. *Describing Early America: Bartram, Jefferson, Crevecoeur, and the Rhetoric of Natural History.* DeKalb: Northern Illinois University Press, 1991.

Ross, Andrew. *The Chicago Gangster Theory of Life: Nature's Debt to Society.* New York: Verso, 1994.

———. *Strange Weather: Culture, Science and Technology in the Age of Limits.* New York: Verso, 1991.

Ryden, Kent C. *Mapping the Invisible Landscape: Folklore, Writing, and the Sense of Place.* Iowa City: Iowa University Press, 1993.

Sedgwick, Eve Kosofsky. *Epistemology of the Closet.* Berkeley: University of California Press, 1990.

Shepard, Paul. *The Subversive Science: Essays towards an Ecology of Man.* Boston: Houghton Mifflin, 1969.

Tallmadge, John. "From Chronicle to Quest: The Shaping of Darwin's 'Voyage of the Beagle,'" *Victorian Studies* (Spring 1980).

Thomas, Brook. *The New Historicism and Other Old-Fashioned Topics.* Princeton: Princeton University Press, 1991.

Thomas, Lewis. *The Lives of a Cell: Notes of a Biology Watcher.* New York: Viking, 1974.

Tudge, Colin. *Global Ecology.* New York: Oxford University Press, 1991.

Weiner, Jonathan. *The Beak of the Finch: A Story of Evolution in Our Time.* New York: Knopf, 1994.

Weissmann, Gerald. *The Woods Hole Cantata: Essays on Science and Society.* New York: Dodd, Mead, 1985.

Wendlen, Albert. *Science, Myth, and the Fictional Creation of Alien Worlds.* Ann Arbor: University of Michigan Research Press, 1985.

Williams, Raymond. *Keywords.* Oxford: Oxford University Press, 1976.

Wilson, Edward O. *Biophilia.* Cambridge, Mass.: Harvard University Press, 1984.

Wilson, Edward O. *The Diversity of Life.* Cambridge, Mass.: Harvard University Press, 1992.

Wood, Denis. *The Power of Maps.* New York: Guilford Press, 1992.

Worster, Donald. *Nature's Economy: A History of Ecological Ideas.* Cambridge: Cambridge University Press, 1985.

Worster, Donald. *The Wealth of Nature: Environmental History and the Ecological Imagination.* New York: Oxford University Press, 1993.

Wright, Will. *Wild Knowledge: Science, Language, and Social Life in a Fragile Environment.* Minneapolis: University of Minnesota Press, 1992.

NEIL EVERNDEN

Beyond Ecology

■ ■ ■

SELF, PLACE, AND THE PATHETIC FALLACY

It is a matter of considerable concern to me that the sector of society we designate as the Arts and Humanities seems to play so minor a role in the environmental movement. There are notable exceptions, to be sure. People like Allan Gussow, Eliot Porter, and Ansel Adams have probably had a discernible effect on public conscience and consciousness. But most commonly the environmentalist is thought of as someone with a background in the natural sciences. This is unfortunate, I think, and explains in part the one-sidedness of environmentalist arguments and their tendency to contain the seeds of the movement's destruction. Failure is inevitable because of the movement's willingness to address the developer's perpetual question: "What good is it?" Accepting the validity of that question entails denying the validity of the preservationist movement.

I recall one incident which seems to me to illustrate the self-destruct mechanism built into the conservationist cause. About fifteen years ago, I was sitting at a long cafeteria table with some other biologists. We were discussing with righteous indignation the proposal that a railroad be built through Wood Buffalo National Park in northern Canada. This line would have run through the nesting ground of the only remaining Whooping Cranes, of which there were only about 18 at the time. It seemed utterly unbelievable to us that anyone could even suggest such a scheme. But we were brought down to earth rather abruptly when someone sitting at the same table, who had been forced to listen to our tirade, turned to us and said "So what—what good are Whooping Cranes?" What annoyed me most was that, for the life of me, I couldn't think of a single use for Whooping Cranes. They don't sing or eat harmful insects—you can't even claim them as a tourist attraction. Instantly, because our entire justification for existence of non-human nature was based on utility, our ability to defend the Whooping Crane disintegrated. To justify the birds, we had to fall back on—dare I say it?—*subjective* arguments, the kind a forester recently condemned as "burdened with sentimentality and impractical attitudes toward natural resource use."[1]

But to some, the conservation movement along with its in-built argument for utility seems to have been made viable again by the higher profile of Ecology. Ecology, they would argue, shows us that we can't do as we wish without paying a price. All of nature has utility, all is important. Hence Ecology, the "subversive science," seems to give much-needed support to the cause of the preservationist. And so it does, to a degree. Yet the "ecology movement" shares the same self-destructive embrace of the utility argument, and inevitably the demand arises for Ecology to *solve* the problem. If we can't proceed with a certain development without undesirable consequences, then obviously it is the role of the ecologist to find a way for us to proceed with the development while avoiding the consequences. Ecology, in general, is about as subversive as the Chamber of Commerce.

But there is, I think, a sense in which Ecology truly *is* subversive, and in which it both supports the preservationist movement and the role of the artist in that movement. The really subversive element in Ecology rests not on any of its more sophisticated concepts, but upon its basic premise: inter-relatedness. But the genuinely radical nature of that proposition is not generally perceived, even, I think, by ecologists. To the western mind, *inter-related* implies a causal connectedness. Things are inter-related if a change in one affects the other. So to say that all things are inter-related simply implies that if we wish to develop our "resources," we must find some technological means to defuse the interaction. The solution to pollution is dilution. But what is actually involved is a genuine *intermingling* of parts of the ecosystem. There are no discrete entities. As Paul Shepard described it in one of his many fine essays, the epidermis of the skin is "ecologically like a pond surface or a forest soil, not a shell so much as a delicate interpenetration."[2]

Ecology begins as a normal, reductionist science, but to its own surprise it winds up denying the subject-object relationship upon which science rests. Ecology undermines not only the growth addict and the chronic developer, but science itself.

At the outset, there seemed little enough risk. Biology has had to contend for years with relationships that contradict the assumptions of discreteness so important in its own taxonomic systems. Evolution itself was a severe blow to the pigeonhole mentality; it's very discouraging to have your species go and change on you after you get them all neatly labeled. But then there were the symbionts, the creatures that habitually co-exist in such close association as to make it difficult or impossible to deal with one without simultaneously dealing with the other. What do you do with creatures such as lichen, composed of two kinds of organism (and not even closely related ones at that)? The algal component provides photosynthetic ability, the fungal component structure and nutrient uptake. The two are mutually dependent on each other. What is a lichen? A plant? A co-operative? And what about colonial organisms, in which different individuals perform different functions so that the community as a whole persists? Is the Portuguese Man-of-War an animal or a colony of animals? Where do you draw the line?

The situation has gotten even more confusing in recent years. Until now it has at least seemed safe to assume that whatever is with a cell belongs to that cell. But now it appears that the chloroplasts within the plant cell behave quite independently of the rest of the cell, and may originally have been separate organisms, like the algae and fungi in lichen.[3] That is to say, what we take for granted to be a single organism controlled by a single set of genes may in fact be more properly thought of as a very dependent kind of symbiosis, a mutualism in which the fate of two (or more) organisms has become so incredibly intertwined as to make them appear inseparable. Is a plant a plant, or a system of formerly independent creatures?

But still more disturbing to the particulate mentality is the fact that even humans seem to share this kind of ambiguity. It has been known for years, of course, that the bacterial flora of the intestine are essential for our survival. But it now appears that some of the organelles in our cells are quite as independent as the chloroplasts. Mitochondria, it turns out, replicate separately and independently of the cells, and are made up of RNA that is quite unlike the RNA of the cells. Apparently the mitochondria move into the cells like colonists, and continue their separate existence within us.[4] And what does that make man? Do we also merit colonial status? But perhaps that seems like mere semantics. What difference does it make that the parts are not what they seemed, so long as they act as an isolated organism? But is it isolated? Perhaps not. In his fascinating review of current bacteriological research, Reanny has outlined the difficulties that have arisen with the realization that mammalian evolution could not have occurred as rapidly as it did by mutation and natural selection alone. There must have been some sort of speeding-up involved, possibly through mechanisms that permit different expression of the genes without having to wait for gross changes in the genes themselves. That is, the genetic keyboard could remain about the same while different selections were performed on it. Such a phenomenon is now known to occur in bacteria. There are "extra-chromasomal elements" that can perform the role of cellular conductors, orchestrating new and resistant strains of bacterial cells to combat the extravagant barrage of antibiotics that flow from the pens of willing medical prescribers. But perhaps the more significant part of this fascinating phenomenon is that these are *extra*-chromasomal elements. They are not a part of what was traditionally regarded as the control center of the cell. They are independent. And they are transferable. That is, an extra-chromasomal element from one cell can be transferred to another. This means that a new evolutionary advance can be spread throughout the population very quickly, without waiting for natural selection. Creatures can "infect" each other with evolutionary transformations. And finally, most remarkable of all is the fact that these elements appear to be transmissible not only between individuals of the same species, but between species as well. This means it is conceivable that groups of species, perhaps even whole communities of organisms, could, in a sense, co-evolve. They are all quite literally inter-related.

And so we return again to the subversive tenet of Ecology: interrelatedness. But, I emphasize again, it is to be taken quite literally, not simply as an indication of causal connectedness. Where do you draw the line between one creature and another? Where does one organism stop and another begin? Is there even a boundary between you and the non-living world, or will the atoms in this page be a part of your body tomorrow? How, in short, can you make any sense out of the concept of man as a discrete entity? How can the proper study for man be man if it is impossible for man to exist out of context? For the ecologist, then, the desire of some in the humanities to deal only with the fragment of reality they term "human" is nonsense.

The social sciences are especially prone to act as if there was a discrete entity of all-consuming importance called *man*. In what I doubt is an isolated incident, one social scientist who had recently joined an environmental studies department was heard to express great surprise that some members of that department were studying natural ecosystems rather than cities and human populations. Even in psychiatry, the social environment is given almost exclusive attention. So far as I know, no recent contributions have been made to the promising start made by Harold Searles in 1960.[5] Searles emphasized the dangers of ignoring the non-human portion of the environment and man's relationship to it. He claimed that a disproportionate number of his schizophrenic patients came from homes in which they were denied the chance to relate to material things. This is not to suggest that such a dependency on the non-human is pathological, but rather that the schizophrenic cannot afford to ignore, as most of us do, the fact that the material objects in one's life are an emotionally meaningful part of it. But even if a start has been made by writers such as Searles, Cobb,[6] and Shepard,[7] the significance of the concept of relatedness to the non-human seems to escape even those who would consider themselves conservationists. It is much easier for us to think in terms of anti-pollution campaigns than to contemplate a fundamental error in our set of cultural assumptions. Allied with this mania for believing in totally separate packages is our tendency to regard experience too as a set of separate factors, some of which are labelled "stimulus" and others "response." This in turn leads to some very unfortunate misunderstandings. Take the case of our current interest in landscape aesthetics, for example. With no discernible leadership from the arts, the scientists and planners have attempted to use their traditional tools—fragmentation and measurement—to describe the aesthetic superiority of one piece of landscape over another.[8] The assumption is that there is something physical "out there" which, when seen by us "in here" produces a pleasurable effect. Obviously, if we can learn to identify and measure those physical factors that lead to the desired effect, we will have a charming new technique to use in environmental impact assessments and cost-benefit analyses. The result, predictably, is a kind of glorified Neilsen rating for nature, which threatens to help legitimize the further homogenization of the landscape by encouraging preservation of the currently popular while the less favored areas are consumed behind cosmetic barriers. Nowhere in the current literature do we find a conception of aesthetics adequate to permit the inclusion of such writers as Edith Cobb.

Cobb speaks of the child's relationship to the natural world as being basically aesthetic. This would be quite meaningless to current landscape researchers who presume a strictly formalist view of aesthetics. But this is a far cry from what Cobb has in mind. In contrast, Cobb's is a world of interactions, much more in line, I think, with the aesthetic theories of

John Dewey than with the assumptions of those currently declaring interest in environmental aesthetics. The aesthetic experience, in Dewey's terminology, lies in the relationship between the individual and the environment, not simply in the object viewed, nor in the mind of the viewer. Rather than a subject-object relationship in which the observer parades before the supposedly beautiful view, we have instead a process, an interaction between the viewer and the viewed, and it is in that joint association that the aesthetic experience lies. Instead of a detachment from the environment, we have a subtle diffusion into it. This concept of aesthetics makes perfect sense if one recognizes that strict categories are an abstraction, not a reality.

Similarly, the question of the role of the environment in the life of the individual is now transformed. Rather than thinking of an individual spaceman who must slurp up chunks of the world—"resources"—into his separate compartment, we must deal instead with the individual-in-environment, the individual as a component of, not something distinct from, the rest of the environment.

Which brings us back again to the question of inter-relatedness. What evidence have we of the relationship between organisms and their environment? Are there demonstrable instances of substantial involvement of an individual with a total environment? There is at least one well-known phenomenon which indicates a strong affinity to a particular place. I'm speaking of "territoriality," but I have no interest in the routine description of it. Instead, I want to approach it from an aspect denied the scientist. I want to ask what it *feels* like to have a territory.

▪ ▪ ▪ Let me remind you of one of the common examples, that of a small fish called a cichlid. Normally, size is of considerable importance—the big guy usually gets his way. But when the breeding season comes along, strange things start to happen; size does not necessarily prevail. It appears that once a small fish has established himself in a territory, he goes quite mad. That is to say, he does not appear to behave rationally. He doesn't seem to respect size at all. He even seems to forget what an insignificant specimen he is, and will attack a much larger intruder.

In short, it's as if he thinks he is as big as his territory. It's as if his boundary of what he considers to be "himself" has expanded to the dimensions of the territory itself. The fish is no longer an organism bounded by skin—it is an organism-plus-environment bounded by an imaginary integument.

The boundary isn't a sharp one, but rather is a gradient. The further you get from its center, the less willing is the fish to attack. It's as if there is a kind of *field* in the territory, with the "self" present throughout but more concentrated toward the center:

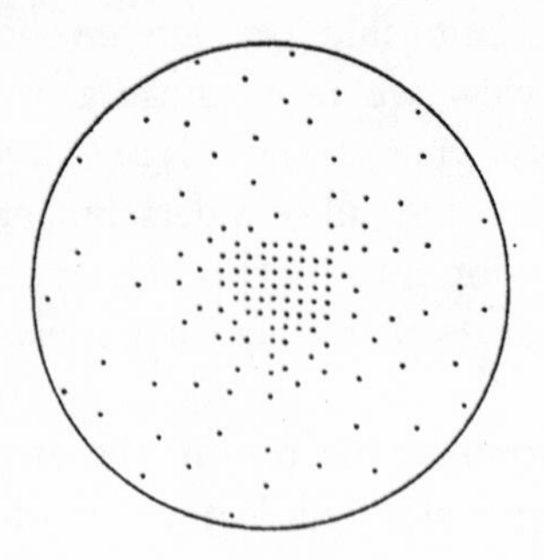

This is in striking contrast to the "normal" state of affairs, in which the fish is *non-properterian* and regards itself as bounded, more or less, by the skin itself:

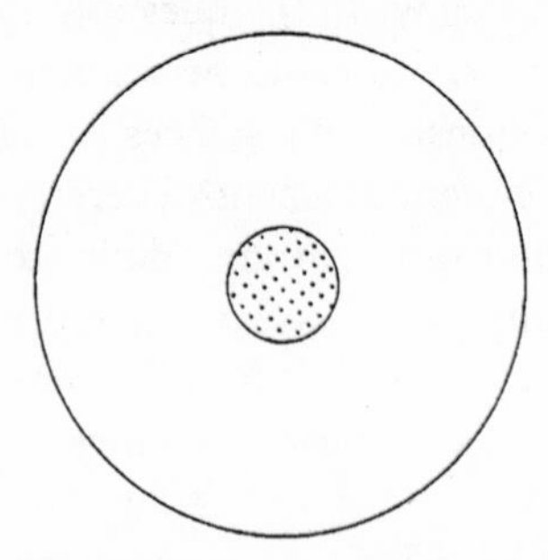

In this case, there is more clearly an individual and an environment.

Now, to take the admittedly precarious step of assuming some analogy, if not homology, between humans and more demonstrably territorial animals, there is an additional phenomenon that becomes immediately apparent. Since Descartes, westerners have been content to take the illustrated procedure a step further. Not only are we not a part of an environment, we are not even part of a *body*. We, the "real" us, is concentrated in some disputed recess of the body, a precious cocoon, separate from the world of matter. Far from extending our "self" into the environment as the territorial fish does, we hoard our ego as tightly as we can.

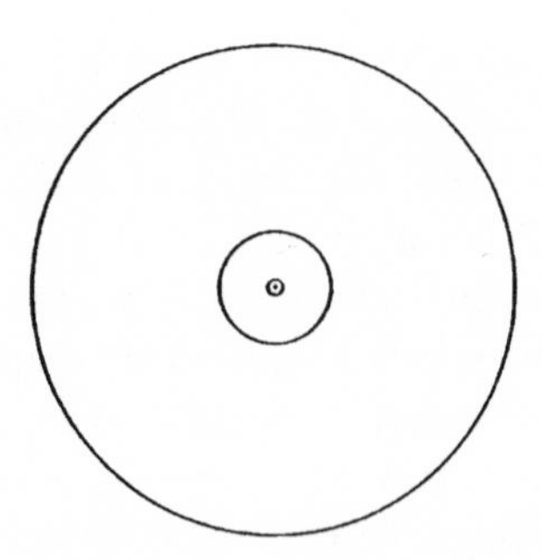

This brings up the question of what we really mean when we speak of man/environment relationships. F. Sparshott has suggested[9] there are several kinds of relationship possible: I-Thou, subject-object, user and used, and so forth. But the only one that is really relevant to a discussion of man and environment is *the relation of self to setting.*

Given this, one who looks on the world as simply a set of resources to be utilized is not thinking of it as an environment at all. Such a man is, according to Sparshott, "blind to all the aspects that make it an environment." The whole world is simply fodder and feces to the consumer, in sharp contrast to the man who is in an environment in which he belongs and is of necessity a part. The tourist can grasp only the superficialities of a landscape, whereas a resident reacts to what has occurred. He sees a landscape not only as a collection of physical forms, but as the evidence of what has occurred there. To the tourist, the landscape is merely a facade, but to the resident it is "the outcome of how it got there and the outside of what goes on inside." The resident is, in short, a part of the place, just as the fish is a part of the territory. And his involvement with that place is, I think, an aesthetic one in the sense that Dewey and Cobb use the term. And perhaps also in the sense in which Northrop Frye uses it when he claims that the goal of art is to "recapture, in full consciousness, that original lost sense of identity with our surroundings, where there is nothing outside the mind of man, or something identical with the mind of man."[10]

We might deduce from this that what the landscape artist is doing is giving us an understanding of what a place would look like to us *if we "belonged" there,* if it were "our place." The artist is not doing landscape paintings; he is doing landscape *portraits,* or place portraits. And, just as the serious portraitist attempts to capture the essential qualities of his subject, qualities which would otherwise be known only to the subject's friends, so the landscape artist gives us a glimpse of the character of the land that would otherwise require long experience to achieve. The artist makes the world personal—known, loved, feared, or whatever, but *not neutral*.

We achieve, then, the sensation of knowing, the sensation of being part of a known place. Perhaps it is a cultural simulation of a sense of place. Whether or not the attachment of humans to place is indeed homologous to territoriality in other animals is not of great importance here—although it is suggestive that such things as territoriality, social hierarchy, and imprinting, along with the ability to personally identify with and remember what is going on in the environment, are functions of the ancient limbic system which we share with these other creatures.[11] It is sufficient that it serve as an analogy for the kinds of attachment we do form, and perhaps for the activities of the serious landscape artist. In other words, there appears to be a human phenomenon, similar in some ways to the experience of territoriality, that is described as aesthetic and which is, in effect, a "sense of place," a sense of knowing and of being a part of a particular place. There's nothing very mysterious about this—it's just what it feels like to be home, to experience a sense of light or of smell that is inexplicably "right." I sometimes imagine that it is also the experience that inspires the homing pigeon to its incredible accomplishments. The scientist, of course, is only permitted to ask the bird how he does it, not why, and certainly not what it feels like. But the salient feature of the phenomenon is not whether the subconscious act of navigation is dependent on stars or magnetism or polarized light, but that the bird must move to correct the tension it feels when it finds itself "out of context." It moves to correct its feeling of placelessness, a defect that will only be corrected when it reaches its roost. The bird is carried by a swirling mental vortex toward the center of the vacuum left by its displacement from its place in the environmental collage, to that small slice of environment in which it fits *and by which it is defined*.

The assumption that there is such a thing as a sense of place brings to light some strange anomalies in our current lifestyle. For instance, we must ask ourselves whether it is truly possible for any creatures in a state of sensory deprivation to form genuine attachments to place. What is the experience one has of an urban environment? What do we see? What do we smell, or hear? Contrary to those who praise the complexity of urban life, I must insist we take seriously Kvaløy's distinction between the complex natural environment and the merely complicated urban one.[12] The environmental repertoire is vastly diminished in urban life, perhaps to the point of making genuine attachment to place very difficult—even assuming a person were to stay in one place long enough to make the attempt at all. In lieu of the opportunity to form a relationship to place, the urbanite is easy prey to the advertisers who promise an easy surrogate, a commercial sop to his need for place, both social and physical. He is encouraged to accept the social place that comes, free of extra charge, with the commodity in question. But an automobile is no real substitute for physical place, no adequate extension of the self, or one so limited in potential as to hopelessly limit the emotional repertoire of the symbiont. What *does* make sense, however, is something that most in our society could not take seriously: animism. For once we engage in the extension of the boundary of the self into the "environment," then of course we imbue it with life and can quite properly regard it as animate—it is animate because we are a part of it. And, following from this, all the metaphorical properties so favored by poets make perfect sense: the Pathetic Fallacy is a fallacy only to the ego clencher. Metaphoric language is an indicator of "place"—an indication that the speaker has a place, feels part of a place. Indeed, the motive for metaphor may be as Frye claims, "a desire to associate, and finally to identify, the human mind with what goes on outside it, because the only genuine joy you can have is in those rare moments when you feel that although we may know in part . . . we are also a part of what we know."[13]

The act of naming may itself be a part of the process of establishing a sense of place. This is fairly easy to understand in a personal sense, that is, giving personal names to special components of a place, but it also may apply in the case of generic names. Perhaps the naturalist, with his penchant for learning the names of everything, is establishing a global place, making the world his home, just as the "primitive" hunter did on the territory of his tribe.

▪ ▪ ▪ But whatever the mechanism, I persist in believing that there is some connection between the individual and his particular place and that, as Paul Shepard says, knowing who you are is impossible without knowing where you are from.[14] The recognition that the establishment of self is impossible without the context of place casts an entirely different light on the significance of the non-human, and underlines the futility of quantitative popularity ratings in the determination of the significance of public landscapes. The significance of place is a very personal thing, and the battle for the right to know "where I am from" is not one to be won by environmental impact assessments and benefit-cost analyses. The right to place, to know where one is from, is a right that is difficult to argue with the tools of the scientist. It is unfortunate, therefore, that those in the environmental sciences are assumed to be the logical choice as advocates in the environmental movement. In fact, many of the most significant arguments cannot be handled by their lexicon. Furthermore, their advocacy is, of necessity, limited to what Kvaløy[15] calls the "shallow ecological movement." The "deep ecological movement," the one that concerns itself with the underlying roots of the environmental crisis rather than simply its physical manifestation, demands the involvement of the arts and humanities. Yet it is the members of those disciplines that seem least frequently involved, with, as I said before, some very notable exceptions. In part this may be due to the reluctance of society to pay attention to anyone who is not a scientist. It may also be partly due to a fear that anyone interested in animals and flowers will be labeled a Romantic. But I fear it stems in part from the old assumption that the proper study for man is man. In accepting this, artists and humanists borrow from the sciences whose reductionism they so often criticize, for to suggest that man can and should be studied exclusive of his environment is as good an example of reductionism as we are likely to find. Hence, there is man, and there is environment. The humanist need feel responsible only for man. If there's a problem with the rest, call in a scientist. Indeed, even the suggestion that man is tied to anything but himself, or that he shares any biological imperatives with other creatures, is seen in some quarters as an affront to humanity. This is doubly unfortunate, I think, for not only does it bespeak a regrettably low opinion of the rest of creation, it also alienates from the environmental movement a portion of the population that could be its most potent force.

I am not advocating some kind of neo-romanticism, but rather an open endorsement of the value of the experience of landscape to counteract the prevailing attitude favoring only the consumption of landscape as a commodity. Far from being a demeaning concept, it should reveal "the self enobled and extended rather than threatened as part of the landscape and the ecosystem, because the beauty and complexity of nature are continuous with ourselves."[16] The subversive nature of Ecology rests on its assumption of literal interrelatedness, not just interdependence. Ecology as a discipline has been called upon to ignore the former and deal with the latter, on the assumption that the patterns of dependence can be shifted, whereas relatedness cannot. It seems to me that an involvement by the arts is vitally needed to emphasize that relatedness, and the intimate and vital involvement of self with place. Ultimately, preservation of the non-human is a very personal crusade, a rejection of the homogenization of the world that threatens to diminish all, including the self. There is no such thing as an individual, only an individual-in-context, individual as a component of place, defined by place. One can scarcely be critical of Ecology if it fails to incorporate such arguments into its equations. There are very severe limits placed on it by virtue of being, or aspiring to be, a science. Aldo Leopold complained that

> A professor may pluck the strings of his own instrument, but never that of another, and if he listens for music he must never admit it to his fellows or his students. For all are restrained by an ironbound taboo which decrees that the construction of instruments is the domain of science, while the detection of harmony is the domain of poets.[17]

It is ironic, then, that when a society finally detects a dissonance in the world around it, it looks to Science for a solution. And so the ecologist mumbles on, picking up the pieces and pretending that the imminent discovery and marketing of a new miracle adhesive will restore the Harmony of the Biosphere. It's no good passing the buck to ecologists—environmentalism involves the perception of values, and values are the coin of the arts. Environmentalism without aesthetics is merely regional planning.

NOTES

1. F. L. Newby, "Man-Nature-Beauty: A Research Dilemma" (Munich: IUFRO-Kongress, 1967) papers 7, section 26: 227–38.
2. Paul Shepard, "Ecology and Man—A Viewpoint," introduction to *The Subversive Science,* ed. P. Shepard and D. McKinley (New York: Houghton Mifflin, 1969).
3. Lewis Thomas, *Lives of a Cell* (New York: Bantam, 1974).
4. D. Reanny, "Extrachromasomal Elements as Possible Agents of Adaptation and Development," *Bacterial Review* 40 (1976): 552–90.
5. Harold Searles, *The Nonhuman Environment in Normal Development and in Schizophrenia* (New York: International Universities Press, 1960).
6. Edith Cobb, *The Ecology of Imagination in Childhood* (New York: Columbia University Press, 1977).

7. Paul Shepard, "Place in American Culture," *North American Review* 262 (Fall 1977): 22–32.

8. L. M. Arthur, T. C. Daniel, and R. J. Boster, "Scenic Assessment: An Overview," *Landscape Planning* 4 (1977): 102–29.

9. F. Sparshott, "Figuring the Ground: Notes on Some Theoretical Problems of the Aesthetic Environment," *Journal of Aesthetic Education* 6.3 (1972): 11–23.

10. Northrop Frye, *The Educated Imagination* (Toronto: CBC, 1961) 9.

11. P. Maclean, "The Paranoid Streak in Man," *Beyond Reductionism*, ed. A. Koestler and J. Smythies (London: Hutchinson, 1969).

12. S. Kvaløy, "Ecophilosophy & Ecopolitics: Thinking and Acting in Response to the Threats of Ecocatastrophe," *North American Review* 260 (Summer 1974): 17–28.

13. Frye 11.

14. Shepard, "Place in American Culture," 32.

15. Kvaløy.

16. Shepard, "Ecology and Man," 2.

17. Aldo Leopold, *A Sand County Almanac and Sketches Here and There* (New York: Oxford University Press, 1949) 153.

WILLIAM RUECKERT

Literature and Ecology

■ ■ ■

AN EXPERIMENT IN ECOCRITICISM

"It is the business of those who direct the activities that will shape tomorrow's world to think beyond today's well being and provide for tomorrow."—Raymond Dasmann, *Planet in Peril*

"Any living thing that hopes to live on earth must fit into the ecosphere or perish."—Barry Commoner, *The Closing Circle*

". . . the function of poetry . . . is to nourish the spirit of man by giving him the cosmos to suckle. We have only to lower our standard of dominating nature and to raise our standard of participating in it in order to make the reconciliation take place. When man becomes proud to be not just the site where ideas and feelings are produced, but also the crossroad where they divide and mingle, he will be ready to be saved. Hope therefore lies in a poetry through which the world so invades the spirit of man that he becomes almost speechless, and later reinvents language."—Francis Ponge, *The Voice of Things*

SHIFTING OUR LOCUS OF MOTIVATION

Where have we been in literary criticism in my time? Well, like Count Mippipopolus in *The Sun Also Rises,* we seem to have been everywhere, seen and done everything. Here are just some of the positions and battles which many of us have been into and through: formalism, neoformalism, and contextualism; biographical, historical, and textual criticism; mythic, archetypal, and psychological criticism; structuralism and phenomenology; spatial, ontological, and—well, and so forth, and so forth. Individually and collectively, we have been through so many great and original minds, that one wonders what could possibly be left for experimental criticism to experiment with just now—in 1976.

Furthermore, there are so many resourceful and energetic minds working out from even the merest suggestion of a new position, that the permutations of even the most complex new theory or methodology are exhausted very quickly these days. If you do not get in on the very beginning of a new theory, it is all over with before you can even think it through, apply it, write it up, and send it out for publication. The incredible storehouse of existing theories and methods, coupled with the rapid aging (almost pre-aging, it seems) of new critical theories and methods, has made for a somewhat curious critical environment. For those who are happy with it, a fabulously resourceful, seemingly limitless, pluralism is available: there is something for everybody and almost anything can be done with it. But for those whose need and bent is to go where others have not yet been, no matter how remote that territory may be, there are some problems: the compulsion toward newness acts like a forcing house to produce theories which are evermore elegant, more baroque, more scholastic, even, sometimes, somewhat hysterical—or/and, my wife insists, testesical.

I don't mean to ridicule this motive; in fact, I have recently defended it rather energetically.[1] I'm really reminding myself of how things can go in endeavors such as this one, so that I can, if possible, avoid the freakism and exploitation latent in the experimental motive. Pluralism, a necessary and valuable position, which is not really a position at all, has certain obvious limitations because one always tries to keep up with what's new but must still work always with what has already been done and is already known. So what is to be done if one wants to do something that is worth doing, that is significant; if one is suffering from the pricks of historical conscience and consciousness; wanting to be "original," to add something new, but wanting to avoid the straining and posturing that often goes with this motive, and above all, wanting to avoid the Detroit syndrome, in which the new model is confused with the better or the intrinsically valuable. Whatever experimental criticism is about, the senseless creation of new models just to displace or replace old ones, or to beat out a competitor in the intellectual marketplace should not be the result. To confuse the life of the mind with the insane economy of the American automobile industry would be the worst thing we could do.

The more I have thought about the problem, the more it has seemed to me that for those of us who still wish to move forward out of critical pluralism, there must be a shift in our locus of motivation from newness, or theoretical elegance, or even coherence, to a principle of relevance. I am aware that there are certain obvious hazards inherent in any attempt to generate a critical position out of a concept of relevance, but that is what experiments are for. The most obvious and disastrous hazard is that of rigid doctrinal relevance—the old party-line syndrome. I have tried to avoid that. Specifically, I am going to experiment with the application of ecology and ecological concepts to the study of literature, because ecology (as a science, as a discipline, as the basis for a human vision) has the greatest relevance to the present and future of the world we all live in of anything that I have studied in recent years. Experimenting a bit with the title of this paper, I could say that I am going to try to discover something about the ecology of literature, or try to develop an ecological poetics by applying ecological concepts to the reading, teaching, and writing about literature. To borrow a splendid phrase from Kenneth Burke, one of our great experimental critics, I am going to experiment with the conceptual and practical possibilities of an apparent perspective by incongruity. Forward then. Perhaps that old pair of antagonists, science and poetry, can be persuaded to lie down together and be generative after all.

LITERATURE AND THE BIOSPHERE

What follows can be understood as a contribution to human ecology, specifically, literary ecology, though I use (and transform) a considerable number of concepts from pure, biological ecology.

The problem now, as most ecologists agree, is to find ways of keeping the human community from destroying the natural community, and with it the human community. This is what ecologists like to call the self-destructive or suicidal motive that is inherent in our prevailing and paradoxical attitude toward nature. The conceptual and practical problem is to find the grounds upon which the two communities—the human, the natural—can coexist, cooperate, and flourish in the biosphere. All of the most serious and thoughtful ecologists (such as Aldo Leopold, Ian McHarg, Barry Commoner, and Garret Hardin) have tried to develop ecological visions which can be translated into social, economic, political, and individual programs of action. Ecology has been called, accurately, a subversive science because all these ecological visions are radical ones and attempt to subvert the continued-growth economy which dominates all emerging and most developed industrial states. A steady or sustainable state economy, with an entirely new concept of growth, is central to all ecological visions. All this may seem rather remote from creating, reading, teaching, and writing about literature; but in fact, it is not. I invoke here (to be spelled out in detail later) the first Law of Ecology: "Everything is connected to everything else." This is Commoner's phrasing, but the law is common to all ecologists and all ecological visions. This need to see even the smallest, most remote part in relation to a very large whole is the central intellectual action required by ecology and of an ecological vision. It is not mind-bending or mind-blowing or mind-boggling; it is mind-expanding. As absurd as this may sound, the paper is about literature and the biosphere. This is no more absurd, of course, than the idea that man does not have the right to do anything he wants with nature. The idea that nature should also be protected by human laws, that trees (dolphins and whales, hawks and whooping cranes) should have lawyers to articulate and defend their rights is one of the most marvelous and characteristic parts of the ecological vision.

ENERGY PATHWAYS WHICH SUSTAIN LIFE

I'm going to begin with some ecological concepts taken from a great variety of sources more or less randomly arranged and somewhat poetically commented upon.

A poem is stored energy, a formal turbulence, a living thing, a swirl in the flow.

Poems are part of the energy pathways which sustain life.

Poems are a verbal equivalent of fossil fuel (stored energy), but they are a renewable source of energy, coming, as they do, from those ever generative twin matrices, language and imagination.

Some poems—say *King Lear, Moby Dick, Song of Myself*—seem to be, in themselves, ever-living, inexhaustible sources of stored energy, whose relevance does not derive solely from their meaning, but from their capacity to remain active in any language and to go on with the work of energy transfer, to continue to function as an energy pathway that sustains life and the human community. Unlike fossil fuels, they cannot be used up. The more one thinks about this, the more one realizes that here one encounters a great mystery; here is a radical differential between the ways in which the human world and the natural world sustain life and communities.

Reading, teaching, and critical discourse all release the energy and power stored in poetry so that it may flow through the human community; all energy in nature comes, ultimately, from the sun, and life in the biosphere depends upon a continuous flow of sunlight. In nature, this solar "energy is used once by a given organism or population; some of it is stored and the rest is converted into heat, and is soon lost" from a given ecosystem. The "one-way flow of energy" is a universal phenomenon of nature, where, according to the laws of thermodynamics, energy is never created or destroyed: it is only transformed, degraded, or dispersed, flowing always from a concentrated form into a dispersed (entropic) form. One of the basic formulations of ecology is that there is a one-way flow of energy through a system but that materials circulate or are recycled and can be used over and over. Now, without oversimplifying these enormously complex matters, it would seem that once one moves out of the purely biological community and into the human community, where language and symbol-systems are present, things are not quite the same with regard to energy. The matter is so complex one hesitates to take it on, but one must begin, even hypothetically, somewhere, and try to avoid victimage or neutralization by simple-minded analogical thinking. In literature, all energy comes from the creative imagination. It does not come from language, because language is only one (among many) vehicles for the storing of creative energy. A painting and a symphony are also stored energy. And clearly, this stored energy is not just used once, converted, and lost from the human community. It is perhaps true that the life of the human community depends upon the continuous flow of creative energy (in all its forms) from the creative imagination and intelligence, and that this flow could be considered the sun upon which life in the human community depends; but it is not true that energy stored in a poem—*Song of Myself*—is used once, converted, and then lost from the ecosystem. It is used over and over again as a renewable resource by the same individual. Unlike nature, which has a single ultimate source of energy, the human community would seem to have many suns, resources, renewable and otherwise, to out-sun the sun itself. Literature in general and individual works in particular are one among many human suns. We need to discover ways of using this renewable energy-source to keep that other ultimate energy-source (upon which all life in the natural biosphere, and human communities, including human life, depends) flowing into the biosphere. We need to make some connections between literature and the sun, between teaching literature and the health of the biosphere.

Energy flows from the poet's language centers and creative imagination into the poem and thence, from the poem (which converts and stores this energy) into the reader. Reading is clearly an energy transfer as the energy stored in the poem is released and flows back into the language centers and creative imaginations of the readers. Various human hungers, including word hunger, are satisfied by this energy flow along this particular energy pathway. The concept of a poem as stored energy (as active, alive, and generative, rather than as inert, as a kind of corpse upon which one performs an autopsy, or as an art object one takes possession of, or as an antagonist—a knot of meanings—one must overcome) frees one from a variety of critical tyrannies, most notably, perhaps, that of pure hermeneutics, the transformation of this stored creative energy directly into a set of coherent meanings. What a poem is saying is probably always less important than what it is doing and how—in the deep sense—it coheres. Properly understood, poems can be studied as models for energy flow, community building, and ecosystems. The first Law of Ecology—that everything is connected to everything else—applies to poems as well as to nature. The concept of the interactive field was operative in nature, ecology, and poetry long before it ever appeared in criticism.

Reading, teaching, and critical discourse are enactments of the poem which release the stored energy so that it can flow into the reader—sometimes with such intensity that one is conscious of an actual inflow; or, if it is in the classroom, one becomes conscious of the extent to which this one source of stored energy is flowing around through a community, and of how "feedback," negative or positive, is working.

Kenneth Burke was right—as usual—to argue that drama should be our model or paradigm for literature because a drama, enacted upon the stage, before a live audience, releases its energy into the human community assembled in the theater and raises all the energy levels. Burke did not want us to treat novels and poems as plays; he wanted us to become aware of what they were doing as creative verbal actions in the human community. He was one of our first critical ecologists.

Coming together in the classroom, in the lecture hall, in the seminar room (anywhere, really) to discuss or read or study literature, is to gather energy centers around a matrix of stored poetic/verbal energy. In some ways, this is the true interactive field because the energy flow is not just a two-way flow from poem to person as it would be in reading; the flow is along many energy pathways from poem to person, from person to person. The process is triangulated, quadrangulated, multiangulated; and there is, ideally, a raising of the energy levels which makes it possible for the highest motives of literature to accomplish themselves. These motives are not pleasure and truth, but creativity and community.

POEMS AS GREEN PLANTS

Ian McHarg—one of the most profound thinkers I have read who has tried to design a new model of reality based upon ecology—says that "perhaps the greatest conceptual contribution of the ecological view is the perception of the world and evolution as a creative process." He defines creation as the raising of matter from lower to higher order. In nature, he says, this occurs when some of the sun's energy is entrapped on its path to entropy. This process of entrapment and creation, he calls—somewhat cacophonously—negentropy, since it negates the negative process of entropy and allows energy to be saved from random dispersal and put to creative ends. Green plants, for example, are among the most creative organisms on earth. They are nature's poets. There is no end to the ways in which this concept can be applied to the human community, but let me stay close to the topic at hand. Poems are green plants among us; if poets are suns, then poems are green plants among us for they clearly arrest energy on its path to entropy and in so doing, not only raise matter from lower to higher order, but help to create a self-perpetuating and evolving system. That is, they help to create creativity and community, and when their energy is released and flows out into others, to again raise matter from lower to higher order (to use one of the most common descriptions of what culture is). One of the reasons why teaching and the classroom are so important (for literature, anyway) is that they intensify and continue this process by providing the environment in which the stored energy of poetry can be released to carry on its work of creation and community. The greatest teachers (the best ecologists of the classroom) are those who can generate and release the greatest amount of collective creative energy; they are the ones who understand that the classroom is a community, a true interactive field. Though few of us—maybe none of us—understand precisely how this idea can be used to the ends of biospheric health, its exploration would be one of the central problems which an ecological poetics would have to address.

THE REMORSELESS INEVITABLENESS OF THINGS

As a classic textbook by E. Odum on the subject tells us, ecology is always concerned with "levels beyond that of the individual organism. It is concerned with populations, communities, ecosystems, and the biosphere." By its very nature it is concerned with complex interactions and with the largest sets of interrelationships. We must remember Commoner's first Law of Ecology: "Everything is connected to everything else." The biosphere (or ecosphere) is the home that life has built for itself on the planet's outer surface. In that ecosphere there is a reciprocal interdependence of one life process upon another, and there is a mutual interconnected development of all of the earth's life systems. If we continue to teach, write, and write about poetry without acknowledging and trying to act upon the fact that—to cite a single example—all the oceans of our home are slowly being contaminated by all the pollutants disposed of in modern communities—even what we try to send up in smoke—then we will soon lose the environment in which we write and teach. All the creative processes of the biosphere, including the human ones, may well come to an end if we cannot find a way to determine the limits of human destruction and intrusion which the biosphere can tolerate, and learn how to creatively manage the biosphere. McHarg and others say that this is our unique creative role, but that as yet we have neither the vision nor the knowledge to carry it out, and that we do not have much more time to acquire both. This somewhat hysterical proposition is why I tried to write this paper and why, true to the experimental motive intrinsic to me as a human being, I have taken on the question of how reading, teaching, and writing about literature might function creatively in the biosphere, to the ends of biospheric purgation, redemption from human intrusions, and health.

As a reader and teacher and critic of literature, I have asked the largest, most important and relevant question about literature that I know how to ask in 1976. It is interesting, to me anyway, that eight years ago, trying to define my position, I was asking questions about the visionary fifth dimension and about how man is *released from the necessities of nature into this realm of pure being by means of literature*. Four years ago, attempting to do the same thing, I was writing about history as a symbol and about being boxed in the void, convinced that there were no viable concepts of or possibilities for the future, and about literary criticism as a necessary, endlessly dialectical process which helps to keep culture healthy and viable throughout history.[2] Nothing about nature and the biosphere in all this. Now, in 1976, here I am back on earth (from my heady space trips, from the rigors and pleasures of dialectic, from the histrionic metaphor of being boxed in the void) trying to learn something about what the ecologists variously call the laws of nature, the "body of inescapable natural laws," the "impotence principles" which are beyond our ability to alter or escape, the remorseless inevitableness of things, the laws of nature which are "decrees of fate." I have been trying to learn something by contemplating (from my vantage point in literature) one of ecology's basic maxims: "We are not free to violate the laws of nature." The view we get of humans in the biosphere from the ecologists these days is a tragic one, as pure and classic as the Greek or Shakespearean views: in partial knowledge or often in total ignorance (the basic postulate of ecology and tragedy is that humans precipitate tragic consequences by acting either in ignorance of or without properly understanding the true consequences of their actions), we are violating the laws of nature, and the retribution from the biosphere will be more terrible than any inflicted on humans by the gods. In ecology, man's tragic flaw is his anthropocentric (as opposed to biocentric) vision, and his compulsion to conquer, humanize, domesticate, violate, and exploit every natural thing. The ecological nightmare (as one gets it in Brunner's *The Sheep Look Up*) is of a monstrously overpopulated, almost completely polluted, all but totally humanized planet. These nightmares are all if/then projections: *if* everything continues as is, *then* this will happen. A common form of this nightmare is Garrett Hardin's ironic population projection: if we continue our present 2% growth rate indefinitely, then in only 615 years there will be standing room only on all the land areas of the world.

To simply absorb this tragic ecological view of our present and possible futures (if nothing occurs to alter our anthropocentric vision) into the doomsday syndrome is a comforting but specious intellectual, critical, and historical response: it dissipates action into the platitudes of purely archetypal and intellectual connections. Better to bring Shakespearean and Greek tragedy to bear upon our own biosphere's tragedy as a program for action than this—any day. I will not attempt to deal here with the responses to the tragic/doomsday ecological view generated by a commitment to the economic growth spiral or the national interest. Others have done it better than I ever could. Let me say here that the evidence is so overwhelming and terrifying that I can no longer even imagine (using any vision) the possibility of ignoring Ian McHarg's mandate in his sobering and brilliant book, *Design With Nature:*

> Each individual has a responsibility for the entire biosphere and is required to engage in creative and cooperative activities.

As readers, teachers, and critics of literature, we are used to asking ourselves questions—often very complex and sophisticated ones—about the nature of literature, critical discourse, language, curriculum, liberal arts, literature and society, literature and history; but McHarg has proposed new concepts of creativity and community so radical that it is even hard to comprehend them. As readers, teachers and critics of literature, how do we become responsible planet stewards? How do we ask questions about literature and the biosphere? What do we even ask? These are overwhelming questions. They fill one with a sense of futility and absurdity and provoke one's self-irony at the first faint soundings of the still largely ignorant, preaching, pontificating voice. How does one engage in responsible creative and cooperative biospheric action as a reader, teacher (especially this), and critic of literature? I think that we have to begin answering this question and that we should do what we have always done: turn to the poets. And then to the ecologists. We must formulate an ecological poetics. We must promote an ecological vision. At best, I can only begin here. Following McHarg and rephrasing a fine old adage, we can say that "where there is no ecological vision, the people will perish." And this ecological vision must penetrate the economic, political, social, and technological visions of our time, and radicalize them. The problem is not national, but global, planetary. It will not stop here. As Arthur Boughey points out, "There is no population, community, or ecosystem left on earth completely independent of the effects of human cultural behavior. Now [this human] influence has begun to spread beyond the globe to the rest of our planetary system and even to the universe itself."

THE CENTRAL PARADOX: POWERLESS VISIONS

One has to begin somewhere. Since literature is our business, let us begin with the poets or creators in this field and see if we can move toward a generative poetics by connecting poetry to ecology. As should be clear by now, I am not just interested in transferring ecological concepts to the study of literature, but in attempting to see literature inside the context of an ecological vision in ways which restrict neither and do not lead merely to proselytizing based upon a few simple generalizations and perceptions which have been common to American literature (at least) since Cooper, and are central to the whole transcendental vision as one gets it in Emerson, Thoreau, Whitman, and Melville. As Barry Commoner points out, "The complex web in which all life is enmeshed, and man's place in it, are clearly—and beautifully—described in the poems of Walt Whitman," in Melville's *Moby Dick* and everywhere in Emerson and Thoreau. "Unfortunately," he says, with a kind of unintentional, but terrible understatement for literary people, "this literary heritage has not been enough to save us from ecological disaster." And here we are back again, before we even start, to the paradoxes which confront us as readers, teachers, and critics of literature—and perhaps as just plain citizens: the separation of vision and action; the futility of vision and knowledge without power.

THE HARSHEST, CRUELEST REALITIES OF OUR PROFESSION

Bringing literature and ecology together is a lesson in the harshest, cruelest realities which permeate our profession: we live by the word, and by the power of the word, but are increasingly powerless to act upon the word. Real power in our time is political, economic, and technological; real knowledge is increasingly scientific. Are we not here at the center of it all? We can race our verbal motors, spin our dialectical wheels, build more and more sophisticated systems, recycle dazzling ideas through the elite of the profession. We can keep going by charging ourselves back up in the classroom. In the end, we wonder what it all comes down to. Reading Commoner's (or almost any other serious ecologist's) statements, knowing they come from a formidable scientific knowledge, from direct involvement with the problems and issue from a deeply committed human being, can we help but wonder what we are doing teaching students to love poetry, to take literature seriously, to write good papers about literature:

> Because the global ecosystem is a connected whole, in which nothing can be gained or lost and which is not subject to overall improvement, anything extracted from it by human effort must be replaced. Payment of this price

cannot be avoided; it can only be delayed. The present environmental crisis is a warning that we have delayed nearly too long.

> . . . we are in an environmental crisis because the means by which we use the ecosphere to produce wealth are destructive of the ecosystem itself. The present system of production is self-destructive. The present course of human civilization is suicidal. In our unwitting march toward ecological suicide we have run out of options. Human beings have broken out of the circle of life, driven not by biological need, but by social organization which they have devised to conquer nature . . .

All my literary training tells me that this is not merely rhetoric, and that no amount of rhetoric or manipulation of the language to political, economic, technological, or other ends will make it go away. It is a substantive, biosphere-wide reality we must confront and attempt to do something about.

THE GENEROSITY OF THE POETS

I will use what I know best and begin with the poets. If we begin with the poets (who have never had any doubts about the seriousness and relevance of what they are doing), they teach us that literature is an enormous, ever increasing, wonderfully diverse storehouse of creative and cooperative energy which can never be used up. It is like the gene-pool, like the best ecosystems. Literature is a true cornucopia, thanks to the continuous generosity of the poets, who generate this energy out of themselves, requiring, and usually receiving, very little in return over and above the feedback from the creative act itself.

This is probably nowhere more evident than in a book such as Gary Snyder's *Turtle Island;* or, to take quite a different kind of text, in Adrienne Rich's *Diving into the Wreck*. What the poets do is "Hold it close" and then "give it all away." What Snyder holds close and gives away in *Turtle Island* is a complete ecological vision which has worked down into every detail of his personal life and is the result of many years of intellectual and personal wandering. Every poem is an action which comes from a finely developed and refined ecological conscience and consciousness. The book enacts a whole program of ecological action; it is offered (like *Walden*) as a guide book. It has in it one of the most useful and complete concepts of renewable, creative human energy which can be put to creative and cooperative biospheric ends that I know of. Its relevance for this paper is probably so obvious that I should not pursue it any longer.

The Generosity of Adrienne Rich's *Diving into the Wreck*

Things are very different in this book of poems, and not immediately applicable to the topic of this paper. But this book is the epitome—for me—of the ways in which poets are generous with themselves and can be used as models for creative, cooperative action. Without exception, the poems in this book are about the ecology of the female self, and they impinge upon the concerns of this paper in their treatment of men as destroyers (here of women rather than of the biosphere, but for remarkably similar reasons). As Margaret Atwood's profound ecological novel, *Surfacing*, makes clear, there is a demonstrable relationship between the ways in which men treat and destroy women and the ways in which men treat and destroy nature. Many of the poems—and in particular a poem such as "The Phenomenology of Anger"—are about how one woman changed and brought this destruction and suppression to an end, and about what changes must occur to bring the whole process to an end. A mind familiar with ecology cannot avoid the many profound and disturbing connections to be made here between women and western history, nature and western history.

The Deconstructive Wisdom of W. S. Merwin's *Lice*

One of the most continuously shattering experiences of my intellectual life has been the reading, teaching, and thenceforth re-reading and re-teaching of this book of poems. This is one of the most profound books of poems written in our time and one of the great ecological texts of any time. Whatever has been argued from factual, scientific, historical, and intellectual evidence in the ecology books that I read is confirmed (and more) by the imaginative evidence of this book of poems. Merwin's generosity consists in the extraordinary efforts he made to deconstruct the cumulative wisdom of western culture and then imaginatively project himself into an almost unbearable future. Again, as with Adrienne Rich, these poems are about the deep inner changes which must occur if we are to keep from destroying the world and survive as human beings. I know of no other book of poems so aware of the biosphere and what humans have done to destroy it as this one. Reading this book of poems requires one to unmake and remake one's mind. It is the most painfully constructive book of poems I think I have ever read. What these poems affirm over and over is that if a new ecological vision is to emerge, the old destructive western one must be deconstructed and abandoned. This is exactly what Rich's poems say about men and women.

The Energy of Love in Walt Whitman's *Song of Myself*

This energy flows out of Whitman into the world (all the things of the world) and back into Whitman from the things of the world in one of the most marvelous ontological interchanges one can find anywhere in poetry. This ontological interchange between Whitman and the biosphere is the energy pathway that sustains life in Whitman and, so far as he is concerned, in the biosphere. There is a complete ecological vision in this poem, just as there is in Whitman's conception of a poetry cycle which resembles the water cycle within the biosphere. Whitman says that poems come out of the poets, go up into the atmosphere to create a kind of poetic atmosphere, come down upon us in the form of poetic rain, nourish us and make us creative and then are recycled. Without this poetic atmosphere and cultural cycle, he says, we would die as human beings. A lovely concept, and true for some of us, but it has not yet resolved the disjunction (as Commoner points out) between vision and action, knowledge and power.

The Biocentric Vision of Faulkner's *Absalom, Absalom!*

Can we not study this great fiction, and its central character, Thomas Sutpen, in relation to one of the most fundamental of all ecological principles: "That nature is an interacting process, a seamless web, that it [nature] is responsive to laws, that it constitutes a value system with intrinsic opportunities and constraints upon human use." There is an ecological lesson for all of us in the ferocious destructiveness of human and natural things brought about by Thomas Sutpen.

Looking upon the World, Listening and Learning with Henry David Thoreau

Does he not tell us that this planet, and the creatures who inhabit it, including men and women, were, have been, are now, and are in the process of becoming? A beautiful and true concept of the biosphere. His model of reality was so new, so radical even in the mid-nineteenth century, that we have still not been able to absorb and act upon it more than a hundred years later.

Entropy and Negentropy in Theodore Roethke's "Greenhouse," "Lost Son," and "North American Sequence"

Was there ever a greater ecological, evolutionary poet of the self than Roethke, one who really believed that ontology recapitulates phylogeny, one so close to his evolutionary predecessors that he experiences an interchange of being with them and never demeans them with personification and seldom with metaphor. Kenneth Burke's brilliant phrase—vegetal radicalism—still takes us to the ecological centers of Roethke, self-absorbed, self-obsessed as he was.

But enough of this. The poets have always been generous. I mean only to suggest a few ecological readings of texts I know well. Teaching and criticism are the central issues here, so let me move on toward some conclusions.

TEACHING AND CRITICAL DISCOURSE AS FORMS OF SYMBIOSIS

"Creativeness is a universal prerequisite which man shares with all creatures." The central, modern idea of the poet, of literature, and of literary criticism is based upon the postulate that humans are capable of genuine creation and that literature is one of the enactments of this creative principle. Taking literature to ecology by way of McHarg's statement joins two principles of creativity so that humans are acting in concert with the rest of the biosphere, but not necessarily to the ends of biospheric health. That has always been the problem. Some of our most amazing creative achievements—say in chemistry and physics—have been our most destructive. Culture—one of our great achievements wherever we have gone—has often fed like a great predator and parasite upon nature and never entered into a reciprocating energy-transfer, into a recycling relationship with the biosphere. In fact, one of the most common antinomies in the human mind is between culture/civilization and nature/wilderness. As Kenneth Burke pointed out some time ago, man's tendency is to become rotten with perfection. As Burke ironically formulated it, man's entelechy is technology. Perceiving and teaching (even writing about) human creativity in this larger ecological context could be done in all literature courses and especially in all creative writing courses. It could only have a salutary effect. It would make the poet and the green plants brothers and sisters; it would charge creative writing and literature with ecological purpose.

Symbiosis, according to McHarg, is the "cooperative arrangement that permits increase in the levels of order"; it is this cooperative arrangement that permits the use of energy in raising the levels of matter. McHarg says that symbiosis makes negentropy possible; he identifies negentropy as the creative principle and process at work in the biosphere which keeps everything moving in the evolutionary direction which has characterized the development of all life in the biosphere. Where humans are involved and where literature provides the energy source within the symbiotic arrangement, McHarg says that a very complex process occurs in which energy is transmuted into information and thence into meaning by means of a process he calls apperception. As McHarg demonstrated in his book, both the process of apperception and the meaning which results from it can be used to creative, cooperative ends in our management of the biosphere. The central endeavor, then, of any ecological poetics would have to be a working model for the processes of transformation which occur as one moves from the stored creative energy of the poem, to its release by reading, teaching, or writing, to its transmutation into meaning, and finally to its application, in an ecological value system, to what McHarg variously calls "fitness and fitting," and to "health"—which he defines as "creative fitting" and by which he means to suggest our creation of a fit environment. This work could transform culture and help bring our destruction of the biosphere to an end.

Now there is no question that literature can do all this, but there are a lot of questions as to whether it does in fact do it, how, and how effectively. All these concerns might well be central for teachers and critics of literature these days. We tend to over-refine our conceptual frameworks so that they can only be used by a corps of elitist experts and gradually lose their practical *relevance* as they increase their theoretical *elegance*. I am reminded here of the stridently practical questions Burke asked all through the thirties and early forties and of the scorn with which they were so often greeted by literary critics and historians of his time. But none of these questions is antithetical to literature and there is a certain splendid resonance which comes from thinking of poets and green plants being engaged in the same creative, life-sustaining activities, and of teachers and literary critics as creative mediators between literature and the biosphere whose tasks include the encouragement of, the discovery, training, and development of creative biospheric apperceptions, attitudes, and actions. To charge the classroom with ecological purpose one has only to begin to think of it in symbiotic terms as a cooperative arrangement which makes it possible to release the stream of energy which flows out of the poet and into the poem, out of the poem and into the readers, out of the readers and into the classroom, and then back into the readers and out of the classroom with them, and finally back into the other larger community in a never ending circuit of life.

BUT . . .

I stop here, short of action, halfway between literature and ecology, the energy pathways obscured, the circuits of life broken between words and actions, vision and action, the verbal domain and the non-verbal domain, between literature and the biosphere—because I can't go any further. The desire to join literature to ecology originates out of and is sustained by a Merwin-like condition and question: how can we apply the energy, the creativity, the knowledge, the vision we know to be in literature to the human-made problems ecology tells us are destroying the biosphere which is our home? How can we translate literature into purgative-redemptive biospheric action; how can we resolve the fundamental paradox of this profession and get out of our heads? How can we turn words into something other than more words (poems, rhetoric, lectures, talks, position papers—the very substance of an MLA meeting: millions and millions of words; endlessly recirculating among those of us in the profession); how can we do something more than recycle WORDS?

Let experimental criticism address itself to this dilemma.

How can we move from the community of literature to the larger biospheric community which ecology tells us (correctly, I think) we belong to even as we are destroying it?

▪ ▪ ▪ *Free us from false figures of speech.*

NOTES

I have not documented all of the quotations from, paraphrases of, and references to ecological works because there are so many of them and I wanted the paper to be read right through. The paper is literally a kind of patchwork of ecological material. I have identified my major sources and resources in the bibliography. The only things I felt should be identified were my own works because the references to them would be obscure and quite incomprehensible otherwise.

1. In "Literary Criticism and History: The Endless Dialectic," *New Literary History* 6 (1974–75): 491–512.

2. Respectively, in (a) "Kenneth Burke and Structuralism," *Shenandoah* 21 (Autumn 1969), 19–28; (b) "Literary Criticism and History"; and (c) "History as Symbol: Boxed in the Void," *Iowa Review* 9.1 (Winter 1978): 62–71.

WORKS CITED

I have drawn upon the following books in a great variety of ways. I list them here to acknowledge some of the ecological resources I have used.

Bates, Marston. *The Forest and the Sea: A Look at the Economy of Nature and the Ecology of Man.* New York: Mentor, 1960.

Bateson, Gregory. *Steps to an Ecology of Mind.* New York: Ballantine, 1972.

Boughey, Arthur S. *Man and the Environment: An Introduction to Human Ecology and Evolution.* Second Edition. New York: Macmillan, 1975.

Commoner, Barry. *The Closing Circle: Nature, Man, and Technology.* New York: Bantam Books, 1972.

The Crisis of Survival. By the editors of the Progressive and the College Division of Scott, Foresman and Company. New York: Morrow, 1970.

Dasmann, Raymond. *Planet in Peril: Man and the Biosphere Today.* New York: World Publishing, 1972.

Hardin, Garrett. *Exploring New Ethics for Survival: The Voyage of the Spaceship Beagle.* New York: Viking Press, 1972.

The House We Live In: An Environmental Reader. New York: Macmillan, 1971.

Kormandy, Edward J. *Concepts of Ecology.* Concepts of Modern Biology Series. Englewood Cliffs, N.J.: Prentice-Hall, 1969.

Leopold, Aldo. *A Sand County Almanac.* 1949. New York: Ballantine, 1966.

McHarg, Ian. *Design with Nature.* 1969. New York: Doubleday/Natural History Press, 1971.

Nearing, Helen, and Scott Nearing. *Living the Good Life: How to Live Sanely and Simply in a Troubled World.* New York: Schocken Books, 1970.

Odum, Eugene. *Ecology.* Modern Biology Series. New York: Holt, Rinehart, Winston, 1963.

Smity, G. J. C., H. J. Steck, and G. Surette. *Our Ecological Crisis: Its Biological, Economic, and Political Dimensions.* New York: Macmillan, 1974.

Snyder, Gary. *Turtle Island.* New York: New Directions, 1974.

The Subversive Science: Essays toward an Ecology of Man. Ed. Shepard and McKinley. Boston: Houghton Mifflin, 1969.

Who Speaks for Earth. Papers from the 1972 Stockholm conference. New York: Norton, 1973.

SUEELLEN CAMPBELL

The Land and Language of Desire

■ ■ ■

WHERE DEEP ECOLOGY AND POST-STRUCTURALISM MEET

In my mind I'd spent the year in the wilderness—dazzled by the desert heat, mushing huskies in the twilit arctic winter, hunting buffalo and antelope on the prairie, exulting on the tops of the Sierras. Back home at last in the West, on sabbatical from my teaching job in Ohio, I'd been hiking and skiing and backpacking—and spending long days on my ancient leather couch reading wilderness narratives and nature essays. American ones, ranging from early travellers like John Bartram and Lewis and Clark, through Thoreau and Muir and Mary Austin and John Van Dyke, to Margaret Murie and David Rains Wallace and Barry Lopez.

So I was disconcerted by an invitation to give an informal talk on the subject of contemporary critical theory to the English faculty at a nearby university. This should have been easy for me—criticism is one of my specialties, and in fact, though the man who asked me to talk didn't yet know it, I was in the midst of applying for a job teaching theory in his department. I couldn't decline, of course, and I knew that my prospects might hinge on what I could come up with, but what really worried me was that nothing could have been further from my current state of mind than contemporary criticism. All those days in the wilderness had taken me about as far as I could be from the crowded cafés and academic closets of theory.

How could I do this talk without tearing myself away from the wilderness? Once before, I remembered, I'd had to face this disjunction between two parts of my own mind. One May a couple of years ago I found myself moving in just a few days from a very theoretical conference at a midwestern university to a friend's remote cabin in the Adirondack mountains. I surrounded myself with ideas about feminism and psychoanalysis and Marxism and deconstruction—all those ideas you could collect under the label "post-structuralism." And then I sat on my friend's porch and gazed down a long, empty lake and read *Arctic Dreams* and *The Klamath Knot*—and immersed myself in all those ideas you could collect under the label "deep ecology." These were two very different worlds, and I didn't understand how I could live in both of them.

I was certainly speaking two languages. Consider these titles, fragments of the language of theory: "Categories for a Materialist Criticism," "Semiology and Rhetoric," "The Novel as Polylogue," "The Supplement of Copula: Philosophy *before* Linguistics," and—amazingly—"Of Structure as an Inmixing of an Otherness Prerequisite to Any Subject Whatever." How different from "Tracks in the Wilderness," "Ice and Light," "Fecundity," "A World of Infinite Variety," "The Heat of Noon: Rock and Tree and Cloud."

I've amused myself imagining what a hard-core theorist and a hard-core nature writer might say about each other. Picture, say, two equally notorious figures: the French philosopher Jacques Derrida, inventor of deconstruction, and the American guru of eco-sabotage, Edward Abbey (the two, as it happens, who wrote the titles on my list with colons—a reminder, perhaps, that Abbey studied philosophy?). "That arrogant, incomprehensible, disembodied lump of brain," Abbey might have said. "He's more convoluted than the Grand Canyon. That deconstruction gibberish, it's so *French*—pretentious and citified and elitist and esoteric. It's about as clear as smog. I bet the closest he ever gets to the real world is a glass of Perrier and a bottle of artificial mesquite smoke." Abbey, Derrida might say (in that complex, multisyllabic, sibylline way I prefer not even to try to imitate), is romantic, escapist, naive, fuzzy-minded, eccentric, a misanthropic American Back-to-Nature primitive. It's nearly impossible to imagine them chatting over lunch. They would almost certainly have reacted to each other with scorn and incomprehension.

Even in the rare cases I've seen when someone from one world really tries to deal with the other, the chasm seems unbridgeable, the languages too different to translate. I think of an essay about *Walden* I read recently by a theorist I admire, Barbara Johnson. She says that by living in the woods Thoreau collapsed the distinction between nature and textuality. Because Walden Pond is real and metaphorical at the same time, she concludes, Thoreau is "obscure" and incomprehensible. From the other side of the chasm is a letter I got this year from a friend who knows a lot about theory but is basically a nature person. He wrote that he'd been reading a book called *Hermeneutics and Deconstruction,* and said, "I didn't get very far before starting to froth. What lives do those people lead that makes them think of those things?"

Yet that week in the Adirondacks I started thinking there must be some way to bridge the gap. Maybe I could figure out how to reconcile these two bodies of thought, or at least how to make sense of their differences. Perhaps this seemed possible because I was just then crossing the dividing line, part of my mind still full of theory, the rest of it with my body in the quiet sunshine. It was the right moment to think theoretically about the natural world, to be post-structuralist and ecological at the same time. After all, I knew from all the theory I'd read that all ideas are historical: surely two such major and contemporary intellectual developments must be somehow related to each other, and I ought to be able to turn my analytic mind to the problem. Surely, too, there must be a reason *I*—with what was really, of course, just one body and just one mind—could be drawn so strongly to both of these ways of thinking about the world. Then there was one other small seed of encouragement. One of the central terms of that midwestern conference, I was surprised to discover, was also one of Barry Lopez's. As I neared the end of *Arctic Dreams,* I found Lopez talking about *desire* in terms that reminded me of what I'd heard a few days before, and I started to wonder whether this word meant something similar in both worlds. If so, might there be other connections? Could my own desire—and what theory and nature writing taught me about it—show me a way to understanding?

▪ ▪ ▪ This is how I came to give a most idiosyncratic talk about the shared premises of post-structuralist theory and ecologically minded nature writing. For almost two years, I stored the problem in the back of my mind and pulled it out every now and then to glance at—often when I felt the differences between these fields most strongly, when I had to set aside Everett Ruess's desert letters to prepare a class on Roland Barthes, but also now and then when something I was reading would echo in my mind, when for a moment the ecologist Aldo Leopold would sound like the post-structuralist historian Michel Foucault. Bit by bit, sometimes tentatively, sometimes decisively, these echoes, these moments of connection, came together, until I realized I had found a kind of answer. All those conspicuous contrasts, I have come to think, do grow out of some important and very basic similarities. This, then, is what I want to discuss here—a shared critical stance and a pair of shared beliefs about the nature of reality, the common ground of post-structuralism and deep ecology, the common source of their differences.

A critical stance. I mean by this two connected things. One is the way writers see themselves standing in relation to tradition and to authority. The other is the way they construct their ideas and arguments, given that position. Both theorists and ecologists (I'll use these terms for short) are at core revolutionary. They stand in opposition to traditional authority, which they question and then reject. All of them begin by criticizing the dominant structures of Western culture and the vast abuses they have spawned. What I once might blithely have called The Establishment is now identified by such ornate epithets as "logocentrism," "phallocentrism," "patriarchy," "technocracy"—those structures of interwoven thought and power, concept and institution, in which humans matter more than other creatures, men more than women, Europeans more than Africans or Asians or Native Americans, logic more than emotion, reason more than dreams or madness. For both theory and ecology, it is axiomatic that knowledge and power, ideas and actions, are inseparable. (Both worlds, not surprisingly, are home to feminists.) "What is at stake," writes the theorist Sandor Goodhart, "is Western humanism at large" (68).

Standing thus opposed to tradition, theory and ecology also share two basic tactics for revealing the flaws of old ideas and building new ones. One is largely polemical—to overturn old hierarchies, to take value from the once dominant and give it to the weak. In both fields feminists sometimes say that feminine values are more life-enhancing than masculine values and that non-linear thought is better than linear thought. Nature writers often imply that aboriginal cultures are simply better than Western culture—that Native Americans, for instance, have always lived in perfect harmony with their surroundings, while Europeans have always destroyed theirs. Literary critics are likely to dismiss as trivial or misleading those aspects of texts that are easy to see, the obvious meanings, and consider only what is hidden between and beneath the lines. And when former director of the National Endowment for the Humanities and Secretary of Education William Bennett rails against professors who no longer think Shakespeare is important, he is responding to the polemical shift of value from the great authors of tradition to others we have long ignored.

The second shared critical tactic is more subtle and more radical. This is to question the concepts on which the old hierarchies are built. Nature and culture, madness and reason, fact and fiction, human and animal, self and other, scientific and unscientific, civilized and primitive, even male and female, good and evil—all these oppositions come under scrutiny, are revealed as artificial, biased, and oversimple, and are then somehow restructured. An especially compelling example is the argument Michel Foucault makes in *Madness and Civilization,* his history of the way Western culture has thought about and treated madness. Reason, he shows, has always defined itself by its opposition to unreason, but neither category has remained constant. From the Middle Ages on, in different ways at different times, we have called mad what we do not want to acknowledge in ourselves, what we do not want in our society—not just delirium and hallucination, not even just hysteria and hypochondria and criminality, but poverty and idleness and discontent. With this kind of argument, the post-structuralist transforms what might once have seemed an unproblematic concept into something that is both thoroughly historical and thoroughly political; the old contrast is transformed into a new and much more complicated kind of opposition, and other similar concepts come into question as a consequence.

For ecologists and nature writers, this kind of critique is often indirect. Barry Lopez, for instance, replaces the distinction between humanized landscapes and uninhabited wilderness by paying attention to how the human imagination—as well as human action—has always interacted with the land. And he questions the usual opposition between the civilized and the primitive when he says, "What is truly primitive in us and them, savage hungers, ethical dereliction, we try to pass over" (217). But the most important challenge to traditional hierarchies in ecology is the concept of biocentrism—the conviction that humans are neither better nor worse than other creatures (animals, plants, bacteria, rocks, rivers) but simply equal to everything else in the natural world. In *The Pathless Way,* Michael Cohen talks about how John Muir gradually learned to see from a biocentric point of view by imagining the opinion of an alligator or a grizzly. "Why," Muir asked, "should man value himself as more than a small part of the one great unit of creation?" (Cohen 20). Old beliefs, old relations of power, old oppositions—ecology, like theory, would restructure them all.

▪ ▪ ▪ A common critical stance, of course, need not imply common ideas. In this case, though, it does. Along with the questioning of authority comes a shared critique of the idea of objectivity. (Authority always pretends to be objective.) Theory and ecology agree: our perceptions are always subjective and we are always involved. Relativity theory and quantum mechanics are surely the root of these beliefs. "According to quantum mechanics," Gary Zukav writes in *The Dancing Wu Li Masters,* "there is no such thing as objectivity. We cannot eliminate ourselves from the picture. We are a part of nature, and when we study nature there is no way around the fact that nature is studying itself" (31). We always affect any system we touch. As Zukav says, "It is not possible to observe reality without changing it" (30).

These assumptions are especially clear in literary theory, where nearly everyone agrees that all readings are "situated." We *always* read from within a system of social, political, economic, cultural, and personal circumstances—and thus a set of conceptual structures—that direct us to a *particular* reading. (This is roughly what post-structuralists mean when they say we are created by "textuality." I'll come back to this later.) Even "facts" are subjective—a fact is only a fact inside an interpretation, and interpretations are human. According to Zukav, one philosophical implication of quantum mechanics is that we not only "influence our reality, but, in some degree, we actually *create* it" (28). Theory agrees: when we read, we create meaning. Without a reader, the words on the page mean nothing—we give them life with our feelings, our experience, our knowledge, our subjectivity.

In the same way, as Lopez says in *Arctic Dreams,* what we think of any landscape depends on what we know, what we imagine, and how we are disposed; each of us puts together the information we have differently, "according to his cultural predispositions and his personality" (243–44). To use an easy example, an oilman's Arctic is not the same as an Eskimo's, neither as an idea nor as a field for action—and so of course their effects on the land will also differ. The oilman will create the landscape he expects or wants or understands, and so will the Eskimo. But for ecology, the belief that we affect what we observe most often means simply that our actions reverberate farther and longer than we can know. Aldo Leopold is a good source for memorable illustrations of this idea. In "The Round River," for example, he describes a hill in Germany whose two slopes once grew the same valuable kind of oak. In the Middle Ages, the south slope was kept by a local bishop as a hunting preserve; the north was cleared and settled. Later, the north slope was replanted for forest. But the oak won't grow there anymore: the soil has lost essential microscopic flora and fauna, and two centuries of forest conservation have not been able to put them back.

All human actions, it seems, will provoke unexpected reactions. We are a part of nature studying and acting on itself.

At this point, though, the comparison gets a bit complicated. For theory, to read—to describe, to interpret—is to act. All the meaning that matters, we create. There are no texts without readers. Our complicity is absolute. But for ecology, simply to observe is not always to act. As Leopold says, "The outstanding characteristic of perception is that it entails no consumption and no dilution of any resource" (290). Of course, how we see will often direct what we do. Yet, ecologists insist, we do not create the land itself or its other inhabitants. "The land retains an identity of its own," Lopez reminds us, "still deeper and more subtle than we can know" (204). It seems to me that this difference repeats the classic opposition between idealism and realism. Like the idealist, the post-structuralist thinks the world into being; like the realist, the ecologist insists that "*out there* is a different world, older and greater and deeper by far than ours" (Abbey 37). (Echoing Samuel Johnson's refutation of Bishop Berkeley, Edward Abbey also says, "To refute the solipsist or the metaphysical idealist all that you have to do is take him out and throw a rock at his head: if he ducks, he's a liar" [Abbey 97].) When Thoreau, student of Emersonian idealism, climbed to the top of Maine's Mount Katahdin, he was stunned by the bare solidity of the rocks. "Think of our life in nature,—" he exclaimed, "daily to be shown matter, to come in contact with it,—rocks, trees, wind on our cheeks! the *solid* earth! the *actual* world! the *common sense! Contact! Contact!*" (71).

One of the important differences between ecology and theory arises from this philosophical contrast. This is a difference in attitude. If we always change what we study, how shall we decide how to act?

Generally, theory sees this situation as liberating. Freed of old illusions, we can ask different questions now: if objectivity has always been subjectivity, and the meanings of texts have never been definite, then we can try to understand *how* we create meaning, and we can take more control over our thinking. Sometimes theorists describe their activities as essentially amoral. Derrida, for instance, once said, "I don't see why I should renounce or why anyone should renounce the radicality of a critical work under the pretext that it risks the sterilization of science, humanity, progress, the origin of meaning, etc. I believe that the risk of sterility and of sterilization has always been the price of lucidity" (271). This is the kind of remark that sometimes gives contemporary theory a bad name. Some critics (the often-maligned "Yale deconstructionists," for instance) do seem to take this position. But I do not see them as central to post-structuralist theory. More often, I think, theorists see what they do as intensely moral (or ethical or political): remember that their critique of authority alerts them to the way abstractions can cause practical abuses. Thus Terry Eagleton argues throughout *Literary Theory* that all criticism is political. We must first decide how we want to affect the world, he says, and then choose our strategies.

The response of ecology is rather different. Our complicity is seen not as liberating but as a call to caution. This response is so pervasive it's difficult to choose an example. It is central to the whole preservation movement: if we can't know everything, if we can't control the effects of our actions, if even the smallest human interference can cause massive natural destruction, then the only way to keep something important is to *preserve* it. The response of caution is implicit in such books as Charles Bowden's *Blue Desert* and Gary Nabhan's *Gathering the Desert,* which outline the complex chain of destruction which has followed our unrestricted use of scarce water in the Southwest. It underlies the suspicion of technology—of the faith that human ingenuity can solve all problems—that is common among ecological nature writers. (Technology is also seen by both theory and ecology as a false authority based on the claim of objectivity.) And it is central to Leopold's immensely influential "land ethic." "A thing is right when it tends to preserve the integrity, stability, and beauty of the biotic community. It is wrong when it tends otherwise" (262). "Preserve" and "stability"—two words uncommon in post-structuralism and central to ecology. A "misread" text and a depleted aquifer present quite different practical problems and raise quite different moral and ethical questions. But they both speak of our intimacy with what surrounds us.

▪ ▪ ▪ Always we are part of systems larger than ourselves. As Fritjof Capra explains in *The Tao of Physics,* the world is "a complicated web of relations between the various parts of the whole" (71). Finally we arrive at what I see as the most comprehensive and most important shared premise of post-structuralist and ecological theory. Both criticize the traditional sense of a separate, independent, authoritative *center* of value or meaning; both substitute the idea of *networks.*

One often-cited source for this idea is the Swiss linguist Ferdinand de Saussure, who argued that meaning in language is created by relationship (by similarity, contiguity, difference, and so on), rather than by a direct connection between a word and what it means. Theory takes this argument and broadens it to apply to all kinds of structures and meanings. Here again Derrida is representative, with his argument that we have always tried to invent a center with concepts like essence, subject, the soul, consciousness, God, man, and so on. In "Structure, Sign, and Play in the Human Sciences," for instance, he looks at how Claude Lévi-Strauss's effort to find one "key myth" at the center of a culture's mythology gives way to the notion of a network of relationships among myths. More generally, the concept of intertextuality also depends on the sense of networks. In the work of such influential theorists as Harold Bloom and Julia Kristeva, texts (and authors) are seen as thoroughly connected to other texts (and here the term text is used very broadly, to include whole systems of relationships and all kinds of discourse) in very complicated and often hidden ways—so thoroughly that no text contains all of its own meaning.

With the questioning of stable centers in physics, linguistics, philosophy, anthropology, and literary criticism, not surprisingly, we also find theory re-examining the idea of the human being as a coherent and self-contained self. Here Freud is important, with his theory of an unconscious, shaped by forces outside ourselves and beyond our knowledge and control, that intrudes on conscious life in all kinds of ways that we don't always recognize—and the corollary that our sense of a more or less simple consciousness at the center of our "self" is illusory. Marx, of course, also exposed this sense as an illusion, though in different terms. More recent theorists have combined the ideas of Freud and Marx with the post-structuralist concept of intertextuality. The psychoanalyst Jacques Lacan, for instance, argues that we are what we are because of the "symbolic order" outside ourselves that creates us—again replacing the traditional humanist notion of a centered self with the idea of an uncentered network. As Foucault puts it, an individual is a "node within a network."

In ecology, the replacement of centers with networks is closely connected to what I've already said about the complicity of the human observer. We can't do anything without causing lots of side effects because everything is connected, nothing is isolated. As Arne Naess says, "Organisms are knots in the biospherical net or field of intrinsic relations" (Tobias 39). (Naess is the Norwegian philosopher responsible for the term "deep ecology.") A deer, for instance, has no being apart from things like the presence or absence of wolves, the kind of forage in its environment, the temperature and snowfall of any given winter, the other animals competing for the available food, the number of hunters with licenses, the bacteria in its intestines that either keep it healthy or make it sick. Theory and ecology agree that there's no such thing as a self-enclosed, private piece of property, neither a deer nor a person nor a text nor a piece of land.

Perhaps the most important idea that follows from this premise is that human beings are no longer the center of value or meaning. The best example of this new belief in theory may be Foucault's argument (at the end of *The Order of Things*) that the concept of "man" as we generally understand it—of individual humans as the centers of intelligence and spirit and therefore value in the world—is a historical one that is now disappearing. In ecology, this premise can be seen in Michael Tobias's remark (in the introduction to the collection *Deep Ecology*) that "From the biosphere's perspective, the whole point of Homo sapiens is their armpits, aswarm with 24.1 billion bacteria" (vii). Similarly, David Quammen points out in a recent essay about all the microscopic creatures that live on and in our skin, "You are an ecosystem . . . a community of flora and fauna" (23). Leopold's frequently quoted statement is still the most direct—that we are plain members and citizens of the land-community, not the rulers of the earth (240). Here the critique of traditional authority comes into play very strongly: ecology rejects as dangerous and unjustifiable hubris the ancient Western idea that—as the 1988 policy statement of the Colorado Farm Bureau puts it—"natural resources are here for the use and enjoyment of mankind." For both post-structuralism and deep ecology, the assumptions underlying "humanism" have become untenable; we need new ways, they agree, to understand our place in the world.

▪ ▪ ▪ While both theory and ecology reject the traditional humanist view of our importance in the scheme of things, though, what they focus on as a replacement is quite different. Theory sees everything as textuality, as networks of signifying systems of all kinds. Foucault sees an idea like madness as a text; Lacan sees a human being as a text; Derrida argues that everything is text in the sense that everything signifies something else. But ecology insists that we pay attention not to the way things have meaning for us, but to the way the rest of the world—the nonhuman part—exists apart from us and our languages. It's central to this insistence that we remember, in David Rains Wallace's words, "that the world is much greater and older than normal human perception of it . . . that the human is a participant as well as a perceiver in the ancient continuum of bears and forests" (7). The systems of meaning that matter are ecosystems.

Both of these perspectives follow pretty directly from the premises I've described. But the difference between them, I think, is the source of almost all the conspicuous differences between theory and ecology.

This is the question, then: how do we choose? What makes one of us care about textuality where another cares about the land? Certainly we can't organize these choices under the traditional hierarchy of good and bad, moral and immoral. Are they perhaps aesthetic or emotional choices? Or is it entirely a matter of practical circumstances? As I've wondered about this question, I've realized that my own vague, unfinished answer is shaped partly by theory and partly by ecology. Theory is right, I think, that what we are depends on all kinds of influences outside ourselves, that we are part of vast networks, texts written by larger and stronger forces. But surely one of the most important of these forces is the rest of the natural world. How close we are to the land as we are growing up and when we are grown, how we learn to see our relationship with it—these things must matter enormously. Our choices, it seems to me, depend on the shape of our lives—where we live, how we spend our days, how we've been taught—and especially on the role the land itself has played in what we might call the writing of our textuality.

So here, at last, I come back to the question of desire. What shapes my desire? And when theory and ecology speak of loss and desire, are they speaking of the same thing?

According to theory, and here Lacan is important, we emerge from the unity of infancy only when we begin to experience ourselves as separate from everything else, especially from our mothers' bodies. This happens at the moment we enter into the network of language, the "symbolic order" that will determine what we become. At the core of our sense of self, then, is our feeling of loss and the desire for unity that is born of loss. Loss makes us what we are, and desire is an empty force (not dependent on any object we might want at any given time) which always drives us but can never be satisfied.

Ecologists also see an experience of lost unity and a desire to regain it as central to our human nature. They are more likely, though, to see it as coming from our separation from the rest of the natural world. As Emerson wrote in *Nature,* "We are as much strangers in nature as we are aliens from God. We do not understand the notes of birds. The fox and the deer run away from us; the bear and tiger rend us" (74). Often this view is the Wordsworthian one that as children we are in perfect harmony with nature, but then lose that harmony as we develop the barrier of a self. (This sense is especially important, for example, in Peter Matthiessen's *The Snow Leopard.*) But there is also a more purely "ecological" version of this view—the one, I think, that is in part behind Barry Lopez's use of the word "desire." Because our culture does not teach us that we are plain citizens of the earth, because we live apart from the natural world and deny our intimacy with it, we have lost the sense of unity that is still possible in other cultures. Our desire marks what we have lost and what we still hope to regain. Desire, for ecology, goes beyond the human.

▪ ▪ ▪ Yesterday I climbed up to a high ridge in Colorado's Medicine Bow Mountains, in a range called Rawah after an Indian word for wilderness, and I thought about how I might close this essay. I might mention that the comparison could be continued, that this is not all there is to be said. I could follow my usual advice to students and make some concrete conclusions, perhaps about how theory and ecology can complement each other, how they reinforce each other's premises and pinpoint each other's blind spots. I should probably mention that I did get a job in that department whose invitation to talk jogged me into thinking, a job I hope will open up the right kind of space—at home in the West—for exploring how to draw on both theory and ecology as I read and write. I could speculate about those suggestive similarities to quantum mechanics and relativity theory, and add to them some of the insights of Zen and Taoism. Or I could simply describe how I've seen illustrations of these ideas everywhere since I started thinking about them—in what may be the most common experience of the world as a web of networks.

But what I really wanted to close with, I realized, was my own desire. Theory helps me to step back from myself, to *think* about desire, to see how it changes shape but still stays the same, to try to understand with my mind. But when I read Lopez or Leopold or Muir, I am immersed in desire. I want to see the land they saw, the way they saw it. I try to imagine how the prairie looked to Lewis and Clark, and how Alaska's Brooks Range looked to Margaret Murie as she crossed it by dogsled on her winter honeymoon. I daydream about how the valley where I live might have been two hundred years ago, when Indians drove herds of buffalo off the cliff in front of my living room window. It is theory that teaches me how to argue that all desire is not human, that we belong not only to networks of language and culture but also to the networks of the land. But it is in nature writing—perhaps almost as much as in the wilderness itself—that I learn to recognize the shape and force of my own desire to be at home on the earth.

WORKS CITED

Abbey, Edward. *Desert Solitaire: A Season in the Wilderness*. New York: McGraw-Hill, 1968.

Capra, Fritjof. *The Tao of Physics*. Oxford, England: Fontana, 1976.

Cohen, Michael P. *The Pathless Way: John Muir and American Wilderness*. Madison: University of Wisconsin Press, 1984.

Derrida, Jacques. "Structure, Sign, and Play in the Human Sciences." *The Structuralist Controversy*. Ed. Richard Macksey and Eugenio Donato. Baltimore: Johns Hopkins University Press, 1972.

Emerson, Ralph Waldo. "Nature." *Selected Essays*. Ed. Larzer Ziff. New York: Penguin, 1982.

Goodhart, Sandor. "Oedipus and Laius' Many Murderers." *Diacritics* (March 1978).

Leopold, Aldo. *A Sand County Almanac, With Essays on Conservation from Round River*. New York: Ballantine, 1970.

Lopez, Barry. *Arctic Dreams: Imagination and Desire in a Northern Landscape*. New York: Bantam, 1987.

Quammen, David. "The Zoo of You." *Outside* (August 1988).

Thoreau, Henry David. *The Maine Woods*. Princeton: Princeton University Press, 1972.

Tobias, Michael, ed. *Deep Ecology*. San Diego: Avant Books, 1984.

Wallace, David Rains. *The Klamath Knot*. San Francisco: Sierra Club Books, 1983.

Zukav, Gary. *The Dancing Wu Li Masters: An Overview of the New Physics*. New York: Bantam, 1980.

DAVID MAZEL

American Literary Environmentalism as Domestic Orientalism

■ ■ ■

I wish to address two possible problems for the criticism of environmental literature. The first of these is the incredible heterogeneity of that literature, the way it cuts across so many genres and the way its language draws upon such a variety of disciplines. The second is the close relationship between ecocriticism, environmental literature, and environmental politics. What is the critic to make of this heterogeneity and this politics? In this paper I propose to make of them an ecocritical theory in which they are not seen as problems at all, but rather as *necessary to* and *constitutive of* the environment itself.

I want to begin with a personal anecdote concerning the recent public television movie, *Land of Little Rain,* about turn-of-the-century novelist Mary Hunter Austin. For this film, the producers needed two principal performers: one to play Austin and one to portray the environment in which she lived and wrote. Her story could not have adequately been filmed otherwise, for, as Austin fans will know, the intermountain desert environment of California's Owens Valley was her home at a crucial point in her career. Ecologically fragile and hauntingly beautiful, this valley not only inspired Austin's first book but also helped transform her into the environmentalist who fought the diversion of valley stream waters to the distant city of Los Angeles. She and her neighbors ultimately lost that fight, with the disastrous ecological and social consequences that now comprise such a sad chapter of our environmental history.[1]

By the time of Austin's death in 1934, the Owens Valley that inspired

Land of Little Rain had all but died. Certainly by the time shooting began for the film in 1987, this environmental morality play's two indispensable performers—environmentalist and environment—had long been unavailable to present themselves to the camera. They had instead to be acted, to be *re*presented. Cast in the role of California's Owens Valley was the San Luis Valley of Colorado, chosen for its resemblance to the Owens Valley of Austin's day—a logical choice, as today's San Luis Valley also possesses a fragile ecology and a spectacular landscape and is also the site of a water-rights conflict, one that again has pitted an overmatched rural environment and populace against the seemingly endless thirst of Los Angeles.[2]

At that time I lived in the San Luis Valley. Like other environmentalists working against the depletion of the local aquifer, I found the completed film admirable but also deeply unsettling. It was not just déjà vu, the sense that some particularly bad environmental history was repeating itself; just as unnerving was the realization that I was watching "my" environment *perform*, that for perhaps millions of viewers it would have a greater reality as something other than itself. As a signifier, detached from its seemingly natural character and place, the San Luis Valley landscape performed convincingly not on its own quite pressing behalf, but in a story whose ending was already so far beyond emendation as already to be suffused with nostalgia. Comfortable as I had been with thinking of my environment as some securely grounded *reality*, it was certainly disturbing to see it suddenly in this alien and performative light, to realize that, like any performer, the environment could be cast in a multiplicity of roles, toward divergent ends, and by different people—not necessarily people with any immediate stake in its welfare, but quite necessarily those with the cultural wherewithal (precisely what we locals seemed to lack) to *make* it perform.

This sense of the environment as a performer had stayed with me over the years, and thus when I recently looked up *environment* in the *Oxford English Dictionary,* I was not wholly surprised to discover that performance is originary to the word itself. A root verb plus a suffix, environment once denoted "the action of environing," that is, surrounding (*OED*). But with the obsolescence of the verb *environ,* this active sense has been lost, so that we no longer hear it the way we do in words such as *judge*ment and *govern*ment—words that still echo with the full senses of the actions and the actors upon which they necessarily follow. What remains of our sense of environment, by contrast, is not any action but a thing; thanks to a nominalizing process that effaces both act and actor, we no longer speak of what *environs* us, but of what our environment *is*. This is not a trivial distinction, for restoring to environment the sense of its originary action allows us to inquire into not only *what* environs us, but *how* it came to do so, by means of what *agency,* and so on—questions crucial to the discussion that follows.

If, as the dictionary suggests, environment originates in action, just what is the nature of the action—and who or what is the actor, that is, the plain and simple noun that can be cast as a grammatical subject? The *OED* is of little help in disentangling environment-as-noun from its antecedent environment-as-verb; it first defines the environment (in its contemporary usage) quite circularly as "that which environs." This circle is not broken when the dictionary attempts a definition-by-enumeration, by telling us the environment is "the objects or region surrounding anything." Here, environment-as-noun is simply yoked to a substitute verb, *surround,* which though not obsolete is more or less synonymous with *environ*. Clearly, whatever the concrete entities enumerated in this way by the dictionary, they do not comprise an environment until and unless they come to environ, and we are no closer than before to knowing what the environment *is* independent of its acts of environing.

The way out of this circle, I suggest, is to tease out the genuine agency at work in acts of environment, to shift our attention from the mere grammatical subject—from the elusive environment-as-noun—to something whose agency is as real in fact as we unwittingly imagine the environment to be in speech. We need to focus on the speaker who is environed, on precisely that component which is left out of the dictionary definition. We need to stop trying to enumerate those elusive properties that comprise our environment and ask instead, "How is it that our environment has come to environ *us*?" The answer, I suggest, lies in the act of entry by the speaker who says, "*my* environment." It is not, after all, any action on the part of our surroundings that has made them *our* surroundings, but the onset of our being here. Environment-as-noun points to and is logically inseparable from an earlier and originary environment-as-action, which in turn points to acts of entry and occupation; all these together account for our being environed, and hence of "having" an environment that we can deploy as a noun.

At this point I wish to examine the way that our language casts the environment as a grammatical subject. Why this strange construction in which a fully agentive humanity is grammatically cast as passive object? Consider briefly what happens when people first enter a region and begin to speak of it as their environment (the process that was repeated over and over again in that crucible of modern environmentalism, the nineteenth-century American West). During this process the region so entered does nothing in particular to transform itself from terra incognita into environment; all that it does of its own accord is to continue being itself, in all its preexisting entities and processes and rhythms. What precipitates environment is rather the action of the entering and occupying humans: to have an environment is to have entered and remained.

To use a suggestive term deliberately, originary acts of environment correspond to simultaneous and logically complementary acts of *penetration*—a word I use consciously to suggest an analogy between the discourses of environmentalism and sexuality. As a variety of feminist critics have pointed out,[3] even though a sexual *penetration* might be thought of as logically complementary to and simultaneous with, say, an *engulfment* or an *immersion,* the preferred term is of course penetration, which is privileged precisely because it foregrounds male sexual agency. Use of terms such as engulfment, with their ascription of sexual agency to the female, is all but forbidden by a code that works to efface female sexuality generally.

In its complementarity to the act of penetration, environment-as-action can be thought of as analogous to engulfment or immersion. Yet within the discourse of environmentalism—unlike that of sexuality—penetration is not foregrounded but backgrounded. Agency is grammatically ascribed to what is in fact the genuinely passive partner in the transaction. This construction seems quite odd, until we notice that it has the rhetorical effect of purging environmental discourse of that sometimes discomfiting history of penetration—of discovery, exploration, conquest—that constituted the American environment-as-action in the first place. The grammar shifts attention from the real actions of human beings and focuses it upon an abstraction that not only lacks agency and presence, but whose very conjuring is a mystification.

Back now to the *OED,* which defines environment-as-noun as the "sum total" of "that which environs; the objects or region surrounding anything." I will deal shortly with the environment's putative *totality;* for now I wish to focus on the definitional primacy of its *externality,* on the way the very idea of environment divides the world into an inside and an outside. The terms here suggest a way of theorizing the environment as it is represented in narrative, specifically, in terms of Jurij Lotman's theory of plot typology. According to Lotman, the mythic text features at root just two types of characters, "those who are mobile, who enjoy freedom with respect to plot-space, who can change their place in the structure of the artistic world and cross the frontier, the basic topological feature of this space, and those who are immobile, who represent, in fact, a function of this space" (167). The plot-space itself "is divided by a single boundary into an external and an internal sphere," and only "a single character has the opportunity to cross that boundary" (167). Thus on the most fundamental narrative level there are, as Donna Haraway puts it, only two characters: "the hero and the limit of his action or the space through which he moves" (234). Haraway deliberately uses "he" here because the narrative hero is the "creator of differences," the one who differentiates his interior from his exterior and as such is "structurally male." The female is "both the space for and the resistance to" such marking (234)—"an element of plot-space," in the words now of Teresa de Lauretis, "a topos, a resistance, matrix and matter" (44).

Though Lotman wrote specifically of myth, de Lauretis of Hollywood cinema, and Haraway of the deep structure of scientific research, it is not difficult to recognize in this "matrix and matter" the environment as it is usually represented in early environmental literature. This is that literature's *narrative* environment, the Grand Canyon of John Wesley Powell or the High Sierra of Clarence King, the landscape that however much it may be exalted is also passive and objectified, like any other female in patriarchal discourse, "fixed in the position of icon, spectacle, the one looked at, in which the subject sees the objectification of *his* action and subjectivity" (Haraway 234).

To the extent that it genders the environment as female, this initial creation of difference, the discrimination of the internal from the external, is already a thoroughly political activity. Here I'll digress from the theoretical discussion and give a concrete example of how this discriminating process need not be confined to gender politics, but can become racial politics as well. In his *Notes on the State of Virginia,* it will be recalled, Thomas Jefferson's discussion of Native Americans appeared in the chapter titled "Productions," that is, as part of the natural environment. In this early early environmental construction, natives were not part of the internal but the external sphere, quite in keeping with prevailing notions of native peoples as "natural," as "children of the forest," and so on. Jefferson's enunciation of racial/environmental difference would then be echoed in certain writings that now, because they presaged the creation of the national parks, are considered formative of modern environmentalism. In 1832, for example, George Catlin called for the creation of "a magnificent park" that would not only protect nonhuman nature but would be a place "where the world could see for ages to come, the native Indian in his classic attire, galloping his wild horse . . . A *nation's Park,* containing man and beast, containing all the fresh[ness] of their nature's beauty!" (261–62). Similarly, Henry David Thoreau asked in 1858 why we should not "have our own national preserves . . . in which the bear and panther, and some even of the hunter race, may still exist . . . ?" (317). We know, of course, that the first national parks were actually formed in regions from which native peoples were being *evicted,* rather than "preserved"; this reflects a generally unremarked and unexamined change in the early racial politics of the environment.

A second layer of environmental politics may be discerned by returning to the second salient feature in the dictionary's definition of environment, that is, the notion of *totality.* This term cannot refer inclusively and exhaustively to the infinity that remains after a discrete unit—Lotman's internal sphere, the self—is subtracted from an infinite surrounding external. I am ultimately concerned here with the environment that can be defined operationally as "that which is the object of the study and concern and political action of environmentalism," and such an environment must be finite and particularized enough to have become manifest in concrete practice. Any politically actionable environmentalist discourse thus requires two creations of difference, both of which can be construed as thoroughly political. First is the discrimination of an outside from an inside (which, as we have just seen, genders and potentially racializes the environment). Such discourse also requires a secondary discrimination, a marking off of some graspable portion of the remaining totality. But what part? Such a selection requires a prior determination of what shall *count* as environment. This is the source of the second layer of politics, for not everyone will agree on what matters. The ecocritic is free here to challenge any claim of universality and objectivity, to ask not only "What has come to *matter?*" but also to ask, "Matters to *whom?*" and to test whether in fact what comes to count as the environment is that which matters to the culturally dominant, and finally to explore whether the construction of the environment is itself an exercise of cultural power.

It should be stressed that all this speaks to the insinuation of politics not into environmentalism—where one expects to find it—but into the *environ-*

ment itself, where it is likely to go unrecognized. I am arguing that ecocriticism should help readers to recognize the existence of and the workings of this deeper politics. Our reading of environmental literature should help us realize that the concerns are not exclusively of the order of "Shall these trees be cut? or "Shall this river be dammed?"—important as such questions are—but also of the order of "What has counted as the environment, and what *may* count? Who marks off the conceptual boundaries, and under what authority, and for what reasons? Have those boundaries and that authority been contested, and if so, by whom? With what success, and by virtue of what strategies of resistance?" These are the levels on which I would like to see ecocriticism theorize the environment.

Pointing as it does toward an environment rooted in human agency, and hinting at an environmentalism that is not solely a resistance to power but also an exercise of it, the discussion thus far suggests a specific path for a poststructuralist theory of literary environmentalism. Paralleling Michel Foucault's theorization of sex and sexuality, I suggest approaching the environment as a construct, not as the prediscursive origin and cause of environmental discourse but rather as the effect of that discourse. In this conception the environment becomes manifest as what Foucault called a *dispositif*, an epistemological category that organizes around itself the otherwise unrelated disciplines that claim (in this case) "the environment" as their common object of study and concern. Out of an otherwise quite heterogeneous collection of words and things that are studied by an equally heterogeneous variety of disciplines, "the environment" produces an appearance of order, relation, and presence. It is no more and no less than that particular abstraction that can be pondered not only by what we commonly think of as environmentalists, but also by the full panoply of artists who pronounce the environment beautiful, of scientists who discover it to be fragile and complex, of theologians who find it spiritually regenerating, of sociologists who recommend it as an antidote to the ills of urban society, and so on.[4]

In the broader sense I am trying to develop here, all of these people are environmentalists, regardless of their particular politics, for I am trying to reconceive of environmentalism not just as a "movement" but as a much larger ensemble of interlocking ideas, texts, people, and institutions—a (by now) sprawling formation within which environmental discourse can appear true and through which it attains an intellectual, popular, and legal authority. As you will probably have recognized by now, I am suggesting that American literary environmentalism be approached as a form of domestic Orientalism, as the latter has been formulated by Edward Said: as a "created body of theory and practice" (6), as the "corporate institution" empowered to deal with the environment "by making statements about it, authorizing views of it, describing it," and even "ruling over it" (3). Rather than treating environmentalism as a conceptually "pure" and unproblematic *resistance to* power, a resistance based upon an objective and disinterested organization of knowledge, I suggest we analyze it as just one of many potential modes for *exercising* power, as a particular "style," both political and epistemological, "for dominating, restructuring, and having authority" (3) over the real territories and lives that the environment displaces and for which it is invoked as a representation.

My comparison of literary environmentalism to Orientalism might be disputed on the grounds that it concerns one's *own* territory rather than foreign lands upon which one has some evil imperial design. However, what we today call environmentalism is generally understood to have had its beginnings in the mid- to late-nineteenth-century American West, a time and a region that place it directly upon the heels of imperial conquest. And even though environmentalism as explicit political practice—as the establishment of national parks, for example—clearly begins *after* conquest, much of what we recognize as literary environmentalism just as clearly begins earlier, as a quite interested style for knowing territory that at the time was *not* undisputed United States soil, a style generally predicated upon an imperial teleology that always took for granted the eventual domination of the region in question.[5]

For me, the larger ecocritical question is whether the emergent political environmentalism of the late nineteenth century might best be understood not as new—not as some sharp break with previous beliefs and practices—but as a seamless refinement of earlier styles for knowing, restructuring, and finally controlling the land and life of the continent.

NOTES

I wish to thank SueEllen Campbell, whose essay "The Land and Language of Desire," which appeared two years ago in *Western American Literature,* prompted me to begin the project of which this paper is a part.

1. On Austin's opposition to the Los Angeles Aqueduct, see her brief allusion to it in *Earth Horizon* (Boston: Houghton Mifflin, 1932) 290 and 307–8. See also

T. M. Pearce, *Literary America 1903-1934: The Mary Austin Letters* (Westport, Conn.: Greenwood, 1979) 12–14; Esther Lanigan Stineman, *Mary Austin: Song of a Maverick* (New Haven: Yale University Press, 1989) 82–83; Benay Blend, "Mary Austin and the Western Conservation Movement, 1900–1927," *Journal of the Southwest* 30 (Spring 1988): 12–34; William L. Kahrl, *Water and Power: The Conflict over Los Angeles's Water Supply in the Owens Valley* (Berkeley: University of California Press, 1982) 104 and 107; and Abraham Hoffman, *Vision or Villainy: Origins of the Owens Valley-Los Angeles Water Controversy* (College Station: Texas A&M University Press, 1981) 103.

2. See "Mary Austin and the Tale of Two Valleys," Alamosa, Colo., *Valley Courier* 3 June 1987: 2, and "Alamosans Taking Part in Filming of 'Land of Little Rain,'" *Valley Courier* 30 June 1987: 10.

3. See, for just one example, Julia Penelope's semantic analysis of sexual discourse in *Speaking Freely: Unlearning the Lies of the Fathers' Tongues* (New York: Pergamon, 1990) 186–87.

4. In *Worldviews and Ecology,* Mary Evelyn Tucker and John A. Grim, eds., (Lewisburg: Bucknell University Press, 1993), Thomas Berry writes:

> General ecological studies can be too abstract or too theoretical to constitute a recognized scientific discipline. Biological and geological studies can be too specialized. Environmental ethics is a much needed study, yet it cannot proceed in any effective manner without a larger understanding of the natural world. The more humanistic realm of poetry and the natural history essay are important to establish the emotional-aesthetic feeling for the wonders of the natural world and to awaken the psychic energies needed. . . . But these humanistic insights are themselves mightily enhanced by a more thorough understanding of the identifying features and intimate modes of functioning of bioregions.
>
> "None of these studies can be done in isolation from the others. . . . *The relationship of humans to the earth requires all these modes of inquiry, all these modes of expression.*" (236, my emphasis)

This fairly typical statement epitomizes the formal and epistemological heterogeneity of environmentalist discourse.

5. George Sessions, for example, considers Henry David Thoreau and John Muir the forerunners of deep ecology (Tucker and Grim 207), as does J. Baird Callicott (30). Frederick O. Waage takes a similar tack in periodizing the first wave of environmentalism as 1864–1920, as he does in *Teaching Environmental Literature* (New York: MLA, 1985). For a sample of Western American environmental literature analyzed in a nineteenth-century imperial context, see Bruce Greenfield, "The Problem of the Discoverer's Authority in Lewis and Clark's *History,*" *Macropolitics of Nineteenth-Century Literature,* Jonathan Arac and Harriet Ritvo, eds. (Philadelphia: University of Pennsylvania Press, 1991) 12–36.

WORKS CITED

Catlin, George. *Letters and Notes on the North American Indian*. Vol. 1. New York: Dover, 1973.

Haraway, Donna. *Primate Visions: Gender, Race, and Nature in the World of Modern Science*. New York: Routledge, 1989.

Lauretis, Teresa de. *Technologies of Gender: Essays on Theory, Film, and Fiction*. Bloomington: Indiana University Press, 1987.

Lotman, Jurij. "The Origin of Plot in the Light of Typology." Trans. Julian Graffy. *Poetics Today* 1 (1979): 161–84.

Said, Edward. *Orientalism*. New York: Pantheon, 1978.

Thoreau, Henry David. "Chesuncook." *Atlantic Monthly* 2 (June, July, and August 1858): 1–12, 224–33, and 305–17.

PART TWO

Ecocritical Considerations of Fiction and Drama

URSULA K. LE GUIN

The Carrier Bag Theory of Fiction

■ ■ ■

In the temperate and tropical regions where it appears that hominids evolved into human beings, the principal food of the species was vegetable. Sixty-five to eighty percent of what human beings ate in those regions in Paleolithic, Neolithic, and prehistoric times was gathered; only in the extreme Arctic was meat the staple food. The mammoth hunters spectacularly occupy the cave wall and the mind, but what we actually did to stay alive and fat was gather seeds, roots, sprouts, shoots, leaves, nuts, berries, fruits, and grains, adding bugs and mollusks and netting or snaring birds, fish, rats, rabbits, and other tuskless small fry to up the protein. And we didn't even work hard at it—much less hard than peasants slaving in somebody else's field after agriculture was invented, much less hard than paid workers since civilization was invented. The average prehistoric person could make a nice living in about a fifteen-hour work week.

Fifteen hours a week for subsistence leaves a lot of time for other things. So much time that maybe the restless ones who didn't have a baby around to enliven their life, or skill in making or cooking or singing, or very interesting thoughts to think, decided to slope off and hunt mammoths. The skillful hunters then would come staggering back with a load of meat, a lot of ivory, and a story. It wasn't the meat that made the difference. It was the story.

It is hard to tell a really gripping tale of how I wrested a wild-oat seed from its husk, and then another, and then another, and then another, and then another, and then I scratched my gnat bites, and Ool said something funny, and we went to the creek and got a drink and watched newts for a while, and then I found another patch of oats. . . . No, it does not compare, it cannot compete with how I thrust my spear deep into the titanic hairy flank while Oob, impaled on one huge sweeping tusk, writhed screaming, and blood spouted everywhere in crimson torrents, and Boob was crushed to jelly when the mammoth fell on him as I shot my unerring arrow straight through eye to brain.

That story not only has Action, it has a Hero. Heroes are powerful. Before you know it, the men and women in the wild-oat patch and their kids and the skills of the makers and the thoughts of the thoughtful and the songs of the singers are all part of it, have all been pressed into service in the tale of the Hero. But it isn't their story. It's his.

When she was planning the book that ended up as *Three Guineas,* Virginia Woolf wrote a heading in her notebook, "Glossary"; she had thought of reinventing English according to a new plan, in order to tell a different story. One of the entries in this glossary is *heroism,* defined as "botulism." And *hero,* in Woolf's dictionary, is "bottle." The hero as bottle, a stringent reevaluation. I now propose the bottle as hero.

Not just the bottle of gin or wine, but bottle in its older sense of container in general, a thing that holds something else.

If you haven't got something to put it in, food will escape you—even something as uncombative and unresourceful as an oat. You put as many as you can into your stomach while they are handy, that being the primary container; but what about tomorrow morning when you wake up and it's cold and raining and wouldn't it be good to have just a few handfuls of oats to chew on and give little Oom to make her shut up, but how do you get more than one stomachful and one handful home? So you get up and go to the damned soggy oat patch in the rain, and wouldn't it be a good thing if you had something to put Baby Oo Oo in so that you could pick the oats with both hands? A leaf a gourd a shell a net a bag a sling a sack a bottle a pot a box a container. A holder. A recipient.

> The first cultural device was probably a recipient. . . . Many theorizers feel that the earliest cultural inventions must have been a container to hold gathered products and some kind of sling or net carrier.

So says Elizabeth Fisher in *Women's Creation* (McGraw-Hill, 1975). But no, this cannot be. Where is that wonderful, big, long, hard thing, a bone, I believe, that the Ape Man first bashed somebody with in the movie and then, grunting with ecstasy at having achieved the first proper murder, flung up into the sky, and whirling there it became a space ship thrusting its way into the cosmos to fertilize it and produce at the end of the movie a lovely fetus, a boy of course, drifting around the Milky Way without (oddly enough) any womb, any matrix at all? I don't know. I don't even care. I'm not telling that story. We've heard it, we've all heard all about all the sticks and spears and swords, the things to bash and poke and hit with, the long, hard things, but we have not heard about the thing to put things in, the container for the thing contained. That is a new story. That is news.

And yet old. Before—once you think about it, surely long before—the weapon, a late, luxurious, superfluous tool; long before the useful knife and ax; right along with the indispensable whacker, grinder, and digger—for what's the use of digging up a lot of potatoes if you have nothing to lug the ones you can't eat home in—with or before the tool that forces energy outward, we made the tool that brings energy home. It makes sense to me. I am an adherent of what Fisher calls the Carrier Bag Theory of human evolution.

This theory not only explains large areas of theoretical obscurity and avoids large areas of theoretical nonsense (inhabited largely by tigers, foxes, and other highly territorial mammals); it also grounds me, personally, in human culture in a way I never felt grounded before. So long as culture was explained as originating from and elaborating upon the use of long, hard objects for sticking, bashing, and killing, I never thought that I had, or wanted, any particular share in it. ("What Freud mistook for her lack of civilization is woman's lack of *loyalty* to civilization," Lillian Smith observed.) The society, the civilization they were talking about, these theoreticians, was evidently theirs; they owned it, they liked it; they were human, fully human, bashing, sticking, thrusting, killing. Wanting to be human too, I sought for evidence that I was; but if that's what it took, to make a weapon and kill with it, then evidently I was either extremely defective as a human being, or not human at all.

That's right, they said. What you are is a woman. Possibly not human at all, certainly defective. Now be quiet while we go on telling the Story of the Ascent of Man the Hero.

Go on, say I, wandering off towards the wild oats, with Oo Oo in the sling and little Oom carrying the basket. You just go on telling how the mammoth fell on Boob and how Cain fell on Abel and how the bomb fell on Nagasaki and how the burning jelly fell on the villagers and how the missiles will fall on the Evil Empire, and all the other steps in the Ascent of Man.

If it is a human thing to do to put something you want, because it's useful, edible, or beautiful, into a bag, or a basket, or a bit of rolled bark or leaf, or a net woven of your own hair, or what have you, and then take it home with you, home being another, larger kind of pouch or bag, a container for people, and then later on you take it out and eat it or share it or store it up for winter in a solider container or put it in the medicine bundle or the shrine or the museum, the holy place, the area that contains what is sacred, and then next day you probably do much the same again—if to do that is human, if that's what it takes, then I am a human being after all. Fully, freely, gladly, for the first time.

Not, let it be said at once, an unaggressive or uncombative human being. I am an aging, angry woman laying mightily about me with my handbag, fighting hoodlums off. However I don't, nor does anybody else, consider myself heroic for doing so. It's just one of those damned things you have to do in order to be able to go on gathering wild oats and telling stories.

It is the story that makes the difference. It is the story that hid my humanity from me, the story the mammoth hunters told about bashing, thrusting, raping, killing, about the Hero. The wonderful, poisonous story of Botulism. The killer story.

It sometimes seems that that story is approaching its end. Lest there be no more telling of stories at all, some of us out here in the wild oats, amid the alien corn, think we'd better start telling another one, which maybe people can go on with when the old one's finished. Maybe. The trouble is, we've all let ourselves become part of the killer story, and so we may get finished along with it. Hence it is with a certain feeling of urgency that I seek the nature, subject, words of the other story, the untold one, the life story.

It's unfamiliar, it doesn't come easily, thoughtlessly to the lips as the killer story does; but still, "untold" was an exaggeration. People have been telling the life story for ages, in all sorts of words and ways. Myths of creation and transformation, trickster stories, folktales, jokes, novels. . . .

The novel is a fundamentally unheroic kind of story. Of course the Hero has frequently taken it over, that being his imperial nature and uncontrollable impulse, to take everything over and run it while making stern decrees and laws to control his uncontrollable impulse to kill it. So the Hero has decreed through his mouthpieces the Lawgivers, first, that the proper shape of the narrative is that of the arrow or spear, starting *here* and going straight *there* and THOK! hitting its mark (which drops dead); second, that the central concern of narrative, including the novel, is conflict; and third, that the story isn't any good if he isn't in it.

I differ with all of this. I would go so far as to say that the natural, proper, fitting shape of the novel might be that of a sack, a bag. A book holds words. Words hold things. They bear meanings. A novel is a medicine bundle, holding things in a particular, powerful relation to one another and to us.

One relationship among elements in the novel may well be that of conflict, but the reduction of narrative to conflict is absurd. (I have read a how-to-write manual that said, "A story should be seen as a battle," and went on about strategies, attacks, victory, etc.) Conflict, competition, stress, struggle, etc., within the narrative conceived as carrier bag/belly/box/house/medicine bundle, may be seen as necessary elements of a whole which itself cannot be characterized either as conflict or as harmony, since its purpose is neither resolution nor stasis but continuing process.

Finally, it's clear that the Hero does not look well in this bag. He needs a stage or a pedestal or a pinnacle. You put him in a bag and he looks like a rabbit, like a potato.

That is why I like novels: instead of heroes they have people in them.

So, when I came to write science-fiction novels, I came lugging this great heavy sack of stuff, my carrier bag full of wimps and klutzes, and tiny grains of things smaller than a mustard seed, and intricately woven nets which when laboriously unknotted are seen to contain one blue pebble, an imperturbably functioning chronometer telling the time on another world, and a mouse's skull; full of beginnings without ends, of initiations, of losses, of transformations and translations, and far more tricks than conflicts, far fewer triumphs than snares and delusions; full of space ships that get stuck, missions that fail, and people who don't understand. I said it was hard to make a gripping tale of how we wrested the wild oats from their husks, I didn't say it was impossible. Who ever said writing a novel was easy?

If science fiction is the mythology of modern technology, then its myth is tragic. "Technology," or "modern science" (using the words as they are usually used, in an unexamined shorthand standing for the "hard" sciences and high technology founded upon continuous economic growth), is a heroic undertaking, Herculean, Promethean, conceived as triumph, hence ultimately as tragedy. The fiction embodying this myth will be, and has been, triumphant (Man conquers earth, space, aliens, death, the future, etc.) and tragic (apocalypse, holocaust, then or now).

If, however, one avoids the linear, progressive, Time's-(killing)-arrow mode of the Techno-Heroic, and redefines technology and science as primarily cultural carrier bag rather than weapon of domination, one pleasant side effect is that science fiction can be seen as a far less rigid, narrow field, not necessarily Promethean or apocalyptic at all, and in fact less a mythological genre than a realistic one.

It is a strange realism, but it is a strange reality.

Science fiction properly conceived, like all serious fiction, however funny, is a way of trying to describe what is in fact going on, what people actually do and feel, how people relate to everything else in this vast sack, this belly of the universe, this womb of things to be and tomb of things that were, this unending story. In it, as in all fiction, there is room enough to keep even Man where he belongs, in his place in the scheme of things; there is time enough to gather plenty of wild oats and sow them too, and sing to little Oom, and listen to Ool's joke, and watch newts, and still the story isn't over. Still there are seeds to be gathered, and room in the bag of stars.

JOSEPH W. MEEKER

The Comic Mode

■ ■ ■

THE BIOLOGY OF COMEDY

Literary criticism has asserted from its beginnings the idea that literature is essentially an imitation of the actions of men. Few have disputed the doctrine of mimesis first spelled out in ancient Greece in Plato's *Republic* and revised in Aristotle's *Poetics,* though subsequent critics have modified the interpretation of the term *mimesis.* Without going into the niceties of the argument, let me merely assume in a simpleminded way that literature does imitate human actions, and consider two examples of such imitation. Both seek to reproduce the same fictional action, but from different historical perspectives and using different literary modes.

The first example is *Oedipus the King,* written in the fifth century B.C. by the Greek dramatist Sophocles. Early in the play Teiresias, the blind seer, confronts the king with the suggestion that the murderer he is seeking is perhaps Oedipus himself.

TEIRESIAS
I say you are the murderer of the king
whose murderer you seek.
OEDIPUS
Not twice you shall
say calumnies like this and stay unpunished.
TEIRESIAS
Shall I say more to tempt your anger more?
OEDIPUS
As much as you desire; it will be said
in vain.

TEIRESIAS

I say that with those you love best
you live in foulest shame unconsciously
and do not see where you are in calamity.

OEDIPUS

Do you imagine you can always talk
like this, and live to laugh at it hereafter?

TEIRESIAS

Yes, if the truth has anything of strength.[1]

In *Giles Goat-Boy,* a novel by the contemporary American novelist John Barth, a central chapter is devoted to the translation of the Oedipus story into the idiom of comedy in a post-Freudian world. Barth's version follows Sophocles' closely, but with rather different effect. The Barth account of the meeting between Gynander (Teiresias) and Taliped Decanus (Oedipus) shows all the solemnity of a vaudeville routine.

GYNANDER

When this play's over you'll
regret you made that silly vow of yours.
You tragic-hero types are bloody bores.
. . . You're
the wretch you want. You'll see, when
Scene Four's done
that you're your daughter's brother,
your own stepson
and foster-father, uncle to your cousin,
your brother-in-law's nephew, and (as
if that wasn't
enough) a parricide—and a matriphile!
Bye-bye now Taliped. You call *me* vile,
But your two crimes will have us all
upchucking:
father-murdering and mother—

TALIPED

Ducking
out won't save you. You'll hear from me!

GYNANDER

You killed your daddy!
You shagged your mommy!
[He is taken away][2]

Both scenes are recognizable imitations of the actions of men, and in this case the action being imitated is the same: the revelation of Oedipus's crimes. But the purposes, the language, the moods, and the contexts of the two passages could hardly contrast more than they do. Sophocles and John Barth are imitating different aspects of human action, and the difference between them illustrates a basic distinction between the tragic and the comic views of human behavior. Sophocles' purpose is to imitate man insofar as he is a creature of suffering and greatness; through his characters he demonstrates the enormous human capacity for creating and for enduring pain, for following a passion to its ultimate end, for employing the power of mind and spirit to rise above the contradictions of matter and circumstance even though one is destroyed by them. Sophocles imitates man as a noble creature. Barth imitates man's absurdity. Barth's version emphasizes the ridiculousness of Oedipus's situation and suggests that the hero is slightly dense for not avoiding the mess he's made of his life. Barth's image shows man's innate stupidity and ignorance and emphasizes the triviality of human passions by reducing them to the level of street-corner disputes.

The tragic view of man has not often been achieved. Whole cultures have lived and died without producing tragedy or the philosophical views that tragedy depends upon. Both as a literary form and as a philosophical attitude, tragedy seems to have been an invention of Western culture, specifically of the Greeks. It is shared by those traditions influenced by Greek thought, though few of the cultures even in the direct line of that influence have produced a significant tragic literature rivaling that of ancient Greece. The intellectual presuppositions necessary to the creation of tragic literature have not been present in all civilizations. It is conspicuously absent, for instance, in Oriental, Middle Eastern, and primitive cultures. The tragic view assumes that man exists in a state of conflict with powers that are greater than he is. Such forces as nature, the gods, moral law, passionate love, the greatness of ideas and knowledge all seem enormously above mankind and in some way determine his welfare or his suffering. Tragic literature and philosophy, then, undertake to demonstrate that man is equal or superior to his conflict. The tragic man takes his conflict seriously, and feels compelled to affirm his mastery and his greatness in the face of his own destruction. He is a triumphant image of what man can be. Outside of ancient Greece and Elizabethan England, few playwrights have been able to produce this image in a convincing manner.

Comedy, on the other hand, is very nearly universal. Comic literature appears wherever human culture exists, and often where it doesn't. Comedy can be universal largely because it depends less upon particular ideologies or metaphysical systems than tragedy does. Rather, comedy grows from the biological circumstances of life. It is unconcerned with cultural systems of morality. As the contemporary American philosopher Susanne Langer has put it, comedy is truly amoral in that it has, literally, "no use" for morality—that is, moral insights play no significant role in the comic experience.[3] Similarly, comedy avoids strong emotions. Passionate love, hate, or patriotism generally appear ridiculous in a comic context, for comedy creates a psychological mood which is incompatible with deep emotions. Great ideas and ideals fare no better at the hands of comedy, which ordinarily treats them as if they were insignificant. When noble idealism does appear in comedy, its vehicle is commonly a Tartuffe (as in Moliere's *Tartuffe: or the Imposter*) or a Malvolio (as in Shakespeare's *Twelfth Night*), whose nobility turns out to be merely a sham to conceal selfish or ignoble motives. The comic view of man demonstrates that men behave irrationally, committing follies which reveal their essential ignorance and ridiculousness in relation to civilized systems of ethical and social behavior. As Aristotle puts it, comedy imitates the actions of men who are subnormal or inferior to the social norm and tragedy imitates the actions of superior men.

It could thus be argued that comedy is basically pessimistic and tragedy basically optimistic, as tragedy shows man's potential strength and greatness. This is true only if it is assumed that the metaphysical morality that encourages man to rise above his natural environment and his animal origins is mankind's best hope for the future. That assumption is seriously in doubt in our time. There are good reasons to suspect the wisdom of the traditions of metaphysical idealism. Philosophy since Nietzsche has demonstrated the poverty of humanistic idealism, evolutionary biology has demonstrated the animality of mankind, and contemporary psychology has shown that the mind is guided by many forces stronger than great ideas. Political philosophies fail daily to meet mankind's simplest needs, and now the environmental crisis raises the possibility that the world itself and all its creatures are in jeopardy because humanity has thought too highly of itself. The tragic view of man, for all its flattering optimism, has led to cultural and biological disasters, and it is time to look for alternatives which might encourage better the survival of our own and other species.

Comedy demonstrates that man is durable even though he may be weak, stupid, and undignified. As the tragic hero suffers or dies for his ideals, the comic hero survives without them. At the end of his tale he manages to marry his girl, evade his enemies, slip by the oppressive authorities, avoid drastic punishment, and to stay alive. His victories are all small, but he lives in a world where only small victories are possible. His career demonstrates that weakness is a common condition of mankind that must be lived with, not one worth dying for. Comedy is careless of morality, goodness, truth, beauty, heroism, and all such abstract values men say they live by. Its only concern is to affirm man's capacity for survival and to celebrate the continuity of life itself, despite all moralities. Comedy is a celebration, a ritual renewal of biological welfare as it persists in spite of any reasons there may be for feeling metaphysical despair.

The Greek demigod Comus, whose name was probably the origin of the word comedy, was a god of fertility in a large but unpretentious sense. His concerns included the ordinary sexual fertility of plants, men, and animals, and also the general success of family and community life insofar as these depend upon biological processes. Comus was content to leave matters of great intellectual import to Apollo and gigantic passions to Dionysus while he busied himself with the maintenance of the commonplace conditions that are friendly to life. Maintaining equilibrium among living things, and restoring it once it has been lost, are Comus's special talents, and they are shared by the many comic heroes who follow the god's example.

Literary comedy depicts the loss of equilibrium and its recovery. Wherever the normal processes of life are obstructed unnecessarily, the comic mode seeks to return to normal. The point can be illustrated by a Greek comic drama from the fifth century B.C., Aristophanes' *Lysistrata:* When the young men all disappear from their wives' beds in order to fight a foolish foreign war, the comic heroine Lysistrata calls a sex strike of all women and bargains for an end to the war in exchange for a restoration of normal sexual activities. Lysistrata counts on her own wit and the natural lecherousness of men to solve her immediate problem. Lysistrata's motive is not peace with honor but peace with love—or at least with lovemaking. Honor belongs to the vocabulary of tragedy and warfare. At best it is irrelevant to peace, at worst destructive of it. As Americans have learned during the Vietnam decade, honor can be dangerous and disruptive when used as a principle of public policy. Lysistrata and her women puncture the inflated rhetoric of warriors and politicians to reassert the comic primacy of sex and its attendant social needs: mutual access of men and women to one another, family wholeness, and the maintenance of normal reproduction, child rearing, and nourishment.

Typical of comic action, *Lysistrata* demonstrates no discovery of a new truth and no permanent conquest over an evil force, but merely a return to a former normalcy. No enemy has been destroyed and no new victories have been won. Success is temporary, and it has been accomplished with the most modest of weapons: wit, luck, persuasion, and a bit of fanciful inventiveness. The antagonists are momentarily reconciled, the killing ceases, the men make love to their wives, and the wives raise children and keep house, which is exactly what they were doing before the heroics of warfare interfered with their lives. Like most significant comedy, *Lysistrata* pretends only to show how mankind can hold its own and survive in a world where both real and artificial threats to survival abound. Comedy is concerned with muddling through, not with progress or perfection.

To people disposed in favor of heroism and idealistic ethics, comedy may seem trivial in its insistence that the commonplace is worth maintaining. The comic point of view is that man's high moral ideals and glorified heroic poses are themselves largely based upon fantasy and are likely to lead to misery or death for those who hold them. In the world as revealed by comedy, the important thing is to live and to encourage life even though it is probably meaningless to do so. If the survival of our species is trivial, then so is comedy.

THE COMEDY OF BIOLOGY

If comedy is essentially biological, it is possible that biology is also comic. Some animal ethologists argue that humor is not only a deterrent to aggression, but also an essential ingredient in the formation of intraspecific bonds. It appears to have a phylogenetic basis in many animals as well as in man.[4] Beyond this behavioral level, structures in nature also reveal organizational principles and processes which closely resemble the patterns found in comedy. Productive and stable ecosystems are those which minimize destructive aggression, encourage maximum diversity, and seek to establish equilibrium among their participants—which is essentially what happens in literary comedy. Biological evolution itself shows all the flexibility of comic drama, and little of the monolithic passion peculiar to tragedy.

Ecology is to a large extent the study of plant and animal succession. Ecologists seek to understand the processes through which interactions among species over long periods of time produce the various biological communities and environments found in the natural world. At an early stage in any given environment, pioneering or invading species dominate the scene. These are highly generalized, flexible, and adaptable creatures capable of surviving despite the inhospitable nature of their environments. Pioneers must be aggressive, competitive, and tough. On an evolutionary time scale, their careers are brief but dramatic episodes, but they make possible the more stable ecosystems which follow them. Many weeds that grow on newly cleared land following fires, volcanic eruptions, or construction projects are pioneer plants such as dandelions and crabgrass. Weekend gardeners know well their tenacity and durability. Rats, too, are pioneers capable of thriving against terrible odds by exploiting the meager resources available, as are starlings and several varieties of eels and carp. Many of the species that men find objectionable—the "weeds," "trash fish," and "nuisance" mammals and birds—are pioneering or invading species whose life styles resemble behavior that men have admired most when they have seen it in other men. We celebrate the qualities in human pioneers that we despise in the pioneers of other plant and animal species.

Ecological pioneering species, like human pioneers, are creatures capable of living without some of the normal needs felt by others of their kind. They are heroic individuals who make their homes where no one else wants to live, and their lives lead the way toward challenging and dangerous horizons. They risk death in order to conquer new territory, and their survival depends on their individual qualities of strength, aggressiveness, and often ruthlessness. Pioneer species are the loners of the natural world, the tragic heroes who sacrifice themselves in satisfaction of mysterious inner commands which they alone can hear.

This may sound like anthropomorphism but it is not. I am not suggesting at all that plants and animals possess human qualities but that much elaborate philosophizing about human behavior has been mere rationalization of relatively common natural patterns of behavior which are to be found in many species of plants and animals. The tragic attitude assumes remarkable behavior to be the result of a remarkable personality and an exclusively human prerogative. But Achilles does no more or less for human posterity than a fireweed growing on a glacial moraine does for the plants that will succeed it. The major difference, perhaps, is that the fireweed will indeed be succeeded by different kinds of plants until ultimately a complex forest emerges, while Achilles will be reincarnated by imitators from among his own species for many centuries, to the grief of many Troys and many Hectors.

The process of ecological succession begun by the pioneer species, if left alone, results in a climax ecosystem. Climax communities of plants and animals are extremely diverse and complicated groupings of living things which exist in a relatively balanced state with one another and with their nonliving environment. A climax ecosystem is much more complicated than any human social organization, if only because it integrates the diverse needs and activities of a very large number of *different* species. Human social systems have only one animal to deal with, man, plus minor adjustments to keep alive the few domesticated plants and animals enslaved to man. But a natural ecosystem accommodates not only the complete life of every species within it, but also provides for relatively harmonious relationships among all its constituent species. In a mature ponderosa pine forest, for instance, thousands of highly specialized types of bacteria maintain stable soil chemistry as each type plays its particular role in the processes of decomposition; insects live upon plants and bacteria and are eaten by birds; small mammals breed in the complex vegetation; larger mammals eat certain specific kinds of plants or prey upon smaller animals; the many highly specialized plants, from small ferns to enormous pines, make up the setting for all other life, provide food and shelter, and in turn depend upon the environmental determinants of weather and geography. It is an unbelievably complicated community in which no individual and no species can survive well unless all other species survive, for all are ultimately dependent upon the completeness of the environment as a whole. The diversity of a climax ecosystem is one of the secrets of its durability.

Life is dangerous for any individual in such a system, for there is always some other individual who needs to eat him. The welfare of individuals is generally subordinated to the welfare of the group. No individuals and no particular species stand out as overwhelmingly dominant, but each performs unique and specialized functions which play a part in the overall stability of the community. It is the community itself that really matters, and it is likely to be an extremely durable community so long as balance is maintained among its many elements.

No human has ever known what it means to live in a climax ecosystem, at least not since the emergence of consciousness which has made us human. We have generally acted the role of the pioneer species, dedicating ourselves to survival through the destruction of all our competitors and to achieving effective dominance over other forms of life. Civilization, at least in the West, has developed as a tragedy does, through the actions of pioneering leaders who break new ground and surmount huge obstacles. Religion and philosophy have usually affirmed the pioneer's faith that only his own kind really counts, and that he has a right—perhaps even an obligation—to destroy or subjugate whatever seems to obstruct his hopes of conquest. Some relatively benevolent societies have provided for wide diversification among men, but none has extended *e pluribus unum* to include other species.

Like comedy, mature ecosystems are cosmopolitan. Whatever life forms may exist seem to have an equal right to existence, and no individual needs, prejudices, or passions give sufficient cause to threaten the welfare of the ecosystem structure as a whole. Necessity, of course, is real. All must eat and in turn be eaten, storms must come and go, and injustices must occur when so many rightful claimants contend. But that is just the point: comedy and ecology are systems designed to accommodate necessity and to encourage acceptance of it, while tragedy is concerned with avoiding or transcending the necessary in order to accomplish the impossible.

One of the tenets of the humanistic tradition is that human beings should try to accomplish whatever the human mind can imagine. Many of our imaginings have been directed toward making ourselves more perfect. The human brain makes it possible to modify human behavior according to conceptual plans which may or may not agree with established natural processes or with human instinctual needs. Unlike other animals, humans can select from a large number of conceptual possibilities the behavior that they prefer for mating, social organization, aggression and defense, rearing of offspring, and the maintenance of food supply.

The capacity to choose one's behavior includes the possibility of choosing erroneously, and many of the environmental problems facing mankind today seem to be the products of mistaken human choices. But what does "mistaken" mean, and how it is possible to know the difference between ecological wisdom and ecological insanity? It is depressing to realize that such questions have been asked seriously only in recent years. Human behavior has generally been guided by presumed metaphysical principles which have neglected to recognize that man is a species of animal whose welfare depends upon successful integration with the plants, animals, and land that make up his environment.

Because they do not have such a wide choice, other animals have more successfully maintained the behavioral patterns which make their own survival possible while contributing to the long-term maintenance of their environments. The recent growth of ethology, the study of animal behavior, is a sign that humans are now beginning to see animals as significant sources of information about living well. Ethologists have consistently discovered that even the simplest of creatures follow exceedingly complicated and often highly sophisticated patterns of behavior, many of which continue to defy human understanding. Animal rituals of reproduction and rearing, defense of territory, maintenance of social systems, nest-building, migrations, and food-gathering are quite as intricate as comparable human activities. The simplest migratory bird has a guidance system that is more subtle and far more reliable than the most sophisticated ICBM, and any pair of whooping cranes has a courtship and sex life at least as complicated as Romeo and Juliet's. We are slowly beginning to realize that we have grossly underestimated the animals.

The truth may be that civilized human life is much simpler than most animal life. We seem to have used our enlarged brain in order to reduce the number of choices facing us, and we have sought the simple way of destroying or ignoring our competition rather than the more demanding task of accommodating ourselves to the forces that surround us. We establish artificial polarities like good and evil, truth and falsehood, pain and pleasure, and demand that a choice be made which will elevate one and destroy the other. We transform complicated wilderness environments into ecologically simple farmlands. We seek unity and we fear diversity. We demand that one species, our own, achieve unchallenged dominance where hundreds of species lived in complex equilibrium before our arrival. In the present environmental dilemma, humanity stands like a pioneer species facing heroically the consequences of its own tragic behavior, with a growing need to learn from the more stable comic heroes of nature, the animals.

Tragedy demands that choices be made among alternatives; comedy assumes that all choice is likely to be in error and that survival depends upon finding accommodations that will permit all parties to endure. Evolution itself is a gigantic comic drama, not the bloody tragic spectacle imagined by the sentimental humanists of early Darwinism. Nature is not "red in tooth and claw" as the nineteenth-century English poet Alfred, Lord Tennyson characterized it, for evolution does not proceed through battles fought among animals to see who is fit enough to survive and who is not. Rather, the evolutionary process is one of adaptation and accommodation, with the various species exploring opportunistically their environments in search of a means to maintain their existence. Like comedy, evolution is a matter of muddling through.

Literary comedy and biological evolution share in common the view that all change is conservative.[5] Organisms and comic heroes change their structure or behavior only in order to preserve an accustomed way of life which has been threatened by changes in the environment. The ancient fish that developed lungs when his home in the sea became untenable was not a radical revolutionary, but a public-spirited preserver of his genetic heritage. The famous peppered moth of Birmingham who changed his color from light gray to black when smoke from the industrial revolution discolored the bark on his native trees may have denied thousands of years of moth tradition, but his adaptation made it possible to preserve moth existence. If there were moral philosophers among the lungfishes and peppered moths, these innovations would very likely have been condemned as threats to the continuity of tradition, or perhaps as shameful immorality. All admiration would no doubt have been reserved for the heroic fish who would rather die than give up his gills and for the moth who nobly faced his end wearing customary gray. Fossilized remains attest to the many extinct animals who insisted upon the propriety of their traditions in the face of a changing world. Of the estimated one billion different species produced so far by evolution, ninety-nine percent have become extinct in such a manner.

To say that change is conservative may confuse anyone who thinks the term is the antonym of liberal and that it describes a mental attitude in favor of traditional social values and customs. The conservative principle in biology is evolutionary; it refers to those variations in structure and behavior which adapt an organism more perfectly to a changing environment, thus conserving its genetic continuity despite changes in form. Whatever may threaten the continuity of life itself is considered by evolution to be expendable and subject to modification, whether it be gills or social rituals. To evolution and to comedy, nothing is sacred but life itself.

The old Italian whoremaster in Joseph Heller's contemporary American novel, *Catch-22,* teaches a similar lesson:

> I was a fascist when Mussolini was on top, and I am an anti-fascist now that he has been deposed. I was fanatically pro-German when the Germans were here to protect us against the Americans, and now that the Americans are here to protect us against the Germans I am fanatically pro-American.[6]

Nately, the naively idealistic American soldier to whom he is talking, sputters in dismay that he is a shameful, unscrupulous opportunist, and the old man replies only: "I am a hundred and seven years old." Young Nately, committed to the idealism of keeping the world safe for democracy, dies in combat before his twentieth birthday. The old man's morality rests upon the comic imperative of preserving life itself at all costs, a principle which overrides all other moral commitments.

Evolution is just such a shameful, unscrupulous, opportunistic comedy, the object of which appears to be the proliferation and preservation of as many life forms as possible without regard for anyone's moral ideas. Successful participants in it are those who remain alive when circumstances change, not those who are best able to destroy competitors and enemies. Its ground rules for participants (including man) are those which also govern literary comedy: organisms must adapt themselves to their circumstances in every possible way, must studiously avoid all-or-nothing choices, must prefer any alternative to death, must accept and encourage maximum diversity, must accommodate themselves to the accidental limitations of birth and environment, and must always prefer love to war—though if warfare is inevitable, it should be prosecuted so as to humble the enemy without destroying him. The events depicted in tragic literature *cannot* occur if these principles are observed. Comic action follows naturally from them.

COMIC SURVIVAL

Oscar Wilde, the nineteenth-century British playwright, offered an important amendment to Aristotle when he observed that life imitates art at least as much as art imitates life. Artists and thinkers, he argued, create images of what life might be like and so provide models for human behavior which men may imitate. Don Quixote was not born a knight-errant, but discovered his profession by reading tales of adventure. People can choose to some extent the roles they wish to play from among the many models preserved by literature and cultural traditions. If people generally see themselves in the tragic mode, it is perhaps because it satisfies their vanity and makes their actions seem important. It is gratifying to think of oneself as a hero, a great sufferer, a martyr, or an oppressed idealist. Oedipus and Hamlet might not have been admired all these centuries if they had not offered illustrious images showing how to bear pain magnificently. But unfortunately, the tragic heroes preserved in literature are the products of metaphysical presuppositions which most people can no longer honestly share, any more than Don Quixote could live up to the requirements of medieval chivalry while living in Renaissance Spain. A post-Freudian world no longer sees incest as an offense against the universe as Oedipus did, nor can we share Hamlet's view that revenge will give peace to the ghost of his slain father. The philosophical props and settings for genuine tragic experience have disappeared. Moderns can only pretend to tragic heroism, and that pretense is painfully hollow and melodramatic in the absence of the beliefs that tragedy depends upon.

Prerequisite to tragedy is the belief that the universe cares about the lives of human beings. There must be a faith that some superior order exists, and that man will be punished if he transgresses against it. It matters little whether this principle takes the form of fate, the gods, or impersonal moral law, for all are symbols of the world's interest in human actions and evidence that the welfare of all creation somehow depends upon what humans do. Corollary to this is the assumption that man is essentially superior to animal, vegetable, and mineral nature and is destined to exercise mastery over all natural processes, including those of his own body. The most respected tragedy further assumes that some truth exists in the universe which is more valuable than life itself. There must be abstract ideas and values which are worth dying and suffering for, otherwise the hero's painful quest for spiritual purity and enlightenment becomes absurd.

"Absurd" is the proper adjective to describe these assumptions, in the rather technical sense in which existential philosophy uses the term. The world has never cared about man, nature has never shown itself to be inferior to humanity, and truth has never been revealed in its awesome majesty except perhaps in the creations of tragic literature. Tragedy does not imitate the conditions of life, but creates artificial conditions which men mimic in their attempts to attain the flattering illusions of dignity and honor. In an age which perceives dignity, honor, truth, law, and the gods as the inventions of egocentric man and not as given facts of the universe, tragedy can only parody itself.

More appropriate to our time are the relatively modest assumptions made by the comic spirit. Man is a part of nature and subject to all natural limitations and flaws. Morality is a matter of getting along with one's fellow creatures as well as possible. All beliefs are provisional, subject to change when they fail to produce harmonious consequences. Life itself is the most important force there is: the proper study of mankind is survival. When the existence of many species, including the human, and the continuity of the biological environment are threatened as they are now, mankind can no longer afford the wasteful and destructive luxuries of a tragic view of life.

As patterns of behavior, both tragedy and comedy are strategies for the resolution of conflicts. From the tragic perspective, the world is a battleground where good and evil, man and nature, truth and falsehood make war, each with the goal of destroying its polar opposite. Warfare is the basic metaphor of tragedy, and its strategy is a battle plan designed to eliminate the enemy. That is why tragedy ends with a funeral or its equivalent. Comic strategy, on the other hand, sees life as a game. Its basic metaphors are sporting events and the courtship of lovers, and its conclusion is generally a wedding rather than a funeral. When faced with polar opposites, the problem of comedy is always how to resolve conflict without destroying the participants. Comedy is the art of accommodation and reconciliation.

Though the comic, ecological view of life may be modest and unheroic, it is anything but simple. Some superrationalists reject the current interest in ecology by arguing that a "return to nature" would be a denial of the mental capacities of mankind, and impossible in a world as complicated and populous as it is today. Their assumption that nature is simple while civilization is complex is one of the sad legacies of romantic thought. Nature is neither an idyll of simplicity and peace populated by noble savages (as pictured by the eighteenth-century French philosopher Jean Jacques Rousseau) nor a bloody battlefield where only the most brutal can survive (as defined by the seventeenth-century British philosopher Thomas Hobbes, and later elaborated by nineteenth-century social Darwinism). Both views drastically oversimplify the intricate processes of nature because they reflect the methods and values of a pioneer species, man, rather than the complexity of the more highly developed species of an ecological climax.

If a "return to nature" were to be based upon the model of a climax ecosystem, civilization would have to become far more complex than anything man has yet produced. Human values could no longer be based on the assumption that man is alone at the center of creation; allowance would have to be made for the welfare of all the plants, animals, and land of the natural environment. Mankind would have to cultivate a new and more elaborate mentality capable of understanding intricate processes without destroying them. Ecology challenges mankind to vigorous complexity, not passive simplicity.

If the lesson of ecology is balance and equilibrium, the lesson of comedy is humility and endurance. The comic mode of human behavior represented in literature is the closest art has come to describing man as an adaptive animal. Comedy illustrates that survival depends upon man's ability to change himself rather than his environment, and upon his ability to accept limitations rather than to curse fate for limiting him. It is a strategy for living which agrees well with the demands of ecological wisdom, and it cannot be ignored as a model for human behavior if man hopes to keep a place for himself among the animals who live according to the comic mode.

NOTES

1. David Grene and Richmond Lattimore, *The Complete Greek Tragedies* (Chicago: University of Chicago Press, 1959), 2:26.
2. John Barth, *Giles Goat-Boy* (New York: Fawcett, 1967), 323.
3. Susanne Langer, *Feeling and Form* (New York: Charles Scribner's Sons, 1953), 345.
4. Konrad Lorenz, *On Aggression* (New York: Bantam Books, 1967), 171–73, 284–87.
5. Charles F. Hockett and Robert Ascher, "The Human Revolution," *Current Anthropology* 5, no. 3 (1964): 140.
6. Joseph Heller, *Catch-22* (New York: Dell, 1961), 251–52.

ANNETTE KOLODNY

Unearthing Herstory

■ ■ ■

AN INTRODUCTION

You don't know what you've got 'til it's gone,
They paved Paradise and put up a parking lot.
—Joni Mitchell, "Big Yellow Taxi"

For the brief space of perhaps two weeks at the end of May 1969, a small plot of deserted ground just south of the University of California campus at Berkeley dominated headlines and news broadcasts across the country. That such an apparently local incident as the "Battle for People's Park" could so quickly and so effectively capture a nation's attention suggests that it had touched off a resonant chord in the American imagination. If the various legal, political, moral, and ecological issues involved in the controversy are as confused and confusing today as they were in 1969, they do at least all seem to cohere around a single unifying verbal image that appeared in almost all of the leaflets, handbills, and speeches printed during the uproar:

The earth is our Mother
 the land
The University put a fence around
 the land—our Mother.[1]

In what has since been partially paved over and designated a parking lot, the advocates of People's Park dared fantasize a natural maternal realm, in which human children happily working together in the spontaneous and unalienated labor of planting and tilling might all be "sod brothers."[2] So powerful was the fantasy, in fact, that many seriously believed that, armed "with sod, lots of flowers, and spirit," those evicted from the park might return and "ask our brothers in the [National] Guard to let us into our park."[3]

If the wished-for fraternity with the National Guard was at least erratically realized, the return to "the land—our Mother," the place, they insisted, "where our souls belong,"[4] was thwarted completely. The disposition of the land through "proper channels"—including city council and university officials—was characterized variously as "the rape of People's Park" or, more graphically, as a case of "The University . . . / fucking with our land."[5] For many, hurt and angered at the massive repression their fantasy had engendered, People's Park became "a mirror in which our society may see itself," a summing up of American history: "We have constituted ourselves socially and politically to conquer and transform nature."[6]

In fact, the advocates of People's Park had asserted another version of what is probably America's oldest and most cherished fantasy: a daily reality of harmony between man and nature based on an experience of the land as essentially feminine—that is, not simply the land as mother, but the land as woman, the total female principle of gratification—enclosing the individual in an environment of receptivity, repose, and painless and integral satisfaction.[7] Such imagery is archetypal wherever we find it; the soul's home, as the People's Park Committee leaflet and three hundred years of American writing before it had asserted, is that place where the conditions of exile—from Eden or from some primal harmony with the Mother—do not obtain; it is a realm of nurture, abundance, and unalienated labor within which all men are truly brothers. In short, the place America had long promised to be, ever since the first explorers declared themselves virtually "ravisht with the . . . pleasant land" and described the new continent as a "*Paradise* with all her Virgin Beauties."[8] The human, and decidedly feminine, impact of the landscape became a staple of the early promotional tracts, inviting prospective settlers to inhabit "valleyes and plaines streaming with sweete Springs, like veynes in a naturall bodie," and to explore "hills and mountaines making a sensible proffer of hidden treasure, neuer yet searched."[9]

As a result, along with their explicit hopes for commercial, religious, and political gains, the earliest explorers and settlers in the New World can be said to have carried with them a "yearning for paradise." When they ran across people living in what seemed to them "the manner of the golden age," and found lands where "nature and liberty affords vs that freely, which in *England* we want, or it costeth vs dearely," dormant dreams found substantial root.[10] When, for instance, Arthur Barlowe's account of his "First Voyage Made to the Coasts of America . . . Anno 1584," described the Indian women who greeted him and his men as uniformly beautiful, gracious, cheerful, and friendly, with the wife of the king's brother taking "great pains to see all things ordered in the best manner she could, making great haste to dress some meat for us to eat," he initiated a habit of mind that came to see the Indian woman as a kind of emblem for a land that was similarly entertaining the Europeans "with all love and kindness and . . . as much bounty." Not until the end of the seventeenth century, when the tragic contradictions inherent in such experience could no longer be ignored, were the Indian women depicted more usually as hag-like, ugly, and immoral. The excitement that greeted John Rolfe's marriage to Pocahontas, in April of 1614, may have been due to the fact that it served, in some symbolic sense, as a kind of objective correlative for the possibility of Europeans' actually possessing the charms inherent in the virgin continent. Similarly, the repeated evocation of the new continent as "some delicate garden abounding with all kinds of odoriferous flowers," and the sometimes strident insistence that early explorers had "made a Garden vpon the top of a Rockie Ile . . . that grew so well,"[11] tantalizes with the suggestion that the garden may in fact be "an abstraction of the essential femininity of the terrain." Paul Shepard undoubtedly has a point when he claims that "we have yet to recognize the full implication of the mother as a primary landscape,"[12] especially since, as psychiatrist Joel Kovel has argued, "the life of the body and the experiences of infancy, . . . are the reference points of human knowledge and the bedrock of the structures of culture."[13]

If the initial impulse to experience the New World landscape, not merely as an object of domination and exploitation, but as a maternal "garden," receiving and nurturing human children, was a reactivation of what we now recognize as universal mythic wishes, it had one radically different facet: *this* paradise really existed, "Whole" and "True," its many published descriptions boasting "the *proofe* of the present benefit this Countrey affoords"[14] (italics mine). All the descriptions of wonderful beasts and strangely contoured humans notwithstanding, the published documents from explorers assured the reader of the author's accuracy and unimpeachable reliability. No mere literary convention this; an irrefutable fact of history (the European discovery of America) touched every word written about the New World with the possibility that the ideally beautiful and bountiful terrain might be lifted forever out of the canon of pastoral convention and invested with the reality of daily experience. In some sense, the process had already begun, as explorer after explorer claimed to have "personally . . . wth diligence searched and viewed these contries" before concluding them to be "the fairest, frutefullest, and pleasauntest of all the worlde."[15] Eden, Paradise, the Golden Age, and the idyllic garden, in short, all the backdrops for European literary pastoral, were subsumed in the image of an America promising material ease without labor or hardship, as opposed to the grinding poverty of previous European existence; a frank, free affectional life in which all might share in a primal and noncompetitive fraternity; a resurrection of the lost state of innocence that the adult abandons when he joins the world of competitive self-assertion; and all this possible because, at the deepest psychological level, the move to America was experienced as the daily reality of what has become its single dominating metaphor: regression from the cares of adult life and a return to the primal warmth of womb or breast in a feminine landscape. And when America finally produced a pastoral literature of her own, that literature hailed the essential femininity of the terrain in a way European pastoral never had, explored the historical consequences of its central metaphor in a way European pastoral had never dared, and, from the first, took its metaphors as literal truths. The traditional mode had embraced its last and possibly its most uniquely revitalizing permutation.

As Joel Kovel points out, of course, "It is one thing to daydream and conjure up wishful images of the way things ought to be in order that one's instinctually-based fantasies may come true"; at the time of America's discovery, this had become the province of European pastoral. "It is quite another matter, and a more important one in cultural terms,"[16] he continues, to begin experiencing those fantasies as the pattern of one's daily activity—as was the case in sixteenth- and seventeenth-century America. For only if we acknowledge the power of the pastoral impulse to shape and structure experience can we reconcile the images of abundance in the early texts with the historical evidence of starvation, poor harvests, and inclement weather.[17] To label such an impulse as "mere fantasy" in order to dismiss it ignores the fact that fantasy is a particular way of relating to the world, even, as R. D. Laing suggests, "part of, sometimes the essential part of, the meaning or sense . . . implicit in action."[18] In 1630 Francis Higginson, "one of the ministers of Salem," claimed that "Experience doth manifest that there is hardly a more healthfull place to be found in the World" and boasted that "since I came hither . . . I thanke God I haue had perfect health, and . . . whereas beforetime I cloathed my self with double cloathes and thicke Wastcoats to keepe me warme, euen in the Summer time, I doe now goe as thin clad as any, onely wearing a light Stuffe Cassocke vpon my Shirt and Stuffe Breeches and one thickness without Linings."[19] The fact that he died the next year of pneumonia, or, as Governor Dudley phrased it, "of a feaver," in no way negates what the good minister claimed his "Experience doth manifest." American pastoral, unlike European, holds at its very core the promise of fantasy as daily reality. Implicit in the call to emigrate, then, was the tantalizing proximity to a happiness that had heretofore been the repressed promise of a better future, a call to act out what was at once a psychological and political revolt against a culture based on toil, domination, and self-denial.

But not many who emigrated yearning for pastoral gratifications shared Higginson's "Experience." Colonization brought with it an inevitable paradox: the success of settlement depended on the ability to master the land, transforming the virgin territories into something else—a farm, a village, a road, a canal, a railway, a mine, a factory, a city, and finally, an urban nation. As a result, those who had initially responded to the promise inherent in a feminine landscape were now faced with the consequences of that response: either they recoiled in horror from the meaning of their manipulation of a naturally generous world, accusing one another, as did John Hammond in 1656, of raping and deflowering the "naturall fertility and comelinesse," or, like those whom Robert Beverley and William Byrd accused of "slothful Indolence," they succumbed to a life of easeful regression, "spung[ing] upon the Blessings of a warm Sun, and a fruitful Soil" and "approach[ing] nearer to the Description of Lubberland than any other."[20] Neither response, however, obviated the fact that the despoliation of the land appeared more and more an inevitable consequence of human habitation—any more than it terminated the pastoral impulse itself. The instinctual drive embedded in the fantasy, which had first impelled men to emigrate, now impelled them both to continue pursuing the fantasy in daily life, and, when that failed, to codify it as part of the culture's shared dream life, through art—there for all to see in the paintings of Cole and Audubon, in the fictional "letters" of Crevecoeur, the fallacious "local color" of Irving's Sleepy Hollow, and finally, the northern and southern contours clearly distinguished, in the Leatherstocking novels of James Fenimore Cooper and in the Revolutionary War romances of William Gilmore

Simms. "Thus," as Joel Kovel argues, "the decisive symbolic elements [of a culture's history] will be those that represent not only repressed content, but ego activity as well."[21]

Other civilizations have undoubtedly gone through a similar history, but at a pace too slow or in a time too ancient to be remembered. Only in America has the entire process remained within historical memory, giving Americans the unique ability to see themselves as the wilful exploiters of the very land that had once promised an escape from such necessities. With the pastoral impulse neither terminated nor yet wholly repressed, the entire process—the dream and its betrayal, and the consequent guilt and anger—in short, the knowledge of what we have done to our continent, continues even in this century, as Gary Snyder put it, "eating at the American heart like acid."[22] How much better might things have turned out had we heeded the advice of an earlier American poet, Charles Hansford, who probably wrote the following lines about the middle of the eighteenth century:

> To strive with Nature little it avails.
> Her favors to improve and nicely scan
> Is all that is within the reach of Man.
> Nature is to be follow'd, and not forc'd,
> For, otherwise, our labor will be lost.[23]

From accounts of the earliest explorers onward, then, a uniquely American pastoral vocabulary began to show itself, releasing and emphasizing some facets of the traditional European mode and all but ignoring others. At its core lay a yearning to know and to respond to the landscape as feminine, a yearning that I have labeled as the uniquely American "pastoral impulse." Obviously, such an impulse must at some very basic level stem from desires and tensions that arise when patterns from within the human mind confront an external reality of physical phenomena. But the precise psychological and linguistic processes by which the mind imposes order or even meaning onto the phenomena—these have yet to be understood. Let us remember, however, that gendering the land as feminine was nothing new in the sixteenth century; Indo-European languages, among others, have long maintained the habit of gendering the physical world and imbuing it with human capacities. What happened with the discovery of America was the revival of that linguistic habit on the level of personal experience; that is, what had by then degenerated into the dead conventions of self-consciously "literary" language, hardly attended to, let alone explored, suddenly, with the discovery of America, became the vocabulary of everyday reality. Perhaps, after all, the world *is* really gendered, in some subtle way we have not yet quite understood. Certainly, for William Byrd, topography and anatomy were at least analogous, with "a Single Mountain [in the Blue Ridge range], very much resembling a Woman's breast" and a "Ledge that stretch't away to the N.E. . . . [rising] in the Shape of a Maiden's Breast."[24]

Or, perhaps, the connections are more subtle still: was there perhaps a *need* to experience the land as a nurturing, giving maternal breast because of the threatening, alien, and potentially emasculating terror of the unknown? Beautiful, indeed, that wilderness appeared—but also dark, uncharted, and prowled by howling beasts. In a sense, to make the new continent Woman was already to civilize it a bit, casting the stamp of human relations upon what was otherwise unknown and untamed. But, more precisely still, just as the impulse for emigration was an impulse to begin again (whether politically, economically, or religiously), so, too, the place of that new beginning was, in a sense, the new Mother, her adopted children having cast off the bonds of Europe, "where mother-country acts the stepdame's part."[25] If the American continent was to become the birthplace of a new culture and, with it, new and improved human possibilities, then it was, in fact as well as in metaphor, a womb of generation and a provider of sustenance. Hence, the heart of American pastoral—the only pastoral in which metaphor and the patterns of daily activity refuse to be separated.

. . . .

All of which indicates how bound we still are by the vocabulary of a feminine landscape and the psychological patterns of regression and violation that it implies. Fortunately, however, that same language that now appalls us with its implications of regression or willful violation also supplies a framework, open to examination, within which the kinds of symbolic functioning we have examined here get maximum exposure. It gives us, to begin with, at least some indication of *how* those peculiar intersections of human psychology, historical accident, and New World geography combined to create the vocabulary for the experience of the land-as-woman. And it gives us, more importantly, another vantage point from which to understand those unacknowledged but mutually accepted patterns by which Americans have chosen to regulate their lives and interactions for over three hundred years now. Our continuing fascination with the lone male in the wilderness, and our literary heritage of essentially adolescent, presexual pastoral heroes, suggest that we have yet to come up with a satisfying model for mature masculinity on this continent; while the images of abuse that have come to dominate the pastoral vocabulary suggest that we have been no more successful in our response to the feminine qualities of nature than we have to the human feminine. But such speculations are only the beginning: the more we understand how we use language and, conversely, how (in some sense) language uses us, the stronger the possibility becomes that we may actually begin to choose more beneficial patterns for labeling and experiencing that mysterious realm of phenomena outside ourselves and, hopefully, with that, better our chances for survival amid phenomena that, after all, we know only through the intercession of our brain's encodings.

We must begin by acknowledging that the image system of a feminine landscape was for a time both useful and societally adaptive; it brought successive generations of immigrants to strange shores and then propelled them across a vast uncharted terrain. For it is precisely those images through which we have experienced and made meaning out of the discrete data of our five senses (and our cerebral wanderings) that have allowed us to put our human stamp on a world of external phenomena and, thereby, survive in the first place in a strange and forbidding wilderness. And the fact that the symbolizations we chose have now resulted in a vocabulary of destructive aggression and in an active expression of frustration and anger should not make us assume that they may not yet again prove useful to us, or, if not, that we have only to abandon them altogether in order to solve our ecological problems. The habits of language are basically conservative, representing what Benjamin Lee Whorf characterizes as "the mass mind." As he points out, language may indeed be "affected by inventions and innovations, but affected little and slowly."[26] The habits of image-laden language such as we have looked at here, especially, inhibit change because they contain within them an extension, in adult mental processes, of experiential and perceptual configurations inherited from infancy; and, because of the various coincidences through which such configurations got projected out onto the American continent, they have come to reflect not only the integration of universal human dilemmas into cultural patterns, but also the psychic content of the group's shared fantasies—however unacknowledged or unconscious these may have been. Students of language, following Whorf and Edward Sapir, are coming more and more to assert the intimate interaction between language, perception, and action, even going so far, as Whorf does, to argue that once particular "ways of analyzing and reporting experience . . . have become fixed in the language as integrated 'fashions of speaking,'" they tend to influence the ways in "which the personality not only communicates, but also analyzes nature, notices or neglects types of relationship and phenomena, channels . . . reasoning, and builds the house of . . . consciousness."[27] "And once such a system of meanings comes into being, it is never simply abandoned or superseded, as Freud and all other developmental psychologists have repeatedly demonstrated."[28]

Still, if this study has suggested anything, it must be that what we need is a radically new symbolic mode for relating to "the fairest, frutefullest, and pleasauntest [land] of all the worlde";[29] we can no longer afford to keep turning "America the Beautiful" into *America the Raped*. The tantalizing possibility that metaphor, or symbolizing in general, both helps to give coherence to the otherwise inchoate succession of discrete sense data and, also, helps us explore the *possibilities* of experience, suggests that we might, on a highly conscious level, call into play once more our evolutionary adaptive ability to create and re-create our own images of reality. The magic, and even salvation, of man may, after all, lie in his capacity to enter into and exit from the images by which, periodically, he seeks to explore and codify the meaning of his experience. Which suggests that the will to freedom and the will to community, the desire for self-fulfillment, and the attractions of passive acceptance, which were always at the base of the pastoral impulse, might, in some other metaphor, prove finally reconcilable.

NOTES

1. Poem credited to Book Jones, printed in a leaflet issued in Berkeley during the last week of May 1969, by the People's Park Committee (hereafter cited as "People's Park Committee leaflet"). For one of the better detailed accounts of this event, see Sheldon Wolin and John Schaar, "Berkeley: The Battle of People's Park," *New York Review of Books*, 19 June 1969, pp. 24–31. A full collection of pamphlets, leaflets, and newspaper articles about People's Park is available in the Bancroft Library, University of California, Berkeley.

2. A red and black sign printed with the words "sod brother" appeared on shop windows and doors in the south campus area to identify their owners as sympathetic to the demands for a People's Park. The words were also lettered on windows

and doors of private homes and became a means of protection from damage by angry and frustrated demonstrators.

3. "People's Park Committee leaflet." While most of the law enforcement groups brought into the area were regarded with hostility both by the student and local communities, the National Guard, which bivouacked on park grounds for two weeks, were more cordially tolerated. Rumors flew that guardsmen were watering the plants behind the fence, and both the underground and establishment local press frequently printed photographs of guardsmen accepting flowers from demonstrators.

4. "People's Park Committee leaflet."

5. Joanna Gewertz, "culturevulture," *Berkeley Monitor*, 31 May 1969, p. 3; "People's Park Committee leaflet."

6. Quoted from leaflet entitled "Ecology and Politics in America," distributed 26–27 May 1969, in Berkeley, by American Federation of Teachers locals 1474 and 1795.

7. The Freudian argument for this approach, with which I only partly concur, but by which my remarks are influenced, is best put forth by Herbert Marcuse, *Eros and Civilization* (1955; reprint ed., New York: Random House, Vintage Books, 1961), pp. 246–47.

8. Robert Johnson, "Nova Britannia: Offering Most Excellent fruites by Planting In Virginia. Exciting all such as be well affected to further the same" (London, 1609), p. 11; Robert Mountgomry, "A Discourse Concerning the design'd Establishment of a New Colony To The South of Carolina In The Most delightful Country of the Universe" (London, 1717), p. 6. Both papers are in *Tracts and Other Papers, Relating Principally to the Origin, Settlement, And Progress of the Colonies in North America, From The Discovery Of The Country To The Year 1776*, comp. Peter Force, 3 vols. (Washington, D.C., 1836–38), vol. 1 (hereafter cited as *Force's Tracts*). All of the papers in *Force's Tracts* are paginated separately.

9. Johnson, "Nova Britannia," p. 11, in *Force's Tracts*, vol. 1.

10. "The First Voyage Made To The Coasts Of America With Two Barks, Wherein Were Captains M. Philip Amadas And M. Arthur Barlowe Who Discovered Part Of The Country Now Called Virginia, Anno 1584. Written By One Of The Said Captains [probably Barlowe, who kept the daily record], And Sent To Sir Walter Raleigh, Knight, At Whose Charge And Direction The Said Voyage Was Set Forth," in *Explorations, Descriptions, and Attempted Settlements of Carolina, 1584–1590*, ed. David Leroy Corbitt (Raleigh: State Department of Archives and History, 1948), pp. 19–20 (hereafter cited as *Explorations of Carolina*); John Smith, "A Description of New England; or, The Observations, and Discoueries of Captain John Smith (Admirall of the Country) in the North of America, in the year of our Lord 1614" (London, 1616), p. 21, in *Force's Tracts*, vol. 2.

11. [M. Arthur Barlowe], "The First Voyage Made to the Coasts of America," in *Explorations of Carolina,* pp. 19, 13; Smith, "A Description of New England," p. 9, in *Force's Tracts,* vol. 2.

12. Paul Shepard, *Man in the Landscape* (New York: Alfred A. Knopf, 1967), pp. 108, 98.

13. Joel Kovel, *White Racism* (New York: Random House, Pantheon Books, 1970), p. 7.

14. Smith, "A Description of New England," title page, in *Force's Tracts,* vol. 2.

15. Richard Hakluyt, "Discourse of Western Planting . . . 1584," in *The Original Writings and Correspondence of the Two Richard Hakluyts,* ed. E. G. R. Taylor, 2d ser. (London: Hakluyt Society, 1935), 77:222 (hereafter cited as *Hakluyt Correspondence*). Hakluyt's note identifies "the work alluded to" as John Ribault's "*The whole and true discouerye of Terra Florida* . . . Prynted at London . . . 1563."

16. Kovel, *White Racism,* p. 99.

17. Most of the original settlers of Jamestown died of either disease or starvation, while only about half of the Pilgrims who landed at Plymouth in December 1620 survived the first winter; of the 900 settlers led by Winthrop to Massachusetts Bay, 200 died during the first year. Howard Mumford Jones has surveyed these materials and pointed out that "it took many years for investors and home officials to learn that you could not found a plantation by dumping a few men on a New World shore. . . . A high percentage of sickness and death accompanied the process of acclimatization" (*O Strange New World* [1952; reprint ed., London: Chatto & Windus, 1965], p. 277).

18. R. D. Laing, *The Politics of Experience* (New York: Random House, Pantheon Books, 1967), pp. 14–15.

19. Thomas Dudley, "Gov. Thomas Dudley's Letter To The Countess of Lincoln, March, 1631," p. 10, in *Force's Tracts,* vol. 2; Francis Higginson, "New-Englands Plantation; or, A Short And Trve Description of The Commodities And Discommodities of that Countrey" (London, 1630), pp. 9, 10, in *Force's Tracts,* vol. 1.

20. John Hammond, "Leah and Rachel; or, The Two Fruitfull Sisters Virginia and MaryLand," in *Narratives of Early Maryland, 1633–1684,* ed. Clayton Colman Hall (New York: Charles Scribner's Sons, 1910), p. 300; Robert Beverley, *The History and Present State of Virginia,* ed. Louis B. Wright (Chapel Hill: University of North Carolina Press, 1947), p. 319; William Byrd, *William Byrd's Histories of the Dividing Line Betwixt Virginia and North Carolina,* ed. William K. Boyd (Raleigh: North Carolina Historical Commission, 1929), p. 92.

21. Kovel, *White Racism,* p. 99. For a fuller discussion, see chap. 5, "The Symbolic Matrix," pp. 93–105.

22. Gary Snyder, *Earth House Hold* (New York: New Directions, 1969), p. 119.

23. Charles Hansford, "My Country's Worth," in *The Poems of Charles Hansford,* ed. James A. Servies and Carl R. Dolmetsch (Chapel Hill: University of North

Carolina Press, 1961), p. 52. Probably born about 1685, Hansford lived in York County, Virginia, and was by trade a blacksmith; when he died, in 1761, he left in manuscript several poems which he called "A Clumsey Attempt of an Old Man to turn Some of his Serious Thoughts into Verse." The poems are printed here for the first time, with titles supplied by the editors.

24. Byrd, *Histories of the Dividing Line*, pp. 214(*H*), 249(*SH*).

25. Philip Freneau, "To Crispin O'Conner, A Back-Woodsman," in *The Poems of Philip Freneau, Poet of the American Revolution*, ed. Fred Lewis Pattee, 3 vols. (Princeton, N.J.: University Library, 1902–7), 3:74–75. The poem was first published in 1792; the text is from the 1809 edition of Freneau's collected *Poems*. Unless otherwise noted, all quotations from Freneau's poems are from the Pattee edition.

26. Benjamin Lee Whorf, *Language, Thought and Reality* (1956; reprint, Cambridge, Mass.: MIT Press, 1969), p. 156.

27. Ibid., pp. 158, 252.

28. Richard M. Jones, *The New Psychology of Dreaming* (New York: Grune and Stratton, 1970), p. 161.

29. Richard Hakluyt, "Discourse of Western Planting . . . 1584," in *Hakluyt Correspondence*, 77:222.

SCOTT RUSSELL SANDERS

Speaking a Word for Nature

■ ■ ■

Why is so much recent American fiction so barren? Putting the question more honestly, why do I find myself reading fewer contemporary novels and stories each year, and why do I so often feel that the work most celebrated by literary mavens (both avant-garde and establishment) is the shallowest? What is missing? Clearly there is no lack of verbal skill, nor of ingenuity in the use of forms. And there is no shortage of writers: if you pause in the checkout line at the supermarket the clerk is likely to drag his manuscript from under the counter and ask your opinion. It is as though we had an ever-growing corps of wizards concocting weaker and weaker spells.

To suggest what is missing, I begin with a passage from D. H. Lawrence's essay about Thomas Hardy. Lawrence argued that the controlling element in *The Return of the Native* is not the human action, but the setting where that action takes place, the wasteland of Egdon Heath: "What is the real stuff of tragedy in the book? It is the Heath. It is the primitive, primal earth, where the instinctive life heaves up. . . . Here is the deep, black source from whence all these little contents of lives are drawn." Lawrence went on to generalize:

> This is a constant revelation in Hardy's novels: that there exists a great background, vital and vivid, which matters more than the people who move upon it. Against the background of dark, passionate Egdon, of the leafy, sappy passion and sentiment of the woodlands, of the unfathomed stars, is drawn the lesser scheme of lives. . . . The vast, unexplored morality of life itself, what we call the immorality of nature, surrounds us in its eternal incomprehensibility, and in its midst goes on the little human morality play, . . . seriously, portentously, till some one of the protagonists chances to look out of the charmed circle . . . into the wilderness raging around.[1]

All fiction is a drawing of charmed circles, since we can write about only a piece of the world. Within that circle, language shines meaning onto every whisper, every gesture and object. All the while, beyond that circle, the universe cycles on. Much contemporary fiction seems to me barren in part because it draws such tiny, cautious circles, in part because it pretends that nothing lies beyond its timid boundaries. Such fiction treats some "little human morality play" as the whole of reality, and never turns outward to acknowledge the "wilderness raging round." And by wilderness I mean quite literally the untrammeled being of nature, which might include—depending on where you look—a woods, a river, an alien planet, the genetic code, a cloud of subatomic particles, or a cluster of galaxies. What is missing from much recent fiction, I feel, is any sense of nature, any acknowledgment of a nonhuman context.

While Lawrence's account seems to me largely true of Hardy, it does not apply to the mainstream of British fiction. In the work of British novelists from Defoe and Fielding through Austen, Dickens, George Eliot, Joyce, and Woolf, up to contemporaries such as Margaret Drabble and Anthony Powell, the social realm—the human morality play—is a far more powerful presence than nature. What Lawrence wrote about Hardy applies more widely and deeply, in fact, to American literature. Hardy glimpsed "the primitive, primal earth" in Dorset, and Wordsworth searched for it in the Lake District, and Lawrence himself found remnants of it amid the coal fields of the industrial Midlands. But these were pockets of wildness surrounded by a domesticated landscape. In America, by contrast, until well into this century—and even, in some desert and mountainous places, still today—writers have not had to hunt for wildness. For over three centuries, from the time of William Bradford in Plymouth Plantation, to William Faulkner in Mississippi, when our writers looked outward from the circle of human activity, they could not help but see "the wilderness raging round." Our feelings toward this wild arena have shifted back and forth between a sense of revulsion as in Bradford and a sense of reverence as in Faulkner; but what has been constant through all except the last few decades of our history is the potent fact of the wilderness itself. Again and again in the great works of American literature, the human world is set against the overarching background of nature. As in Hardy's novels, this landscape is no mere scenery, no flimsy stage set, but rather the energizing *medium* from which human lives emerge and by which those lives are bounded and measured.

Soon after writing his essay on Hardy, Lawrence undertook a study of American literature, attracted by the same quality he had identified in *The Return of the Native*. In the works of Melville, Cooper, Hawthorne, Crevecoeur, and Thoreau he found a divided consciousness: on the surface they were concerned with the human world, with towns and ships and cultivated land, with households and the spiderwebs of families; but underneath they were haunted by nature. Thus Melville seemed to Lawrence "more spell-bound by the strange slidings and collidings of Matter than by the things men do." Cooper sentimentalized the New York frontier in his Leatherstocking tales, yet wildness kept breaking through. This divided consciousness arose, Lawrence argued, because in America "there is too much menace in the landscape."[2]

By the time his *Studies in Classic American Literature* appeared, Lawrence had moved to a ranch in New Mexico, and he could write from direct experience that, "when one comes to America, one finds . . . there is always a certain slightly devilish resistance in the . . . landscape."[3] In *St. Mawr* (1925), a short novel written during his American stay, the heroine flees from England, where every scrap of country has been "humanized, occupied by the human claim"; and she settles as Lawrence did on a mountain overlooking the desert. Here she "felt a certain latent holiness in the very atmosphere, . . . such as she had never felt in Europe, or in the East. . . . The landscape lived, and lived as the world of the gods, unsullied and unconcerned. . . . Man did not exist for it."[4] Something like Lawrence's awestruck encounter with the American landscape has been recorded time and again in our literature. By sampling this tradition, we can see more vividly the sort of nature-awareness that has largely disappeared from contemporary fiction.

▪ ▪ ▪ Lawrence's response to the land as holy, as a source of meaning and energy, while it is an ancient view among Indians, is a fairly recent view for white people. The earliest responses to the wilderness were typically those of horror and revulsion. Here, for example, is William Bradford, writing sometime after 1620 about the Pilgrims' first impression of their new land:

> [W]hat could they see but a hideous and desolate wilderness, full of wild beasts and wild men. . . . [W]hich way soever they turned their eyes (save upward to the heavens) they could have little solace or content in respect of any outward objects. . . . [A]ll things stand upon them with a weatherbeaten face, and the whole country, full of woods and thickets, represented a wild and sav-

> age hue. If they looked behind them, there was the mighty ocean which they had passed and was now a main bar and gulf to separate them from all the civil parts of the world.[5]

One feels that in Bradford's devout eyes the wilderness was, if anything, more certain a presence than heaven itself. Merely because a writer is overwhelmingly *aware* of the American landscape, however, is no guarantee that he or she will know what to make of it. None of the intellectual gear that Bradford had carried with him from "the civil parts of the world," least of all his Puritan theology, had equipped him to see this New World with any clarity. Like many who followed in his religious tradition, including Hawthorne two centuries later, Bradford looked at the wilderness and saw the *un*holy, the *dis*ordered. It was all a menacing blur.

Since the time of Bradford, many of our writers—reluctant or unable to invent a fresh language of nature—have tried to squeeze American landscape into a European frame. Washington Irving, for example, taking a tour of the prairies in 1835 shortly after his return from a stay in Europe, described the Oklahoma frontier in terms of classical mythology, royal gardens, and French and Dutch painting. He laid out the countryside as if on canvas, with dark bands of trees or prairie in the foreground, lighter river valley or hills in the middle ground, and hazy sky in the distance, the whole suffused, as he remarked at one point, with "the golden tone of one of the landscapes of Claude Lorraine." The western forests reminded him of Gothic cathedrals, "those vast and venerable piles, and the sound of the wind sweeping through them supplie[d] the deep breathings of the organ." Later in his account of the frontier expedition, Irving made his Old World frame explicit:

> The prairies bordering on the rivers are always varied in this way with woodland, so beautifully interspersed as to appear to have been laid out by the hand of taste; and they only want here and there a village spire, the battlements of a castle, or the turrets of an old family mansion rising from among the trees, to rival the most ornamented scenery of Europe.[6]

The "hand of taste" is evident here and throughout *A Tour on the Prairies,* rearranging the rude Oklahoma countryside to make it more nearly conform to the landscape of England or France.

Irving was only one in a long line of American writers who gazed at the wild countryside and regretted the absence of human "ornament." Even so keen an observer of our landscape as Thomas Cole voiced a complaint similar to Irving's after returning (in 1832) from his own European sojourn: "Although American scenery is often so fine, we feel the want of associations such as cling to scenes in the old world. Simple nature is not quite sufficient. We want human interest, incident and action to render the effect of landscape complete."[7] Half a century later, in a notorious essay on Hawthorne, Henry James listed all the ornaments that were missing from the American scene. It is a long list, including castles and kings. By comparison with the Old World, the New had little to offer except raw nature. And James had no more idea than Bradford what to make of a wild landscape. He felt at ease only in Europe, where nature had long since been cut into a human quilt. Still today, although young writers may no longer feel compelled to live in Paris or London, most who grow up in the backwoods or on the prairies—in Oklahoma, say, or Indiana—eventually pack their bags and head for the cities of the East Coast or the West, as if the land in between were too poor to support crops of fiction.

While some writers were trying to squeeze New World landscapes into Old World frames, others tried to discover a fresh way of seeing the "primitive, primal earth" that was laid bare in America. One of the earliest inventors of this homegrown vision was William Bartram, the vagabond naturalist, who gazed at the American countryside on the eve of the Revolution. Here is Bartram, camped in a Florida swamp:

> The verges and islets of the lagoon were elegantly embellished with flowering plants and shrubs; the laughing coots with wings half spread were tripping over the little coves, and hiding themselves in the tufts of grass; young broods of the painted summer teal, skimming the surface of the waters, and following the watchful parent unconscious of danger, were frequently surprised by the voracious trout; and he, in turn, as often by the subtle greedy alligator. Behold him rushing forth from the flags and reeds. His enormous body swells. His plaited tail brandished high, floats upon the lake. The waters like a cataract descend from his opening jaws. Clouds of smoke issue from his dilated nostrils. The earth trembles with his thunder.[8]

Darwin would not have had much to teach this intrepid naturalist on the subject of violence in nature. Despite these dragon-like alligators with their smoking nostrils, Bartram stuck around long enough to explore the swamps. Everywhere on his travels he learned what he could of the Indians, plants, soil, and beasts. He was helping, in fact, to invent scientific observation, a way of seeing and speaking of nature as separate, orderly, obeying its own laws. He treated the lagoons and rivers and forests through which he traveled as a sequence of habitats, although of course he did not use that newfangled word.

The works of Bartram circulated widely in Europe, where a new generation of writers, including Wordsworth, Coleridge, and Chateaubriand, feeling encumbered by civilization, were eager for these glimpses of wild and wondrous territory. What often happened to American literary landscapes when they were transported across the ocean may be suggested by looking at Chateaubriand's New World romance, *Atala* (1801). Unlike most European Romantics, Chateaubriand actually traveled to America, spending the winter of 1791–2 in upstate New York. Not content to write about the landscape he had actually seen, however, he borrowed heavily from Bartram's *Travels* and from his own fancy to produce descriptions such as this one, of the Mississippi River:

> [W]hile the middle current sweeps the dead pines and oaks to the sea, one can see, on the side currents, floating isles of pistia and water lilies, whose pinkish yellow flowers, rising like little banners, are carried along the river banks. Green serpents, blue herons, pink flamingoes, young crocodiles sail like passengers on the flower-ships, and the colony, unfolding its golden sails to the wind, lazily drifts into some hidden bend of the river.[9]

The bend must have been very well hidden, since no other traveler on the Mississippi has ever discovered a scene remotely like that one. Along those fabulous shores, the Frenchman noted mountains, Indian pyramids, caribou, bears drunk on grapes, and snakes that disguised themselves as vines to catch birds. While Bartram was given to exaggeration, especially in the vicinity of alligators, he always checked his enthusiasm against what his eyes were telling him; Chateaubriand suffered no such inhibitions.

Like Lawrence and many other European writers, Chateaubriand was lured to America by the very qualities in our landscape that drove Cooper, Irving, and James to Europe. This contrary movement has been going on now for two centuries. I imagine that right this minute, in the air over the Atlantic, jumbo jets are crossing paths, the eastbound ones carrying Americans to Europe in search of castles and gravestones, the westbound ones carrying Europeans to America in search of redwoods and waterfalls.

Emerson had a look at landscapes on both sides of the ocean, and decided that the native variety was the one best suited to his imagination. His *Nature* (1836) seems to me still the most eloquent manifesto for a way of seeing appropriate to the New World setting. In the essay he urged American writers to cast off the conventions of thought inherited from Europe, that stuffy old wardrobe of hand-me-down ideas, and "to look at the world with new eyes." But how? By turning away from "the artificial and curtailed life of cities" and going back to the source of all thought and language, to nature itself:

> Hundreds of writers may be found in every long-civilized nation, who for a short time believe, and make others believe, that they see and utter truths, who do not of themselves clothe one thought in its natural garment, but who feed unconsciously on the language created by the primary writers of the country, those, namely, who hold primarily on nature. But wise men pierce this rotten diction and fasten words again to visible things.[10]

This advice is easier to accept than to apply, as Emerson's own verbal landscapes demonstrate. In *Nature* itself, whenever he began to fasten words onto visible things—seeing, for instance, "The leafless trees become spires of flame in the sunset, with the blue east for their background, and the stars of the dead calices of flowers, and every withered stem and stubble rimed with frost,"—he interrupted himself to ask a question or to drag in some of that discarded European baggage: "What was it that nature would say? Was there no meaning in the live repose of the valley behind the mill, and which Homer or Shakespeare could not re-form for me in words?"[11] Listening for what nature had to say, Emerson was always a little too eager to hear the cultural mutterings of his own well-stocked mind, and thus his landscapes are less substantial than those drawn by many of the writers who followed his precepts—including, most famously, Thoreau.

However much we might quarrel about who belongs on the short list of primary writers—those who renew our language and vision by fastening words to nature—I hope we would agree to include the name of Thoreau. His descriptions of the Concord River, the Maine woods, Cape Cod, and Walden Pond are among the most vigorous and penetrating accounts of our landscape ever written. One of his prime motives for undertaking the experiment in living beside Walden Pond was to train himself to *see:* "It is something to be able to paint a particular picture, or to carve a statue, and so to make a few objects beautiful; but it is far more glorious to carve and paint the very atmosphere and medium through which we look." In passage after passage of *Walden,* Thoreau portrayed a dynamic nature—frozen sand melting and sliding down the railroad embankment, ice breaking up on the pond, geese circling overhead and muskrats burrowing underfoot. Watching this energetic landscape was his chief business:

> Sometimes, in a summer morning, having taken my accustomed bath, I sat in my sunny doorway from sunrise till noon, rapt in a revery, amidst the pines and hickories and sumachs, in undisturbed solitude and stillness, while the birds sang around or flitted noiseless through the house, until by the sun falling in at my west window, or the noise of some traveller's wagon on the distant highway, I was reminded of the lapse of time. I grew in those seasons like corn in the night, and they were far better than any work of the hands would have been.[12]

Thoreau situated himself *within* nature, and drew upon all the senses—he devoted an entire chapter to sounds, for example—to convey what was going on around him in the green world. The forces at work in pond and forest he found also at work in himself. An entry in his journal catches this feeling memorably: "A writer, a man writing, is the scribe of all nature; he is the corn and the grass and the atmosphere writing."[13]

In Thoreau we find no conflict between the scientist's method of close, reasoned observation and the poet's free play of imagination. Since Thoreau's time, however, as the products of reason have come to dominate and efface the natural landscape, writers have found it more and more difficult to combine these two ways of seeing. In *Life on the Mississippi* (1883), for example, Samuel Clemens wrote about having to learn every mile of the shifting river by heart. He studied hard, and eventually became a professor of the river, but at a price:

> Now when I had mastered the language of this water and had come to know every trifling feature that bordered the great river as familiarly as I knew the letters of the alphabet, I had made a valuable acquisition. But I had lost something, too. I had lost something which could never be restored to me while I lived. All the grace, the beauty, the poetry had gone out of the majestic river![14]

However, we can see from *Huckleberry Finn* (1885), published two years after *Life on the Mississippi,* that he was in fact able to fuse an adult's rational knowledge and a child's fresh emotion in his vision of the river. Here is Huck, for example, watching the sun rise over the Mississippi:

> The first thing to see, looking away over the water, was a kind of dull line—that was the woods on t'other side—you couldn't make nothing else out; then a pale place in the sky; then more paleness, spreading around; then the river softened up, away off, and warn't black any more, but gray; . . . and you see the mist curl up off of the water, and the east reddens up, and the river, and you make out a log cabin in the edge of the woods . . . ; then the nice breeze

> springs up, and comes fanning you from over there, so cool and fresh, and sweet to smell, on account of the woods and the flowers; . . . and next you've got the full day, and everything smiling in the sun, and the song-birds just going it![15]

To sustain this vision of nature unsullied, Clemens had to push his narrative back into the time of his own childhood, some forty years earlier.

Faulkner did something similar in his short novel, *The Bear* (1942). Although written near the beginning of World War II, it deals with events from a time sixty years earlier, when patches of wilderness still lingered in Mississippi. In order to see Old Ben, the fabled bear, Faulkner's young hero must leave behind his gun, his compass, his watch, every mechanical contrivance, and yield himself to the woods. At length he is granted his vision:

> Then he saw the bear. It did not emerge, appear: it was just there, immobile, fixed in the green and windless noon's hot dappling, not as big as he had dreamed it but as big as he had expected, bigger, dimensionless against the dappled obscurity, looking at him. Then it moved. It crossed the glade without haste, walking for an instant into the sun's full glare and out of it, and stopped again and looked back at him across one shoulder. Then it was gone. It didn't walk into the woods. It faded, sank back into the wilderness without motion as he had watched a fish, a huge old bass, sink back into the dark depths of its pool and vanish without even any movement of its fins.[16]

In the course of the novel Old Ben is killed, the last of the half-Indian hunters dies, and the stand of virgin timber is sold to lumber companies and invaded by railroads and whittled away by the surrounding farms. Faulkner was concerned in *The Bear* not so much with the conflict between reason and imagination in our ways of seeing nature, as with reason's wholesale assault upon nature itself. His fable reminds us that, in a little over a century, our wilderness continent was transformed into one of the most highly industrialized landscapes in the world.

▪ ▪ ▪ And thus we come, by way of a far too-sketchy history, to our own time. In an age of strip mines, nuclear plants, urban sprawl, interstate highways, factory farms, chemical dumps, mass extinction of plant and animal species, oil spills, and "development" of the few remaining scraps of wilderness, many of us have come to view our situation in a manner exactly contrary to that of William Bradford. The landscapes that we ourselves have fashioned often appear "hideous and desolate." We can no longer cut ourselves off from the "civil parts of the world," however much we might wish to.

What has become of nature in recent American writing? A decent answer would be far longer than this entire essay, and even then could only touch on a few literary landscapes—Wendell Berry's Kentucky, say, and Eudora Welty's Mississippi, the Roanoke Valley of Annie Dillard, Edward Hoagland's Vermont, John McPhee's Alaska, Thomas McGuane's Montana, the deserts of Edward Abbey and Barry Lopez, the alien planets of Ursula Le Guin, the Africa and Nepal of Peter Matthiessen, the great plains of N. Scott Momaday and Wright Morris, the fabulous Antarctic of John Calvin Batchelor and the Central American jungle of Paul Theroux, the microscopic arenas of Lewis Thomas. All of these writers seek to understand our life as continuous with the life of nature; they project "the little human morality play" against the "wilderness raging round."

Notice that most of them work outside the braided literary currents that critics, reviewers, and publishers regard as the "mainstream" of contemporary fiction. They work in the essay (Abbey, Lopez, Hoagland, McPhee, Dillard, Thomas); in science fiction or fantasy or fable (all of Le Guin, Batchelor's *The Birth of the People's Republic of Antarctica,* Theroux's *Mosquito Coast*); in travel writing (Matthiessen, Theroux); or in "regional" fiction (meaning, so far as I can tell, fiction set in a recognizable landscape that is not a city: Berry, Welty).

Consider one brief example that stands for a larger pattern. Bobbie Ann Mason's *Shiloh and Other Stories* and the revision of Wendell Berry's *A Place on Earth* came out within a year of one another (1982 and 1983, respectively). Both are set in western Kentucky; both dwell on the breakup of rural lifeways. For Mason, nature supplies an occasional metaphor to illustrate a character's dilemma—a tulip tree cut down when it was about to bloom, a rabbit with crushed legs on the highway—exactly as K-Mart or Cat Chow or the Phil Donahue Show supply analogues. For Berry, no matter how much the land has been neglected or abused, no matter how ignorant of their environment people may have become, nature is the medium in which life transpires, a prime source of values and meaning and purpose. Whereas *Shiloh and Other Stories* was widely praised and imitated and briskly sold, *A Place on Earth*—a far more searching and eloquent book—was generally neglected; when reviewed at all, it was treated as an old-fashioned view of an out-of-the-way place.

That a deep awareness of nature has been largely excluded from "mainstream" fiction is a measure of the narrowing and trivialization of that fashionable current. It is also, of course, and more dangerously, a measure of a shared blindness in the culture at large. Not long ago, while camping in the Great Smoky Mountains, I had a nightmare glimpse of the modern reader. It was late one afternoon in May, the air sweet and mild. I left my tent and crossed the parking lot of the campground on my way to a cliff, where I planned to sit with my legs dangling over the brink and stare out across the westward mountains at the sunset. Already the sky was throbbing with color and the birds were settling down for their evening song. The wind smelled of pines. Near the center of the parking lot, as far as possible from the encircling trees, a huge camping van squatted. There were chocks under the tires, but the motor was running. The air-conditioner gave a high frantic squeal. The van had enough windows for a hothouse, but every one was curtained, even the windshield. Lights glowed around the edges and threw yellow slashes onto the blacktop. What could keep the passengers shut up inside that box on such an afternoon, in such a place? Passing by, I saw through a gap in the curtains a family clustered in front of a television as if in front of a glowing hearth, and I heard the unmistakable banshee cry of Tarzan, King of the Apes.

Whenever I am feeling gloomy about the prospects of making nature *present* to contemporary readers, I think of those campers. They had driven their rolling house to a mountaintop overlooking an awesome sweep of land, and had parked there, with engine running and curtains drawn, to watch a movie starring an Olympic swimmer playing an English lord swinging through a Hollywood jungle. If the Great Smoky Mountains could not lure them from their box, how could words on a page ever stir them? Could such people be made to see, through stories, where it is we actually dwell, what sort of ship we ride through space?

Of course, readers have always been willing to pull on their mental boots and journey to places in books they would never think of visiting in the flesh. Millions have read *Walden* and *Life on the Mississippi*, yet how many have built a hut in the woods or rafted down a river? What is new about contemporary readers is not their preference for an indoor life, but how far indoors they are able to retreat and how long they are able to stay there. The boxes that shut us off from nature have become more perfect, more powerful, from all-electric mansions in the suburbs to glass towers in the city, from space shuttles to shopping malls. Today, the typical adult reader leaves a humming house in the morning, drives an air-conditioned car to a sealed office, works eight hours under fluorescent lights, stops on the way home at night to buy dyed vegetables and frozen meat wrapped in plastic, enters the house through the garage and locks the door. Except for lawns, which are fertilized and purified to an eery shade of green, and a smoky sky, and a potted plant or two, everything this reader sees all day has been made by human beings. Only the body itself stubbornly upholds the claims of biology, and even this biological datum our reader treats with chemicals designed to improve or delay the workings of nature.

Reading this account, perhaps with a canoe strapped to the roof of your car and a compass dangling by a thong around your neck, you may scuff your boots on the floor, impatient with my dark picture. But, with all due respect, I think my campers watching a Tarzan movie in their van are more typical of the age than are the regulars on the Audubon bird count. Despite the sale of recreational gear and the traffic jams in National Parks, I believe that, on the whole, Americans today have less direct experience of nature than at any time in our history. I am not talking about occasional visits to the woods or zoo, as one might visit Grandmother in the country, but of day-to-day living contact with the organic world.

You can see this ignorance of land and landscape illustrated in the stylish fiction of our time. Read Raymond Carver's collection *What We Talk About When We Talk About Love* (1981), for example, and, aside from references to fish, deer, and geese as prey, here is the most elaborate account of nature you will find: "A big moon was laid over the mountains that went around the city. It was a white moon and covered with scars."[17] (Read, for an instructive contrast, Thomas McGuane's *Nobody's Angel,* also published in 1981, which opens with the line, "You would have to care about the country," and over which the Montana landscape presides.) In Don DeLillo's *White Noise*—the most honored novel of 1985—the only time you are reminded that anything exists beyond the human realm is when his characters pause on the expressway to watch a sunset, and even the sunset interests them only because a release of toxic gases from a nearby plant has poisoned it into technicolor. (For a contrast to *White Noise,* read Ursula Le Guin's novel of the same year, *Always Coming Home,* which summons up an entire culture and cosmology governed by the most intricate and lively understanding of nature.)

Sample the novels and stories published in America today, and in the opening pages you are likely to find yourself trapped inside a room—a kitchen, perhaps, or a psychiatrist's office, a bedroom, a bar, a motel—with characters talking. When they pause in their talk, it is usually to shift into another room, where they raise their voices once again. Some might say it is inevitable that our fiction should have such an indoor cast, given that we live in an age and a place dominated by cities; inevitable that characters should display such ignorance of nature, given the shabby way we treat the environment. Of course DeLillo, Carver, Mason and their less able imitators are reporting on our condition: surrounded by artifacts of our own making, engulfed by human racket, illiterate in the language of the cosmos. But durable art, art that matters, has never merely reproduced the superficial consciousness of an age. Cervantes did not limit himself to the platitudes of feudalism, nor Melville to Puritanism, nor Faulkner to racism, nor García Márquez to nationalism and capitalism. They quarreled with the dominant ways of seeing, and in that quarreling with the actual they enlarged our vision of the possible.

However accurately it reflects the surface of our times, fiction that never looks beyond the human realm is profoundly false, and therefore pathological. No matter how urban our experience, no matter how oblivious we may be toward nature, we are nonetheless animals, two-legged sacks of meat and blood and bone dependent on the whole living planet for our survival. Our outbreathings still flow through the pores of trees, our food still grows in dirt, our bodies decay. Of course, of course: we all nod our heads in agreement. The gospel of ecology has become an *intellectual* commonplace. But it is not yet an *emotional* one. For most of us, most of the time, nature appears framed in a window or a video screen or inside the borders of a photograph. We do not feel the organic web passing through our guts, as it truly does. While our theories of nature have become wiser, our experience of nature has become shallower. And true fiction operates at a level deeper than shared intellectual slogans. Thus, any writer who sees the world in ecological perspective faces a hard problem: how, despite the perfection of our technological boxes, to make us feel the ache and tug of that organic web passing through us, how to *situate* the lives of characters—and therefore of readers—in nature.

How we inhabit the planet is intimately connected to how we imagine the land and its creatures. In the history of American writing about landscape, we read in brief the history of our thinking about nature and our place in the natural order. Time and again, inherited ways of seeing have given way before the powerful influence of the New World landscape. If such a revolution in vision is to occur in our time, writers will have to free themselves from human enclosures, and go outside to study the green world. It may seem quaint, in the age of megalopolis, to write about wilderness or about life on farms and in small towns; and it may seem escapist to write about distant planets where the environment shapes every human gesture; but such writing seems to me the most engaged and forward-looking we have. If we are to survive, we must look outward from the charmed circle of our own works, to the stupendous theatre where our tiny, brief play goes on.

NOTES

1. "Study of Thomas Hardy," *Phoenix: The Posthumous Papers of D. H. Lawrence* (London: Heinemann, 1936) 415, 419.

2. *Studies in Classic American Literature* (1924; reprinted London: Mercury Books, 1965) 138, 48.

3. *Studies in Classic American Literature* 52–53.

4. *St. Mawr* (1925; reprinted and bound with *The Virgin and the Gypsy,* Harmondsworth, England: Penguin, 1950) 109, 147.

5. *Of Plymouth Plantation,* Book 1, Ch. 9 (written 1630–50; first published 1856; reprinted in Sculley Bradley et al., eds., *The American Tradition in Literature,* Vol. 1, third edition; New York: Norton, 1967) 19.

6. *A Tour on the Prairies* (1835), in William Kelly, ed., *Selected Writings of Washington Irving* (New York: Modern Library, 1984) 462, 436, 495.

7. Quoted in Roderick Nash, *Wilderness and the American Mind* (rev. ed., New Haven: Yale University Press, 1973) 80.

8. *Travels of William Bartram* (1791), ed. Mark Van Doren (New York: Dover, n.d.) 115.

9. *Atala* (1801), trans. Walter J. Cobb (New York: New American Library, 1961) 16.

10. *Nature* (1836; reprinted in Sculley Bradley et al., eds., *The American Tradition in Literature,* Vol. 1, third edition; New York: Norton, 1967) 1075–76.

11. *Nature* 1069–70.

12. *Walden,* ed. J. Lyndon Shanley (Princeton: Princeton University Press, 1973) 90, 111.

13. *H. D. Thoreau: A Writer's Journal,* ed. Laurence Stapleton (New York: Dover, 1960) 66.

14. *Life on the Mississippi,* in Guy Cardwell, ed., *Mark Twain: Mississippi Writings* (New York: Library of America, 1982) 740–41.

15. *Huckleberry Finn,* in Guy Cardwell, ed. *Mark Twain: Mississippi Writings* (New York: Library of America, 1982) 740–41.

16. *The Bear,* in *Three Famous Short Novels* (New York: Vintage, 1961) 202–3.

17. *What We Talk about When We Talk about Love* (New York: Knopf, 1981) 31.

CYNTHIA DEITERING

The Postnatural Novel

■ ■ ■

TOXIC CONSCIOUSNESS IN FICTION OF THE 1980s

During the 1980s—the decade that began amid anxious speculation about long-term consequences of the nuclear accident at Three Mile Island and drew to a close amid congressional hearings on the greenhouse effect—U.S. novelists showed an increasing concern with the pervasive problem of toxic waste, a concern that is reflected in what I propose to be a new "toxic consciousness" in recent American fiction. Fiction of the 1980s, in its sustained and various representations of pollution, offers insight into a culture's shifting relation to nature and to the environment at a time when the imminence of ecological collapse was, and is, part of the public mind and of individual imaginations. This paper first offers a brief descriptive survey of recent American fiction in order to illustrate a progressive preoccupation with what British novelist Martin Amis has called the "toiletization of the planet"; it then speculates on these texts as they mirror a shift in our cultural identity—a shift from a culture defined by its production to a culture defined by its waste; lastly, it examines the way in which the toxic landscape functions in these novels as a metaphor for the pollution of the natural world, and attempts to show how that contamination inevitably transmogrifies one's experience of the earth itself.

In 1982, prior to the toxic catastrophe of the Union Carbide incident in Bhopal, India, and in what now seems an age of relative innocence in regard to the global contamination of the environment, three of the year's most notable novels thematized, to some extent, a concern with the poisoning of the American landscape. In Saul Bellow's *The Dean's December,* the protagonist is asked by an eminent geophysicist to collaborate on a project to set before the public apocalyptic evidence that three industrial centuries of lead dispersal into the air, water and soil have resulted in the stupefaction of the West. John Cheever's final novella, *Oh What a Paradise It Seems,* focuses on an aging protagonist's symbolic efforts to restore Beazley's Pond—now a toxic dumpsite—to its original purity. And in John Gardner's *Mickelsson's Ghosts* (also a final novel), Peter Mickelsson's newly purchased farmhouse in a remote mountain community turns out to be contaminated by illegally dumped chemicals. By the mid 1980s, this concern with chemical contamination had become a novelistic preoccupation, figuring as an important theme in texts such as Don DeLillo's *White Noise,* Walker Percy's *The Thanatos Syndrome,* Paul Theroux's *O-Zone,* T. Coraghessan Boyle's *World's End,* and Richard Russo's *Mohawk,* and figuring, too, as an important subtext in such novels as Saul Bellow's *More Die of Heartbreak,* Margaret Atwood's *The Handmaid's Tale,* and William Gaddis's *Carpenter's Gothic.* Although a tendency toward apocalyptic themes may be partly due to the historical moment—"the countdown to a millenium"[1]—a preoccupation with the toxic environment in American fiction of the 1980s seems to involve more than millennial ethos. Rather, toxic waste seems to function in recent fiction both as cultural metaphor for a society's most general fears about its collective future and as expression of an ontological rupture in its perception of the Real.

What I see as a new "toxic consciousness" in fiction reflects a fundamental shift in historical consciousness; for at some point during the Reagan-Bush decade, something happened, some boundary was crossed beyond which Americans perceived themselves differently in their relation to the natural world and the ecosystems of the American Empire. What happened, I believe, is that we came to perceive, perhaps inchoately, our own complicity in postindustrial ecosystems, both personal and national, which are predicated on pollution and waste. My premise is that during the 1980s we began to perceive ourselves as inhabitants of a culture defined by its waste, and that a number of American novels written during this period reflect this ontological transformation. I shall illustrate my point here chiefly through two novels, Don DeLillo's *White Noise* and John Updike's *Rabbit at Rest.*

White Noise, published in 1985, depicts a society whose most distinguishing feature is its waste. In the following passage, DeLillo's narrator, Jack Gladney, sifts through his family's compacted garbage, speculating about this middle-class domestic glut as the underside of consumer capitalism:

> I jabbed at it with the butt end of a rake and then spread the material over the concrete floor. I picked through it item by item, mass by shapeless mass, wondering why I felt guilty, a violator of privacy, uncovering intimate and perhaps shameful secrets. It was hard not to be distracted by some of the things they'd chosen to submit to the Juggernaut appliance. But why did I feel like a household spy? Is garbage so private? Does it glow at the core with a personal heat, with signs of one's deepest nature, clues to secret yearnings, humiliating flaws? What habits, fetishes, addictions, inclinations? What solitary acts, behavioral ruts? . . . I found a banana skin with a tampon inside. Was this the dark underside of consumer consciousness?[2]

By fathoming his family's garbage, it seems, Gladney might fathom not only the consciousness of consumer capitalism, but also the individual identities of his wife and children. By understanding the forms of their trash, he might glimpse their true selves as idiosyncratic producers of waste. Here the familiar notion of finding one's identity in commodity products is transformed into the notion of finding one's identity not in the commodities themselves but in their configuration as waste products. A similar transformation is reflected in Gladney's descriptions of the commodities he purchases and eventually discards. Though he feels himself "grow in value and self worth" as a result of these purchases, it is nonetheless only when he ferrets through the house looking for commodity objects to throw away that he uses language which connects his identity to the commodities he owns. In other words, it is when these commodities are perceived as trash that he sees them as extensions of himself, discarding them while "trying to say goodby to himself."[3] DeLillo's characterization here of a man who is, in one sense, defined by his garbage capsulizes this new shift in ontological representation I have suggested. In a postindustrial economy which depends upon the expeditious transformation of goods into waste (thereby enabling the quick purchase of replacement goods), we have come to see in our garbage parts of ourselves, of our personal histories. On some level, perhaps, we have begun to comprehend our seminal role as producers of waste.

Conversely, we have evolved a new way of seeing—a sort of x-ray vision—with which we perceive the waste forms inherent in the landscape and material objects around us. This new way of seeing our environment might be considered as a second stage of what Martin Heidegger discussed in 1953 as the essence of technology whereby what we call the Real is revealed as what Heidegger called the "standing reserve" of industrial and consumer resources. Heidegger, in his essay "The Question Concerning Technology," contended that the Western cultural perception of nature and material objects was that of "standing reserve" whereby a tract of land was revealed and represented as a coal mining district, a mineral deposit; or a river was regarded and represented as a supplier of water power; or an airplane standing on the runway was viewed as a machine poised to insure the possibility of transportation.[4] What has happened recently, as evidenced in a number of novels written since 1980—perhaps most strikingly in John Updike's *Rabbit at Rest*—is a transmutation of Heidegger's essence of technology in which what we have previously regarded and represented as the standing reserve of nature and material objects has been virtually used up. Thus, what we call the Real is now represented not as the standing-reserve but as the already-used-up. The tract of land is now represented as a possible site of contaminated waste, left over from coal mining operations. The river is now represented as a possible waste receptacle for the by-products of a nuclear plant. The airplane is now represented as flaming debris. In other words, what is revealed now is the waste of the empire.

John Updike's 1990 novel, *Rabbit at Rest,* provides a useful example of a narrative point of view which instinctively perceives the "already-used-up." As several critics have remarked, Updike's Rabbit novels read as "decade-end-reports"[5] not only on the character of Harry "Rabbit" Angstrom but on the state of the nation in the Fifties (with *Rabbit Run*), the Sixties (with *Rabbit Redux*), the Seventies (with *Rabbit is Rich*), and now the Eighties (with *Rabbit at Rest*). This fourth and final of the Rabbit quartet reflects the nation in a state of decay, America as "postnatural" land whose ethos is best represented as the "story of a stomach,"[6] the story of an empire voraciously consuming itself and its future. "We're using it all up. The world," thinks 55-year-old Rabbit as he looks around the streets of his hometown of Brewer, Pa. The novel opens in the last week of the last year of Ronald Reagan's reign, when in Rabbit's view "everything is falling apart, airplanes, bridges, eight years under Reagan of nobody minding the store, making money out of nothing. . . ."[7]

At the novel's outset, we learn that Rabbit is heart-frail; having undergone open-heart surgery, he regularly ingests Nitrostat pills, registering the tiny explosions in his chest. Perhaps because Rabbit Angstrom is himself in a state of physical decay, he instinctively perceives the process of decay in the objects, the people, and the landscape around him. For example, what Rabbit sees through the window of the Southwest Florida Regional Airport as he awaits the approaching plane carrying his son and grandchildren is not the "standing reserve" of a machine enabling transportation, but the flaming debris of the machine falling apart. Deeply shaken by the explosion over Lockerbie, Scotland, of the Pan Am 747, Rabbit visualizes his son's approaching flight "exploding in a ball of red flame" and is shocked to find within himself not much emotion, just a kind of "bleak wonder at the fury of chemicals."[8]

Similarly, in *Rabbit at Rest,* the body itself is obsessively perceived and represented as a vessel of contamination, an organism in the accelerated process of wasting away. For example, when Rabbit regards the face of his long-time friend and lover, Thelma Harrison, who is now dying of lupus, his gaze is set on the disease in her countenance. He notes the "sallow tinge of her face now deepened with jaundice; he can observe through the makeup she uses to soften her butterfly rash, a reddening the disease has placed like a soreness across her nose and beneath her eyes."[9]

Finally, when he views the landscape of his Florida retirement community, Rabbit sees *through* the paradisical facade to the decay and pollution contained therein. With eyes alert to his domestic "riskscape,"[10] Rabbit sees palm trees dying from the drought; sees a sky "dirtied by jet trails that spread and wander";[11] sees ultraviolet rays which he envisages to be "cooking his squamous cells into skin cancer";[12] and sees an atmospheric haze that makes it difficult to breathe ("Too much ozone or a lack of ozone?" Rabbit wonders).[13] *Rabbit at Rest* is typical of much U.S. fiction to come out of the 1980s in that it delineates our unique position as Americans at what Fredric Jameson has described as the "historical moment of a radical eclipse of Nature itself," when human enterprise has subsumed what was once the privileged category of Nature itself into the province of the artificial.[14]

▪ ▪ ▪ *White Noise, Rabbit at Rest,* and other recent novels informed by what I call a "toxic consciousness" depict a society that has fouled its own nest; hence, the pollution of the natural world, as represented in these novels, inevitably transmogrifies one's experience of the earth as primal home. A number of characters in these texts express the peculiar displacement of a generation poised on the precipice of an epistemic rupture—between knowing the earth as "the landforms, flora and fauna which are the home in which life is set"[15] and knowing the earth as toxic riskscape. We might imagine these characters as environmental exiles of a sort who while resolutely acknowledging their polluted environments, nonetheless hold fast to the *imago* of what John Fowles calls the *bonne vaux*—that pastoral home site associated with innocence and harvest.[16] The paradox of these characters is that they remain "dreamers of nests"[17] even though theirs may be fouled.

Whereas the literary construct of nature during much of the nineteenth century mirrored that of a society with a profound need of nature as spiritual healer, and the literary conception of nature for much of the twentieth century mirrored that of a society which valued nature as an economic resource, the most recent literary version of nature reflects that of a society which at some level understands itself to be living in what Bill McKibben has termed a "postnatural world" and whose conscious need for nature is merely superficial, as McKibben has suggested in his book *The End of Nature*.[18] What is important about American fiction of the 1980s is that it represents the first literary expressions to come out of this postnatural world.

Nature is no longer a central presence in the world of the novel, no longer the "life-sustaining air" that Mary McCarthy claimed the nineteenth-century novel breathed.[19] Rather, the novel of the 1980s reflects a world in which the air is in fact no longer necessarily life-sustaining. Nature in these novels is usually extraneous to the Real, though often it evokes nostalgia and a sense of exile, for the planet itself no longer feels like home to a number of characters: the private experiences which formed their metaphysical definitions of home are no longer available in the 1980s. One way into the novel of the 1980s is to study this new variety of displacement from the earth that *was* home, earth as it is depicted in Don DeLillo's 1983 short story, "Human Moments in World War III." In this story, two astronauts look out the window of their spaceship, while the narrator remarks that the view of Earth is "endlessly fulfilling":

> It satisfies whatever earth sense he possesses, the neural pulse of some wilder awareness, a sympathy of beasts, whatever belief in an immanent vital force, . . . whatever wishfulness and simplehearted hope, . . . whatever burning urge to escape responsibility and routine, escape his own overspecialization, the circumscribed and inward-spiralling self, . . . his fantasies of happy death, whatever sybaritic leanings, lotus-eater, smoker of grasses and herbs, blue-eyed gazer into space—all these are satisfied, all collected and massed in that living body, the sight he sees from the window.[20]

This is earth as metaphysical home. But just as DeLillo's astronauts can apprehend this earth-home only from a distance, from another world, characters in recent American fiction sit poised between worlds, looking back home from an exile they've brought upon themselves as creatures of their culture.

In conclusion, I recall Stendhal's definition of the novel as "a mirror walking down the roadway." Ultimately, I read these novels which are informed by a "toxic consciousness" as political texts: insomuch as they provide representations of a postnatural world, of a culture defined by its waste, and of a nation that has fouled its own nest, these novels do much to raise the environmental consciousness of the society that sees itself in the mirror.

NOTES

1. Susan Sontag discusses the tendency toward end-of-an-era apocalyptic thinking as it pertains to the rhetoric of AIDS in *AIDS and Its Metaphors* (New York: Farrar, Straus, Giroux, 1988).

2. Don DeLillo, *White Noise* (New York: Penguin, 1986), p. 259.

3. DeLillo, p. 294.

4. Martin Heidegger, *Basic Writings,* ed. David Farrel Krell (New York: Harper and Row, 1977), pp. 296–99.

5. I borrow the phrase from Garry Wills's essay on the Rabbit quartet, "Long-Distance Runner," in *New York Review of Books,* 37, No. 16 (Oct. 25, 1990), pp. 11–14.

6. I borrow the phrase from Lewis Lapham's cogent essay on the decline of the American Empire, "Noises Off," in *Harper's,* October 1986.

7. John Updike, *Rabbit at Rest* (New York: Alfred Knopf, 1990), p. 9.

8. Updike, pp. 8 and 10.

9. Updike, p. 193.

10. Susan Cutter, a Rutgers University geographer, coined the term "riskscape" to describe landscapes at risk to acute airborne toxics.

11. Updike, p. 66.

12. Updike, p. 65.

13. Updike, p. 501.

14. Fredric Jameson, "Postmodernism, or The Cultural Logic of Late Capitalism," *New Left Review* 146, July/August 1984, pp. 71–72.

15. Holmes Rolston, *Philosophy Gone Wild: Environmental Ethics* (Buffalo: Prometheus, 1989).

16. Fowles uses this term in his novel *Daniel Martin* (Boston: Little, Brown, 1977), in chapter one, entitled "The Harvest."

17. Gaston Bachelard, in his book *The Poetics of Space,* refers often to "dreamers of nests" in chapter four, "Nests," trans. Maria Jolas (New York: Orion, 1964).

18. Bill McKibben, *The End of Nature* (New York: Random House, 1989), p. 60.

19. Mary McCarthy, in a 1970 essay published in *The New Yorker* (Jan. 24, 1970), wrote that Nature was a central presence in the nineteenth-century novel, "supplying the atmosphere in an almost literal sense; it was the air the novel breathed, like the life-sustaining air surrounding Mother Earth."

20. DeLillo, "Human Moments in World War III," in *Esquire* (July 1983), p. 126.

DANA PHILLIPS

Is Nature Necessary?

■ ■ ■

I'd like to begin asking whether nature is necessary indirectly, by appealing initially to its familiar antithesis—by seeking an answer first in culture: in literature, rather than the natural sciences. The following passage is from Hemingway's 1925 story "Big Two-Hearted River: Part II."

> Nick took his fly rod out of the leather rod-case, jointed it, and shoved the rod-case back into the tent. He put on the reel and threaded the line through the guides. He had to hold it from hand to hand, as he threaded it, or it would slip back through its own weight. It was a heavy, double tapered fly line. Nick had paid eight dollars for it a long time ago. It was made heavy to lift back in the air and come forward flat and heavy and straight to make it possible to cast a fly which has no weight. Nick opened the aluminum leader box. . . . In the damp pads the gut leader had softened and Nick unrolled one and tied it by a loop at the end to the heavy fly line. He fastened a hook on the end of the leader. It was a small hook; very thin and springy. . . . He tested the knot and the spring of the rod by pulling the line taut. It was a good feeling. He was careful not to let the hook bite into his finger.
>
> He started down to the stream, holding his rod, the bottle of grasshoppers hung from his neck. . . .

Now consider a passage from Carl Hiaasen's best-selling mystery *Double Whammy* (1987):

> Like a surgeon inspecting his instruments, Dennis Gault laid out his tournament bass tackle on the pile carpet and took inventory: six Bantam Magnumlite 2000 GT plugging reels, eight Shimano rods, four graphite Ugly Stiks, three bottles of Happy Gland bass scent, a Randall Knife, two cutting stones, Sargent stainless pliers, a diamond-flake hook sharpener, Coppertone sunblock, a telescopic landing net, two pairs of Polaroid sunglasses (amber and green), a certified Chatillion scale and, of course, his tacklebox. The tacklebox

> was the suitcase-size Plano Model 7777, with ninety separate compartments. As was everything in Dennis Gault's tournament artillery, his bass lures were brand-new. For top-water action he had stocked up on Bang-O-Lures, Shad Raps, Slo Dancers, Hula Poppers, and Zara Spooks; for deep dredging he had armed himself with Wee Warts and Whopper Stoppers and the redoubtable Lazy Ike. For brushpiles he had unsheathed the Jig-N-Pig and Double Whammy, the Bayou Boogie and Eerie Dearie, plus a rainbow trove of Mister Twisters. As for that most reliable of bass rigs, the artificial worm, Dennis Gault had amassed three gooey pounds. He had caught fish on every color, so he packed them all: the black-grape crawdad, the smoke-sparkle lizard, the flip-tale purple daddy, the motor-oil moccasin, the blue-berry gollywhomper, everything.

I reproduce these two roughly similar passages at length in order to demonstrate their difference. In Hiaasen's paragraph, an explosion of content has occurred, and the muted restraint characteristic of Hemingway's writing has been abandoned in favor of an esthetic of excess: number and adjective have proliferated; a fecundity once associated with the creations of nature has been granted to the products of tackle manufacturers. In the passage from Hemingway, Nick Adams's careful attention to technique is a means to uncover a more fundamental reality. While Hiaasen's initial comparison of Dennis Gault to a surgeon seems to suggest equally painstaking care, and perhaps a similar quest, his extended lists instead present us with a puzzling, weird array: a new and bizarre reality, featuring an alien technology and hybrid life forms (flip-tale purple daddies), is recorded in Hiaasen's bionic, day-glo bestiary. But more is at stake here than the stylistic or temperamental differences between Hemingway, Great American Writer, and Hiaasen, columnist for the *Miami Herald* and author of ecothrillers. The import of comparing the two passages is cultural and historical: these differences are those between modernism and postmodernism.

Hemingway's evocations of sport are modernist. Sport, particularly so-called "blood sport" (bullfighting, big game hunting, fishing, war), serves Hemingway as a vehicle for his version of the modernist project: the affirmation of the self in a transcendant moment of realization in which the dross of culture (language, sexuality, history) is clarified, melting away to reveal the roots of culture in nature, and human nature. Trout fishing, Hemingway writes, makes Nick Adams feel "happy," it makes him feel that he has "left everything behind, the need for thinking, the need to write, other needs." Hemingway's stripped-down, spare modernism has as its goal a basic transformation, like Nick's, effected through a redemptive artistic project or therapeutic experience.

Hiaasen's description of Dennis Gault kneeling on his carpet before piles of tackle suggests that a transformation of the sort Hemingway celebrates is no longer at stake. Nick Adams is *using* his minimal equipment, which is "used" or old, some of it homemade, and using it almost ritually (he sacrifices live bait). But Gault is only inspecting his fishing gear: his actions do not mean a return to the "good place," as Nick's did. There is no equivalent for Gault of Nick's campsite by the river. Nature plays a small part, or no part at all, in the inventory he conducts on his living room floor, where nature is so far absent as to be not even missed.

This inventory foregrounds the essence of postmodernist sport: it occurs in a simulated plenum, where nature is smoke-sparkle, rather than red in tooth and claw. Representation has supplanted presence. Gault's fishing lures, ostensibly mere imitations, have taken on a strange life of their own. Some of them seem to be inspired by cartoon or video game characters rather than by old-fashioned, organic fishbait (worms, minnows, crickets). Lazy Ike and Mister Twister are personalities of sorts—perhaps even celebrities, like the Teenage Mutant Ninja Turtles (these lures are not Hiaasen's inventions, I should add, but are actually available commercially). Gault's display of hardware is suggestive of a celebrity gala, or of window-dressing in a "bait shop" (to use a term that now begins to resonate across a broader cultural spectrum), and he kneels before it as if he were engaging in that second-most fundamental of consumer activities, as if he were "just looking"—and this is so even though he has just bought all that tackle.

Gault's gaze, moreover, is not contemplative: contemplation belongs to an older, bygone humanist tradition of sport fishing (Walton, Thoreau), of which Hemingway now appears as a final avatar. Gault's gaze is that of a new kind of commodity fetishist: he is having an attack of conspicuous consumption that has to do not with his own status, but with that of the totems he has purchased—totems of which he has become a mere function.

Pathetic as he is, it seems fitting that Dennis Gault suffers a strikingly perverse fate: he is killed during a competitive fishing tournament sponsored by the Outdoor Christian Network, when an enormous bass pulls him out of his boat into the whirring stainless-steel propellor of his outboard motor. For Hiaasen, Gault represents everything wrong with contemporary Florida: he's a rich real estate developer with a contradictory taste (contradictory in more ways than one) for the outdoors, for the natural splendor he has helped spoil. But Hiaasen misreads the new Florida landscape (Disney World, condos, shopping malls, golf courses), when he suggests that it is merely the product of the cynicism and greed of men like Gault. Florida is rather an exemplar of the postmodern, which has changed, perhaps forever, our relationship to the landscapes we inhabit.

Accounts of postmodernism tend to focus on urban centers (often Los Angeles), and usually cite changes in architecture and the visual arts as the primary signs of the postmodern. Postmodernism seems to be happening downtown, and almost nowhere else. Analyses of postmodernism are usually skewed, I think, by what might be called "urbocentrism," and leave open the response that good country people will have none of this thing called the postmodern, which would seem irrelevant to their experience.

But the classic distinction between city and country may no longer hold true, as Guy Debord suggests in *The Society of the Spectacle* (1970): "Economic history, which developed entirely around the opposition between town and country, has arrived at a level of success which simultaneously annihilates both terms." The "new and historically original penetration of Nature and the Unconscious" of which Fredric Jameson, in his 1984 essay "Postmodernism, or the Cultural Logic of Late Capitalism," says "one is tempted to speak," is now a reality. The recent cultural and natural history of Florida suggests that such is the case, and that analyses of postmodernism (like Hiaasen's, or Baudrillard's) focus too exclusively on spectacle, becoming tentative when faced with evidence of real behavioral and material changes. These changes have little to do with style, and their historical roots run deep into our past; although, as I will argue in the second section of this essay, we now have reached a point where they have achieved a sort of critical mass.

First, however, I want to investigate the subculture, to most readers no doubt rather alien, of professional bass fishing. "Professional bass fishing" means just that: bass fishermen get paid, and they are also celebrities. (They are a cross between baseball players—they wear caps, chew tobacco, and speak an arcane jargon which seems to be more than half the attraction—and golfers, whom they resemble athletically. The blond and perennial Roland Martin, whose home lake is Okeechobee in Florida, is the sport's answer to golf's Jack Nicklaus.) That a sport like bass fishing can become a spectator sport, one which attracts huge audiences both live and via television, underscores the transformative power of this new cultural practice.

Overseeing the professionalization of the sport has been the mission of the Bass Anglers Sportsman Society. BASS conducts fishing tournaments around the country, but mostly in the Deep South, where the sport has achieved its definitive form, and where the largemouth bass—*Micropterus salmoides*—has its native and most ardent constituency, because southern bass more often grow to monstrous—"lunker" or "hawg"—dimensions. But bass fishing is extremely popular all over the country, north and south; the largemouth's qualities—it is an omnivorous feeder, and easier to catch than the quirkier and more scarce smallmouth bass—give it broad appeal demographically. It is heavily stocked by most state wildlife programs and tirelessly promoted by fishing industry flacks.

BASS was founded in the late 1960s by Ray Scott, Jr., of Alabama. He recently reiterated, in his editor's column in *Bassmaster Magazine*, the importance of professionalization to bass fishing: "At the outset, my announced goal in forming Bass Anglers Sportsman Society 23 years ago was to 'elevate bass fishing to a par with golf.' " Scott's recollection provides a pretext for his disapproval of a golfer and erstwhile bass fisherman in Memphis, who seems to have dispatched a twenty-six-inch bass weighing nine pounds and two ounces—"a trophy by anyone's standards," Scott says—with a golf club. This is not the kind of association with golf Scott originally had in mind: "The latest link between golf and bass fishing," he writes, "doesn't do either sport any good. Bass fishing has its own set of rules, and clubbing a 'hapless fish senseless' with a 3-wood is not among them. The black bass deserves better." But Scott's evocation of this "noble game fish" seems not only maudlin, but false (as mistaken, in its own way, as Hiaasen's contempt for Dennis Gault). The noble bass in question was surely already somewhat travestied by its presence in the links-and-lakes landscape of a suburban golf course. That landscape might better be the object of Scott's ire, but like Hiaasen, he misreads postmodern symptoms—in this case, imitation run wild (bassers imitating golfers imitating bassers)—as merely the aberrant behavior of a single misguided sportsman. He appeals to standards of sport already undermined by the practice of sport.

Despite its unsanctioned death, the hapless bass has been mounted (ironically enough, by Tennessee conservation officials) and is proudly on display in the clubhouse at the Edmund Orgill Golf Course. It has become a material image of the cultural order which brought about its death, which occurred in the zombie world of what Guy Debord calls the "American way of death." Both taxidermy and mortuary science insist on the dead's "capacity to maintain in this encounter the greatest possible number of *appearances* of life," Debord suggests. "This social absence of death is identical to the social absence of life." In modernist sport as practiced by Hemingway, death was purposeful, one had to feel the other's death in order to confirm one's own life; in postmodernist sport, death is irrelevant—the other is irrelevant, as is one's self. The concept of the "trophy" cannot mean what it meant for Hemingway, since taxidermists now regularly use fiberglass replicas of gamefish—they come in all sizes—to "mount" their client's catches, discarding most of the actual fish, or working entirely from photographs of fish that were caught and released. The fiberglass fish look more like live fish than stuffed fish ever did. Of course, such trophies memorialize much more than a great day afield: they are monuments to a disappearing natural world.

This erasure of the distinction between life and death, nature and culture, is equally clear in the promotion of a new form of fishing practice called CPR, which stands not for "cardiopulmonary resuscitation," although the associated images of revivification are apt, but for "Catch, Photograph, and Release." Under the guise of responsible conservation, and faced with a decreasing fish population of increasing levels of toxicity, bass fishermen are being urged—quite sensibly—to set free a majority of the fish they boat. But in order to help them remember each fish, BASS suggests that fishermen photograph their catch before release, noting all the pertinent data (date, place, weight of the fish, etc.) on the back of each snapshot. As one advertisement has it, "Probably the only thing more satisfying than landing an ornery bass is showing off a stringer full of lunkers. And now, Polaroid, along with B.A.S.S., makes it easier than ever to bring home the catch of the day, while leaving the fish behind. . . . The best way to save the bass is to catch them. With a Polaroid camera." The ad features a photograph of a hand and forearm holding up a stringerful of Polaroids, in which grinning fishermen present lunker bass to the lens of the camera—all of which suggests the infinite regress of the event itself.

The spectacularization of nature—the doubling of our alleged alienation from it in new and ever more encapsulated forms—could scarcely be more clearly documented, when documentation itself, the substitution of the snapshot for memory (just as Walter Benjamin feared), has become the privileged form of our interaction with it. This cycle of reflexivity brings together, in a more or less closed circuit, the Bass Anglers Sportsman Society, the Polaroid corporation, readers of *Bassmaster,* a man and a camera—and a fish, as the last vestige of what used to be thought essential to the experience.

Experience may seem a problematic category in my analysis, continually reintroducing the dicey notion of individuality as a factor which might undermine and undo the conditions I describe by offering escape from them, a retreat to the safe house of personal consciousness (much like that which Nick Adams makes in Hemingway's story). But my argument is that little or no solace is available that way, because the self is not only invaded but shaped by that which it would escape. Cognitive dissonance comes with the territory, all territory, the terrain of the self not excluded. We don't know ourselves in these new behaviors, and how we feel about them is not the issue: cultural power these days is invested elsewhere, in the name of what sometimes seems to be an alien totality that we cannot (as individuals) sign off from merely by canceling the social contract, and going "back to nature." This impossibility is, partially, what is indicated when Jameson speaks of a new "penetration" of "Nature and the Subconscious." Postmodern "experience" is not a psychological category, but a collective one, though hardly in the utopian sense.

Our old assumptions about the self and nature are out of sync with both our new social practices and the objective conditions of that very Nature which used to serve us as something like a last court of appeal. The professionalization of bass fishing, for example, entails the institution of rules of conduct (an ethos), the election of governing bodies, and the organization, from above and below at once, of an activity formerly characterized by its relative aimlessness, by its leisure. This benignly Foucauldian regime also requires the administration of a system which disciplines and punishes, but most importantly, *rewards* its subjects: tournament victories can mean hundreds of thousands of dollars in prize money and commercial endorsements. Bass fishermen participate eagerly in this new cultural form. But their subjectivity has a new meaning: subjectivity means membership in BASS, which can be seen as a collective but dispersed metasubject in its own right, one which in matters requiring judgment or comment retains the right of final authority. Displays of what formerly might have been seen as charming or amusing individuality—a golfer's killing a fish with a golf club—may occasion official wrath. Refusing to accept the authority of organizations like BASS, or other authorities, such as those that sell fishing licenses, might amount to a sort of social banditry, for which poaching of course offers a classic paradigm. But such a refusal would be politically irrelevant, a mere romantic gesture, as well as a crime inviting potentially severe punishment (seizure of one's boat, jail time). In any case, bass bandits will find the pro tour more lucrative than poaching: bass aren't really prized as table fare. They have been marketed more as a result of their catchability than their edibility.

Consider one final example of our misapprehension of nature, the fisherman in his bass boat. The bass boat's array of data processing equipment renders archaic the older virtues of the fisherman: sense of place is beside the point, if Loran can chart his course for him; his good eye for weather need not be open, if the weather radio warns him of storms before he glimpses the red sky at morning; he needn't worry about being out of his depth, if his depth finder watches the lake bottom for him. He'll catch some fish, if his underwater probe reports favorable pH, temperature, and turbidity; he would be "actually handicapped without" the Multi-C-Lector, because "any fisherman is!"—pro basser Woo Daves told him so in the Multi-C-Lector ad in *North Carolina Game & Fish*. Its "totally automated fishing information," as Jimmy Houston, top pro and TV show host, says in the same ad, gives him "better information in minutes than trial-and-error [or even experience] ever did." So seated in his pedestal chair, his new "sensitive" graphite rod in his hand, he makes his first cast, fishing a "creature" lure, a Root Beer and Black Flake Cabela's Weedless Do Sump'n Stand-Up Jig by Mister Twister. It's drenched in FS-454, the fish feeding stimulant from Aquanautics Corporation (if bass "don't eat this, they don't eat food!"). He's got a frogbait tied on his other rod, a lure designed by the Bass Professor, Doug Hannon, and his wife—"wildlife sculptress" Lynn Hannon. The professor has caught over five hundred bass of ten pounds or more; if he could fish like that, maybe Razor boats—they're "now accepting resumes" for their "pro staff fishing team"—will hire him, and give him one of their new boats with the $\frac{3}{16}$" bullet-proof all-welded aluminum hull. If that happens, he'll buy his wife that pair of silk "Kiss My Bass!" panties, and his son the "Lake Mead" version of Rick Tauber's Bass Champ Computer Game.

This little vignette borrows information and language (as does *Double Whammy*) directly from bassing magazines and equipment catalogs, and is meant to suggest how both nature, and ourselves, have undergone a real phenomenological reduction. Our living quarters and our imaginations have been overrun and colonized by more than a simple exponential increase in available commodities, but by new possibilities for behavior, and what we might call "designer" epistemologies, marketed by members of subcultural elites like the Bass Professor. I say "our imaginations" because the bass fisherman is, of course, Everyman. The theme song to the television program "Fishin' with Orlando Wilson" puts the case for his lack of acquaintance with nature most succinctly.

> I hitched my boat onto the back of my truck,
> I called a friend and said let's go try our luck,
> He said, I'm sorry buddy I can't go,
> I'm watching the Orlando Wilson fishin' show!

The song is, of course, a joke, but I would argue that since this sort of joke tends to recur again and again in the literature and other media productions of the bass fishing subculture, it is one of those jokes that has a kernel of serious truth to it: these campy fishermen may never go camping again. Bassers may be laughin' to keep from cryin' over the loss Orlando's theme song implies.

The changes these sad figures embody are so far-reaching that the older dualisms break down. Man and machine, city and country, nature and culture, all merge in the figure of the bass boat: floating avatar of the dispersed urban center, this water-borne police cruiser is piloted by a cyborg dressed in a Goretex jumpsuit covered with the emblems of the new multinational order (Yamaha, Shimano, Mercury, Du Pont). He sits monitoring his surveillance equipment, his probes and prostheses: his experience is structured not by the vicissitudes of nature (which has been all but factored or filtered out of the equation) but by those of the marketplace: the tackle shops, the electronics, marine, and oil industries, print and video fishing magazines, wildlife agencies, and the Army Corps of Engineers.

Professional bass fishing is part of a social order which has brought nature to market hook, line, and sinker. The politics of this regime are more demographic than democratic: you are free to buy Tom Mann's Jelly Worms, to hunt bass on your Tom Mann Hawkeye model fish locator from Microsonics, and to tune in, if you are a paid cable subscriber, to "Tom Mann's America" (on ESPN, the network of postmodern sports). The *depth* of experience, for which fishing used to be an apt metaphor, has been replaced by the endless extension of its *surface,* which is everywhere the same, in a glass of water the same as in a Corps of Engineers reservoir (a favored site of bass fishing tournaments, and the environment for which most of the pro's equipment is designed). We can no longer speak of "culture," of lives rooted in time and place, only of strange new demographic formations like BASS—or the Fellowship of Christian Anglers Society (FOCAS), whose spokesman, pro fisherman Uncle Homer Circle, notes that the fellowship's efforts "to promote and develop the spiritual growth, family strength, and fishing skills of men and women everywhere" are "worthy of fishing tackle industry support."

Given new combinations, like these, of sports, religion, entertainment, technology, industry, and ersatz nationalism (George Bush, incidentally, is one of Ray Scott's fishing buddies, and a member of BASS), the question is whether there can be, in Tom Mann's America, an effective oppositional politics, a politics with environmental goals. Or do these conditions mark the emergence of what seems to be a postpolitical and thoroughly unnatural age? Is all this as depressing as it sounds? Are we all doomed to watch reruns of the Orlando Wilson fishin' show, until somebody (its sponsors) pulls the plug?

The fate of Skink, the hero of *Double Whammy,* suggests that such may be the case. Hiaasen counters the postmodern condition by posing against it a portrait of true individuality. Skink lives in a shack by one of Florida's remaining natural lakes, eating roadkill or the occasional bass, the catching of which he expedites with a twelve-gauge shotgun. Skink rejects the pretense of the new consumer culture by happily violating its commodity taboos (by fishing with buckshot instead of a spinnerbait), and practices an authentic Cracker politics. Uncompromised by complicity with the big-business New South, and untainted by allegiance to the unreconstructed values of the Old South (his best friend is a black highway patrolman), Skink is a true native son. Perhaps Hiaasen means his evocation of a Green-Redneck politics to be hopeful: in an era when culture has subsumed nature, perhaps only an equally hybrid political practice can survive, and awaken nature from its culturally induced coma.

"Skink," however, is actually Clinton Tyree, a decorated Vietnam War hero and the former governor of Florida. When Tyree couldn't stand corrupt Florida politics any longer, he ran away from the governor's mansion and went into hiding, making what might be called "a separate peace" with Tallahassee. Tyree now wants nothing more than to read and to collect dead possums from the highway; he dresses in fluorescent orange coveralls, and calls himself by an appropriately lower-order zoological name (the blue-tailed skink is a species of lizard).

But Tyree's alter ego, who at first appears to be merely a strange man of uncanny if socially unacceptable talents, and is then revealed as a hero (admittedly parodic) cut to Hemingway's dimensions, is nevertheless compromised by the new order of things in Florida, which again overwhelms him: keeping his true identity secret does not protect him. At the novel's end, Skink has lost an eye to muggers, and replaces it with a great yellow glass ball from the eyesocket of a taxidermied owl, thus incorporating an ultimate sign of simulated nature into his own body. He also inadvertently poisons his thirty-pound, world-record-size pet bass Queenie, whom he refers to as "the fucking monster-beastie of all time"—a phrase which may equate her with the great modernist symbols of natural redemption (Hemingway's trout, Faulkner's bear). As part of a scheme to sabotage a pro bass tournament (she is the fish who pulls Dennis Gault to his death), Queenie spends the day in a "Lunker Lake" at one of the Outdoor Christian Network's residential sports-fishing complexes, where she is exposed to polychlorinated biphenyls. Skink's sabotage of OCN's bassfishing tournament is a pyrrhic victory: he cannot turn the new cultural order to his own ends.

With the dying Queenie in his arms, Skink crosses what he calls "the moral seam of the universe," a thin dike separating Lunker Lake Number Seven from the Everglades. Together they swim out of the novel and into the mythical element, the figurative eternity, from which both derive their values. But this is merely a literary metasolution: Hiaasen's "moral seam" is a fiction. Even Everglades bass contain high levels of mercury, those that haven't died as a result of the recent drought of several years' duration. Hiaasen's response to the dystopian conditions of present-day life comes too late. Despite *Double Whammy*'s postmodern decor, its hero is modeled on an untenable modernist paradigm (i.e., Nick Adams), and in the end his eccentricity only mirrors the decentered and distorted social fabric he abhors.

▪ ▪ ▪ "Nature" may seem to be a notion disqualified by everything said in the preceding pages. Can an expression like "the natural world" have any meaning, if we have solved the puzzle of our estrangement from nature by making strange nature itself? In one New England state, biologists stock some streams with hatchery-bred albino trout ("mutants"): albino trout are popular with anglers, who find them easier to catch because they're so easy to see. This kind of fishery is called a "put and take": albino trout are stocked in streams just as hamburger is stocked in grocery stores, except that the hamburger probably has a longer shelf-life (predators find the trout easy to see, too). Such encounters with artifice, where one expects to find only the real thing, suggest that we have found a substitute for "the natural world": in the postmodern world, nature no longer seems to be necessary.

In suggesting that nature seems to be no longer necessary, I don't mean that we can dispense with nature altogether, having put behind us the childish anxieties of our longing for authenticity and utopia in favor of the absentee landlord rule of the multinational corporate state. I don't mean we no longer have to worry about nature: I think it's going to be on our minds, all the time. Bill McKibben has described this new state of affairs as entailing "The End of Nature" (in his recent book of that title), by which he also doesn't mean "the end of the world," but the obsolescence of "a certain set of human ideas about the world and our place in it . . . the death of these ideas begins with concrete changes in the reality around us." The ideas McKibben refers to are the old ones of nature as a green and pleasant space that was always there outside culture, a space into which we might someday pass over or return, in a moment of utmost pleasure (or, as a darker vision of nature has it, of terror). This idea of a "natural world" may have operated as a set of constraints upon our actions. However, the changes McKibben mentions, such as the recently discovered damage done by chlorofluorocarbons to the ozone layer, acid rain, and the mutations engineered by genetic researchers, give the lie to our old ideals: they weren't much else. But McKibben is no Chicken Little: his argument isn't that the sky is falling, but that the sky we see up there is not the same sky it used to be, not the sky we still fondly believe it to be: "these changes," he claims, "clash with our perceptions."

Though McKibben does not use the term, I believe these changes are consistent with the condition of postmodernity. The essential character of the postmodern order with regard to the place of nature in it is not simply put. Superficially, it has to do with the fact that landscapes are now treated identically irrespective of place; on the surface, such spaces become indistinguishable one from another and thus not properly separate "spaces" at all. Suburban housing developments, for example, typically bear no distinctive markers of place: if you have seen the green lawns of Jacksonville, you have seen the green lawns of Phoenix. And an even greater uniformity is now observable in "nature": in the pine forests of the timber industry, or the wheat, corn, and soybean monocultures of agribusiness, which has little use for barnyard variety.

In a global village of this sort, the idea of landscape has no meaning: "every inch and every hour" of the planet has the same markings, McKibben argues, and "the world outdoors" means "the same thing as the world indoors" (because both are, in effect, carpeted). But this goes well beyond the matter of how nature *looks*. And thus analyses of postmodernism, because of their emphasis on visual representation, often fall short of a full appreciation of just how *different* a world the real world has become. If acid rain falls equally on the just and the unjust; if a desert sun peeps, through a hole in the ozone, at both Phoenix and Jacksonville; and if the corn in the field you're driving past has "designer genes," that's because nature is now man-made. We may not see it, but nature wears a brand, McKibben argues; it is "a steer, not a deer." The rain, the sun, the corn, and the deer may not look any different, but they perform differently in the "natural" order: the rain erodes the waxy coating of evergreen leaves, the sun changes age-old weather patterns, the corn blankets the field in uniformity, the deer stand around and eat the corn, like cows.

More abstractly, and even harder for us to see, postmodernity results from a shift in the epistemological basis not only of the human relationship to nature, but of human relationships altogether. Debord puts it this way: "Everything that was directly lived has moved away into a representation." For the first time in history, he argues, human experience on all fronts is organized and represented back to us in the form of inventories of the possible. One now has a life in much the same sense one has lunch: by consuming it à la carte. Having a "lifestyle" means exercising our freedom of choice as consumers, not merely in the literal sense of purchasing this or that item, but by attending such and such a school, working in this or that profession, living here or there. However, these narratives are largely predetermined for us: our freedom is rather spurious, constrained as it is by a narrow range of options (the range itself is not so optional).

In this new economy of experience, alienation has become so basic a phenomenon that "concepts such as anxiety and alienation"—(concepts key to experience as defined by Hemingway)—"are no longer appropriate," according to Jameson. Why? Because subjectivity goes the same way as place in the postmodern world: if experience is dispensed in the form of the commodity, then one experience is much like another, as perfectly exchangeable as one commodity with another. Experience is made to trade; it no longer has the markings of the personal: "the alienation of the subject" has been "displaced by the fragmentation of the subject," Jameson concludes. We don't know the difference, because memory is debased in a world where it is daily replaced by the artificial repositories of the snapshot, the video, and the credit rating; these things have changed the meaning and structure of memory itself.

What is being described here should not be taken as referring merely to the feeling one might have of dread or anomie while wandering through a shopping mall or watching a bass tournament on television. Rather, the postmodern has to do more with the new ways knowledge is developed by, and simultaneously develops, the technological and natural world, the way cognition—and not merely emotion—has had to adjust and will have to adjust to the drastic changes described by McKibben, and many others, and the new ways in which these conditions recruit our actions. The darker aspects of the postmodern imply something like an unimaginable Copernican shift, "the moment of a radical eclipse of Nature itself," Jameson suggests, in which even the timeless natural order cannot be taken as assured. We may, nevertheless, still feel at home in this world because we no longer know or can tell the difference between nature and culture. Whatever remains of nature, in its former significance as wilderness, exists as such precisely because it is, if only for the time being, unknown to us. It falls outside our ken, it isn't a "resource," and is therefore (blessedly, perhaps) irrelevant, or not "nature" at all, insofar as our workaday habits are concerned. But as McKibben points out, even this nature which we have "preserved" already has our fingerprints all over it: it is smudged with our pollutants, just like anywhere and everywhere else. That wilderness is something of an optical illusion, crucial as its preservation may be, is an irony those who care for it have already lived with a long time.

I want to underscore the historicity of the changes I've described, and further illuminate the preceding remarks as well, by considering what can be read as a parable of the postmodern, from Martin Heidegger's essay, "The Question Concerning Technology":

> The forester who measures the felled timber in the woods and who to all appearances walks the forest path in the same way his grandfather did is today ordered by the industry that produces commercial woods, whether he knows it or not. He is made subordinate to the orderability of cellulose, which for its part is challenged forth by the need for paper, which is then delivered to newspapers and illustrated magazines. The latter, in their turn, set public opinion to swallowing what is printed, so that a set configuration of opinion becomes available on demand.

Heidegger's point is not that the forester's experience is somehow *felt* as radically different from that of his grandfather (though it may be), but that it *is* different apart from any consideration of the merely personal or psychological. The forester, and the forest, are subsumed in a new form of social and natural organization in which everything, literally everything, is one way or another answerable to human need, or deeply rooted in hegemonic forms: "available on demand." This demand is all-encompassing: nature and human nature, the forest and the forester, become part of what Heidegger calls "the standing-reserve," which "assumes the rank of an inclusive rubric"—which is to say that "whatever stands by in the sense of standing-reserve no longer stands over against us as object," but is already understood as a potential human artifact. This mediation—seeing the whole world as raw material—is the *essence* of technology, which Heidegger says is "by no means anything technological." He means that "technology" isn't itself a machine, but one of the many forms of *logos* itself. The essential tools are intellectual: the binary opposition is more important than the opposable thumb. Accordingly, we have resolved the old dilemma of not seeing the forest for the trees by eliminating the category of forest, by bringing nature into culture boardfoot by boardfoot—or fish by fish, as the case may be.

It might be said that although Heidegger is right about the forest *today*, things used not to be this way. This objection does not take into account the true force of Heidegger's definition of technology as the mediation of nature, a mental operation which surely, to note the contradiction in his thinking, must have been performed by the forester's grandfather, too. There is more to the story than a simple, but crucial, shift in worldview. Seeing nature (if one sees it at all) as something other than a mere "standing-reserve" cannot mean a return to a romantic, prelapsarian relationship with it, nor a repudiation of "technology" in Heidegger's sense of the term. We can't just change our mind about nature, because its problems did not begin just there, and nowhere else. They began, to put the case crudely, in the conjunction of Heideggerian "technology" and technology in the usual sense. They began when the will had the means, in the intersection of the mind and the tool at a point we might call that of no return, of totality: the *global* mechanisms of nature (the oceans and the atmosphere, for example) are the last frontiers. We know which technologies have taken us past these boundaries: coal-fired power plants, petroleum production, spray-can accelerants. What we haven't yet accepted is that some things won't be "available on demand" forever, and ought to be refused, even if they are.

Our thinking about nature should not be limited to strategies based on alternative worldviews (like Skink's). We haven't half understood our current worldview just yet: the apocalyptic word *post* in the compound *postmodernism* implies that one cannot get out ahead of its curve. And if McKibben is right, nature may soon begin dictating a new worldview of its own, setting harsher limits to our thinking, and our behavior, for us. Meanwhile, we ought to begin what Jameson has called "the practical reconquest of a sense of place," a practice he terms "cognitive mapping." Cognitive mapping entails the establishment of "an *imaginary* relation to the *real*": which I understand to mean the imagination of the real *as real,* as something that *matters,* to use a verb with possibly Heideggerian resonances. However, although Jameson uses the word *reconquest,* I want to suggest that the imagination of the real as real, and treating it as such, would be an historically original act. Whatever our reverence for nature may have been in the past, only recently have we begun to understand it in rich enough detail for the sort of cognitive mapping we must do.

If to imagine nature as something real, treat it accordingly, and understand why it is important to do so, is something new, then the revolutionary slogans for the future must abandon older formulas: if in smashing the multinational corporate state, you have nothing to lose but your chainsaws, the loss is nonetheless real and possibly quite painful, however necessary. "The sacrifices demanded may be on a scale we can't imagine and won't like," McKibben says. Such assertions may seem to reintroduce precisely the sort of totalizing hubris which brought on the state of affairs they would overthrow, but ecological thinking necessitates a certain regard for totalities—but they are different, and limited, totalities ("wholes," as ecologists like to call them, are perhaps among the first things needing to be mapped). It does not mean a return to Eden or the Everglades, to myth, nor is it simply a matter of what the analyst of postmodern malaise Andreas Huyssen calls "blue-eyed enthusiasm for peace and nature." It means a truly materialist version—ecologically rather than economically based—of "cognitive mapping," which must entail wiping our fingerprints off the landscape as we redraw the maps in our minds.

"Cognitive mapping" is of course a metaphor, one which resonates with Heidegger's notion of "building dwelling thinking": both suggest topographic and domestic considerations which are apt. To object that by speaking metaphorically we remain still too much locked within the realm of the textual, of *mere* metaphor, and even less concretely, of thought, misses the point, which is a polemical one. Let me explain what I mean by turning to the work—and not just the words—of another critic of our culture, Wendell Berry, who shares a distrust of our culture with Heidegger, Debord, and Jameson, but uses other idioms to express himself. Poet, novelist, essayist, and farmer, Berry has recently argued that "global" solutions to the problems of natural recovery cannot succeed. He might be suspicious of the grand sweep of theoretical notions like cognitive mapping, or of the very idea of postmodernism itself, for that matter. But his insistence that localities all around the globe must be involved in the effort to heal nature, seems to reintroduce the very category he rejects: "all of us," he complains in his essay "The Futility of Global Thinking," are "living either partly wrong or almost entirely wrong."

Berry's caution seems well-advised, if one recalls the global heroics of the era of modernity (big business, fascism, and Stalinism being particularly unhappy examples), and the potential erasure of natural and cultural differences under postmodernity. Both modernism and postmodernism celebrate historical rupture, as the periodizing effect of such labeling suggests; both institute forms of individuality that are either fractious or fractured. Neither gives historical and natural continuity much respect or thought. Berry's practice is by contrast regional, historical, and collective: words which do not necessarily imply bluebirds and happiness for him, since his ideal is outlined in a portrait of a Kentucky farm community in the midst of the Great Depression. This small community serves Berry as an ideal not because it was wholly successful (it no longer exists, after all) but because it offers him a model of conscious, hard-won awareness of the differences between nature and culture, and of the limits to their interrelationships, as well as a model of what might be called chastened individuality.

More than the other cultural critics I have mentioned, Berry, because he is a farmer, offers specifics for the treatment of postmodern conditions. We must, he says, abandon the sole standard of measure we have applied in our long history of relations with nature, the standard of productivity. Berry thinks we must learn to take another measure—reproductivity—as our standard of what we might cautiously call use-value. Nature is necessary, Berry argues, in that it is necessity itself: however much has been said about the "social production" of needs and the disappearance of use-value, the use-value of breathable air and drinkable water is not socially produced, nor can either be "simulated" once they are all gone. In another recent essay ("Taking Nature's Measure"), Berry suggests that "the use of nature as measure proposes an atonement between ourselves and our world, between economy and ecology, between the domestic and the wild . . . a conscious and careful recognition of the interdependence between ourselves and nature that in fact has always existed and, if we are to live, must always exist." For Berry and those with whom he lives, this has meant the restoration of the soil on his Kentucky hillside farm, a years-long effort to build up the depth and richness that poor farming practices and erosion had carried away, as well as years of writing about that effort and others like it. He argues that the soil is our heritage, our history. That is, the soil is also to be read, interpreted, taught, learned from, handed down to the next generation, and kept from becoming mere dirt. For Berry, farming is the deliberate but restrained process of turning nature into culture—and culture into nature.

For the state of Florida, whose topography I have been surveying throughout this essay, taking nature's measure has meant the decision to rechannel the Kissimmee River in its original flood plain, "to return the river," as one newspaper story put it, "to its natural state." Twenty years ago, the Army Corps of Engineers converted the one hundred miles of the Kissimmee into a fifty-two-mile drainage canal (collapsing space in the most postmodern manner: the river has been compared to an airport runway). In the segments of the river restored so far, native plants, animals, birds, and fish have returned, and are flourishing. On current maps the Kissimmee is shown flowing in nearly straight lines to Lake Okeechobee, bass fishing capital of the state, and near neighbor to Disney World. But those maps will need to be redrawn.

What effect the rechanneling of the Kissimmee will have on the area's bass fishing remains to be seen. But public works of this sort (things like asbestos removal, or efforts to clean up toxic waste; a more benign example might be Wes Jackson's efforts to farm prairie grasses) seem to me to offer metaphors for current cultural conditions. In a sense, public work of this sort is not unlike the great dam-building and skyscraper construction projects which offered symbols for the cultural diagnosis of fifty years ago. But the difference is that today's symbols are not so readily exploited for propaganda: they are dystopian, rather than utopian. At best they might represent breaking even with history; this is, I think, partly what Berry means by reproductivity (and what the Marxist idea of use-value ought to imply). Today's cultural energy must be largely devoted to coping with the negative effects of yesterday's: the symbols and successes of fifty years ago are often today's environmental disasters, and may prove harder to repair or unmake than they were to create, hard as that may have been.

Unmaking history seems to me to be the sober prospect postmodernism offers us, and is more difficult than making it. The special difficulty of unmaking what used to be called natural history is compounded by our ignorance of human complicity in it, and revising it is going to take more than just good writing or vigorous demonstration. But thinking and working our way through the past, and the perhaps unthinkable, impossible future of nature, may be our last best hope for building dwelling thinking here and now.

PART THREE

Critical Studies of Environmental Literature

GLEN A. LOVE

Revaluing Nature

TOWARD AN ECOLOGICAL CRITICISM

Describing the early rejection of the manuscript for his widely admired book, *A River Runs Through It,* Norman Maclean recalls in his acknowledgments the cool dismissal from one New York publisher: "These stories have trees in them."

The renowned English historian Arnold Toynbee, in his narrative history of the world entitled *Mankind and Mother Earth,* published in 1976 at the end of his long career and also at the time of the first worldwide recognition of the possibility of environmental disaster, concluded somberly that our present biosphere is the only habitable space we have, or are ever likely to have, that mankind now has the power to "make the biosphere uninhabitable, and that it will, in fact, produce this suicidal result within a foreseeable period of time if the human population of the globe does not now take prompt and vigorous concerted action to check the pollution and the spoliation that are being inflicted upon the biosphere by short-sighted human greed" (9). In the intervening decade-plus since Toynbee's statement, we have seen little in the way of the prompt and vigorous concerted action which he calls for, and we must consider ourselves further along the road to an uninhabitable earth.

The catalogue of actual and potential horrors is by now familiar to us all: the threats of nuclear holocaust, or of slower radiation poisoning, of chemical or germ warfare, the alarming growth of the world's population (standing room only in a few centuries at the present rate of growth), mounting evidence of global warming, destruction of the planet's protective ozone layer, the increasingly harmful effects of acid rain, overcutting of the world's last remaining great forests, the critical loss of topsoil and groundwater, overfishing and toxic poisoning of the oceans, inundation in our own garbage, an increasing rate of extinction of plant and animal species. The doomsday potentialities are so real and so profoundly important that a ritual chanting of them ought to replace the various nationalistic and spiritual incantations with which we succor ourselves. But rather than confronting these ecological issues, we prefer to think on other things. The mechanism which David Ehrenfeld calls "the avoidance of unpleasant reality" remains firmly in place (243). For the most part, our society goes on with its bread and circuses, exemplified by the mindless diversion reflected in mass culture and the dizzying proliferation of activity among practitioners of literary research. In the face of profound threats to our biological survival, we continue, in the proud tradition of humanism, to, as Ehrenfeld says, "love ourselves best of all," to celebrate the self-aggrandizing ego and to place self-interest above public interest, even, irrationally enough, in matters of common survival (238–39).

One would hope and expect that our field of English would respond appropriately to the radical displacements accompanying ecological catastrophe. Consider, however, that our society as a whole and our profession in particular have, as Cheryll Burgess [Glotfelty] points out, been faced with three crises in the last thirty years: civil rights, women's liberation, and environmental degradation (2). All three of these problem areas have been the subject of widespread social concern. All have become, to a greater or lesser extent, world issues. The discipline of English has addressed the concerns of civil rights, equality for minorities, and women's liberation through widespread attention and no small amount of action in such crucial areas as hiring and promotion practices, literary theory and criticism, and canon-formation. Race, class, and gender are the words which we see and hear everywhere at our professional meetings and in our current publications. But curiously enough, as Burgess points out, the English profession has failed to respond in any significant way to the issue of the environment, the acknowledgment of our place within the natural world and our need to live heedfully within it, at peril of our very survival.

Curiosity must give way to incredulity at our unconcern when one reflects that in this area the problem-solving strategies of the past are increasingly ineffectual. We have grown accustomed to living with crises, and to outliving them, or to resolving them in some manner or other with comparatively little harm to business as usual. But, as Lord Ashby explains, environmental degradation is more than just another crisis. As he describes it, "a crisis is a situation that will pass; it can be resolved by temporary hardship, temporary adjustment, technological and political expedients. What we are experiencing is not a crisis, it is a climacteric." (Quoted in Sheffer, p. 100.) For the rest of human history on the earth, says Ashby, we will have to live with problems of population, resources, and pollution.

Given the fact that most of us in the profession of English would be offended at not being considered environmentally conscious and ecologically aware, how are we to account for our general failure to apply any sense of this awareness to our daily work? One explanation might be that we care about these issues, but we don't care enough. It is our second most vital concern, the first position being reserved, as Mark Twain reminds us in "Corn-Pone Opinions," for that which immediately affects our personal economic livelihood. A diminished environment is, for the present, a postponable worry. Without in any way discounting the issues to which we have given first priority, however, there will clearly come a time, and soon, when we will be forced to recognize that human domination—never mind the subdivisions of human—of the biosphere is the overriding problem.

I find myself siding here with the contemporary "deep" ecologists, who argue that we must break through our preoccupation with mediating between only human issues, the belief that, as Warwick Fox puts it, "all will become ecologically well with the world if we just put this or that interhuman concern first" (18). Theodore Roszak, in *Person/Planet,* states that

> we have an economic style whose dynamism is too great, too fast, too reckless for the ecological systems that must absorb its impact. It makes no difference to those systems if the oil spills, the pesticides, the radioactive wastes, the industrial toxins they must cleanse are socialist or capitalist in origin; the ecological damage is not mitigated in the least if it is perpetrated by a 'good society' that shares its wealth fairly and provides the finest welfare programs for its citizens. The problem the biosphere confronts is the convergence of all urban-industrial economies as they thicken and coagulate into a single planet-wide system everywhere devoted to maximum productivity and the unbridled assertion of human dominance. (33)

The decision of those of us who profess English has been, by and large, that the relationship between literature and these issues of the degradation of the earth is something that we won't talk about. Where the subject unavoidably arises, it is commonly assigned to some category such as "nature writing," or "regionalism," or "interdisciplinary studies," obscure pigeonholes whose very titles have seemed to announce their insignificance. Consider the curious nonreception from our profession of Joseph Meeker's seminal book, published in 1974, *The Comedy of Survival: Studies in Literary Ecology.* Launched by a major publisher at a time of widespread public concern for the environment, with a challenging introduction by the distinguished ethologist Konrad Lorenz, this provocative book offered the first genuinely new reading of literature from an ecological viewpoint. Meeker wrote, "Human beings are the earth's only literary creatures. . . . If the creation of literature is an important characteristic of the human species, it should be examined carefully and honestly to discover its influence upon human behavior and the natural environment—to determine what role, if any, it plays in the welfare and survival of mankind and what insight it offers into human relationships with other species and with the world around us. Is it an activity which adapts us better to the world or one which estranges us from it? From the unforgiving perspective of evolution and natural selection, does literature contribute more to our survival than it does to our extinction?" (3–4)

Meeker's principal contribution in *The Comedy of Survival* is a challenging rereading of tragedy and comedy from an ecological viewpoint. The book was virtually ignored by reviewers—made uncomfortable, no doubt, by its cross-disciplinary approach. (Nature, unfortunately for the organization of academia, is vexingly interdisciplinary.) But its significance is that it confronts the essential issues which are being forced upon us—and does so even more strongly today, after fifteen years in which the problems it addresses have grown more serious in being deliberately ignored.

Recent historical studies such as Donald Worster's *Nature's Economy* and Roderick Nash's *The Rights of Nature* narrate the history of ecological thinking. Nash's book, in particular, records the powerful influence of environmentalism in a number of intellectual fields. He describes the greening of liberal thought, the greening of religion and philosophy, even law. (Contemporary events underscore Nash's analysis. Alaska's wildlife, for example, will sue the Exxon Corporation for damages as a result of the March 1989 oil spill in Prince William Sound. A San Francisco law firm will claim that bears, otters, birds, salmon, and other animals should have legal standing in court actions against Exxon ["Unusual claim"]). The question of rights for non-human organisms is one of the most vital areas of concern in several disciplines today. Congressional passage of the Endangered

Species Act of 1973 has extended ethical and legal rights to some species of plants and animals, and has thus projected ecological thinking into central public policy. Other fields, such as architecture and urban planning, have been powerfully influenced by such environmental awareness. History, our sister discipline, displays a lively new interest in the origin and progress of conservation movements, in the backgrounds of ecological thought, as the Worster and Nash books indicate. Clearly, a general shift of consciousness is taking place in many fields as past paradigms are found to be irrelevant or even harmful in the face of new circumstances.

In the context of this widespread disciplinary revaluation, why, one wonders, have literary criticism and theory remained so peculiarly unaffected, so curiously unwilling or unable to address questions which are at the forefront of public concern, which occupy the discourse of a number of our related contemporary disciplines, and which are—most important of all—engaged implicitly or explicitly in the body of works to which we have given our professional lives? Why are our theory and methodology so oddly untouched by all of this? Why, as Cheryll Burgess [Glotfelty] asks, are there no Professors of Literature and the Environment? (10) Why no prestigious chairs, or even jobs? There are half a dozen English graduate students at my university—and I hear continually of others elsewhere—who, like Ms. Burgess [Glotfelty], wish to work in the field of literature and ecology, and they wonder why none of the fashionable critics and theorists are addressing these vital matters. How can the discipline of English—which purports to deal with the human value systems of the past and the present, which seemingly engages literary representations of our relationship with our surroundings, and which thus both influences, and is influenced by, that relationship—fail to address such issues? Why are the activities aboard the *Titanic* so fascinating to us that we give no heed to the waters through which we pass, or to that iceberg on the horizon?

Besides our tendency to postpone or relegate to lesser priority ecological considerations, we must also recognize, in our failure to consider the iceberg, our discipline's limited humanistic vision, our narrowly anthropocentric view of what is consequential in life. The extension of human morality to the non-human world discussed above suggests that the time is past due for a redefinition of what is significant on earth. In our thinking, the challenge that faces us in these terms is to outgrow our notion that human beings are so special that the earth exists for our comfort and disposal alone. Here is the point at which a nature-oriented literature offers a needed corrective, for one very important aspect of this literature is its regard—either implicit or stated—for the non-human. While critical interpretation, taken as a whole, tends to regard ego-consciousness as the supreme evidence of literary and critical achievement, it is eco-consciousness which is a particular contribution of most regional literature, of nature-writing, and of many other ignored forms and works, passed over because they do not seem to respond to anthropocentric—let alone modernist and postmodernist—assumptions and methodologies. In such a climate of opinion, for example, Hemingway's *The Sun Also Rises,* which is little occupied with ecological considerations, is widely taught in college classes, while his *The Old Man and the Sea,* which engages such issues profoundly, is not.

In what follows, I will be turning increasingly to that nature-oriented literature in which most of us spend much of our professional lives, western American literature (though one could as well focus on other examples, as does John Alcorn on rural England in *The Nature Novel from Hardy to Lawrence,* or on various landscapes, as do Leonard Lutwack in *The Role of Place in Literature* and John Elder in *Imagining the Earth*). Fred Erisman made the point over ten years ago in an essay entitled "Western Fiction as an Ecological Parable," that much western American literature is an implicit plea for ecological awareness and activism. Even earlier, Thomas J. Lyon had posited hopefully that "the West's great contribution to American culture will be in codifying and directing the natural drive toward ecological thought, a flowering of regional literature into literally world-wide attention and relevance" (118). I think that many of us have found ourselves drawn to western literature by such a sense of its significance. Perversely enough, it is just this sort of literature rooted in a real world which is ignored or devalued by such modish surveys as the recently published *Columbia Literary History of the United States* (See Maguire).

It is one of the great mistaken ideas of anthropocentric thinking, and thus one of the cosmic ironies, that society is complex while nature is simple. The statement "These stories have trees in them" conveys the assumption that modern readers have outgrown trees. That literature in which nature plays a significant role is, by definition, irrelevant and inconsequential. That nature is dull and uninteresting while society is sophisticated and interesting. Ignoring, for the moment, the fact that there is a good deal of human society in Maclean's book, we might examine these assumptions which underlie the editor's put-down. If we are to believe what modern ecology is telling us, the greatest of all intellectual puzzles is the earth and the myriad systems of life which it nourishes. Nature reveals adaptive strategies far more complex than any human mind could devise. Surely one of the great challenges of literature, as a creation of human society, is to examine this complexity as it relates to the human lives which it encompasses. Indeed, in the pastoral tradition we have a long and familiar heritage in literature which purports to do just that. But the pastoral mode, in an important sense, reflects the same sort of anthropocentric assumptions which are in such dire need of reassessment. Literary pastoral traditionally posits a natural world, a green world, to which sophisticated urbanites withdraw in search of the lessons of simplicity which only nature can teach. There, amid sylvan groves and meadows and rural characters—idealized images of country existence—the sophisticates attain a critical vision of the good, simple life, a vision which will presumably sustain them as they return at the end to the great world on the horizon.

While the impetus, the motivation, for pastoral is perfectly relevant and understandable, no less today than it was 2,300 years ago, the terms by which pastoral's contrastive worlds are defined do, from an ecological viewpoint, distort the true essence of each. (This is as true for ironic versions of pastoral, even anti-pastorals, as it is for the conventional pastoral described above.) The green world becomes a highly stylized and simplified creation of the humanistic assumptions of the writer and his audience. Arcadia has no identity of its own. It is but a temporary and ephemeral release from the urban world, which asserts its mastery by its linguistic creation and manipulation of the generic form itself, and by its imposition of its own self-centered values upon the contrastive worlds. The lasting appeal of pastoral is, I think, a testament to our instinctive or mythic sense of ourselves as creatures of natural origins, those who must return periodically to the earth for the rootholds of sanity somehow denied us by civilization. But we need to redefine pastoral in terms of the new and more complex understanding of nature.

Western American literature provides us with some appropriate versions of new pastoral. Consider the case of a latter-day western writer, Joseph Wood Krutch. Krutch for many years lived in New York City, where he achieved a major reputation as a literary and dramatic critic and scholar. In his later years, he moved to the New England countryside, and then to Arizona, and became—can it be stated without hearing a snicker from Maclean's dismissing editor?—a nature-writer. In this latter role, Krutch authored a book on Thoreau, and many other volumes, including *The Twelve Seasons, The Desert Year, The Voice of the Desert, The Great Chain of Life,* and other works on the Grand Canyon, on Baja California, and on other aspects of the natural world. Having argued in his famous early book, *The Modern Temper,* that contemporary science had sucked dry modern life of its moral and spiritual values, Krutch went on to become something of a scientist himself, but a scientist of a natural world in which he found many of the values which he had presumed to be lost. He became a writer of natural history who, under the influence of Thoreau and Aldo Leopold, came to reassess his dualistic view of man's nature.

Describing how his own version of ego-consciousness had gradually changed to eco-consciousness, Krutch tells of his growing sense that mankind's ingenuity had outpaced its wisdom: "We have engineered ourselves into a position where, for the first time in history, it has become possible for man to destroy his whole species. May we not at the same time have philosophized ourselves into a position where we are no longer able to manage successfully our mental and spiritual lives?" (*The Measure of Man,* 28). Although Krutch remained in many respects a traditional humanist all his life, he found that his investigation of what he calls "the paradox of Man, who is a part of nature yet can become what he is only by being something also unique," led him to expand his vision of what is significant (*More Lives Than One,* 313). The realization came to be summed up for him in the words with which he found himself responding to the announcement of Spring by a chorus of frogs: "We are all in this together." This sentence, he recalls in his autobiography, *More Lives Than One,* "was important to me because it stated for the first time a conviction and an attitude which had come to mean more to me than I realized and, indeed, summed up a kind of pantheism which was gradually coming to be an essential part of the faith—if you can call it that—which would form the basis of an escape from the pessimism of *The Modern Temper* upon which I had turned my back without ever conquering it" (294–95). This growing awareness of interconnectedness between humankind and the non-human world led Krutch to risk being labelled with what he calls "the contemptuous epithet 'nature-lover' " (*More Lives Than One,* 338). He might have noted that his adoption of the desert Southwest as the subject of his books left him open, also, to the contemptuous epithet "western writer," or, worse yet, "regionalist."

This pattern is not an unfamiliar one. One thinks of Jack Schaefer, who wrote *Shane,* the definitive formula Western, without ever being further west than Ohio. Yet, in later life, Schaefer moved west, also to the desert, and gave us a new kind of western, a book about the animals of the desert, *An American Bestiary,* whose introduction tells of his own loss of innocence: "I had become ashamed of my species and myself. I understood at last that . . . I was part of the deadly conquest called civilization . . ." (xi). One may find a similar pattern of awareness in the works of urbanites like Edward Hoagland and Gretel Ehrlich, who seem to slough off their New York or L.A. skins when they confront western landscapes. The tug of eco-consciousness as a corrective to ego-consciousness is a familiar feature of their work, as it is in the great preponderance of those whom we consider western writers by birthright or by long association, writers like Cather and Austin and Silko, Jeffers and Stegner and Snyder. "What disregards people does people good," concludes William Stafford of the wild coastal setting in his 1950 poem, "An Address to the Vacationers at Cape Lookout." The chastisement, as in the works of Robinson Jeffers, identifies itself particularly with western settings and the writers of those settings, whose life and work is characterized, to no small degree, by its recognition of a natural otherness, a world of land and sky and organic life which exists outside human life, yet seems to command its allegiance. "These stories have trees in them." Much of what it means to be a western writer is to risk the contemptuous epithet, nature-lover.

The risk is worth taking, indeed must be taken, if it focuses attention on what appears to be nothing less than an ecologically suicidal path by the rest of the culture. Freud, in *Civilization and Its Discontents,* Erich Fromm in *The Sane Society,* and Paul Shepard in *Nature and Madness,* all confront the question of whether a society itself can be sick. All conclude that it indeed can be. The fact that millions of people share the same neurosis does not make them sane, as Fromm and Shepard remind us (Shepard xi). And, as Freud says, the means for curing a communal neurosis cannot come from those afflicted by the neurosis. Rather, it must come from elsewhere (Alcorn 108). John Alcorn finds this "elsewhere" in the English literature of place as revealed in the nature novels of Hardy and Lawrence (108). For others of us, the literature of the American West constitutes that sort of an alternative, as is demonstrated most recently by Harold P. Simonson in his *Beyond the Frontier.* For still others, it is in the literature of some other piece of earth. One place, properly regarded, serves as well as another. As anthropologist-writer Richard Nelson says, "What makes a place special is the way it buries itself inside the heart, not whether it's flat or rugged, rich or austere, wet or arid, gentle or harsh, warm or cold, wild or tame. Every place, like every person, is elevated by the love and respect shown toward it, and by the way in which its bounty is received" (xii). We become increasingly aware, as our technological world begins to crack beneath our feet, that our task is not to remake nature so that it is fit for humankind, but as Thoreau says, to make humankind right for nature.

Recent studies of pastoral ideology reveal the pervasive and tenacious appeal of pastoralism in American literature. Leo Marx, in reconsidering the conclusions he reached in his seminal 1964 study, *The Machine in the Garden,* now allows what western American literature has always suggested, that American pastoral did not retreat into insignificance with the rise of modern industrial urbanism. In a 1986 essay, Marx re-examines pastoralism and acknowledges its continuing relevance today. Unfortunately, he continues to underestimate its significance, seeing it only as another in a set of competing political ideologies. Marx does not consider whether the very real loomings of ecological catastrophe preclude pastoral's classification as just another value system ("Pastoralism in America"). Lawrence Buell, in a significant and wide-ranging survey of pastoralism in American literature and criticism, explores the experience of American pastoral in a variety of frames and contexts—social, political, gender-based, aesthetic, pragmatic, and environmental. (For further contemporary reconsiderations of pastoral, see Meeker and Howarth.) Buell gives more attention than Marx to the emergent threat of ecological holocaust, and he sees environmental pressures as tending to increase the importance of pastoralism as a literary and cultural force in the future. Obviously, I agree with him on this last point, although it needs to be said that such an outcome will require a more radical revaluation than any achieved thus far by pastoral's interpreters. Aldo Leopold's "land ethic," proposed in his environmental classic, *A Sand County Almanac,* might well be the litmus test for the new pastoralism: "A thing is right when it tends to preserve the integrity, stability, and beauty of the biotic community. It is wrong when it tends otherwise" (262). An ideology framed in such terms, with the human participants taking their own place in, and recognizing their obligation to, the shared natural world, will be an appropriate pastoral construct for the future. Whether we can accept it or not will say much about our chances for survival.

The redefinition of pastoral, then, requires that contact with the green world be acknowledged as something more than a temporary excursion into simplicity which exists primarily for the sake of its eventual renunciation and a return to the "real" world at the end. A pastoral for the present and the future calls for a better science of nature, a greater understanding of its complexity, a more radical awareness of its primal energy and stability, and a more acute questioning of the values of the supposedly sophisticated society to which we are bound. These are the qualities which distinguish much of our best western American literature, where writers characteristically push beyond the pastoral conventions to confront the power of a nature which rebuffs society's assumptions of control. Much of the elemental dignity of Willa Cather's fiction, for example, resides in her refusal to limit her conception of the significant in western life to that which can be encompassed in the humanistic preconceptions of the pastoral tradition. She never ignores the primal undercurrent, the wild land that kicks things to pieces, while it may also yield the pastoral farms of Alexandra and Ántonia. Nature says, "I am here still, at the bottom of things, warming the roots of life; you cannot starve me nor tame me nor thwart me; I made the world, I rule it, I am its destiny" (*The Kingdom of Art* 95).

Indeed, the western version of pastoral may be said to reverse the characteristic pattern of entry and return so that it is the green world which asserts its greater significance to the main character, despite the intrusion of societal values and obligations. This reversal is implicit in Barry Lopez's claim "that this area of writing [nature writing] will not only one day produce a major and lasting body of American literature, but that it might also provide the foundation for a reorganization of American political thought" (297).

While such predictions may be considered visionary, a reasonable observer must conclude that either through some ecological catastrophe of massive proportions or through a genuinely enlightened new sense of environmental awareness, our profession must soon direct its attention to that literature which recognizes and dramatizes the integration of human with natural cycles of life. The time cannot be far off when an ecological perspective will swim into our ken. Just as we now deal with issues of racism or sexism in our pedagogy and our theory, in the books which we canonize, so must it happen that our critical and aesthetic faculties will come to reassess those texts—literary and critical—which ignore any values save for an earth-denying and ultimately destructive anthropocentrism. And it does not seem unreasonable to suggest that the potential significance of such an awareness for the reinterpretation and reformation of the literary canon could be far greater than any critical movement which we have seen thus far. At a time when the discipline of literary criticism retreats ever further from public life into a professionalism characterized by its obscurity and inaccessibility to all but other English professors, it seems necessary to begin asking elemental questions of ourselves and the literature which we profess.

In anticipation of that inevitable day, I would offer three observations related to the future role of the Western Literature Association:

First, that the discipline of western American literature belongs in the forefront of the predicted critical shift. Its authority to lead such a movement arises not only from the work of its established writers and scholars, but also from the contributions of its younger practitioners like Carl Bredahl, Cheryll Burgess [Glotfelty], and SueEllen Campbell, who have already begun the thrust into contemporary critical fields.

Second, that the revaluation of nature will be accompanied by a major reordering of the literary genres, with realist and other discourse which values unity rising over post-structuralist nihilism. Certainly we shall see a new attention to nature writing. Although the growing interest in nature writing is by no means confined to the American West, writers and scholars from this region have been at the forefront in the surge of recent publications on nature writing. Important new anthologies, such as Thomas J. Lyon's *This Incomperable Lande,* Robert C. Baron and Elizabeth Darby Junkin's *Discovery and Destiny,* and Ann Ronald's *Words for the Wild,* have come out of the West recently along with the influential volume, *On Nature,* edited by Daniel Halpern and published by North Point Press of San Francisco. Two recent books of interviews and exchanges with nature writers, Stephen Trimble's *Words From the Land* and Edward Lueders's *Writing Natural History,* further underscore the growing interest in nature writing in the West, as does the burgeoning number of conferences on the topic throughout the region.

Add these to such evidence of national interest as the new *Norton Book of Nature Writing,* edited by Robert Finch and John Elder, and Alicia Nitecki's recently launched *American Nature Writing Newsletter,* and one might find the basis for some signs of environmental life in the profession. The call for papers for this year's MLA meeting lists two proposed sessions of interest to ecologically minded critics and teachers, evidence that voices crying in—and for—the wilderness will perhaps be heard at last within the halls of influence, voices asserting the significance of a value-laden landscape and a meaningful earth. These are small steps, but they may mark a beginning.

Third, that western American literature is not unique in its ecological perspective and that we need to recognize our kinship with nature-oriented writers in New England, in Canada, in Europe, in South and Central America, in Africa, in Australia, everywhere. Ecological issues are both regional and global. They transcend political boundaries. What is required is more interdisciplinary scholarship and more inter-regional scholarship on common issues. Deb Wylder has suggested the possibility of an international meeting of the Western Literature Association. Such a meeting, with significant participation from scholars in other countries, would be well-suited to examining and exploring the literary-ecological connections raised here. Because the American West is a region recognized everywhere through books and film, it now seems appropriate to focus upon the new West and other global regions of threatened landscapes, and upon how current environmental perceptions alter forever our sense of lighting out for the wide open spaces. With the seriousness of these issues, it is perhaps time for Melville's shock of recognition which runs the whole world round.

The distinguished cell biologist Lewis Thomas has cautioned us recently that it is time for us as human beings "to grow up as a species." Because of our unique gift of consciousness (to which should be added our concomitant gift of language), Thomas observes that "it is up to us, if we are to become an evolutionary success, to fit in, to become the consciousness of the whole earth. We are the planet's awareness of itself, and if we do it right we have a very long way to go" (52). As members of a discipline whose defining characteristics are consciousness and language, we in English are particularly involved here. We have indeed a very long way to go, and we seem remarkably loathe to begin the journey.

The most important function of literature today is to redirect human consciousness to a full consideration of its place in a threatened natural world. Why does nature writing, literature of place, regional writing, poetry of nature, flourish now—even as it is ignored or denigrated by most contemporary criticism? Because of a widely shared sense—outside the literary establishment—that the current ideology which separates human beings from their environment is demonstrably and dangerously reductionist. Because the natural world is indubitably real and beautiful and significant.

Paradoxically, recognizing the primacy of nature, and the necessity for a new ethic and aesthetic embracing the human and the natural—these may provide us with our best hope of recovering the lost social role of literary criticism.

WORKS CITED

Alcorn, John. *The Nature Novel from Hardy to Lawrence*. New York: Columbia University Press, 1977.

Baron, Robert C., and Elizabeth Darby Junkin, eds. *Discovery and Destiny: An Anthology of American Writers and the American Land*. Golden, Colorado: Fulcrum, 1986.

Bredahl, Carl. *New Ground: Western American Narrative and the Literary Canon*. Chapel Hill: University of North Carolina Press, 1989.

Buell, Lawrence. "American Pastoral Ideology Reappraised." *American Literary History* 1:1 (Spring 1989): 1–29.

Campbell, SueEllen. "The Land and Language of Desire: Where Deep Ecology and Post-Structuralism Meet." *Western American Literature* 24:3 (November 1989): 199–211.

Cather, Willa. *The Kingdom of Art: Willa Cather's First Principles and Critical Statements 1893–1896*. Ed. Bernice Slote. Lincoln: University of Nebraska Press, 1966.

Ehrenfeld, David. *The Arrogance of Humanism*. New York: Oxford University Press, 1978.

Elder, John. *Imagining the Earth: Poetry and the Vision of Nature*. Urbana: University of Illinois Press, 1985.

Erisman, Fred. "Western Fiction as an Ecological Parable." *Environmental Review* 6 (1978): 15–23.

Finch, Robert, and John Elder, eds. *The Norton Book of Nature Writing*. New York: W. W. Norton, 1990.

Fox, Warwick. "The Deep Ecology–Feminism Debate and Its Parallels." *Environmental Ethics* 11:1 (Spring 1989): 5–25.

[Glotfelty], Cheryll Burgess. "Toward an Ecological Literary Criticism." Western American Literature Meeting, Coeur d' Alene, Idaho, 13 October 1989.

Halpern, Daniel. *On Nature: Nature, Landscape, and Natural History*. San Francisco: North Point Press, 1987.

Howarth, William. "Country Books, City Writers: America's Rural Literature." *National Rural Studies Committee: A Proceedings*. Hood River, Ore., 24–25 May 1988: 11–21.

Krutch, Joseph Wood. *The Measure of Man*. New York: Bobbs-Merrill, 1954.

———. *More Lives Than One*. New York: William Sloane Associates, 1962.

Leopold, Aldo. *A Sand County Almanac*. San Francisco: Sierra Club/Ballantine, 1970.

Lopez, Barry. "Barry Lopez." *On Nature*. Ed. Daniel Halpern. San Francisco: North Point Press, 1987. 295–97.

Lueders, Edward, ed. *Writing Natural History: Dialogues with Authors*. Salt Lake City: University of Utah Press, 1989.

Lutwack, Leonard. *The Role of Place in Literature*. Syracuse, New York: Syracuse University Press, 1984.

Lyon, Thomas J. "The Ecological Vision of Gary Snyder." *Kansas Quarterly* 2 (Spring 1970): 117–24.

———, ed. *This Incomperable Lande*. Boston: Houghton Mifflin, 1989.

Maclean, Norman. *A River Runs Through It and Other Stories*. Chicago: University of Chicago Press, 1976.

Maguire, James H. "The Canon and the 'Diminished Thing.'" *American Literature* 60:4 (December 1988): 643–52.

Marx, Leo. *The Machine in the Garden*. New York: Oxford University Press, 1964.

———. "Pastoralism in America." *Ideology and Classic American Literature*. Ed. Sacvan Bercovitch and Myra Jehlen. Cambridge: Cambridge University Press, 1986. 36–69.

Meeker, Joseph. *The Comedy of Survival: Studies in Literary Ecology*. New York: Charles Scribner's Sons, 1974.

Nash, Roderick Frazier. *The Rights of Nature: A History of Environmental Ethics*. Madison: University of Wisconsin Press, 1989.

Nelson, Richard. *The Island Within*. San Francisco: North Point Press, 1989.

Nitecki, Alicia, ed. *The American Nature Writing Newsletter*. Department of English, Bentley College, Waltham, Mass. 02154-4705.

Ronald, Ann, ed. *Words for the Wild*. San Francisco: Sierra Club Books, 1987.

Roszak, Theodore. *Person/Planet: The Creative Disintegration of Industrial Society*. Garden City, New York: Doubleday, 1978.

Schaefer, Jack. *An American Bestiary*. Boston: Houghton Mifflin, 1975.

Sheffer, Victor B. "Environmentalism: Its Articles of Faith." *The Northwest Environmental Journal* 5:1 (Spring/Summer 1989): 99–109.

Shepard, Paul. *Nature and Madness*. San Francisco: Sierra Club Books, 1982.

Simonson, Harold P. *Beyond the Frontier: Writers, Western Regionalism and a Sense of Place*. Fort Worth: Texas Christian University Press, 1989.

Thomas, Lewis. "Are We Fit to Fit In?" *Sierra* 67:2 (March/April 1982): 49–52.

Toynbee, Arnold. *Mankind and Mother Earth*. New York: Oxford University Press, 1976.

Trimble, Stephen, ed. *Words from the Land: Encounters with Natural History*. Salt Lake City: Peregrine Smith, 1989.

Twain, Mark. "Corn-Pone Opinions." *Great Short Works of Mark Twain*. Ed. Justin Kaplan. New York: Harper and Row Perennial Classics, 1967. 188–92.

"Unusual claim includes wildlife in oil spill suit." *The Register-Guard*, Eugene, Oregon. 18 August 1989: 3A.

Worster, Donald. *Nature's Economy: A History of Ecological Ideas*. New York: Cambridge University Press, 1977.

PAULA GUNN ALLEN

The Sacred Hoop

■ ■ ■

A CONTEMPORARY PERSPECTIVE

Literature is one facet of a culture. The significance of a literature can be best understood in terms of the culture from which it springs, and the purpose of literature is clear only when the reader understands and accepts the assumptions on which the literature is based. A person who was raised in a given culture has no problem seeing the relevance, the level of complexity, or the symbolic significance of that culture's literature. We are all from early childhood familiar with the assumptions that underlie our own culture and its literature and art. Intelligent analysis becomes a matter of identifying smaller assumptions peculiar to the locale, idiom, and psyche of the writer.

The study of non-Western literature poses a problem for Western readers, who naturally tend to see alien literature in terms that are familiar to them, however irrelevant those terms may be to the literature under consideration. Because of this, students of traditional American Indian literatures have applied the terms *primitive, savage, childlike,* and *pagan* to these literatures. Perceiving only the most superficial aspects of American Indian literary traditions, Western scholars have labeled the whole body of these literatures *folklore,* even though the term specifically applies only to those parts of the literatures that are the province of the general populace.

The great mythic[1] and ceremonial cycles of the American Indian peoples are neither primitive, in any meaningful sense of the word, nor necessarily the province of the folk; much of the literature, in fact, is known only to educated, specialized persons who are privy to the philosophical, mystical, and literary wealth of their own tribe.

Much of the literature that was in the keeping of such persons, engraved perfectly and completely in their memories, was not known to most other men and women. Because of this, much literature has been lost as the last initiates of particular tribes and societies within the tribes died, leaving no successors.

Most important, traditional American Indian literature is not similar to Western literature because the basic assumptions about the universe and, therefore, the basic reality experienced by tribal peoples and by Western peoples are not the same, even at the level of folklore. This difference has confused non-Indian students for centuries. They have been unable or unwilling to accept this difference and to develop critical procedures to illuminate the materials without trivializing or otherwise invalidating them.

For example, American Indian and Western literary traditions differ greatly in the assumed purposes they serve. The purpose of traditional American Indian literature is never simply pure self-expression. The "private soul at any public wall" is a concept alien to American Indian thought. The tribes do not celebrate the individual's ability to feel emotion, for they assume that all people are able to do so. One's emotions are one's own; to suggest that others should imitate them is to impose on the personal integrity of others. The tribes seek—through song, ceremony, legend, sacred stories (myths), and tales—to embody, articulate, and share reality, to bring the isolated, private self into harmony and balance with this reality, to verbalize the sense of the majesty and reverent mystery of all things, and to actualize, in language, those truths that give to humanity its greatest significance and dignity. To a large extent, ceremonial literature serves to redirect private emotion and integrate the energy generated by emotion within a cosmic framework. The artistry of the tribes is married to the essence of language itself, for through language one can share one's singular being with that of the community and know within oneself the communal knowledge of the tribe. In this art, the greater self and all-that-is are blended into a balanced whole, and in this way the concept of being that is the fundamental and sacred spring of life is given voice and being for all. American Indian people do not content themselves with simple preachments of this truth, but through the sacred power of utterance they seek to shape and mold, to direct and determine, the forces that surround and govern human life and the related lives of all things.

An old Keres song says:

> I add my breath to your breath
> That our days may be long on the Earth

That the days of our people may be long
That we may be one person
That we may finish our roads together
May our mother bless you with life
May our Life Paths be fulfilled.

In this way one learns how to view oneself and one's tradition so as to approach both rightly. Breath is life, and the intermingling of breaths is the purpose of good living. This is in essence the great principle on which all productive living must rest, for relationships among all the beings of the universe must be fulfilled; in this way each individual life may also be fulfilled.

This idea is apparent in the Plains tribes' idea of a medicine wheel[2] or sacred hoop.[3] The concept is one of singular unity that is dynamic and encompassing, including all that is contained in its most essential aspect, that of life. In his introduction to Geronimo's autobiography, Frederick Turner III incorrectly characterizes the American Indian cultures as static.[4] Stasis is not characteristic of the American Indians' view of things. As any American Indian knows, all of life is living—that is, dynamic and aware, partaking as it does in the life of the All Spirit and contributing as it does to the continuing life of that same Great Mystery. The tribal systems are static in that all movement is related to all other movement—that is, harmonious and balanced or unified; they are not static in the sense that they do not allow or accept change. Even a cursory examination of tribal systems will show that all have undergone massive changes while retaining those characteristics of outlook and experience that are the bedrock of tribal life.[5] So the primary assumptions tribespeople make can be seen as static only in that these people acknowledge the essential harmony of all things and see all things as being of equal value in the scheme of things, denying the opposition, dualism, and isolation (separateness) that characterize non-Indian thought. Christians believe that God is separate from humanity and does as he wishes without the creative assistance of any of his creatures, while the non-Christian tribal person assumes a place in creation that is dynamic, creative, and responsive. Further, tribal people allow all animals, vegetables, and minerals (the entire biota, in short) the same or even greater privileges than humans. The Indian participates in destiny on all levels, including that of creation. Thus this passage from a Cheyenne tale in which Maheo, the All Spirit, creates out of the void four things—the water, the light, the sky-air, and the peoples of the water:

"How beautiful their wings are in the light," Maheo said to his Power, as the birds wheeled and turned, and became living patterns against the sky.

The loon was the first to drop back to the surface of the lake. "Maheo," he said, looking around, for he knew that Maheo was all about him, "You have made us sky and light to fly in, and you have made us water to swim in. It sounds ungrateful to want something else, yet still we do. When we are tired of swimming and tired of flying, we should like a dry solid place where we could walk and rest. Give us a place to build our nests, please, Maheo."

"So be it," answered Maheo, "but to make such a place I must have your help, all of you. By myself, I have made four things . . . Now I must have help if I am to create more, for my Power will only let me make four things by myself."[6]

In this passage we see that even the All Spirit, whose "being was a Universe,"[7] has limited power as well as a sense of proportion and respect for the powers of the creatures. Contrast this spirit with the Judeo-Christian God, who makes everything and tells everything how it may and may not function if it is to gain his respect and blessing and whose commandments make no allowance for change or circumstance. The American Indian universe is based on dynamic self-esteem, while the Christian universe is based primarily on a sense of separation and loss. For the American Indian, the ability of all creatures to share in the process of ongoing creation makes all things sacred.

In Paradise, God created a perfect environment for his creatures. He arranged it to their benefit, asking only that they forebear from eating the fruit of one particular tree. In essence, they were left with only one means of exercising their creative capacities and their ability to make their own decisions and choices. Essentially, they were thus prevented from exercising their intelligence while remaining loyal to the creator. To act in a way that was congruent with their natural curiosity and love of exploration and discovery, they were forced to disobey God and thus be exiled from the perfect place he had made for them. They were severely punished for exercising what we might call liberty—Eve more than Adam, for hers was the greater sin (or so the story goes):

And the Lord God commanded the man, saying, Of every tree of the garden thou mayest freely eat:

But of the tree of the knowledge of good and evil, thou shalt not eat: for in the day that thou eatest thereof thou shalt surely die. (Gen. 2:16–17)

The Cheyennes' creator is somewhat wiser. He gives his creatures needs so that they can exert their intelligence and knowledge to satisfy those needs by working together to solve common problems or attain common goals. Together Maheo, the creator, and the water beings create the earth, and with the aid of these beings, Maheo creates first man and first woman and the creatures and environment they will need to live good and satisfying lives. These creation stories demonstrate the basic ordering principles of two different cultures. The Judeo-Christian view is hierarchical. God commands first; within the limits of those commands, man rules; woman is subject to man, as are all the creatures, for God has brought them to Adam for him to name (Gen. 2:18–24, 3:16). In this scheme, the one who is higher has the power to impose penalties or even to deny life to those who are lower:

> And the Lord God said, Behold, the man is become as one of us, to know good and evil; and now, lest he put forth his hand, and take also of the tree of life, and eat, and live for ever;
>
> Therefore, the Lord God sent him forth from the garden of Eden to till the ground from whence he was taken. (Gen. 3:22–23)

The sin Adam and Eve committed in the Garden of Eden was attempting to become knowledgeable. Their attempt opened the further possibility that, with knowledge, they might become immortal. This, apparently, was not acceptable, not because knowledge and immortality were sinful but because the possession of them by human beings would reorder the hierarchical principles on which the Judeo-Christian universe is posited. Those reared in a Christian society are inclined to perceive social relationships—and literary works—in this context; they order events and phenomena in hierarchical and dualistic terms. Those reared in traditional American Indian societies are inclined to relate events and experiences to one another. They do not organize perceptions or external events in terms of dualities or priorities. This egalitarianism is reflected in the structure of American Indian literature, which does not rely on conflict, crisis, and resolution for organization, nor does its merit depend on the parentage, education, or connections of the author. Rather, its significance is determined by its relation to creative empowerment, its reflection of tribal understandings, and its relation to the unitary nature of reality.

The way the loon prays in the Cheyenne creation story is indicative of that difference. The loon looks around him as he addresses Maheo, "for he knew that Maheo was all about him," just as earlier in the story the snow-goose addressed Maheo in these words: "I do not know where you are, but I know you must be everywhere."[8]

Another difference between these two ways of perceiving reality lies in the tendency of the American Indian to view space as spherical and time as cyclical, whereas the non-Indian tends to view space as linear and time as sequential. The circular concept requires all "points" that make up the sphere of being to have a significant identity and function, while the linear model assumes that some "points" are more significant than others. In the one, significance is a necessary factor of being in itself, whereas in the other, significance is a function of placement on an absolute scale that is fixed in time and space. In essence, what we have is a direct contradiction of Turner's notion about the American Indian universe versus that of the West: the Indian universe moves and breathes continuously, and the Western universe is fixed and static. The Christian attitude toward salvation reflects this basic stance: one can be "saved" only if one believes in a Savior who appeared once and will not come again until "the end of time." The idea "once a saint, always a saint" is another expression of the same underlying perception and experience.

The notion that nature is somewhere over there while humanity is over here or that a great hierarchical ladder of being exists on which ground and trees occupy a very low rung, animals a slightly higher one, and man (never woman)—especially "civilized" man—a very high one indeed is antithetical to tribal thought. The American Indian sees all creatures as relatives (and in tribal systems relationship is central), as offspring of the Great Mystery, as cocreators, as children of our mother, and as necessary parts of an ordered, balanced, and living whole. This concept applies to what non-Indian Americans think of as the supernatural, and it applies as well to the more tangible (phenomenal) aspects of the universe. American Indian thought makes no such dualistic division, nor does it draw a hard and fast line between what is material and what is spiritual, for it regards the two as different expressions of the same reality, as though life has twin manifestations that are mutually interchangeable and, in many instances, virtually identical aspects of a reality that is essentially more spirit than matter or, more correctly, that manifests its spirit in a tangible way. The closest analogy in Western thought is the Einsteinian understanding of matter as a special state or condition of energy. Yet even this concept falls short of the American Indian understanding, for Einsteinian energy is believed to be unintelligent, while energy according to the Indian view is intelligence manifested in yet another way.

Many non-Indians believe that human beings possess the only intelligence in phenomenal existence (often in any form of existence). The more abstractionist and less intellectually vain Indian sees human intelligence as rising out of the very nature of being, which is of necessity intelligent in and of itself, as an attribute of being. Again, this idea probably stems from the Indian concept of a circular, dynamic universe in which all things are related and are of one family. It follows that those attributes possessed by human beings are natural attributes of *all* being. The Indian does not regard awareness of being as an abnormality peculiar to one species, but, because of a sense of relatedness to (instead of isolation from) what exists, the Indian assumes that this awareness is a natural by-product of existence itself.

In English, one can divide the universe into two parts: the natural and the supernatural. Humanity has no real part in either, being neither animal nor spirit—that is, the supernatural is discussed as though it were apart from people, and the natural as though people were apart from it. This necessarily forces English-speaking people into a position of alienation from the world they live in. Such isolation is entirely foreign to American Indian thought. At base, every story, every song, every ceremony tells the Indian that each creature is part of a living whole and that all parts of that whole are related to one another by virtue of their participation in the whole of being.

In American Indian thought, God is known as the All Spirit, and other beings are also spirit—more spirit than body, more spirit than intellect, more spirit than mind. The natural state of existence is whole. Thus healing chants and ceremonies emphasize restoration of wholeness, for disease is a condition of division and separation from the harmony of the whole. Beauty is wholeness. Health is wholeness. Goodness is wholeness. The Hopi refer to a witch—a person who uses the powers of the universe in a perverse or inharmonious way—as a two-hearts, one who is not whole but is split in two at the center of being. The circle of being is not physical, but it is dynamic and alive. It is what lives and moves and knows, and all the life forms we recognize—animals, plants, rocks, winds—partake of this greater life. Acknowledgment of this dynamic unity allows healing chants such as this from the Night Chant to heal (make a person whole again):

Happily I recover.
Happily my interior becomes cool.
Happily I go forth.
My interior feeling cool, may I walk.
No longer sore, may I walk.
As it used to be long ago, may I walk.
Happily, with abundant dark clouds, may I walk.
Happily, with abundant showers, may I walk.
Happily, with abundant plants, may I walk.
Happily, on a trail of pollen, may I walk.
Happily, may I walk.[9]

Because of the basic assumption of the wholeness or unity of the universe, our natural and necessary relationship to all life is evident; all phenomena we witness within or "outside" ourselves are, like us, intelligent manifestations of the intelligent universe from which they arise, as do all things of earth and the cosmos beyond. Thunder and rain are specialized aspects of this universe, as is the human race. Consequently, the unity of the whole is preserved and reflected in language, literature, and thought, and arbitrary divisions of the universe into "divine" and "worldly" or "natural" and "unnatural" beings do not occur.

Literature takes on more meaning when considered in terms of some relevant whole (like life itself), so let us consider some relationships between specific American Indian literary forms and the symbols usually found in them. The two forms basic to American Indian literature are the ceremony and the myth. The ceremony is the ritual enactment of a specialized perception of a cosmic relationship, while the myth is a prose record of that relationship. Thus, the wiwanyag wachipi (sun dance) is the ritual enactment of the relationship the Plains people see between consecration of the human spirit and Wakan Tanka as manifested as Sun, or Light, and Life-Bestower. Through purification, participation, sacrifice, and supplication, the participants act as instruments or transmitters of increased power and wholeness, which bestows health and prosperity, from Wakan Tanka.

The formal structure of a ceremony is as holistic as the universe it purports to reflect and respond to, for the ceremony contains other forms such as incantation, song (dance), and prayer, and it is itself the central mode of literary expression from which all allied songs and stories derive. The Lakota view all the ceremonies as related to one another in various explicit and implicit ways, as though each were one face of a multifaceted prism.

This interlocking of the basic forms has led to much confusion among non-Indian collectors and commentators, and this complexity makes all simplistic treatments of American Indian literature more confusing than helpful. Indeed, the non-Indian tendency to separate things from one another—be they literary forms, species, or persons—causes a great deal of unnecessary difficulty with and misinterpretation of American Indian life and culture. It is reasonable, from an Indian point of view, that all literary forms should be interrelated, given the basic idea of the unity and relatedness of all the phenomena of life. Separation of parts into this or that category is not agreeable to American Indians, and the attempt to separate essentially unified phenomena results in distortion.

For example, to say that a ceremony contains songs and prayers is misleading, for prayers are one form of address and songs are another. It is more appropriate to say that songs, prayers, dances, drums, ritual movements, and dramatic address are compositional elements of a ceremony. It is equally misleading to single out the wiwanyag wachipi and treat it as an isolated ceremony, for it must of necessity include the inipi (rite of purification) and did at one time contain the hanblecheyapi (vision quest), which was how the Lakota learned about it in the first place.[10] Actually, it might best be seen as a communal vision quest.

The purpose of a ceremony is to integrate: to fuse the individual with his or her fellows, the community of people with that of the other kingdoms, and this larger communal group with the worlds beyond this one. A raising or expansion of individual consciousness naturally accompanies this process. The person sheds the isolated, individual personality and is restored to conscious harmony with the universe. In addition to this general purpose, each ceremony has its own specific purpose. This purpose usually varies from tribe to tribe and may be culture-specific. For example, the rain dances of the Southwest are peculiar to certain groups, such as the Pueblos, and are not found among some other tribes, while war ceremonies, which make up a large part of certain Plains tribes' ceremonial life, are unknown among many tribes in California.[11] But all ceremonies, whether for war or healing, create and support the sense of community that is the bedrock of tribal life. This community is not made up only of members of the tribe but necessarily includes all beings that inhabit the tribe's universe.

Within this context the dynamic characteristics of American Indian literature can best be understood. The structures that embody expressed and implied relationships between human and nonhuman beings, as well as the symbols that signify and articulate them, are designed to integrate the various orders of consciousness. Entities other than the human participants are present at ceremonial enactments, and the ceremony is composed for their participation as well as for that of the human beings who are there. Some tribes understand that the human participants include members of the tribe who are not physically present and that the community as a community, not simply the separate persons in attendance, enact the ceremony.

Thus devices such as repetition and lengthy passages of "meaningless" syllables take on significance within the context of the dance. Repetition has an entrancing effect. Its regular recurrence creates a state of consciousness best described as "oceanic," but without the hypersentimental side effects implied by that term. It is hypnotic, and a hypnotic state of consciousness is the aim of the ceremony. The participants' attention must become diffused. The distractions of ordinary life must be put to rest and emotions redirected and integrated into a ceremonial context so that the greater awareness can come into full consciousness and functioning. In this way the participants become literally one with the universe, for they lose consciousness of mere individuality and share the consciousness that characterizes most orders of being.

In some sense repetition operates like the chorus in Western drama, serving to reinforce the theme and to focus the participants' attention on central concerns while intensifying their involvement with the enactment. One suits one's words and movements (if one is a dancer) to the repetitive pattern. Soon breath, heartbeat, thought, emotion, and word are one. The repetition integrates or fuses, allowing thought and word to coalesce into one rhythmic whole, which is not as jarring to the ear as rhyme.

Margot Astrov suggests that this characteristic device stems from two sources, one psychic and one magical:

> . . . this drive that forces man to express himself in rhythmic patterns has its ultimate source in psychic needs, for example the need of spiritual ingestion and proper organization of all the multiform perceptions and impressions rushing forever upon the individual from without and within . . . Furthermore, repetition, verbal and otherwise, means accumulation of power.[12]

Astrov finds evidence that the first, the need to organize perception, predominates in the ceremonies of some tribes, such as the Apaches, and that the second, a "magically creative quality," is more characteristic of others, such as the Navajo. In other words, some tribes appear to stress form while others stress content, but either way a tribe will make its selection in terms of which emphasis is most likely to bring about fusion with the cosmic whole in its group and environment. This fusion depends on the emphasis that is most congenial to the aesthetic and psychic sense of the tribe.

One should remember, when considering rhythmic aspects of American Indian poetic forms, that all ceremony is chanted, drummed, and danced. American Indians often refer to a piece of music as a dance instead of a song because song without dance is very rare, as is song without the use of a drum or other percussion instrument. One must also note that the drum does not "accompany" the song, for that implies separation between instrument and voice where no separation is recognized. Words, structure, music, movement, and drum combine to form an integral whole, and accompaniment per se is foreign to the ceremony, though it is common in Western music. The ceremony may be enacted before people who are neither singing nor dancing, but their participation is nevertheless assumed. Participation is a matter of attention and attunement, not of activity.

Repetition is of two kinds, incremental and simple. In the first, variations will occur. A stanza may be repeated in its entirety four times—once for each of the directions—or six times—once for each lateral direction plus above and below—or seven times—once for each direction plus the center "where we stand." Alternatively, the repetition may be of a phrase only, as in the Yei be chi, or of a phrase repeated four times with one word—the ceremonial name for each of four mountains, say, or the names of significant colors, animals, or powers—inserted in the appropriate place at each repetition, as in this Navajo Mountain Chant:

Seated at home behold me,
Seated amid the rainbow;
Seated at home behold me,
Lo, here, the Holy Place!
        Yea, seated at home behold me.
At Sisnajinni, and beyond it,
        Yea, seated at home behold me;
The Chief of Mountains, and beyond it,
        Yea, seated at home behold me;
In Life Unending, and beyond it,
        Yea, seated at home behold me;
In Joy Unchanging, and beyond it,
        Yea, seated at home behold me.

Seated at home behold me,
Seated amid the rainbow;
Seated at home behold me,
Lo, here, the Holy Place!
        Yea, seated at home behold me.
At Tsodschl, and beyond it,
        Yea, seated at home behold me;
The Chief of Mountains, and beyond it,
        Yea, seated at home behold me;
In Life Unending, and beyond it,
        Yea, seated at home behold me;
In Joy Unchanging, and beyond it,
        Yea, seated at home behold me.

Seated at home behold me,
Seated amid the rainbow;
Seated at home behold me,
Lo, here, the Holy Place!
        Yea, seated at home behold me.
At Doko-oslid, and beyond it,
        Yea, seated at home behold me;
The Chief of Mountains, and beyond it,
        Yea, seated at home behold me;
In Life Unending, and beyond it,
        Yea, seated at home behold me;
In Joy Unchanging, and beyond it,
        Yea, seated at home behold me.

Seated at home behold me,
Seated amid the rainbow;
Seated at home behold me,
Lo, here, the Holy Place!
        Yea, seated at home behold me.
At Depenitsa, and beyond it,
        Yea, seated at home behold me;
The Chief of Mountains, and beyond it,
        Yea, seated at home behold me;
In Life Unending, and beyond it,
        Yea, seated at home behold me;
In Joy Unchanging, and beyond it,
        Yea, seated at home behold me.[13]

Some critics have said that this device results from the oral nature of American Indian literature, that repetition ensures attention and makes the works easy to remember. If this is a factor at all, however, it is a peripheral one, for nonliterate people have more finely developed memories than do literate people. The child learns early to remember complicated instructions, long stories—often verbatim—multitudes of details about plants, animals, kinship and other social relationships, privileges, and responsibilities, all "by heart." For a person who can't run to a bookshelf or a notebook to look up either vital or trivial information, reliance on memory becomes very important in everyday life. This highly developed everyday memory is not likely to fail on ceremonial occasions, so the use of repetition for ease of memorization is not significant.

Astrov, in her discussion of the "psychic" basis of the device, touches on another reason folklorists give for the widespread use of repetition in oral ceremonial literature:

> A child repeats a statement over and over for two reasons. First, in order to make himself familiar with something that appears to him to be threateningly unknown and thus to organize it into his system of familiar phenomena; and, second, to get something he wants badly.[14]

Astrov implies that repetition is childish on two counts: that it (rather than rational thought) familiarizes and defuses threat and that the person, irrationally, believes that oral repetition of a desire will ensure its gratification. Let us ignore the obvious fact that shamans, dancers, and other adult participants in the ceremony are not children and concentrate on actual ceremonies to see whether they contain factors that are or might appear "threatening" to the tribe or whether they simply repeat wishes over and over. Nothing in the passages quoted so far could be construed as threatening, unless beauty, harmony, health, strength, rain, breath, life unending, or sacred mountains can be so seen. Nor are any threatening unknowns mentioned in the songs and chants Astrov includes in her collection; there are threats implicit in death or great powers, but while these constitute unknowns to many civilized people, they are familiar to the tribes. And, by Astrov's own admission, the works approach death or severe illness in positive ways, as in this death song:

> From the middle
> Of the great water
> I am called by the spirits.[15]

"Light as the last breath of the dying," she comments, "these words flutter out and seem to mingle with the soft fumes and mists that rise from the river in the morning"—hardly a threatening description. She continues:

> It is as though the song, with the lightness of a bird's feather, will carry the departing soul up to where the stars are glittering and yonder where the rainbow touches the dome of the sky.[16]

Nowhere in her discussion of Indian songs does Astrov indicate that the singers feel threatened by the chants. Instead, she points out that they express serenity and even joy in the face of what might seem frightening to a child. Nor do there appear any passages, in her extensive collection, that are the equivalent of "Lord, Won't You Buy Me a Color TV," and the absence of such material weakens the childhood-magic theory of repetition. In fact, the usual American Indian perception of humanity (collectively, not individually) as cocreator discourages the people from perceiving the deity as a sort of cosmic bellhop who alone is responsible for their personal well-being. This perception simultaneously discourages people from setting themselves up as potentates, tyrants, dictators, or leaders of any other kind.

The failure of folklorists to comprehend the true metaphysical and psychic nature of structural devices such as ceremonial repetition is a result of the projection of one set of cultural assumptions onto another culture's customs and literatures. People of the Western cultures, particularly those in professions noted for their "objectivity" and intellectual commitment to Freudian tenets, are likely not to interpret psychic components of ceremonial literature in its extramundane sense but rather in its more familiar psychological sense. The twin assumptions that repetition serves to quiet childish psychological needs and to assure participants in a ceremony that they are exerting control over external phenomena—getting something they want badly—are projections. The participants do indeed believe that they can exert control over natural phenomena, but not because they have childishly repeated some syllables. Rather, they assume that all reality is internal in some sense, that the dichotomy of the isolate individual versus the "out there" only appears to exist, and that ceremonial observance can help them transcend this delusion and achieve union with the All Spirit. From a position of unity within this larger Self, the ceremony can bring about certain results, such as healing one who is ill, ensuring that natural events move in their accustomed way, or bringing prosperity to the tribe.

The westerner's bias against nonordinary states of consciousness is as unthinking as the Indian's belief in them is said to be. The westerner's bias is the result of an intellectual climate that has been carefully fostered in the west for centuries, that has reached its culmination in Freudian and Darwinian theories, and that only now is beginning to yield to the masses of data that contradict it. This cultural bias has had many unfortunate side effects, only one of which is deep misunderstanding of tribal literatures that has for so long marked the learned and popular periodicals that deal with tribal culture.

In his four-volume treatise on nonordinary reality, Carlos Castaneda has described what living in the universe as a shaman is like. Unfortunately, he does not indicate that this experience is rather more common to ordinary than to extraordinary people, that the state of consciousness created through ceremony and ritual and detailed in mythic cycles is exactly that of the "man of knowledge," or sage. He makes the whole thing sound exotic, strange, beyond the reach of most persons, yet the great body of American Indian literature suggests quite a different conclusion. This literature can best be approached as a psychic journey. Only in the context of the consciousness of the universe can it be understood.

American Indian thought is essentially mystical and psychic in nature. Its distinguishing characteristic is a kind of magicalness—not the childish sort described by Astrov but rather an enduring sense of the fluidity and malleability, or creative flux, of things. This is a reasonable attitude in its own context, derived quite logically from the central assumptions that characterize tribal thought. The tribal person perceives things not as inert but as viable and alive, and he or she knows that living things are subject to processes of growth and change as a necessary component of their aliveness. Since all that exists is alive and since all that is alive must grow and change, all existence can be manipulated under certain conditions and according to certain laws. These conditions and laws, called "ritual" or "magic" in the West, are known to American Indians variously. The Sioux refer to them as "walking in a sacred manner," the Navajo as "standing in the center of the world," and the Pomo as "having a tradition." There are as many ways of referring to this phenomenon as there are tribes.

The symbolism in American Indian ceremonial literature, then, is not symbolic in the usual sense; that is, the four mountains in the Mountain Chant do not stand for something else. They are those exact mountains perceived psychically, as it were, or mystically. The color red, as used by the Lakota, doesn't stand for sacred or earth, but it is the quality of a being, the color of it, when perceived "in a sacred manner" or from the point of view of the earth itself. That is, red is a psychic quality, not a material one, though it has a material dimension, of course. But its material aspect is not its essential one. As the great metaphysician Madame Blavatsky put it, the physical is not a principle; or, as Lame Deer the Lakota shaman suggests, the physical aspect of existence is only representative of what is real:

> The meat stands for the four-legged creatures, our animal brothers, who gave of themselves so that we should live. The steam [from the stewpot] is living breath. It was water; now it goes up to the sky, becomes a cloud again . . .
>
> We Sioux spend a lot of time thinking about everyday things, which in our mind are mixed up with the spiritual. We see in the world around us many symbols that teach us the meaning of life. We have a saying that the white man sees so little, he must see with only one eye. We see a lot that you no longer notice. You could notice if you wanted to, but you are usually too busy. We Indians live in a world of symbols and images where the spiritual and the commonplace are one. To you symbols are just words, spoken or written in a book. To us they are part of nature, part of ourselves, even little insects like ants and grasshoppers. We try to understand them not with the head but with the heart, and we need no more than a hint to give us the meaning.[17]

Not only are the "symbols" statements of perceived reality rather than metaphorical or poetic statements but the formulations that are characterized by brevity and repetition are also expressions of that perception. One sees life as part of oneself; a hint as to which particular part is all that is needed to convey meaning. This accounts for the "purity" and "simplicity" that apparently characterize traditional American Indian literatures. The works are simple in that they concern themselves with what is known and familiar, not in that they are childlike or unsophisticated.

In a sense, the American Indian perceives all that exists as symbolic. This outlook has given currency to the concept of the Indian as one who is close to the earth, but the closeness is actual, not a quaint result of savagism or childlike naiveté. An Indian, at the deepest level of being, assumes that the earth is alive in the same sense that human beings are alive. This aliveness is seen in nonphysical terms, in terms that are perhaps familiar to the mystic or the psychic, and this view gives rise to a metaphysical sense of reality that is an ineradicable part of Indian awareness. In brief, we can say that the sun or the earth or a tree is a symbol of an extraordinary truth.

This attitude is not anthropomorphic. No Indian would regard personal perception as the basic, or only, unit of universal consciousness. Indians believe that the basic unit of consciousness is the All Spirit, the living fact of intelligence from which all other perceptions arise and derive their power:

> I live, but I will not live forever.
> Mysterious moon, you only remain,
> Powerful sun, you alone remain,
> Wonderful earth, you remain forever.
> All of us soldiers must die.[18]

This attitude is not superstitious, though it can degenerate into superstition when the culture disintegrates. It is based very solidly on experience, and most members of the tribe share that experience to some degree. The experience is verified by hundreds and thousands of years of experience and is a result of actual perception—sight, taste, hearing, smell—as well as more indirect social and natural phenomena. In the West, if a person points to a building and says, "There is a building," and if other people looking in the direction indicated agree, and if that building can be entered, walked through, touched, then the building is said to be really there.

In the same way, traditional American Indians encounter and verify metaphysical reality. No one's experience is idiosyncratic. The singer who tells of journeying to the west and climbing under the sky speaks of a journey that many have taken in the past and will take in the future. Every traveler will describe the same sights and sounds and will enter and return in like fashion.

Generations of Western observers have noticed this peculiarity of psychic travel, and many attempt to explain it in psychoanalytic terms, referring to Jung's "collective unconscious," for example, or to Freud's notion of the projection of repressed conflict. Nevertheless, the evidence, however one interprets it, suggests that the psychic life of all humanity is the same. Western sophisticates presume that the experiences—sights, sounds, and beings encountered on psychic journeys—are imaginary and hallucinatory; they are equally inclined to presume that thoughts are idiosyncratic events of no real consequence. Nowhere in the literature on ceremonialism have I encountered a Western writer willing to suggest that the "spiritual and the commonplace are one."[19] Many argue that these "hallucinations" are good, others that they are the product of diseased minds,[20] but none suggests that one may *actually* be "seated amid the rainbow."

Symbols in American Indian systems are not symbolic in the usual sense of the word. The words articulate reality—not "psychological" or imagined reality, not emotive reality captured metaphorically in an attempt to fuse thought and feeling, but that reality where thought and feeling are one, where objective and subjective are one, where speaker and listener are one, where sound and sense are one.

The many kinds of American Indian literature can be categorized in various ways, but, given the assumptions behind the creation and performance of the literature, a useful division might be along functional lines rather than along more mechanical ones.

It might be said that the basic purpose of any culture is to maintain the ideal status quo. What creates differences among cultures and literatures is the way in which the people go about this task, and this in turn depends on, and simultaneously maintains, basic assumptions about the nature of life and humanity's place in it. The ideal status quo is generally expressed in terms of peace, prosperity, good health, and stability. Western cultures lean more and more heavily on technological and scientific methods of maintenance, while traditional cultures such as those of American Indian tribes tend toward mystical and philosophical methods. Because of this tendency, literature plays a central role in the traditional cultures that it is unable to play in technological ones. Thus, the purpose of a given work is of central importance to understanding its deeper significance.

We can divide traditional literature into two basic genres: ceremonial and popular, as opposed to the Western prose and poetry distinction. Ceremonial literature includes all literature that is accompanied by ritual actions and music and that produces mythic (metaphysical) states of consciousness and/or conditions. This literature may appear to the westerner as either prose or poetry, but its distinguishing characteristic is that it is to some degree sacred. The word *sacred,* like the words *power* and *medicine,* has a very different meaning to tribal people than to members of technological societies. It does not signify something of religious significance and therefore believed in with emotional fervor—"venerable, consecrated, or sacrosanct," as the Random House dictionary has it—but something that it is filled with an intangible but very real power or force, for good or bad. Lame Deer says in his discussion of symbolism:

> *Four* is the number that is most wakan, most sacred. Four stands for Tatuye Tope—the four quarters of the earth. One of its chief symbols is Umane, which looks like this:

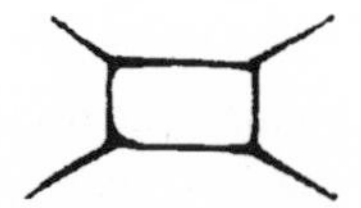

> It represents the unused earth force. By this I mean that the Great Spirit pours a great unimaginable amount of force into all things—pebbles, ants, leaves, whirlwinds—whatever you will . . .
>
> This force is symbolized by the Umane. In the old days men used to have an Umane altar made of raised earth in their tipis on certain special occasions. It was so *wakan* you couldn't touch it or even hold your hand over it.[21]

Lame Deer is not saying that one was forbidden to touch the altar; he is saying that one *could not* touch it. The Umane does not represent the power; it *is* the power. *Sacred, power,* and *medicine* are related terms. Having power means being able to use this extra force without being harmed by it. This is a particular talent that human beings possess to greater or lesser degree, and *medicine* is a term used for the personal force through which one possesses power. Medicine is powerful in itself, but its power can be used only by certain persons, under certain conditions, and for certain purposes.

Ceremonial literature is sacred; it has power. It frequently uses language of its own: archaisms, "meaningless" words, or special words that are not used in everyday conversation. It can be divided into several subcategories, some of which appear in some tribes but not in others, and others that can be found throughout Indian America. Ceremonial literature includes songs for many occasions: healing; initiation; planting, harvesting, and other agricultural pursuits; hunting; blessing new houses, journeys, and undertakings. There are also dream-related songs; war songs; personal power songs; songs for food preparation, purification, and vision seeking. The subjects of the major ceremonial cycles include origin and creation, migration, celebration of new laws, and commemoration of legendary or mythic occurrences. Each serves to hold the society together, create harmony, restore balance, ensure prosperity and unity, and establish right relations within the social and natural world. At base the ceremonials restore the psychic unity of the people, reaffirm the terms of their existence in the universe, and validate their sense of reality, order, and propriety. The most central of these perform this function at levels that are far more intense than others, and these great ceremonies, more than any single phenomenon, distinguish one tribe from another.

Every tribe has a responsibility to the workings of the universe; today as yesterday, human beings play an intrinsic role in the ongoing creation. This role is largely determined by the place where the tribe lives, and the role changes when the tribe moves. In the Southwest, for example, the Zuñi dance Shalako every winter at the solstice so that the sun will turn in its course and move once again toward summer. Cosmic cycles such as Shalako or Wúwuchim relate to life processes on earth and, by virtue of natural relationship, within the universe. They aim toward forces far bigger than the community or the individual, though each is inescapably dependent on the other—"circles within circles," as Lame Deer says, "with no beginning and no end."[22]

The greater and lesser symbols incorporated into the ceremonies take their meaning from the context of the ceremony—its purpose and its meaning. Attempts to understand ceremonial literature without knowledge of this purpose often have ludicrous results. The symbols cannot be understood in terms of another culture, whether it be that of Maya or of England, because those other cultures have different imperatives and have grown on different soil, under a different sky within the nexus of different spirits, and within a different traditional context. "Owl" in one situation will have a very different significance from "owl" in another, and a given color—white or blue—will vary from place to place and from ceremony to ceremony in its significance, intensity, and power. In other words, the rules that govern traditional American Indian literatures are very different from those that govern Western literature, though the enormity of the difference is, I think, a fairly recent development. Literature must, of necessity, express and articulate the deepest perceptions, relationships, and attitudes of a culture, whether it does so deliberately or accidentally. Tribal literature does this with a luminosity and clarity that are largely free of pretension, stylized "elegance," or show. Experiences that are held to be the most meaningful—from those that completely transcend ordinary experience to those that are commonplace—are celebrated in the songs and ceremonial cycles of the people.

The more commonplace experiences are celebrated in popular tales and songs, which may be humorous, soothing, pedagogical, or entertaining. In this category are lullabies, corn-grinding and ditch-digging songs, jokes, pourquoi tales, "little" stories, and stories with contemporary settings. Included here, too, are those delightful dances called '49s.[23] All but the '49s appear in collections of Indian lore, sometimes masquerading as true myths or simple songs. This masquerade, of course, does little to clear up misunderstandings regarding American Indian literature, for frequently those "myths" that seem childlike are forms developed for children and bear only a slight resemblance to the true mythic chants from which they derive.

Between the trivial, popular forms and the ceremonial works are songs and stories such as various games; incantations and other simple forms of magic; prose cycles such as the Trickster tales recorded by Paul Radin; and some journey and food-related songs and legends.

Individual songs may be difficult to classify, though the level of symbolism they contain and the amount of prescribed ritual and associated ceremony, the number and special qualifications of the celebrants, and the physical setting and costume can help distinguish one kind from another. To classify any given song, though, one needs more than a nodding acquaintance with the locality and the tribe whose song or story is under consideration.

Another important factor to consider in classification of a song is the relative secrecy of parts or all of the ceremony, especially when tourists, cameras, or tape recorders are present. The amount of secrecy will vary to some extent from tribe to tribe, some being more open than others, but some secrecy is nearly always the rule.

Another such indicator, particularly valuable for classroom work, is the source of the song or story. Only very erudite tomes are likely to have much that is really sacred, and even those have usually been altered in some way. Popular books are likely to carry mainly popular literature, with a few selections from the next more powerful category. It would be well to mention, in this connection, that the use of really sacred materials by ordinary mortals and publishers is generally forbidden. Also, these works do not make good classroom materials for a variety of reasons: they are arcane; they are usually taboo; they tend to confuse non-Indian students; they may cause resentment among Indian students; and they create questions and digressions that are usually beyond the competence of the teacher or of the academic setting. Frequently they lead to ridicule, disrespect, and belittlement; non-Indian students are not inclined by training or culture to view the sacred as that which has power beyond that of economics, history, or politics.

Underlying all their complexity, traditional American Indian literatures possess a unity and harmony of symbol, structure, and articulation that is peculiar to the American Indian world. This harmony is based on the perceived harmony of the universe and on thousands of years of refinement. This essential sense of unity among all things flows like a clear stream through the songs and stories of the peoples of the western hemisphere. This sense is embodied in the words of an old man:

> There are birds of many colors—red, blue, green, yellow—yet it is all one bird. There are horses of many colors—brown, black, yellow, white—yet it is all one horse. So cattle, so all living things—animals, flowers, trees. So men: in this land where once were only Indians are now men of every color—white, black, yellow, red—yet all one people. That this should come to pass was in the heart of the Great Mystery. It is right thus. And everywhere there shall be peace.[24]

So Hiamove said, more than fifty years ago. It remains for scholars of American Indian literature to look at this literature from the point of view of its people. Only from this vantage can we understand fully the richness, complexity, and true meaning of a people's life; only in this way can we all learn the lessons of the past on this continent and the essential lesson of respect for all that is.

NOTES

1. *Mythic:* 1. narratives that deal with metaphysical, spiritual, and cosmic occurrences that recount the spiritual past and the "mysteries" of the tribe; 2. sacred story. The *Word* in its cosmic, creative sense. This usage follows the literary meaning rather than the common or vernacular meaning of "fictive" or "not real narrative dealing with primitive, irrational explanations of the world." 3. translational.

2. Hyemehosts Storm, *Seven Arrows* (New York: Harper and Row, 1972), p. 4.

3. John G. Neihardt, *Black Elk Speaks* (Lincoln: University of Nebraska Press, 1961), p. 35.

4. Frederick Turner III, Introduction, *Geronimo: His Own Story,* by Geronimo, ed. S. M. Barrett (New York: Ballantine, 1978), p. 7.

5. D'Arcy McNickle, *Native American Tribalism: Indian Survivals and Renewals* (New York: Oxford University Press, 1973), pp. 12–13.

6. Alice Marriott and Carol K. Rachlin, *American Indian Mythology* (New York: New American Library, 1972), p. 39.

7. Marriott and Rachlin, *American Indian Mythology,* p. 39.

8. Natalie B. Curtis, *The Indians' Book: Songs and Legends of the American Indians* (New York: Dover, 1968), pp. 8, 7.

9. From a prayer of the Night Chant of the Navajo people.

10. I am making this inference from the account of the appearance of White Buffalo Cow Woman to Kablaya as recounted by Black Elk in *The Sacred Pipe: Black Elk's Account of the Seven Rites of the Oglala Sioux,* ed. Joseph Eyes Brown (Baltimore: Penguin, 1971), pp. 67–100.

11. T. Kroeber and Robert F. Heizer, *Almost Ancestors: The First Californians,* ed. F. David Hales (San Francisco: Sierra Club, 1968), pp. 28–30.

12. Margot Astrov, *American Indian Prose and Poetry* (New York: Capricorn, 1962), p. 12.

13. Curtis, *Indians' Book,* p. 356. I have reproduced this part of the chant in its entirety, although the Curtis version has only one stanza with a note regarding the proper form.

14. Astrov, *American Indian Prose,* p. 12.

15. Astrov, *American Indian Prose,* p. 50.

16. Astrov, *American Indian Prose,* p. 50.

17. John (Fire) Lame Deer and Richard Erdoes, *Lame Deer: Seeker of Visions* (New York: Touchstone, 1972), pp. 108–9.

18. Crazy Dog Society song of the Kiowa people. This version appears in Alice Marriott, *Kiowa Years: A Study in Culture Impact* (New York: Macmillan, 1968), p. 118.

19. Lame Deer and Erdoes, *Lame Deer,* p. 115.

20. Sigmund Freud, *Totem and Taboo,* trans. James Strachey (New York: Norton, 1952), p. 14.

21. Lame Deer and Erdoes, *Lame Deer,* p. 115.

22. Lame Deer and Erdoes, *Lame Deer,* p. 112.

23. '49 songs were sung (danced) just before a war party went out. They are widely enjoyed today after a powwow has officially ended after midnight. One '49 song goes like this:

> When the dance is ended sweetheart
> I will take you home.
> *He-he-he-ya*
> *He-ya he-he-ya.*

24. Curtis, *Indians' Book,* p. x.

LESLIE MARMON SILKO

Landscape, History, and the Pueblo Imagination

■ ■ ■

FROM A HIGH ARID PLATEAU IN NEW MEXICO

You see that after a thing is dead, it dries up. It might take weeks or years, but eventually if you touch the thing, it crumbles under your fingers. It goes back to dust. The soul of the thing has long since departed. With the plants and wild game the soul may have already been borne back into bones and blood or thick green stalk and leaves. Nothing is wasted. What cannot be eaten by people or in some way used must then be left where other living creatures may benefit. What domestic animals or wild scavengers can't eat will be fed to the plants. The plants feed on the dust of these few remains.

The ancient Pueblo people buried the dead in vacant rooms or partially collapsed rooms adjacent to the main living quarters. Sand and clay used to construct the roof make layers many inches deep once the roof has collapsed. The layers of sand and clay make for easy grave digging. The vacant room fills with cast-off objects and debris. When a vacant room has filled deep enough, a shallow but adequate grave can be scooped in a far corner. Archaeologists have remarked over formal burials complete with elaborate funerary objects excavated in trash middens of abandoned rooms. But the rocks and adobe mortar of collapsed walls were valued by the ancient people. Because each rock had been carefully selected for size and shape, then chiseled to an even face. Even the pink clay adobe melting with each rainstorm had to be prayed over, then dug and carried some distance. Corn cobs and husks, the rinds and stalks and animal bones were not regarded by the ancient people as filth or garbage. The remains were merely resting at a midpoint in their journey back to dust. Human remains are not so different. They should rest with the bones and rinds where they all may benefit living creatures—small rodents and insects—until their return is completed. The remains of things—animals and plants, the clay and the stones—were treated with respect. Because for the ancient people all these things had spirit and being.

The antelope merely consents to return home with the hunter. All phases of the hunt are conducted with love. The love the hunter and the people have for the Antelope People. And the love of the antelope who agree to give up their meat and blood so that human beings will not starve. Waste of meat or even the thoughtless handling of bones cooked bare will offend the antelope spirits. Next year the hunters will vainly search the dry plains for antelope. Thus it is necessary to return carefully the bones and hair, and the stalks and leaves to the earth who first created them. The spirits remain close by. They do not leave us.

The dead become dust, and in this becoming they are once more joined with the Mother. The ancient Pueblo people called the earth the Mother Creator of all things in this world. Her sister, the Corn Mother, occasionally merges with her because all succulent green life rises out of the depths of the earth.

Rocks and clay are part of the Mother. They emerge in various forms, but at some time before, they were smaller particles or great boulders. At a later time they may again become what they once were. Dust.

A rock shares this fate with us and with animals and plants as well. A rock has being or spirit, although we may not understand it. The spirit may differ from the spirit we know in animals or plants or in ourselves. In the end we all originate from the depths of the earth. Perhaps this is how all beings share in the spirit of the Creator. We do not know.

FROM THE EMERGENCE PLACE

Pueblo potters, the creators of petroglyphs and oral narratives, never conceived of removing themselves from the earth and sky. So long as the human consciousness remains *within* the hills, canyons, cliffs, and the plants, clouds, and sky, the term *landscape*, as it has entered the English language, is misleading. "A portion of territory the eye can comprehend in a single view" does not correctly describe the relationship between the human being and his or her surroundings. This assumes the viewer is somehow *outside* or *separate from* the territory he or she surveys. Viewers are as much a part of the landscape as the boulders they stand on. There is no high mesa edge or mountain peak where one can stand and not immediately be part of all that surrounds. Human identity is linked with all the elements of Creation through the clan: you might belong to the Sun Clan or the Lizard Clan or the Corn Clan or the Clay Clan.* Standing deep within the natural world, the ancient Pueblo understood the thing as it was—the squash blossom, grasshopper, or rabbit itself could never be created by the human hand. Ancient Pueblos took the modest view that the thing itself (the landscape) could not be improved upon. The ancients did not presume to tamper with what had already been created. Thus *realism,* as we now recognize it in painting and sculpture, did not catch the imaginations of Pueblo people until recently.

The squash blossom itself is *one thing:* itself. So the ancient Pueblo potter abstracted what she saw to be the key elements of the squash blossom—the four symmetrical petals, with four symmetrical stamens in the center. These key elements, while suggesting the squash flower, also link it with the four cardinal directions. By representing only its intrinsic form, the squash flower is released from a limited meaning or restricted identity. Even in the most sophisticated abstract form, a squash flower or a cloud or a lightning bolt became intricately connected with a complex system of relationships which the ancient Pueblo people maintained with each other, and with the populous natural world they lived within. A bolt of lightning is itself, but at the same time it may mean much more. It may be a messenger of good fortune when summer rains are needed. It may deliver death, perhaps the result of manipulations by the Gunnadeyahs, destructive necromancers. Lightning may strike down an evil-doer. Or lightning may strike a person of good will. If the person survives, lightning endows him or her with heightened power.

Pictographs and petroglyphs of constellations or elk or antelope draw their magic in part from the process wherein the focus of all prayer and concentration is upon the thing itself, which, in its turn, guides the hunter's hand. Connection with the spirit dimensions requires a figure or form which is all-inclusive. A "lifelike" rendering of an elk is too restrictive.

* Clan—A social unit composed of families sharing common ancestors who trace their lineage back to the Emergence where their ancestors allied themselves with certain plants or animals or elements.

Only the elk *is* itself. A *realistic* rendering of an elk would be only one particular elk anyway. The purpose of the hunt rituals and magic is to make contact with *all* the spirits of the Elk.

The land, the sky, and all that is within them—the landscape—includes human beings. Interrelationships in the Pueblo landscape are complex and fragile. The unpredictability of the weather, the aridity and harshness of much of the terrain in the high plateau country explain in large part the relentless attention the ancient Pueblo people gave the sky and the earth around them. Survival depended upon harmony and cooperation not only among human beings, but among all things—the animate and the less animate, since rocks and mountains were known to move, to travel occasionally.

The ancient Pueblos believed the Earth and the Sky were sisters (or sister and brother in the post-Christian version). As long as good family relations are maintained, then the Sky will continue to bless her sister, the Earth, with rain, and the Earth's children will continue to survive. But the old stories recall incidents in which troublesome spirits or beings threaten the earth. In one story, a malicious ka'tsina, called the Gambler, seizes the Shiwana, or Rainclouds, the Sun's beloved children.* The Shiwana are snared in magical power late one afternoon on a high mountain top. The Gambler takes the Rainclouds to his mountain stronghold where he locks them in the north room of his house. What was his idea? The Shiwana were beyond value. They brought life to all things on earth. The Gambler wanted a big stake to wager in his games of chance. But such greed, even on the part of only one being, had the effect of threatening the survival of all life on earth. Sun Youth, aided by old Grandmother Spider, outsmarts the Gambler and the rigged game, and the Rainclouds are set free. The drought ends, and once more life thrives on earth.

THROUGH THE STORIES WE HEAR WHO WE ARE

All summer the people watch the west horizon, scanning the sky from south to north for rain clouds. Corn must have moisture at the time the tassels form. Otherwise pollination will be incomplete, and the ears will

* Ka'tsina—Ka'tsinas are spirit beings who roam the earth and who inhabit kachina masks worn in Pueblo ceremonial dances.

be stunted and shriveled. An inadequate harvest may bring disaster. Stories told at Hopi, Zuni, and at Acoma and Laguna describe drought and starvation as recently as 1900. Precipitation in west-central New Mexico averages fourteen inches annually. The western pueblos are located at altitudes over 5,600 feet above sea level, where winter temperatures at night fall below freezing. Yet evidence of their presence in the high desert plateau country goes back ten thousand years. The ancient Pueblo people not only survived in this environment, but many years they thrived. In A.D. 1100 the people at Chaco Canyon had built cities with apartment buildings of stone five stories high. Their sophistication as sky-watchers was surpassed only by Mayan and Inca astronomers. Yet this vast complex of knowledge and belief, amassed for thousands of years, was never recorded in writing.

Instead, the ancient Pueblo people depended upon collective memory through successive generations to maintain and transmit an entire culture, a world view complete with proven strategies for survival. The oral narrative, or "story," became the medium in which the complex of Pueblo knowledge and belief was maintained. Whatever the event or the subject, the ancient people perceived the world and themselves within that world as part of an ancient continuous story composed of innumerable bundles of other stories.

The ancient Pueblo vision of the world was inclusive. The impulse was to leave nothing out. Pueblo oral tradition necessarily embraced all levels of human experience. Otherwise, the collective knowledge and beliefs comprising ancient Pueblo culture would have been incomplete. Thus stories about the Creation and Emergence of human beings and animals into this World continue to be retold each year for four days and four nights during the winter solstice. The "humma-hah" stories related events from the time long ago when human beings were still able to communicate with animals and other living things. But, beyond these two preceding categories, the Pueblo oral tradition knew no boundaries. Accounts of the appearance of the first Europeans in Pueblo country or of the tragic encounters between Pueblo people and Apache raiders were no more and no less important than stories about the biggest mule deer ever taken or adulterous couples surprised in cornfields and chicken coops. Whatever happened, the ancient people instinctively sorted events and details into a loose narrative structure. Everything became a story.

▪ ▪ ▪ Traditionally everyone, from the youngest child to the oldest person, was expected to listen and to be able to recall or tell a portion, if only a small detail, from a narrative account or story. Thus the remembering and retelling were a communal process. Even if a key figure, an elder who knew much more than others, were to die unexpectedly, the system would remain intact. Through the efforts of a great many people, the community was able to piece together valuable accounts and crucial information that might otherwise have died with an individual.

Communal storytelling was a self-correcting process in which listeners were encouraged to speak up if they noted an important fact or detail omitted. The people were happy to listen to two or three different versions of the same event or the same humma-hah story. Even conflicting versions of an incident were welcomed for the entertainment they provided. Defenders of each version might joke and tease one another, but seldom were there any direct confrontations. Implicit in the Pueblo oral tradition was the awareness that loyalties, grudges, and kinship must always influence the narrator's choices as she emphasizes to listeners this is the way *she* has always heard the story told. The ancient Pueblo people sought a communal truth, not an absolute. For them this truth lived somewhere within the web of differing versions, disputes over minor points, outright contradictions tangling with old feuds and village rivalries.

A dinner-table conversation, recalling a deer hunt forty years ago when the largest mule deer ever was taken, inevitably stimulates similar memories in listeners. But hunting stories were not merely after-dinner entertainment. These accounts contained information of critical importance about behavior and migration patterns of mule deer. Hunting stories carefully described key landmarks and locations of fresh water. Thus a deer-hunt story might also serve as a "map." Lost travelers, and lost piñon-nut gatherers, have been saved by sighting a rock formation they recognize only because they once heard a hunting story describing this rock formation.

The importance of cliff formations and water holes does not end with hunting stories. As offspring of the Mother Earth, the ancient Pueblo people could not conceive of themselves without a specific landscape. Location, or "place," nearly always plays a central role in the Pueblo oral narratives. Indeed, stories are most frequently recalled as people are passing by a specific geographical feature or the exact place where a story takes place. The precise date of the incident often is less important than the place or location of the happening. "Long, long ago," "a long time ago," "not too long ago," and "recently" are usually how stories are classified in terms of time. But the places where the stories occur are precisely located, and prominent geographical details recalled, even if the landscape is well-known to listeners. Often because the turning point in the narrative involved a peculiarity or special quality of a rock or tree or plant found only at that place. Thus, in the case of many of the Pueblo narratives, it is impossible to determine which came first: the incident or the geographical feature which begs to be brought alive in a story that features some unusual aspect of this location.

There is a giant sandstone boulder about a mile north of Old Laguna, on the road to Paguate. It is ten feet tall and twenty feet in circumference. When I was a child, and we would pass this boulder driving to Paguate village, someone usually made reference to the story about Kochininako, Yellow Woman, and the Estrucuyo, a monstrous giant who nearly ate her. The Twin Hero Brothers saved Kochininako, who had been out hunting rabbits to take home to feed her mother and sisters. The Hero Brothers had heard her cries just in time. The Estrucuyo had cornered her in a cave too small to fit its monstrous head. Kochininako had already thrown to the Estrucuyo all her rabbits, as well as her moccasins and most of her clothing. Still the creature had not been satisfied. After killing the Estrucuyo with their bows and arrows, the Twin Hero Brothers slit open the Estrucuyo and cut out its heart. They threw the heart as far as they could. The monster's heart landed there, beside the old trail to Paguate village, where the sandstone boulder rests now.

It may be argued that the existence of the boulder precipitated the creation of a story to explain it. But sandstone boulders and sandstone formations of strange shapes abound in the Laguna Pueblo area. Yet most of them do not have stories. Often the crucial element in a narrative is the terrain—some specific detail of the setting.

A high dark mesa rises dramatically from a grassy plain fifteen miles southeast of Laguna, in an area known as Swanee. On the grassy plain one hundred and forty years ago, my great-grandmother's uncle and his brother-in-law were grazing their herd of sheep. Because visibility on the plain extends for over twenty miles, it wasn't until the two sheepherders came near the high dark mesa that the Apaches were able to stalk them. Using the mesa to obscure their approach, the raiders swept around from both ends of the mesa. My great-grandmother's relatives were killed, and the herd lost. The high dark mesa played a critical role: the mesa had compromised the safety which the openness of the plains had seemed to assure. Pueblo and Apache alike relied upon the terrain, the very earth herself, to give them protection and aid. Human activities or needs were maneuvered to fit the existing surroundings and conditions. I imagine the last afternoon of my distant ancestors as warm and sunny for late September. They might have been traveling slowly, bringing the sheep closer to Laguna in preparation for the approach of colder weather. The grass was tall and only beginning to change from green to a yellow which matched the late-afternoon sun shining off it. There might have been comfort in the warmth and the sight of the sheep fattening on good pasture which lulled my ancestors into their fatal inattention. They might have had a rifle whereas the Apaches had only bows and arrows. But there would have been four or five Apache raiders, and the surprise attack would have canceled any advantage the rifles gave them.

Survival in any landscape comes down to making the best use of all available resources. On that particular September afternoon, the raiders made better use of the Swanee terrain than my poor ancestors did. Thus the high dark mesa and the story of the two lost Laguna herders became inextricably linked. The memory of them and their story resides in part with the high black mesa. For as long as the mesa stands, people within the family and clan will be reminded of the story of that afternoon long ago. Thus the continuity and accuracy of the oral narratives are reinforced by the landscape—and the Pueblo interpretation of that landscape is *maintained*.

THE MIGRATION STORY: AN INTERIOR JOURNEY

The Laguna Pueblo migration stories refer to specific places—mesas, springs, or cottonwood trees—not only locations which can be visited still, but also locations which lie directly on the state highway route linking Paguate village with Laguna village. In traveling this road as a child with older Laguna people I first heard a few of the stories from that much larger body of stories linked with the Emergence and Migration.* It may be coincidental that Laguna people continue to follow the same route which, according to the Migration story, the ancestors followed south from the Emergence Place. It may be that the route is merely the shortest and best

* The Emergence—All the human beings, animals, and life which had been created emerged from the four worlds below when the earth became habitable.
The Migration—The Pueblo people emerged into the Fifth World, but they had already been warned they would have to travel and search before they found the place they were meant to live.

route for car, horse, or foot traffic between Laguna and Paguate villages. But if the stories about boulders, springs, and hills are actually remnants from a ritual that retraces the creation and emergence of the Laguna Pueblo people as a culture, as the people they became, then continued use of that route creates a unique relationship between the ritual-mythic world and the actual, everyday world. A journey from Paguate to Laguna down the long incline of Paguate Hill retraces the original journey from the Emergence Place, which is located slightly north of the Paguate village. Thus the landscape between Paguate and Laguna takes on a deeper significance: the landscape resonates the spiritual or mythic dimension of the Pueblo world even today.

Although each Pueblo culture designates a specific Emergence Place—usually a small natural spring edged with mossy sandstone and full of cattails and wild watercress—it is clear that they do not agree on any single location or natural spring as the one and only true Emergence Place. Each Pueblo group recounts its own stories about Creation, Emergence, and Migration, although they all believe that all human beings, with all the animals and plants, emerged at the same place and at the same time.*

Natural springs are crucial sources of water for all life in the high desert plateau country. So the small spring near Paguate village is literally the source and continuance of life for the people in the area. The spring also functions on a spiritual level, recalling the original Emergence Place and linking the people and the spring water to all other people and to that moment when the Pueblo people became aware of themselves as they are even now. The Emergence was an emergence into a precise cultural identity. Thus the Pueblo stories about the Emergence and Migration are not to be taken as literally as the anthropologists might wish. Prominent geographical features and landmarks which are mentioned in the narratives exist for ritual purposes, not because the Laguna people actually journeyed south for hundreds of years from Chaco Canyon or Mesa Verde, as the archaeologists say, or eight miles from the site of the natural springs at Paguate to the sandstone hilltop at Laguna.

The eight miles, marked with boulders, mesas, springs, and river cross-

* Creation—Tse'itsi'nako, Thought Woman, the Spider, thought about it, and everything she thought came into being. First she thought of three sisters for herself, and they helped her think of the rest of the Universe, including the Fifth World and the four worlds below. *The Fifth World* is the world we are living in today. There are four previous worlds below this world.

ings, are actually a ritual circuit or path which marks the interior journey the Laguna people made: a journey of awareness and imagination in which they emerged from being within the earth and from everything included in earth to the culture and people they became, differentiating themselves for the first time from all that had surrounded them, always aware that interior distances cannot be reckoned in physical miles or in calendar years.

The narratives linked with prominent features of the landscape between Paguate and Laguna delineate the complexities of the relationship which human beings must maintain with the surrounding natural world if they hope to survive in this place. Thus the journey was an interior process of the imagination, a growing awareness that being human is somehow different from all other life—animal, plant, and inanimate. Yet we are all from the same source: the awareness never deteriorated into Cartesian duality, cutting off the human from the natural world.

The people found the opening into the Fifth World too small to allow them or any of the animals to escape. They had sent a fly out through the small hole to tell them if it was the world which the Mother Creator had promised. It was, but there was the problem of getting out. The antelope tried to butt the opening to enlarge it, but the antelope enlarged it only a little. It was necessary for the badger with her long claws to assist the antelope, and at last the opening was enlarged enough so that all the people and animals were able to emerge up into the Fifth World. The human beings could not have emerged without the aid of antelope and badger. The human beings depended upon the aid and charity of the animals. Only through interdependence could the human beings survive. Families belonged to clans, and it was by clan that the human being joined with the animal and plant world. Life on the high arid plateau became viable when the human beings were able to imagine themselves as sisters and brothers to the badger, antelope, clay, yucca, and sun. Not until they could find a viable relationship to the terrain, the landscape they found themselves in, could they *emerge*. Only at the moment the requisite balance between human and *other* was realized could the Pueblo people become a culture, a distinct group whose population and survival remained stable despite the vicissitudes of climate and terrain.

Landscape thus has similarities with dreams. Both have the power to seize terrifying feelings and deep instincts and translate them into images—visual, aural, tactile—into the concrete where human beings may more readily confront and channel the terrifying instincts or powerful emotions into rituals and narratives which reassure the individual while reaffirming cherished values of the group. The identity of the individual as a part of the group and the greater Whole is strengthened, and the terror of facing the world alone is extinguished.

Even now, the people at Laguna Pueblo spend the greater portion of social occasions recounting recent incidents or events which have occurred in the Laguna area. Nearly always, the discussion will precipitate the re-telling of older stories about similar incidents or other stories connected with a specific place. The stories often contain disturbing or provocative material, but are nonetheless told in the presence of children and women. The effect of these interfamily or interclan exchanges is the reassurance for each person that she or he will never be separated or apart from the clan, no matter what might happen. Neither the worst blunders or disasters nor the greatest financial prosperity and joy will ever be permitted to isolate anyone from the rest of the group. In the ancient times, cohesiveness was all that stood between extinction and survival, and, while the individual certainly was recognized, it was always as an individual simultaneously bonded to family and clan by a complex bundle of custom and ritual. You are never the first to suffer a grave loss or profound humiliation. You are never the first, and you understand that you will probably not be the last to commit or be victimized by a repugnant act. Your family and clan are able to go on at length about others now passed on, others older or more experienced than you who suffered similar losses.

The wide deep arroyo near the Kings Bar (located across the reservation borderline) has over the years claimed many vehicles. A few years ago, when a Vietnam veteran's new red Volkswagen rolled backwards into the arroyo while he was inside buying a six-pack of beer, the story of his loss joined the lively and large collection of stories already connected with that big arroyo. I do not know whether the Vietnam veteran was consoled when he was told the stories about the other cars claimed by the ravenous arroyo. All his savings of combat pay had gone for the red Volkswagen. But this man could not have felt any worse than the man who, some years before, had left his children and mother-in-law in his station wagon with the engine running. When he came out of the liquor store his station wagon was gone. He found it and its passengers upside down in the big arroyo. Broken bones, cuts and bruises, and a total wreck of the car. The big arroyo has a wide mouth. Its existence needs no explanation. People in the area regard the arroyo much as they might regard a living being, which has a certain character and personality. I seldom drive past that wide deep arroyo without feeling a familiarity with and even a strange affection for this arroyo. Because as treacherous as it may be, the arroyo maintains a strong connection between human beings and the earth. The arroyo demands from us the caution and attention that constitute respect. It is this sort of respect the old believers have in mind when they tell us we must respect and love the earth.

Hopi Pueblo elders have said that the austere and, to some eyes, barren plains and hills surrounding their mesa-top villages actually help to nurture the spirituality of the Hopi *way*. The Hopi elders say the Hopi people might have settled in locations far more lush where daily life would not have been so grueling. But there on the high silent sandstone mesas that overlook the sandy arid expanses stretching to all horizons, the Hopi elders say the Hopi people must "live by their prayers" if they are to survive. The Hopi way cherishes the intangible: the riches realized from interaction and interrelationships with all beings above all else. Great abundances of material things, even food, the Hopi elders believe, tend to lure human attention away from what is most valuable and important. The views of the Hopi elders are not much different from those elders in all the Pueblos.

The bare vastness of the Hopi landscape emphasizes the visual impact of every plant, every rock, every arroyo. Nothing is overlooked or taken for granted. Each ant, each lizard, each lark is imbued with great value simply because the creature is there, simply because the creature is alive in a place where any life at all is precious. Stand on the mesa edge at Walpai and look west over the bare distances toward the pale blue outlines of the San Francisco peaks where the ka'tsina spirits reside. So little lies between you and the sky. So little lies between you and the earth. One look and you know that simply to survive is a great triumph, that every possible resource is needed, every possible ally—even the most humble insect or reptile. You realize you will be speaking with all of them if you intend to last out the year. Thus it is that the Hopi elders are grateful to the landscape for aiding them in their quest as spiritual people.

THOMAS J. LYON

A Taxonomy of Nature Writing

"... this incomperable lande"—Jean Ribaut, *The Whole & True Discouerye of Terra Florida* (London, 1563)

If we first describe nature writing in quasi-taxonomic terms, that in a general way can help us see what is important about the genre and how its themes are developed. I must introduce a cautionary note, though, before laying out a proposed classification scheme of American nature literature: the types I have listed tend to intergrade, and with great frequency. This may be somewhat irritating to lovers of neatness who would like their categories to be immutable, but nature writing is not in truth a neat and orderly field. Nevertheless, we can make a few sound and, I hope, helpful generalizations. First and most fundamentally, the literature of nature has three main dimensions to it: natural history information, personal responses to nature, and philosophical interpretation of nature. The relative weight or interplay of these three aspects determines all the permutations and categories within the field. If conveying information is almost the whole intention, for example (see the left edge of the spectrum in the chart "Writing About Nature: A Spectrum"), the writing in question is likely to be a professional paper or a field guide or handbook, most of which are only intermittently personal or philosophical and also, perhaps, literary only in spots. A good example is Roger Tory Peterson's *A Field Guide to Western Birds* (1961). The brief description of the canyon wren's song, among other little gems in the book, immediately suggests something more than just accuracy. "Voice: A gushing cadence of clear curved notes tripping down the scale."[1] That single line may evoke the entire ambience of a shaded, slickrock canyon somewhere in the Southwest on a June morning. But few people would expect a field guide to be a literary effort.

When expository descriptions of nature, still the dominant aspect of a book, are fitted into a literary design, so that the facts then give rise to some sort of meaning or interpretation, then we have the basic conditions for the natural history essay. The themes that make natural history information into a coherent, literary whole may be stated by the author in the first person, as in John Hay's *Spirit of Survival* (1974), where Hay found in the life histories of terns wonderfully cogent statements of the beauty and vulnerability of life itself—the life we share with these birds; or they may emerge from the facts as related in a third-person, more or less objective fashion. This latter way was Rachel Carson's choice in *The Sea Around Us* (1950, 1961); she arranged the facts of oceanography and marine biology tellingly, so that the drama and interplay of forces pointed inescapably toward a holistic, ecological view of nature. William O. Pruitt used a similar artistic strategy in *Animals of the North* (1967). By concentrating upon the central fact of the cold of the Arctic and showing the myriad adaptations such a climate requires, he brought out the theme of relationship, which is perhaps the essence of ecology.

The defining characteristic of the natural history essay is that whatever the method chosen for presentation, the main burden of the writing is to convey pointed instruction in the facts of nature. As we move toward the right on the spectrum, the role and relative importance of the author loom a bit larger: experience in nature—the feel of being outdoors, the pleasure of looking closely, and the sense of revelation in small things closely attended to—takes an equal or almost equal place with the facts themselves. Where the natural history and the author's presence are more or less balanced, we have the "ramble." This is a classic American form. The author goes forth into nature, usually on a short excursion near home, and records the walk as observer-participant. Almost the entire work of John Burroughs, to take a prominent example, fits into the category of the ramble, from his earliest published bird walks in *Wake-Robin* (1871). Burroughs's own personality and way of responding to the natural scene were very much a part of his writing and were important to his popular success. His intense feeling for the woods and fields of his home ground—there may never have been such a homebody, in all of American literature, as Burroughs—is also a distinguishing mark of the "ramble" type of nature writing. Burroughs became identified with the patchwork of farms and woods in the vicinity of the Catskill Mountains in New York. The writer of rambles usually does not travel far, and seldom to wilderness; he or she is primarily interested in a

Writing About Nature: A Spectrum

			Essays on Experiences in Nature			
Field Guides and Professional Papers	*Natural History Essays*	*Rambles*	*Solitude and Back-Country Living*	*Travel and Adventure*	*Farm Life*	*Man's Role in Nature*
Clarence King, *Systematic Geology* (1878)	John Muir, *Studies in the Sierra* (1874–1875)	John D. Godman, *Rambles of a Naturalist* (1828)	Henry David Thoreau, *Walden* (1854)	William Bartram, *Travels* (1791)	Hector St. John de Crèvecoeur, *Letters from an American Farmer* (1782)	John Burroughs, *Accepting the Universe* (1920)
Olaus Murie, *A Field Guide to Animal Tracks* (1954)	Rachel Carson, *The Sea Around Us* (1950)	John Burroughs, *Wake-Robin* (1871)	Henry Beston, *The Outermost House* (1928)	Henry David Thoreau, *The Maine Woods* (1865)	Liberty Hyde Bailey, *The Harvest of the Year to the Tiller of the Soul* (1927)	Joseph Wood Krutch, *The Great Chain of Life* (1956)
Roger Tory Peterson, *A Field Guide to Western Birds* (1961)	Ann Zwinger and Beatrice Willard, *The Land Above the Trees* (1972)	John K. Terres, *From Laurel Hill to Siler's Bog* (1969)	Sigurd F. Olson, *Listening Point* (1958)	Charles Sheldon, *The Wilderness of the Upper Yukon* (1911)	Wendell Berry, *A Continuous Harmony* (1972)	John Hay, *In Defense of Nature* (1969)
	John Hay, *Spirit of Survival* (1974)	Annie Dillard, *Pilgrim at Tinker Creek* (1974)	Edward Abbey, *Desert Solitaire* (1968)	Edward Hoagland, *Notes from the Century Before* (1969)		
				Barry Lopez, *Arctic Dreams* (1986)		

loving study of the near, and often the pastoral. To say that the ramble is local, however, or that it often takes place on worked-over ground, is not to imply that it is in any way superficial. As Annie Dillard showed in *Pilgrim at Tinker Creek* (1974), deep familiarity with the most ordinary landscapes can blossom into immense themes.

Continuing rightward on the spectrum, we begin to move away from the primacy of natural history facts to a clear emphasis on the writer's experience. In essays of experience, the author's first-hand contact with nature is the frame for the writing: putting up a cabin in the wilderness (as Richard Proenneke did, in *One Man's Wilderness,* 1973), canoeing down a clear, wild river (John McPhee, *Coming into the Country,* 1977), walking the beach at night (Henry Beston, *The Outermost House,* 1928), rebuilding the soil of a rundown farm (Louis Bromfield, *Malabar Farm,* 1948), or contemplating a desert sunset (Edward Abbey, *Desert Solitaire,* 1968). And much else. Instruction in natural history is often present in the "nature experience" essay, but it is not what structures the book. We are placed behind the writer's eyes here, looking out on this interesting and vital world and moving through it with the protagonist.

Within the broad category of the essay of experience in nature, there are three fairly well-defined subtypes, each with a distinctive avenue for philosophical reflection. Essays of solitude or escape from the city, as might be expected, work much with the contrast between conventional existence and the more intense, more wakeful life in contact with nature. This subtype, like the ramble, is a classic American form, but it tends to be much more critical and radical—compare Thoreau at Walden, anathematizing the false economy of society, and Abbey in the desert, waiting until the engineers drive away in their jeep, then pulling up and throwing away the stakes they had pounded into the ground to mark the location for a new, paved road.

Accounts of travel and adventure (which usually have a strong element of solitude in them) often present the same sort of contrast between the too-safe, habituated existence left behind and the vivid life of discovery. The travel and adventure writer often seems like a ramble writer gone wild; there is less emphasis on natural history and more on movement, solitude, and wildness. Often, the account is framed on the great mythic pattern of departure, initiation, and return,[2] and always the account gains meaning from the basic American circumstance that wilderness, where the traveler and adventurer usually go, has always in our history been considered a realm apart. It is true that some travelers, such as William Bartram, have been deeply interested in the natural history of the new territories they explored: for example, in the *Travels* (1791), Bartram made extensive lists of the species he encountered. Nonetheless, the exhilaration of release from civilization, the sense of self-contained and self-reliant movement, and above all, the thrill of the new, are the prominent qualities here.

The farm essay, with its rooted and consistent emphasis upon stewardship and work (rather than study, or solitude, or discovery), may seem at first to be unrelated to the nature essay. It might be argued, too, that since farming is "only" about ten thousand years old, whereas our connections with wilderness are unimaginably deeper, the entire sensibility may be different. The sublime, so important to the aesthetic of the traveler, and even to the rambler, seems somehow foreign to the farm. But we should be alert to blendings. In practice, American farm writers from Hector St. John de Crèvecoeur in the late eighteenth century to Wendell Berry in the present day have paid close attention to the wildlife on and around their places, and have conveyed the deep, poetic pull of nature on the spirit. Berry, for example, describes how observing some birds at his family's land in Kentucky became instrumental in his development of a "placed" point of view. Stewardship, so prominent in farm literature, also has ecological ramifications; the common understanding of American farm writers is that fitting into natural patterns, rather than imposing some sort of abstract order upon them, is the farmer's proper role. In this ethical commitment, nature writers with an agrarian point of view join with the mainstream philosophy of American nature writing.

On the right-hand edge of the spectrum are the analytic and comprehensive works on man and nature. In these works, interpretation predominates, and the natural history facts or the personal experiences are decidedly secondary. They are illustrations for the argument. Here, philosophy is all. The actual points that are made, typically, are not different from those made in natural history essays, or personal-experience essays, but the mode of presentation tends to be more abstract and scholarly.

I need to add here that the usual terminology covering all of the forms of nature writing tends to lump them. They have all, at one time or another, been called "natural history essays" or "nature essays" interchangeably. I see no real problem in this state of affairs, and not much practical benefit in any attempt to promote an academically rigorous classification. Nature writing itself, in any case, would not rest easily in any static system, prizing as it does vitality and variety, the virtues of its subject. The categories offered here are meant simply to show the breadth of the spectrum and to help indicate some of the special powers each type within the genre may possess.

Whatever the artistic means chosen, and whatever the type of essay we may choose to call a certain piece of nature writing, the fundamental goal of the genre is to turn our attention outward to the activity of nature. This is so, across the spectrum. The literary record time and again displays the claim that there is a lifting and a clarifying of perception inherent in this refocusing, which opens up something like a new world. The sense of wonder conveyed is perhaps very much in the American grain; it may eventually be seen as a more important discovery beyond the finding of new lands.

NOTES

1. Roger Tory Peterson, *A Field Guide to Western Birds* (Boston: Houghton Mifflin, 1961), p. 223.

2. See Joseph Campbell, *The Hero with a Thousand Faces* (Princeton: Princeton University Press, 1949). I am grateful to Professor Joe Gordon of the Colorado College for pointing out this pattern's ubiquity in nature writing.

MICHAEL BRANCH

Indexing American Possibilities

■ ■ ■

THE NATURAL HISTORY WRITING OF BARTRAM, WILSON, AND AUDUBON

During the half-century between the publication of Thomas Jefferson's *Notes on the State of Virginia* (1785) and Ralph Waldo Emerson's *Nature* (1836), American natural history was a flourishing discipline that helped nurture the emergence of a culture distinctively contingent upon the land.[1] This period, which I identify as "early romantic," has received little attention from ecocritics, who more often focus upon Henry Thoreau and his literary descendants—a distinguished lineage that includes figures such as John Muir, John Burroughs, Aldo Leopold, and Edward Abbey. We too often forget that Thoreau is the descendant of a literary tradition as certainly as he is the progenitor of one, and that nature writing from *Walden* on is prefigured and indirectly influenced by a rich tradition of late-eighteenth- and early-nineteenth-century natural history writing.[2]

In this essay I wish to survey briefly early romantic ideas about nature in the New World, and raise some questions about the status and function of American natural history studies around the turn of the century. How is the early romantic enthusiasm for natural history a product of the changing intellectual climate of period? If, as I would argue, natural history writing should be viewed as *both* science and as belles lettres, what is the larger relationship between American natural history studies and the rise of a distinctively American culture during the early romantic period?[3] How do naturalists' representations of the relationship between human and non-human nature contribute to the ecological awareness that has inspired and sustained the American nature-writing tradition? Using the work of botanist William Bartram, ornithologist Alexander Wilson, and painter John

James Audubon, I wish to suggest that early romantic natural history introduced a number of ideas that are essential to the post-Thoreauvian literature of nature. Before we turn to Bartram, Wilson, and Audubon, however, let us make a broad sketch of how changing perceptions of nonhuman nature made their writing possible.

▪ ▪ ▪ During the eighteenth century the confluence of several currents of European thought helped to mitigate the American aversion to wild nature expressed by the Puritan icon of "the howling wilderness." Of primary importance was the influence of deism, the rationalist "natural religion" that held that the creator's hand was evident in the intricate perfection of the natural world. Behind the deist association of God and nature were the century's vast accomplishments in natural science, which continued to reveal the complex precision of geological and astronomical systems. Indeed, natural theologians including John Ray and William Paley had already begun to accord nature a kind of scriptural status, as is apparent from the title of Ray's influential book, *The Wisdom of God Manifested in the Works of the Creation* (1691). According to deism, the "wilderness pleases" because it is the landscape least encumbered by humans, and therefore most directly illustrative of the creator. In America, where Puritan orthodoxy had been a primary source of enmity toward wilderness, deist theology precipitated a radical revision of the human relationship to nonhuman nature.[4]

Once deism had introduced the maxim that nature was an expression of divinity, a rescission of the seventeenth-century notion of "howling wilderness" was inevitable. A primary catalyst for change in this perception of nature came in 1756, with the publication of Edmund Burke's treatise upon the sublime and beautiful. Reviving Longinus's concept of the sublime from antiquity, Burke's influential distinction reshaped conventional aesthetic categories to include as ennobling the feelings of awe and terror. In one sense, the reintroduction of the sublime was simply a backlash against the excessive rigidity of conventional eighteenth-century aesthetics; like the vogue for literary and architectural Gothic and the popular interest in primitivism as espoused by Rousseau and Defoe, the rise of the sublime was a reaction to the rationalist sensibility of the age. In addition to challenging the severity of neoclassical aesthetics, Burke's thesis also legitimized the feelings so often induced by the vast, untamed wilderness of the New World. Significantly, the concept of the sublime also shifted emphasis from the qualities of the landscape toward the feelings the landscape engendered in the observer. As the fear produced by Niagara's cataract came to seem more worthy of experience than the repose occasioned by an impeccably ordered courtly garden, the aesthetic of the sublime established a dynamic, emotional connection between the human spirit and the grandeur of wild nature.[5]

The early romantic connection between human and nonhuman nature also helped nurture the rise of natural history studies in America. If the national faith was to be based upon the vast, uncorrupted wilderness of the new continent, it became imperative to explore, survey, and describe that wilderness as a means both of appraising and expressing American prospects. Just as Thomas Jefferson had suggested that the diversity and size of American animals was emblematic of the republic's rising glory, turn-of-the-century America looked increasingly to natural history as an index of American possibilities. The call for a national literature—which was ubiquitous in the early nineteenth century—was consistently expressed *in terms of* American nature. In an impulse we might call the "topographical imperative," Americans demanded a culture that would be commensurate with the greatness of the land: as expansive as its prairies, as lofty as its mountains, as prolific as its forests. In short, natural history functioned as an expression of America's need to discover the means by which its national destiny would be enacted.[6]

Of course, there were other important reasons for the growth and influence of American natural history studies. The work of establishing America's independence had been finished, and citizens could devote more attention to the arts and sciences. This consequent leisure was also manifest in the vogue for "scenic tours," and for amateur naturalism such as the casual bird-watching which was so popular during the period. Before the end of the eighteenth century, a gentleman or lady could not have considered natural history to be within the domain of their proper affairs, but deism and enlightenment science had widely disseminated the idea that nature could be learned *from* as well as *about*. From every corner of Western culture, the nexus of natural history and literature was receiving the blessing of romanticism. Coleridge in England, Goethe in Germany, and Rousseau in France were exemplars of just how provocative and productive the blend could be. Thanks largely to the influence of Gilbert White's *Natural History of Selborne* (1789) in England and William Bartram's *Travels* (1791) in America, the nature essay began to develop toward the turn of the century into a genre of its own—an informative and stylistically accomplished convergence of science and romanticism.

To some extent, the early nineteenth century turn to the land functioned as an apology for a lack of American culture, and to some degree the vogue for natural history expressed a need to compensate for a dearth of cultural history. But the anxiety of European influence had begun to wane, and there grew in Americans a very real sense that—however unlikely the concept—wilderness would itself inspire culture. The American continent had perpetually been viewed as regenerative, and just as seventeenth-century Americans believed that an oppressed Protestant might begin anew in Massachusetts, or an impoverished laborer might begin anew in Virginia, nineteenth-century Americans believed that culture itself could begin anew, that its seed would germinate and flourish in the rich soil of the New World.

In order to prosper, however, American natural history would have to liberate itself from the colonial impulse to defer to British authority in the field. Until the late eighteenth century, most Americans assumed that British museums were the proper repository for specimens gathered on either side of the Atlantic, and the idea of maintaining permanent natural history collections in America was entertained by only a few. By the early nineteenth century, however, Americans were demanding of their science—just as they were demanding of their art and literature—a purging of European influence and a turning to the uncorrupted cultural resources of the American land. One critic urged naturalists to "study and examine for themselves, instead of blindly using the eyes of foreign naturalists, or bowing implicitly to a foreign bar of criticism." Just as the topographical imperative enjoined a literature commensurate with the greatness of the land, American naturalists were urged to construct monuments to science that would "rise beautifully as our hills, imperishable, and lofty as their summits, which tower sublimely above the clouds."[7]

As a kind of artistic and scientific correlative to the idea of manifest destiny, the topographical imperative decisively associated prospects for American culture with the land itself. By the early nineteenth century, Americans had concluded that indigenous species should be studied and housed in America, and that funding for conducting surveys, creating permanent collections, and publishing natural history at home was essential to nurturing the emergence of American culture. Efforts to establish

American natural history were successfully carried forward on the wave of romantic nationalism which swept early-nineteenth-century America, and the opinion that wilderness was both a natural and a cultural resource finally struck roots in the scientific and literary imagination of the young republic.

The work of William Bartram, Alexander Wilson, and John James Audubon illustrates the important contributions made by natural history writers during the early romantic period. Indeed, many of their characteristic thematic concerns became essential to both nineteenth- and twentieth-century environmental literature. First, their brand of natural history helped to define a uniquely American subject and style; these writers turned west in an attempt to define the "distinctively American" in terms of the impressive natural resources of the young nation. Second, the romantic natural historians helped to relocate divinity in wilderness; elaborating upon the deistic presupposition that the creator is manifest in nature, they affirmed America's moral advantage over domesticated Europe by emphasizing God's sublime presence in the New World landscape. Third, these naturalists were partially motivated by an impulse to document the natural history of an evanescent frontier and its nonhuman inhabitants; early romantic naturalists attempted to delineate a wilderness and to mourn its irrevocable loss before the march of westward expansion. Finally, Bartram, Wilson, and Audubon helped introduce a pattern of ecological thinking in American culture; through emphasis upon a feeling of membership in a natural community and upon the morally regenerative qualities of nature, these writers offered an alternative to the dominant and dominating expansionary ethos of the age, and thereby helped initiate a minority tradition of environmental concern into American intellectual history.

▪▪▪ In considering the cultural value of natural history studies, we should begin with William Bartram, whose *Travels* (1791) is widely recognized as both a scientific and a literary classic of the period.[8] His father was John Bartram of Philadelphia, whom Linnaeus called "the greatest natural botanist in the world" (Elman 26), and whose famous botanical garden at Kingsessing (just outside Philadelphia) was the finest in the colonies. William grew under his father's tutelage to become the greatest American naturalist of his age. As a boy William had learned to identify and sketch plants with prodigious skill and had accompanied his father on several arduous botanical excursions into the wilderness. Using these experiences as his guide,

William set out alone in March 1773 on the four years of wanderings that inspired *Travels*. From a natural historical standpoint, the record of Bartram's journey provided an encyclopedic catalogue of the flora and fauna of the American wilderness, and he returned with specimens and drawings that were invaluable to scientists both in America and abroad.

Although Bartram discovered and described a variety of species that were new to science, his book's greater contribution is the narrative itself—the thoughtful and enthusiastic account of a person fully immersed in the experience of American wilderness. Indeed, Bartram's descriptions are so spontaneous and sincere, so precise in their depictions, so reflective of nature's wonders and of a sensibility capable of appreciating them, so free of the influence of European literary models, that *Travels* stands as a landmark accomplishment in American literature. A vernacular relative of the decorous eighteenth-century "ramble," Bartram's book also helped establish the American genre of the nature essay that, from Thoreau to Barry Lopez, has been an important vehicle for American literary aspirations. And like his friend Thomas Jefferson's *Notes on the State of Virginia,* Bartram's *Travels* had considerable influence upon the literary as well as the scientific minds of Europe. As an exception to the rule that literary capital moved westward across the Atlantic, Bartram's influence appears in the work of Coleridge and Wordsworth and, to a lesser extent, Shelley, Carlyle, and Blake as well. Coleridge described Bartram's *Travels* as "a work of high merit every way," and even wrote to Emerson that "all American libraries ought to provide themselves with that kind of book; and keep them as a future *biblical* article."[9]

Coleridge's farsighted recognition of *Travels* as a seminal American text is rendered even more prescient by his allusion to the book as a kind of Holy Writ. Indeed, it was Bartram's devout faith in the divinity of nature that distinguished his work from most scientific tracts and consequently helped open the way for American literature to explore the spiritual resources of the wilderness. Like his fellow Quaker John Woolman, Bartram was sensitive to signs of divinity in his surroundings; as a naturalist, and as the son of an ardently anticlerical naturalist, he believed divinity to be immanent in that wilderness which so constantly awakened his sense of wonder.[10] Bartram's philosophy was a natural extension of the Quaker "doctrine of light": he insisted that plants and animals, as well as slaves and Indians, had been touched by God with the "dignity, propriety, and beauty of virtue." As Ernest Earnest has observed, Bartram's doctrine of love for nature "is not merely the tender-hearted benevolence of the sensibility school; it is part of his radical view of the nature of animal creation" (151, 144). In the "Introduction" to his *Travels,* which is itself an early example of the nature essay in America, Bartram observed:

> We admire the mechanism of a watch, and the fabric of a piece of brocade, as being the production of art; these merit our admiration, and must excite our esteem for the ingenious artist or modifier; but nature is the work of God omnipotent; and an elephant, nay even this world, is comparatively but a very minute part of his works. If then the visible, the mechanical part of the animal creation, the mere material part, is so admirably beautiful, harmonious, and incomprehensible, what must be the intellectual system? that inexpressibly more essential principle, which secretly operates within? that which animates the inimitable machines, which gives them motion, empowers them to act, speak, and perform, this must be divine and immortal? (21)

Bartram's appreciation for the wonderful intricacy of natural systems and his belief that every living thing manifests "the divine and inimitable workmanship" (17) combined to produce a sensibility that may be described as proto-ecological. Throughout the *Travels* Bartram's incisive observations reveal and celebrate the fabric of interrelationships that he recognized in the wilderness. Most refreshing is Bartram's awareness of his own membership in the natural community. His pantheistic diction constantly suggests a sense of familial relationship with the flora and fauna whom he considered his "ingenious . . . & esteemed Associates" (Seavey 32). Whether describing conversations with his pet crow or relating narrow escapes from hungry alligators in the swamps of Florida, he was always attuned to the effects his presence had upon the balance of the natural community. As Bartram's introduction to his *Travels* reveals, he was a man who not only delighted in watching spiders, but who was sensitive enough to know when the spiders were watching him.[11]

Beyond this sensitivity to interconnectedness, there is in Bartram a strain of radical nonanthropocentrism which clearly distinguishes him from his contemporaries. The ecophilosophical metaphysic that informs the *Travels* is made even more explicit in one of Bartram's unpublished manuscripts:

> I cannot be so impious; nay my soul revolts, is destroyed by such conjectures as to desire or imagine that man who is guilty of more mischief and wickedness than all the other animals together in this world, should be exclusively

> endowed with the knowledge of the Creator. . . . There is something so aristocratic if a philosopher use the expression or the epithet of the *Dignity of Human Nature*. Because a man as viewed in the chain of animal beings according to the common notions of philosophers, acts the part of an absolute tyrant. His actions and movements must, I think, impress such an idea on the minds of all animals, or intelligent beings.[12]

Philosophically closer to the late-twentieth- than the late-eighteenth-century view of the human place in the cosmos, Bartram's advocacy of nature and his criticism of anthropocentric pretensions to superiority clearly prefigure the "ecocentric egalitarianism" of much contemporary ecophilosophy; his criticism of the traditional hierarchical paradigm of the chain of being suggests a respect for the *dignity* of *all* nature, and powerfully expresses the romantic belief that divinity is diffused throughout nature. By uniting natural history with literature, science with spirit, Bartram exemplified the "enlightened naturalist" whom Emerson and Thoreau—as well as Coleridge and Goethe—held in such high esteem.

Although Bartram was an invaluable mentor to naturalists such as Barton, Nuttall, and Michaux, his most accomplished protégé was the ornithologist Alexander Wilson. In 1794, at the age of twenty-eight, Wilson emigrated from Scotland, where he had been a weaver, reformer, poet, painter, and peddler in the mill town of Paisley. In 1802 he had the good fortune to secure employment as a teacher at the Union School in Kingsessing, close to Bartram's botanical garden. Wilson quickly became friends with Bartram, from whom he received encouragement and instruction in drawing and in the study of natural history. Immediately inspired by the beauty and diversity of American birds, Wilson soon devoted his life to their study, and began traveling many thousands of miles on foot in search of undiscovered species. By the time of his death only eleven years after meeting Bartram, Alexander Wilson was the nation's foremost authority on birds, and had completed nearly all nine volumes of his monumental *American Ornithology* (1808–29).[13]

Given his Scottish heritage, it is interesting that Wilson's prodigious accomplishment was motivated largely by his desire to help ground American culture upon the land. Like Jefferson and Bartram before him—both of whom he acknowledged as ornithological predecessors in the introduction to his *American Ornithology*—Wilson assumed very deliberately that his natural history was a contribution not only to science, but to the cultural identity of the nation. According to historian Robert Elman, Wilson expressed

> a somewhat mystical belief . . . that the living riches of America's wilderness formed a common heritage—a kind of unifying fabric—linking all the peoples of diverse ancestry and background to a single destiny in a young, vigorous nation. (65)

Wilson had promised that if "the generous hand of patriotism be stretched forth to assist and cherish the rising arts and literature of our country . . . [they will] increase and flourish with a vigor, a splendor and usefulness inferior to no other on earth." Thomas Paine and (then President) Thomas Jefferson, both of whom were early subscribers to Wilson's unprecedented volumes, would have agreed that the "unifying fabric" of nature was a crucial determinant of America's evolving national character.[14]

As with Bartram, Wilson's considerable scientific acumen was always entwined with an engaged literary sensibility. If he was a weaver by trade and a peddler by necessity, he was a poet by inclination, and had published his verse long before he began his study of the birds. Wilson's ornithological opus is itself a literary accomplishment, for in addition to eloquent prose describing the appearance and habits of the birds, it also interpolates lyrics of his own composition. Like earlier naturalists including Linnaeus, Wilson understood the study of nature to be an ennobling pursuit that spontaneously engendered a poetic response.

This promising unification of literature and science—an impulse we might call the "poetics of natural history"—is most evident in "The Foresters," Wilson's romantic narrative poem about his twelve hundred mile foot-journey to the falls of Niagara. Although it was over twenty-two hundred lines long, the poem was published serially from July 1809 through March 1810 in the Philadelphia *Port Folio,* and was well received.[15] Although literary history does not remember Wilson as a poet, "The Foresters" is an excellent example of how thoroughly enmeshed were his literary and natural historical sensibilities. The poem's exordium invites readers to "explore/ Scenes new to song, and paths untrod before":

> To Europe's shores, renowned in deathless song,
> Must all the honors of the bard belong?
> . . . .
> While bare black heaths, and brooks of half a mile
> Can rouse the thousand bards of Britain's isle,

. . . .
Our western world, with all its matchless floods,
Our vast transparent lakes and boundless woods,
. . . .
Spread their wild grandeur to the unconscious sky,
In sweetest seasons pass unheeded by;
While scarce one Muse returns the songs they gave,
Or seeks to snatch their glories from the grave.
(*Poems* 147–48, st. 2)

The poem finally reaches its crescendo at Niagara, where the travelers gaze with "holy awe" upon the sublime falls that recall the walls of Mecca. Both as ornithologist and as romantic poet, Wilson responded to the unsung beauty of the American wilderness by leading readers on a pilgrimage into the heart of their own country.

Wilson's writing was often informed by an environmentalist critique of human pretensions to control over the natural world. For example, in "Verses, occasioned by seeing two men sawing timber in an open field, in defiance of a furious storm," Wilson criticized the seemingly indefatigable human urge to destroy nature regardless of the consequences. The speaker of this poem tries in vain to save two sawyers who, bent upon their work and the harvest they have come to reap, refuse to desist from their work during a mounting gale. Heedless of the speaker's warnings and of the power of the natural forces they believe they can dominate, the men are crushed beneath the falling tree:

Now see, ye misbelieving sinners,
Your bloody shins—your saw in flinners,
And roun' about your lugs the ruin,
That your demented foly drew on.
(*Poems* 67, st. 2)

Although Wilson's verse here is mediocre, his objection to the sawyers' self-destructive folly is patent: rather than walking with humility in the natural world, these men have been literally crippled by the "sin" of their arrogant determination to destroy that world.

Wilson's literary brand of natural history also displayed an incipient ecological sensibility, especially in its emphasis upon the crucial role that each species plays in "the economy of nature." For example, in his treatment of the bluebird in *American Ornithology,* Wilson includes a poem explaining to readers that the bird "drags the vile grub from the corn he devours," and should therefore be suffered to visit their crops unmolested (2:161). As an early conservationist, he made pioneering studies of wildlife populations and fatefully projected the devastating impact human settlement would have upon native habitat. Because Wilson could identify and extol the singing of *individual* birds in his neighboring woods, he was uniquely qualified to remark and lament the extirpation of species that inevitably followed the westward movement of the American frontier.

Wilson was even capable of activism on behalf of the birds. When in 1807 good sense would not prevail with merchants who were killing thousands of robins to satisfy the genteel palates of Philadelphia, he wrote an anonymous article to city newspapers explaining that robin flesh was unhealthy because of the birds' heavy diet of pokeberries; though Wilson knew the claim to be entirely false, it effectively curtailed the slaughter of robins for the Philadelphia market.[16] Because Wilson, like his mentor Bartram, understood natural history to be "the contemplation and worship of the *Great First Cause,*" ornithology was a devout mission and protection of fellow creatures an article of faith. Believing that what he studied would inspire American culture because it was inspired by God, Wilson combined his scientific and literary talents in order to record the national treasure of America's birds (*American Ornithology* 2).

▪ ▪ ▪ The idyllic vision of America as a regenerative wilderness had a remarkable incarnation in the career of Jean Jacques Rabin Fougere Audubon, the dandified, aristocratic Frenchman who was reborn in the New World as John James Audubon, the self-styled "American Woodsman." Like Wilson, who had come to America to avoid the Scottish mill masters determined to silence his socialist poetry, Audubon came to the land of the second chance as a wayward youth, leaving behind the history of his illegitimate birth to a French slave trader and his Creole mistress. Audubon arrived in America in 1803, where he weathered business misfortunes and poverty for a quarter century while painting the birds of his adopted homeland. Like Bartram and Wilson before him, Audubon traveled thousands of wilderness miles in order to discover, study, and document native species. Finally, in 1826, he made his startlingly successful debut before the artistic community; the next ten years saw the momentous publication of the 435 plates of the mammoth, double elephant folio edition of *The Birds of America*.[17]

Although his considerable fame has rested upon his outstanding accomplishments as an artist, Audubon was also a talented writer whose colorful descriptions of life on the frontier deserve a permanent place in our literature.[18] His "Episodes," or "Delineations of American Scenery and Character," sixty short essays that cover travel adventures from 1808 to 1834, provide remarkable glimpses of the evanescent phenomenon of the frontier and clearly demonstrate why this renowned "naturalist" should be seen in the context of American romantic literature. For example, "Kentucky Sports" tells of a competition between candle-snuffing, nail-driving masters of the long rifle, and is similar to the marksmanship scenes in Cooper's *The Pioneers*. "The Turtlers" is a detailed account of the mysterious beast that Melville was to record in "The Encantadas." In "Niagara" we read of Audubon's adventures to the cataract so celebrated by William Cullen Bryant and other romantic poets.[19] The rough justice administered to an apprehended confidence man in "The Regulators" recalls the misadventures of the King and the Duke from Twain's *Adventures of Huckleberry Finn*. In "Scipio and the Bear," the exciting details of the hunt prefigure the mature treatment Faulkner would give the subject in "The Bear." Throughout the Episodes, Audubon blends natural and social history into narrative tales designed to provide representative vignettes of life in the American wilderness.[20]

Like Bartram and Wilson, Audubon understood the role of natural historian to be complementary with that of romantic author.[21] In "The Ohio," the very first of his Episodes, Audubon makes explicit his vision of the link between American literary accomplishments and the need for documenting a disappearing wilderness condition:

> I feel with regret that there are on record no satisfactory accounts of the state of that portion of the country, from the time when our people first settled in it. This has not been because no one in America is able to accomplish such an undertaking. Our Irvings and our Coopers have proved themselves fully competent for the task. It has more probably been because the changes have succeeded each other with such rapidity, as almost to rival the movements of their pen. However, it is not too late yet. . . . I hope . . . [t]hey will analyze, as it were, into each component part, the country as it once existed, and will render the picture, as it ought to be, immortal. (*Delineations* 5)

Audubon's own painting and prose were dedicated to just such a project, and in recognition of his talents and objectives, Washington Irving sought government patronage for his work in 1836. Like the work of Bryant,

Cooper, and Irving, Audubon's writing is unmistakably characterized by elements of early romanticism in America: a fondness for the picturesque in natural scenery; a powerful attraction to "the American sublime"; a propensity for melodramatic sentimentality; an enduring interest in Native Americans and in the quotidian existence of settlers, trappers, and woodsmen; an incipient impulse to distinguish nature as a source of moral authority; a stylistic tendency to romanticize characters; and a dramatic inclination to set the scene of his stories upon the threshold of wilderness and civilization.

Also interesting is the peculiar way in which Audubon connects romantic literature and natural history by casting the naturalist in the role of romantic hero. Like Bartram, whose *Travels* influenced Coleridge, and like Wilson, who was probably the model for Wordsworth's peddler in "The Excursion," Audubon was the romantic type of the solitary wanderer—the lonely figure who carried a higher vision of nature on his pilgrimage into the wilderness.[22] In fact, distinctions between the period's romanticized folk heroes and its itinerant naturalists sometimes seem arbitrary. William Bartram's woodsmanship and belief in the divinity of wilderness also distinguish the character of Cooper's Natty Bumppo. Wilson's extensive and perilous explorations are reminiscent of Meriwether Lewis, whose mysterious death he investigated in 1810.[23] The tireless Audubon, forever in search of adventure, resembles the mythicized figure of Daniel Boone, with whom the naturalist claimed to have hunted in Kentucky.

Audubon provides the most fascinating study of the naturalist as romantic hero because he so self-consciously cultivated the identity. Like his own hero, Benjamin Franklin, who played the noble American rustic to great effect in the French court, Audubon depended for his success upon his mastery of the role of American Woodsman. Although taught to excel at the aristocratic arts of dancing, fencing, and sporting finery, he visited European drawing rooms clothed in fringed buckskins, carrying a walking stick, and wearing his hair long and dressed with bear grease.[24] An enthusiastic reader of Byron and Scott, as well as Cooper and Irving, Audubon knew—in his various roles as a writer, naturalist, painter, and public figure—how to satisfy his audience's romantic appetite for wilderness. In many of the Episodes, Audubon simply writes himself into the leading role in narratives he heard while traveling the riverboats, wagon paths, and Indian trails of the old Southwest. It is not surprising, therefore, that he has been received into American culture according to the romantic American Woodsman persona he projected. Eudora Welty's short story "A Still Moment" (1943), Jessamyn West's play *A Mirror for the Sky* (1948), Robert Penn Warren's poem series *Audubon: A Vision* (1969), and Scott Russell Sanders's novel *Wonders Hidden* (1984) all commemorate and perpetuate the image of Audubon the romantic.

Alton Lindsey has coined the term *ornitheology* to denote bird study as the "popular faith" of which "John James Audubon [was] the original prophet" (137). Although Audubon was an accomplished scientific naturalist who pioneered bird-banding experiments and contributed to our knowledge of the nesting, mating, feeding, and migration habits of birds, he is perhaps best remembered as a purveyor of "ornitheology." Through his paintings and his prose, Audubon effectively brought the vanishing wilderness before a popular audience. Although many critics fault him for his zealousness as a hunter, his message from the wilderness remains one of devout enthusiasm and concern—a genuine love of nature tempered by a scrupulous fear for its destruction. Indeed, Audubon's ecological anxieties often result in what Leo Marx would call "the episode of the interrupted idyll"—a narrative moment in which the pastoral enjoyment of nature is invaded, in this case by a disconcerting awareness of its inevitable disappearance.[25]

This elegiac "interrupted idyll" is illustrated in the Episode "Scipio and the Bear," which energetically relates the story of a bear hunt, but ends abruptly by lamenting the needless cruelty of man toward his fellow creatures. After hunting and hounding a family of bears that sometimes visited a farmer's field, the hunting party ends by "smoking" two of the bears in the tree where the animals had retreated for safety:

> At length the tree assumed the appearance of a pillar of flame. The Bears mounted to the top branches. When they had reached the uppermost, they were seen to totter, and soon after, the branch cracking and snapping across, they came to the ground, bringing with them a mass of broken twigs. They were cubs, and the dogs soon worried them to death. The [hunting] party returned to the house in triumph. . . . But before we had left the field, the horses, dogs [. . . and] fires, had destroyed more corn within a few hours, than the poor bear and her cubs had, during the whole of their visits. (*Delineations* 109–10)

Audubon leaves little doubt that the crop damage done by the bears in no way warrants the cruel treatment the animals receive. Indeed, the fact that the hunters are more destructive to their fields than are the bears suggests that the hunt is motivated primarily by an excessive desire to harry and control nonhuman nature. In response to the very real loss of wildlife that is represented in such tales, Audubon became an early advocate of government intervention as a means of halting the "war of extermination" upon native species; in spite of such efforts, he often despaired that "Nature herself seems perishing."[26]

Much of Audubon's writing laments the swiftness with which wilderness was being lost. Consider this poignant passage in which he reflects upon his early rambles along the Ohio River:

> When I think of these times, and call back to my mind the grandeur and beauty of those almost uninhabited shores; when I picture to myself the dense and lofty summits of the forest, that everywhere spread along the hills, and overhung the margins of the stream, unmolested by the axe of the settler . . . when I see that no longer any Aborigines are to be found there, and that the vast herds of elks, deer and buffaloes which once pastured on these hills and in these valleys, making for themselves great roads to the several salt-springs, have ceased to exist; when I reflect that the grand portion of our Union, instead of being in a state of nature, is now more or less covered with villages, farms, and towns, where the din of hammers and machinery is constantly heard; that the woods are fast disappearing under the axe by day, and the fire by night . . . when I remember that these extraordinary changes have taken place in the short period of twenty years, I pause, wonder, and, although I know all to be fact, can scarcely believe its reality. (*Delineations* 4)

As Audubon correctly recognized, the impulse toward domination and extermination of wild nature was fast becoming the ecological legacy of the American frontier.

Although the environmental ethic of these early romantic naturalists would not be considered ecocentric by the standards of contemporary ecophilosophy, it is important to recognize that their sensitivity to the natural world and their concern for its preservation is an essential precursor to the ethics of modern American environmental concern. Like Bartram and Wilson before him, Audubon was inspired by the divine beauty of nature, and his study of natural history resulted in contributions to romantic literature and environmental awareness, as well as to science. Audubon's fear for nature's preservation was the combined product of his romantic sensibility, his naturalistic vocation, and the historical moment in which he pursued his studies. His life in America (1803–51) spanned the most active years of frontier expansion, a time when wilderness and the settlement of it were fiercely competing interpretations of a single landscape. By the time Henry Thoreau—who wrote that he read Audubon "with a thrill of delight"—had removed himself to Walden Pond, the American Woodsman had already asked in his journal: "Where can I go now, and visit nature undisturbed?"[27]

▪ ▪ ▪ Although ecocriticism has often been slow to recognize the value and influence of the pre-Thoreauvian literature of nature, the work of William Bartram, Alexander Wilson, and John James Audubon makes clear that early romantic natural history literature is an essential source of the American nature-writing tradition. In addition to indexing the possibilities for American culture in the fecund wilderness of the New World, these writers also helped relocate divinity from ecclesiastical institutions to the natural landscape and its nonhuman inhabitants. Sharing a poignant sense of the impending loss of biodiversity that attended settlement of the frontier, each was motivated by a desire to represent the beauty of American wilderness on the eve of its inexorable destruction. Most important, Bartram, Wilson, and Audubon celebrated their kinship with nonhuman nature, thereby introducing into American letters the proto-ecological sensibility upon which further developments in the genre of natural history writing would depend. Their artistic blending of natural history and belles lettres prefigured—and to a great extent engendered—the justly famous accomplishments of such literary descendants as Henry Thoreau, John Muir, Mary Austin, Annie Dillard, and Barry Lopez.

NOTES

Several passages in this essay also appear in Michael Branch's chapter "Early Romantic Natural History Literature," in *American Nature Writers,* ed. John C. Elder (Scribners, forthcoming).

1. *Notes* was published privately in 1785 and publicly in 1789.

2. Early natural history writing is often included in anthologies of nature writing (for example, see Robert Finch and John Elder, *The Norton Book of Nature Writing* [New York: Norton, 1990]), but is much less often the subject of critical study. For an analysis that has not forgotten the importance of early natural history writing, see Thomas J. Lyon, ed., *This Incomperable Lande* (Boston: Houghton Mifflin, 1989).

3. For a good, recent study of eighteenth-century natural history writing which offers a view very different from my own, see Pamela Regis, *Describing Early America* (DeKalb: Northern Illinois University Press, 1992). In short, Regis argues that the work of a writer such as William Bartram should be considered science *rather than* belles lettres (xi).

4. The new perspective on nature was carried to America in the writings of such deists as Shaftesbury and Pope, who were widely read in the colonies. It was Shaftesbury whose passion for wild nature prompted him to reject the "feigned wilderness" of palace gardens, and Pope who, in his "Essay on Man," encouraged readers to "look up through nature to Nature's God" (Hans Huth, *Nature and the American* [Lincoln: University of Nebraska Press, 1957] 10).

5. Burke's sublime enjoyed great currency in America, and was joined shortly by William Gilpin's concept of the "picturesque." Like the sublime, the idea of the picturesque was widely disseminated in American culture, and Gilpin's work was known to nineteenth-century authors including Emerson, Thoreau, Hawthorne, and Poe (Huth 12). While it may be said that the cult of the sublime and picturesque deteriorated rather rapidly into a clichéd response to the landscape, these new aesthetic categories played a vital role in reversing the seventeenth-century aversion to wilderness. Working in concert with deist assumptions about nature, the sublime and picturesque helped establish as divinely inspiring and aesthetically redeeming the fear and trembling generated by the American land.

6. Naturalists of this period turned away from European cultural standards and toward the scientific and literary possibilities of the American land. An excellent example of the American response to the call for a native natural history is provided by the career of Charles Wilson Peale, whose Philadelphia Museum, established in 1786, had a tremendous influence upon the Americanization of the field.

7. The quotations are Dr. James DeKay and Dr. Daniel Drake, respectively, and are quoted in Merle Curti, *The Growth of American Thought*, 2d ed. (New York: Harper & Bros., 1951) 252–53.

8. The full title of Bartram's book is *Travels Through North & South Carolina, Georgia, East & West Florida, the Cherokee Country, the Extensive Territories of the Muscogulges, or Creek Confederacy, and the Country of the Chactaws; Containing an Account of the Soil and Natural Productions of Those Regions, Together With Observations on the Manners of the Indians*. An English edition was published the following year (1792) in London.

9. The first praise is from Coleridge's *Table Talk;* the passage from the letter to Emerson may be found in the "Editor's Note" (5) of *Travels of William Bartram*, edited by Mark Van Doren. For a thorough discussion of Bartram's influence upon the English romantics, see N. Bryllion Fagin, *William Bartram* (Baltimore: Johns Hopkins University Press, 1933).

10. William's father John subscribed to a personal brand of deism which caused

him to be disowned by the Darby Meeting of the Society of Friends. Although his fellow Quakers left the charge against him deliberately vague, it seems to have been John's defiant claims on behalf of nature that unsettled the Darby Meeting. For instance, John once claimed that animals "possess higher qualifications and more exalted ideas than our traditional mystery mongers [preachers] are willing to allow." For further discussion of John Bartram's theology, see Robert Elman, *First in the Field* (New York: Van Nostrand Reinhold, 1977) 35–37; Ernest Earnest, *John and William Bartram* (Philadelphia: University of Pennsylvania Press, 1940) 66–67.

11. The delightful account of Bartram and the spider is an excellent example of Bartram's ecological consciousness. After describing how the spider stalked a bumblebee while "at the same time keeping a sharp eye upon me," Bartram observes that "perhaps before night [the spider] became himself the delicious evening repast of a bird or lizard" (24–25).

12. The untitled manuscript, which is collected with Bartram's papers at the Historical Society of Pennsylvania, is cited in Earnest 143, 144.

13. When Wilson died on 23 August 1813, he had published seven volumes, and had completed the eighth and some of the ninth. Wilson's friend George Ord saw volume eight through to publication in 1814 and, with a great deal of help from French ornithologist Charles Lucien Bonaparte, published the final volume in 1829.

14. Indeed, many of Wilson's accomplishments were inspired by his early patriotism. Even before he became an American citizen in 1804 Wilson had delivered an "Oration on the Power and Value of National Liberty" to celebrate Jefferson's election to the Presidency, and had composed a popular song entitled "Jefferson and Liberty." For information on Wilson's republican orations, see Clark Hunter, *The Life and Letters of Alexander Wilson* (Philadelphia: American Philosophical Society, 1983) 3. For Wilson's acknowledgment of Bartram and Jefferson, see *American Ornithology,* (Philadelphia: Porter & Coates, 1870) 8. Wilson's call for patriotic support is related by George Ord in his "Biographical Sketch of Alexander Wilson"; see Charlotte M. Porter, *The Eagle's Nest* (University: University of Alabama Press, 1986) 47.

15. See Porter 164.

16. This incident is documented by Elman 65–66.

17. For a fascinating account of how European audiences immediately proclaimed Audubon an "American genius," see Audubon's own 1826 Journal. *The Birds of America* was unprecedented in size and expense. The 435 plates were printed on sheets 26½ inches by 39½ inches and depicted over one thousand individual birds; the cost for the set was a thousand dollars (Elman 103). Audubon's artistic fame does not rest entirely upon his paintings of birds, however; his *Viviparous Quadrupeds of North America* (1845–48), though less famous, is also a classic of wildlife art.

18. Since 1985, the bicentennial of his birth, a critical reappraisal of Audubon's

career has begun to emphasize the importance of his writing. See Alton A. Lindsey, *The Bicentennial of John James Audubon* (Bloomington: Indiana University Press, 1985); and Scott Russell Sanders, *Wonders Hidden: Audubon's Early Years* (Santa Barbara: Capra Press, 1984). Audubon's writing may be roughly organized into three categories. His descriptions of the birds, published in the five-volume *Ornithological Biography* (1831–39), provide a rich account of the American wilderness and its nonhuman inhabitants. His voluminous journals (published in 1897)—although bowdlerized to suit the Victorian pieties of his granddaughter, Maria Audubon—recount with vivid immediacy the story of Audubon's remarkable life and adventures. It is his "Episodes," however, which have the greatest literary interest and merit. The sixty Episodes were originally interpolated into the first three volumes of the *Ornithological Biography,* where they were placed so that one followed every five articles on ornithology in order to relieve the tedium of the hundreds of consecutive bird descriptions. They were later collected as *Delineations of American Scenery and Character.*

19. For example, see Bryant's translation of José María de Heredia's "Niagra," which he called "the best which has been written about the Great American Cataract" (quoted in Charles H. Brown, *William Cullen Bryant* [New York: Charles Scribner's Sons, 1971] 155).

20. As a source of cultural history about the frontier, Audubon provides detailed descriptions of frontier activities such as ox-plowing contests and Independence Day picnics, as well as frontier skills such as hunting a raccoon, poling a flatboat, navigating a canebreak, or salting a buffalo with gunpowder.

21. In style as well as subject, Audubon's Episodes are an important contribution to the literature of the period. For example, his use of lore, tall tales, boasting, and pranks makes him a relative of the Southwest Humorists, who were writing in the same region at the same time.

22. For speculation about Wilson as model for Wordsworth's peddler, see Porter, 41 and Fagin 128–62.

23. See Hunter 100–101.

24. See Sanders 8. In a letter to his wife (from Edinburgh, 22 December 1826), Audubon commented that "My hairs are now as beautifully long and curly as ever and I assure they do as much for me as my talent for painting" (Sanders 206).

25. The best discussion of the breaking of Audubon's pastoral pattern is Annette Kolodny, *The Lay of the Land* (Chapel Hill: University of North Carolina Press, 1975) 74–88. Audubon's ecological or conservationist impulses are also discussed in Lindsey, chap. 8; Francis Hobart Herrick, *Audubon the Naturalist,* 2 vols. (New York: D. Appleton, 1917) xii; Sanders (9–10). Discussion of the "interrupted idyll" will be found in Leo Marx, "Pastoral Ideals and City Troubles," in *Western Man and Environmental Ethics,* ed. Ian G. Barbour (Reading: Addison-Wesley, 1973) 109.

26. Quoted in Lindsey 120.

27. Cited in Sanders 10.

WORKS CITED

Audubon, John James. *Delineations of American Scenery and Character.* New York: G. A. Baker & Company, 1926.

———. *Ornithological Biography, or An Account of the Habits of the Birds of the United States of America.* 5 vols. (This is the text meant to accompany the plates of *The Birds of America.*) Philadelphia: J. Dobson, 1831 (vol. 1); Boston: Hilliard, Gray & Co., 1835 (vol. 2); Edinburgh: A. & C. Black, 1835–39 (vols. 3–5).

———. *The Viviparous Quadrupeds of North America,* with John Bachman. 2 vols. of plates, New York: 1845–46. 3 vols. of text, New York: 1846–54.

Audubon, Maria R. *Audubon and His Journals.* 2 vols. 1897. Reprint, New York: Dover, 1986.

Bartram, William. *Travels.* Ed. Mark Van Doren. New York: Dover, 1955.

Brown, Charles H. *William Cullen Bryant.* New York: Charles Scribner's Sons, 1971.

Burke, Edmund. *Of the Sublime and Beautiful. Works.* Bohn edition, 1854. ii.5.

Curti, Merle. *The Growth of American Thought.* 2d ed. New York: Harper & Bros., 1951.

Earnest, Ernest. *John and William Bartram: Botanists and Explorers.* Philadelphia: University of Pennsylvania Press, 1940.

Elman, Robert. *First in the Field: America's Pioneering Naturalists.* New York: Van Nostrand Reinhold, 1977.

Emerson, Ralph Waldo. *Nature.* Boston: J. Munroe, 1836.

Fagin, N. Bryllion. *William Bartram: Interpreter of the American Landscape.* Baltimore: Johns Hopkins University Press, 1933.

Finch, Robert, and John Elder. *The Norton Book of Nature Writing.* New York: Norton, 1990.

Herrick, Francis Hobart. *Audubon the Naturalist: A History of His Life and Time.* 2 vols. New York: D. Appleton, 1917.

Hunter, Clark. *The Life and Letters of Alexander Wilson.* Philadelphia: American Philosophical Society, 1983.

Huth, Hans. *Nature and the American: Three Centuries of Changing Attitudes.* Lincoln: University of Nebraska Press, 1957.

Jefferson, Thomas. *Notes on the State of Virginia.* Chapel Hill: University of North Carolina Press, 1955.

Kolodny, Annette. *The Lay of the Land: Metaphor as Experience and History in American Life and Letters.* Chapel Hill: University of North Carolina Press, 1975.

Lindsey, Alton A. *The Bicentennial of John James Audubon.* Bloomington: Indiana University Press, 1985.

Lyon, Thomas J., ed. *This Incomperable Lande: A Book of American Nature Writing.* Boston: Houghton Mifflin, 1989.

Marx, Leo. "Pastoral Ideals and City Troubles." In *Western Man and Environmen-*

tal Ethics: Attitudes toward Nature and Technology. Ed. Ian G. Barbour. Reading: Addison-Wesley, 1973. 18–30.

Porter, Charlotte M. *The Eagle's Nest: Natural History and American Ideas, 1812–1842*. Tuscaloosa: University of Alabama Press, 1986.

Ray, John. *The Wisdom of God Manifested in the Works of the Creation*. London: Innys and Manby, 1735.

Regis, Pamela. *Describing Early America: Bartram, Jefferson, Crevecoeur, and the Rhetoric of Natural History*. DeKalb: Northern Illinois University Press, 1992.

Sanders, Scott Russell, ed. *Audubon Reader: The Best Writings of John James Audubon*. Bloomington: Indiana University Press, 1986.

———. *Wonders Hidden: Audubon's Early Years*. Santa Barbara: Capra Press, 1984.

Seavey, Ormond. "William Bartram." *Dictionary of Literary Biography* 37:31–38.

Warren, Robert Penn. *Selected Poems, 1923–1975*. New York: Random House, 1976.

Welty, Eudora. *Collected Stories of Eudora Welty*. San Diego: Harcourt Brace, 1982.

White, Gilbert. *The Natural History and Antiquities of Selborne*. N.p., 1789.

Wilson, Alexander. *American Ornithology or, the Natural History of the Birds of the United States*. (Complete in one volume.) Philadelphia: Porter & Coates, 1870.

———. *The Poetical Works of Alexander Wilson*. Belfast: J. Henderson, 1857.

DON SCHEESE

Desert Solitaire

■ ■ ■

COUNTER-FRICTION TO THE MACHINE IN THE GARDEN

Let your life be a counter friction to stop the machine.—Henry David Thoreau, "Resistance to Civil Government"

I first encountered the work of Edward Abbey during a cross-continental train trip in December 1977. To help me endure the wintry, interminable monotones of the Great Plains, a friend suggested a few books to take along. I can recall but one of them now: Edward Abbey's *Desert Solitaire*.

"How many a man has dated a new era in his life from the reading of a book," Thoreau wrote in *Walden* (107). After reading *Desert Solitaire* a new era began in my life: I made it my vocation both to study the nature-writing tradition *and* devote a significant portion of time to living in the wild. I took up Abbey's suggestions in the introduction to *Abbey's Road* on whom to read—Edward Hoagland, Joseph Wood Krutch, Wendell Berry, Annie Dillard, John McPhee, Ann Zwinger, and Peter Matthiessen (xx)—and followed his example of inhabiting the wilderness: for the past ten summers I have worked as a fire lookout for the Forest Service in Idaho. While living in the woods I have had ample time in which to read hundreds of works of nature writing (to paraphrase Thoreau, in "Natural History of Massachusetts," "Books of natural history make the most cheerful [summer] reading") and meditate upon the significance of one of America's great contributions to world literature.

The label "nature writer" is one that Abbey has resisted. "This is a title I have not earned, never wanted, do not enjoy," he writes in a new preface to *Desert Solitaire* (1988: 12).[1] Many of his self-assessments remind one of what D. H. Lawrence wrote in *Studies in Classic American Literature:* "Never trust the artist. Trust the tale. The proper function of a critic is to save the tale from the artist who created it" (8). The truth of the matter is that Abbey, for all his disclaimers, *is* a nature writer. Like Thoreau, John Muir, and Aldo Leopold, all of whom sought to transcend natural history's purpose of merely naming and classifying natural phenomena, Abbey understood his role to be that of culture critic. "The few such writers whom I wholly admire," he continues, "are those, like Thoreau, who went far beyond simple nature writing to become critics of society, of the state, of our modern industrial culture. . . . It is not enough to understand nature; the point is to save it" (12). Abbey's disclaimers notwithstanding, he falls squarely in the tradition of nature writing established by Thoreau and carried on by Muir and Leopold—those leading figures in the conservation movement whose works we turn to most frequently for inspiration and insight. All four writers sought to instill a land ethic in the American public. Abbey is yet one more inhabitor of the wild—with two important distinctions. The environment he chose to inhabit was the desert; and he is the most radical, iconoclastic figure of the lot.

▪ ▪ ▪ Prior to his death in March 1989, Edward Abbey wrote nineteen works of fiction and non-fiction. (*Hayduke Lives!*, a sequel to *The Monkey Wrench Gang*, was published posthumously in 1990.) Most of Abbey's writing is about the American West, and most of the writing about the American West is about the Southwest. The desert. Born in the Allegheny Mountains of Pennsylvania, he first visited the region as a seventeen-year-old in 1944 while hitchhiking and riding the rails cross-country, prior to his induction in the armed services. In Arizona he encountered

> a land that filled me with strange excitement: crags and pinnacles of naked rock, the dark cores of ancient volcanoes, a vast and silent emptiness smoldering with heat, color, and indecipherable significance, above which floated a small number of pure, hard-edged clouds. For the first time I felt I was getting to the West of my deepest imaginings—the place where the tangible and the mythical become the same. ("Hallelujah" 5)

Following a stint in the Army, Abbey moved to the Southwest permanently (more or less) in 1947. He enrolled at the University of New Mexico under the GI Bill, taking ten years to earn a master's degree in philosophy, for which he wrote a thesis on "Anarchism and the Morality of Violence." Like Thoreau, Muir, and (to a lesser extent) Leopold, he was troubled by the quest for a suitable vocation, faced with the difficult choice of earning "bread money" (Muir's phrase) to provide for his succession of families (he was married five times and fathered five children), *and* finding work he found fulfilling. For a time he resolved the dilemma by working as a seasonal employee with the Park Service. In 1956 and 1957, and again several years later, he worked as a ranger at Arches National Monument in Utah, spending April through September maintaining trails, greeting the public and collecting campground fees, and generally functioning as "sole inhabitant, usufructuary, observer, and custodian" (*Desert Solitaire* 1968: 5). He stored his gear and food in a housetrailer provided by the government, and ate and slept outdoors under a ramada he constructed himself. For three six-month periods he observed the passage of the seasons and inhabited 33,000 acres of slickrock wilderness, accumulating four volumes of notes and sketches. His first three works, all novels, were commercial failures; so, following the advice of a New York publisher to "write about something you know," he typed up an account of "those [first] two seamless perfect seasons" at Arches and sent it to his agent (*Abbey's Road* xix; *Desert Solitaire* 1988: 9–11). Thus *Desert Solitaire* was born.

Like *Walden* and Part I of *A Sand County Almanac, Desert Solitaire* is an example of what Thomas Lyon in his taxonomy of nature writing calls "Solitude and Backcountry Living" (4–6). Other similarities exist among the three works. *Desert Solitaire* represents "compressed time," the distillation of years of experience into a seamless account of intimate participation in the cycle of the seasons; and in recording a significant portion of one's life it also qualifies as a work of autobiography (Sayre 19). Most importantly, Abbey's work, like that of Thoreau, Muir, and Leopold, presents the author as an exemplary inhabitor of the wild. Abbey's term, "usufructuary," is crucial in understanding the advantages of immersion in the wild while simultaneously formulating and adhering to a land ethic. The resulting encounter with nature becomes a myth of self-education, a realization of autobiography and ecotopia, and heartens the receptive reader "by showing us new and true possibilities and how much may be achieved in life and art by conscious endeavor" (Paul 233).

Abbey's specific contributions to the genre of nature writing are threefold: following in the tradition of John Wesley Powell, John C. Van Dyke, Mary Austin, and Joseph Wood Krutch, he popularized an aesthetic of a different kind in celebrating the harsh beauty of the desert landscape; he articulated new arguments, distinguished by a rhetoric of rage, for wilderness preservation; and he advocated political activism in order to defend wild nature. Since the publication of *Desert Solitaire* nature writing and environmental politics have been significantly transformed. Abbey's life and work have become a counterfriction against those forces that would destroy the wilderness.

▪ ▪ ▪ The opening line, "This is the most beautiful place on earth," affirms Abbey's joy at the prospect of living in a desiccated Eden and places him in a relatively brief tradition of desert appreciation (Limerick 7). "What is the peculiar quality or character of the desert that distinguishes it, in spiritual appeal, from other forms of landscape?" (240) he asks, mentioning the handful of American writers who have dealt with this question: Powell, Austin, Van Dyke, and Krutch. Powell, along with his crew of nine the first (in 1869) so far as we know to run the length of the Colorado River through the Grand Canyon, wrote *The Exploration of the Colorado River and Its Canyons,* the record of a journey which Abbey partially retraces in *Desert Solitaire*. In a pantheon of anti-pioneers Abbey praises Powell (along with Thoreau and Muir) for recognizing in nature "something more than merely raw material for pecuniary exploitation" (168). In his book on exploring the Grand Canyon, and later in his career as head of the Bureau of Ethnology, Powell tried to dispel the myth of the American West as Garden by pointing to its low rainfall totals and suggesting that if settlement were to take place the best approach would be communitarian rather than the individualistic style characteristic of much of American frontier development (Stegner 202–42).

Subsequent writers also came to terms with the crucial fact of the desert's aridity. Mary Austin's *The Land of Little Rain* (1903) is based on nearly two decades of residence in the Mojave Desert of eastern California. Austin treats such themes as the harmonious adaptations of animals and Indians to sparse resources, the need to dwell on the land for a significant period of time in order to understand its rhythms, and the careless exploitation of natural resources by Anglo-Americans. The white man, she observes, "is a great blunderer going about in the woods. . . . The cunningest hunter is hunted in turn, and what he leaves of his kill is meat for some other. That is the economy of nature, but with it all there is not sufficient account taken of the works of man. There is no scavenger that eats tin cans, and no wild thing leaves a like disfigurement on the forest floor" (40).

John C. Van Dyke treated themes also taken up by Abbey. An art critic, Van Dyke emphasized the aesthetic value of desert landforms. He found the adaptation of the flora and fauna to the harsh climatic conditions particularly beautiful. He denounced the settlement of the Sonoran, Mojave, and Chihuahan deserts through which he traveled at the turn of the century, declaring that they "should never be reclaimed. They are the breathing-spaces of the west and should be preserved forever" (59). But not only for utilitarian reasons did he believe that the desert should not be over-exploited. In *The Desert* (1901) he argues that regardless of whether or not humans ever witness the beauty of the desert Southwest it has a right to exist.

The same pellucid skies celebrated by Van Dyke, literary critic Joseph Wood Krutch sought out after leaving New York City in 1950. But Krutch quickly discovered that the sunny climate of the Southwest was attracting increasingly greater numbers of Eastern immigrants like himself, leading to the befouling of the air and overcrowding of the land. He tempered his anger over the desecration of the desert environment by suggesting in a number of works how to best appreciate the fragile ecosystem. In distinguishing between the tourist's and the resident's perceptions–"In nature, one never really sees a thing for the first time until one has seen it for the fiftieth" (*Desert Year* 4)—he was both harkening back to Austin and anticipating Abbey in their emphasis on keen perception fostered by long periods of inhabitation.

Desert Solitaire thus owes significant debts to these earlier writers. Yet the work is unique for its passionate defense of the antipastoral environment. Although the writing is overtly autobiographical, with Abbey's ego looming large in almost every chapter, the perspective is more *eco-* than *ego*-centered, emphasizing the harmony and delicate balance of the desert ecosystem. Chapter three, which bears the oxymoronic title "The Serpents of Paradise," nicely illustrates this theme. Abbey presents a desert aesthetic, an explanation of how to appreciate a land that, though antithetical to the traditional notion of the pastoral, is lovely for its spareness and openness and efficiency. Absent are humans, verdure, domestic animals; in their place are rattlesnakes, malevolent (if colorful) cacti, and naked red rock. Slickrock country.

Drinking coffee one morning on the steps of his housetrailer, Abbey looks between his feet and discovers a rattlesnake. What to do? The snake obviously represents a physical threat. But as a ranger he is by law duty-bound to protect all creatures within the park. Moreover by predilection he cannot compel himself to kill the rattler. Paraphrasing a line from Robinson Jeffers's "Hurt Hawks," he says, "I prefer not to kill animals. I'm a humanist; I'd rather kill a man than a snake" (17). So he chooses an ecological alternative. He captures a gopher snake, a species known to drive off rattlers, and keeps it as his pet in the trailer and on his person while patrolling the park. His affinity for wild creatures is further revealed when the gopher snake escapes, only to be rediscovered by Abbey during an elaborate *pas de deux* mating ritual with another member of its species. What follows is a fine example of participation in the wild, comparable to, say, Muir's joy while swaying in a treetop during a violent storm. A shameless voyeur, Abbey approaches the snakes at ground level, mesmerized by their slithering caduceus-like glide. Though he is reminded that humans have lost their wildness when he is repelled "by a fear too ancient and powerful to overcome" (21), he does learn a valuable lesson. He acquires a biocentric outlook, the knowledge of the deep ecologist (Sessions and Devall 65–108). "We are obliged, therefore, to spread the news, painful and bitter though it may be for some to bear, that all living things on earth are kindred" (21).

The integrity, stability, and beauty of the desert are the dominant concerns of *Desert Solitaire*. Integrity, stability, beauty: these criteria of ecological health were established by Aldo Leopold in "The Land Ethic," the concluding essay of *A Sand County Almanac*. The ultimate concern of both nature writers is the preservation of the land, its harmony, and the equilibrium of natural relationships in a particular environment. This becomes evident on another occasion in Abbey's work when he points out how predator control conducted by the government on behalf of the livestock industry (in which Leopold had participated while he worked with the Forest Service in the Southwest) led to an extermination campaign against coyotes, mountain lions, and wolves, and caused an irruption of the deer population. The warfare practiced by the exterminators, with all their modern military apparatus, is contrasted with the solitary quest of the hunter seeking his prey. To illustrate the distinction Abbey performs an experiment of sorts. He hurls a rock at a rabbit to determine whether he could survive in the wild by dint of his physical skills. The projectile lands true to its mark and kills the rabbit; after the initial shock passes, Abbey experiences a mild elation. "I try but cannot feel any sense of guilt. I examine my soul; white as snow. Check my hands: not a trace of blood. No longer do I feel so isolated from the sparse and furtive life around me, a stranger from another world. I have entered into this one." Some might consider the rabbit's death gratuitous. Not Abbey. By killing it he participates again in the natural environment; he becomes part and parcel of nature's economy; he is now a bona fide member of the desert's biotic community. Whether he eats the rabbit or not (he doesn't, fearing the prospect of tularemia) doesn't matter. His point is that, unlike the indiscriminate slaughter committed by the agents of predator control, he has engaged in the noble, one-on-one pursuit of the hunt.[2] "We are kindred all of us, killer and victim, predator and prey, me and the sly coyote, the soaring buzzard, the elegant gopher snake, the trembling cottontail, the foul worms that feed on our entrails, all of them, all of us. Long live diversity, long live the earth!" (34).

Leopold of course later recanted his "sin" against predators in "Thinking Like a Mountain." He would have appreciated Abbey's fear of the consequences of overpopulating the desert, the taxing of natural resources to an ecologically unhealthy degree. The perceived threat of a water shortage prompts this reaction from Abbey: "There is no shortage of water in the desert but exactly the right amount" (126). But a significant difference between the two writers is in tone; Leopold rarely displayed anger or impatience while Abbey denounces mass migration to the Sunbelt region with an extravagance that has become his trademark: "Growth for the sake of growth is the ideology of the cancer cell" (127).

The uses to which facts about the desert's natural history are put remind us of Abbey's ultimate purpose in nature writing. Unlike Thoreau and Leopold who are detailed record-keepers of phenology, the study of seasonal fluctuations of plants and animals, Abbey in his journals is more impressionistic, more interested in the impression a fact of natural history makes upon him than the fact itself (to be sure, the same is true of much of Thoreau's *Journal*). Not that the scientific information recorded by Abbey is inaccurate; as he explains in one of his works, "All the technical information was stolen from reliable sources and I am happy to stand behind it" (introduction to *Journey Home* xiii). Yet for all the precise floral, faunal, and geological description, "the desert figures more as medium than as material" (xii) in *Desert Solitaire*. As in all compelling nature writing, the account of the relationship between self and nature, nature and culture, evokes important truths about self and society. Abbey does indeed write works of personal history. But I suggest that they are works of cultural criticism as well. And it is in his role of culture critic, defender of wildness and wilderness, that his rhetoric becomes increasingly more vociferous. As Patricia Limerick observes, "An extreme and intractable landscape might . . . appeal to a more extreme and intractable man" (149).

▪▪▪ "In wildness is the preservation of the world," Thoreau writes in "Walking." "From the forests and wilderness come tonics and barks which brace mankind" (112). The value of wildness Thoreau deems most important is spiritual (Nash, *Wilderness* 88). "When I would recreate myself, I seek the darkest wood, the thickest and most interminable and, to the citizen, most dismal swamp. I enter a swamp as a sacred place, a *sanctum sanctorum.* There is the strength, the marrow of Nature" ("Walking" 116). Wild places are where spiritual re-creation—recreation we now call it—takes place. Muir echoes Thoreau's declaration when he writes in his journal that "In God's wildness lies the hope of the world—the great fresh unblighted, unredeemed wilderness" (*John of the Mountains* 317). During the era of conservation at the turn of the century, Muir reiterated Thoreau's belief in the spiritual value of wildness, but he also enhanced its worth by giving ecological reasons for wilderness preservation; in the 1890s he insisted that forest reserves be created in the West to protect watersheds (Cohen 151–204). Leopold reprises these arguments in *A Sand County Almanac,* paraphrasing Thoreau in "Thinking Like a Mountain" to read "In wildness is the salvation of the world" (133). In addition to making a case for the aesthetic, spiritual, and recreational values of the wild, Leopold believes it has a "split-rail" or cultural-historical significance for Americans. He also suggests that there is a scientific value in that wilderness functions "as a base datum of normality," "a laboratory for the study of land health" (196).

To these multivalent qualities of the wild Edward Abbey adds yet another: wilderness should be preserved for political reasons, "as a refuge from authoritarian government," because "history demonstrates that personal liberty is a rare and precious thing" (130). Citing as contemporary examples Vietnam, Cuba, and Algeria, Abbey points to the existence of wilderness in these countries as a haven for revolutionaries, a base for guerillas to mount effective resistance to totalitarian regimes. Although he professes a love for cities and, indeed, plans to return to one come season's end, he fears that the urban setting, "which should be the symbol and center of civilization, can also be made to function as a concentration camp" (131). Readers familiar with Abbey's *oeuvre* know well his obsession with an Orwellian scenario. George Washington Hayduke, the most militant of the four "eco-raiders" of *The Monkey Wrench Gang* and *Hayduke Lives!*, fears the prospect of a military-industrial takeover of the American West. In a later tour de force essay, "The Second Rape of the West," Abbey writes of encountering businessmen and U.S. Army officials near a Montana strip mine. This prompts him to remark, "There is something in the juxtaposition of big business, big military, and big technology that always rouses my most paranoid nightmares, visions of the technological superstate, the Pentagon's latent fascism, IBM's laboratory torture chambers, the absolute computerized fusion-powered global tyranny of the twenty-first century" (181). This vision succinctly describes the plot and setting of his later novel *Good News* (1980), which depicts the Southwest in horrific straits, a military dictatorship in control of Phoenix and at war with renegades who remain at large in the wilderness.

"A wild place without dangers is an absurdity," Abbey once wrote in defense of grizzly bears in Glacier National Park ("Fire Lookout" 33). A larger truth is that a world without wilderness is a dangerous place in which to live. Leopold expresses a similar idea in "Thinking Like a Mountain": "Too much safety seems to yield only danger in the long run" (133). He is referring to the personal cost of cautiousness to the individual; Abbey extends the argument by concluding that in wildness also lay the hope for continued preservation of political freedom in the world. To those skeptical of his argument he asks: "What reason have we Americans to think that our own society will necessarily escape the world-wide drift toward the totalitarian organizations of men and institutions?" (130). Evidence of wilderness invaded by the U.S. government already existed in his most cherished place: Glen Canyon.

Why are river accounts so often elegiac? I raise this question in response to "Down the River," the longest chapter of the book, which describes Abbey's farewell journey through Glen Canyon, an exquisite wilderness along the Colorado River prior to its damming. The paeans to rivers which come to mind—Thoreau's *A Week on the Concord and Merrimack Rivers*, John Graves's *Goodbye to a River*, Norman Maclean's *A River Runs Through It*—all possess an elemental sadness. In Abbey's case the sadness is not over a lost brother, as in the works of Thoreau and Maclean, but (as in Graves's) a lost river; and so, as Patricia Limerick says, his excursion is another *jornada del muerto*, a journey of death. Even as Abbey was writing *Desert Solitaire* Glen Canyon Dam took shape, and he capitalizes on this historical circumstance to create a double-vision, a retrospective celebration of the past conjoined with a foreboding view of the present and future. He chronicles a trip from ecotopia to dystopia.

Leopold elegizes the Flambeau River in Wisconsin in *A Sand County Almanac* after encountering two young men on a canoe trip. Learning that they are about to be inducted into the army, Leopold realizes the motif of their journey: it is "the first and last taste of freedom, an interlude between two regimentations: the campus and the barracks." He concludes that "perhaps every youth needs an occasional wilderness trip, in order to learn the meaning of this particular freedom" (113). But future wilderness excursions will have to be experienced elsewhere; the Flambeau was dammed following World War II.

Abbey writes partly with the same elegiac purpose. But his intent is also clearly polemical. His elation in realizing freedom when putting in on the river is juxtaposed against his rage over the regimentation of recreation now enforced by the federal government on the stagnant slackwater of the reservoir. "The delirious exhilaration of independence" has been replaced by a system of play spelled out clearly in official signs: "PLAY SAFE SKI ONLY IN CLOCKWISE DIRECTION: LET'S ALL HAVE FUN TOGETHER!" (152) Abbey once wrote (echoing Thoreau in *Walden*) that in modern society "all men must march to the beat of the same drum, like it or not" ("Numa Ridge" 36), and here his worst fears of an Orwellian future seem to be realized. As a member of the countercultural movement of the 1960s he prefers a form of recreation that runs counter to the type promoted by the government, one which allows for his *re-creation*. He chooses not to waterski (even counter-clockwise) since to do so would be to engage in a form of motorized transportation in a wilderness where motors should be prohibited. In order to re-create himself spiritually he must participate in the environment, and the difference between a float trip—leisurely exploration of a river—and waterskiing—fast-paced thrill-seeking—is the difference between perception and blindness, immersion and non-participation. As Leopold writes: woodcraft in the modern era has become the art of using gadgets. To use too many is to interfere with one's perception. "The outstanding characteristic of perception," Leopold claims, "is that it entails no consumption and no dilution of any resource. . . . To promote perception is the only truly creative part of recreational engineering" (173).

Abbey sets an example of how to participate in the wilderness by floating down the river for two weeks. He and his male companion immerse themselves in its details—exploring the side canyons, discovering the landscape's sparse human history of Indian petroglyphs, Mormon trails, and mining camps—and in the process experience what Abbey calls "intersubjectivity":

> We are merging, molecules getting mixed. Talk about intersubjectivity—we are both taking on the coloration of river and canyon, our skin as mahogany as the water on the shady side, our clothing coated with silt, our bare feet caked with mud and tough as lizard skin, our whiskers bleached as the sand—even our eyeballs, what little you can see of them between the lids, have taken on a coral pink, the color of the dunes. And we smell, I suppose, like catfish. (185)

However, with the intrusion of motor culture, desecration occurs. Abbey recounts his six-mile hike to Rainbow Bridge, one of the most famous natural spans in the canyon, and predicts that its beauty will be lessened once the waters of the reservoir make it accessible to motorboats. When the hike is replaced by an effortless motorized excursion, "the Bridge will be no more than an isolated geological oddity, an extension of that museumlike diorama to which industrial tourism tends to reduce the natural world" (192). Actually, as Abbey records in a later work, a worse contingency comes to pass: the convenience of motorboat camping along the shores of Lake Powell, the reservoir formed by the dam, leads to extensive littering ("Lake Powell" 90).

Abbey attempts to dismiss such desecration by taking a long view of things, professing a natural philosophy of sorts when he concludes that "Men come and go, cities rise and fall, whole civilizations appear and disappear—[yet] the earth remains, slightly modified" (194). This view is something of a sham, however, because the reality and longevity of the dam, considered in human as opposed to geologic time, loom long and large. So he fantasizes over its destruction even while he celebrates his final trip through the canyon. "Some unknown hero," he schemes, "will descend into the bowels of the dam" (165) and blow it up.

As others have noted (Ronald, *New West* 203), this fantasy anticipates a theme of *The Monkey Wrench Gang*. It is the great desire of the four protagonists to "blow that dam to shitaree" (66). Abbey's rage over the building of the dam and his fanatical quest to "deconstruct" it is a recurrent theme in a number of his other works.[3] Not only is he more outrageous in tone than most other nature writers; he has also transformed the genre by openly advocating and participating in violent acts to preserve wilderness.

▪ ▪ ▪ Nowhere is Abbey's rage more evident than in an extended diatribe against industrial tourism in "Episodes and Visions." Wendell Berry points out that Abbey's contribution as a nature writer has been to make clear that the root of our ecological crisis is cultural. "Our country is not being destroyed [merely] by bad politics," Berry writes, "it is being destroyed by a bad way of life" ("Few Words" 10). The Labor Day influx of tourists provokes this outburst over the sedentary experience of most visitors to national parks:

> What can I tell them? Sealed in their metallic shells like molluscs on wheels, how can I pry the people free? The auto as tin can, the park ranger as opener. Look here, I want to say, for godsake folks get out of them there machines, take off those fucking sunglasses and unpeel both eyeballs, look around; throw away those goddamned idiotic cameras! For chrissake folks what is this life if full of care we have no time to stand and stare? eh? Take off your shoes for a while, unzip your fly, piss hearty, dig your toes in the hot sand, feel that raw and rugged earth, split a couple of big toenails, draw blood! Why not? Jesus Christ, lady, roll that window down! You can't see the desert if you can't smell it. Dusty? Of course it's dusty—this is Utah! But it's good dust, good red Utahn dust, rich in iron, rich in irony. Turn that motor off. Get out of that piece of iron and stretch your varicose veins, take off your brassiere and get some hot sun on your old wrinkled dugs! You sir, squinting at the map with your radiator boiling over and your fuel pump vapor-locked, crawl out of that shiny hunk of GM junk and take a walk—yes, leave the old lady and those squawling brats behind for a while, turn your back on them and take a long quiet walk straight into the canyons, get lost for a while, come back when you damn well feel like it, it'll do you and her and them a world of good. Give the kids a break too, let them out of the car, let them go scrambling over the rocks hunting for rattlesnakes and scorpions and anthills—yes sir, let them out, turn them loose; how dare you imprison little children in your goddamned upholstered horseless hearse? Yes, sir, yes madam, I entreat you, get out of those motorized wheelchairs, get off your foam rubber backsides, stand up straight like men! like women! like human beings! and walk—*walk*—WALK upon our blessed land! (233)

I quote this passage because it is representative of Abbey's harsh, iconoclastic, extravagant narrative voice; no other sample of his prose indicates better the difference in temperament between him and most other nature writers. Yet the outrageous rhetoric should not distract from the message: rid yourself of gadgets which interfere with participation in the natural environment. Afford the time to allow for prolonged engagement with and meditation on nature. Enter the wilderness and experience freedom. Be alive to the redemptive possibilities of the wild.

It is the machine in the garden which provokes Abbey's outrage. Leo Marx has observed that "the ominous sounds of machines, like the sound of the steamboat bearing down on the raft or of the train breaking in upon the idyll at Walden, reverberate endlessly in our literature" (16). In *Desert Solitaire* the machine figures most prominently in "Polemic: Industrial Tourism and the National Parks," of which Abbey has written: "it protrudes, like an enflamed member, in the midst of an otherwise simple pastorale" (1988: 12). Rapt in a revery one spring evening, enjoying the moonrise, Abbey suddenly hears

> the discordant note, the snarling whine of a jeep in low range and four-wheel drive. . . . The jeep came in sight from beyond some bluffs, turned onto the dirt road, and came up the hill toward the entrance station. Now operating a motor vehicle of any kind on the trails of a national park is strictly forbidden, a nasty bureaucratic regulation which I heartily support. My bosom swelled with the righteous indignation of a cop: by God, I thought, I'm going to write these sons of bitches a ticket. I put down the drink and strode to the housetrailer to get my badge.(43)

This passage describes a paradigmatic encounter with the machine. The jeep represents the intrusion of modern technology into the wilderness garden. It also stands for industrial tourism and everything that is wrong with the philosophy of the Park Service. For the jeep belongs to the federal government—the Bureau of Public Roads—and is driven by government employees whose job is to survey a route for a paved road that will attract more visitors to Arches. The surveyors are fulfilling part of the Park Service's "Mission 66" goal to increase dramatically the carrying capacity of the national parks by improving roads and constructing tourist accommodations (Runte 173). One can almost hear the distant voice of Aldo Leopold: "To build a road is so much simpler than to think of what the country really needs" (101).

Marx argues that in many classic works of American literature when the machine invades the garden "discord replaces harmony and the tranquil mood vanishes" (225). Certainly Abbey is outraged by the jeep's intrusion. Yet Marx's conclusion "that American writers seldom, if ever, have designed satisfactory resolutions for their pastoral fables" does not hold true for *Desert Solitaire* or for most works of nature writing in general. Contrast Marx's characterization of the typical fate of the American hero, "either dead or totally alienated from society, alone and powerless" (364), with Abbey's reaction to the work of the surveyors. He spends little time arguing with them, for he knows that "one brave deed is worth a thousand books" (*Beyond the Wall* xvi). After the jeep departs he waits for the full moon to illuminate the terrain and then retraces the route of the surveyors, uprooting their stakes along the way. "A futile effort, in the long run," he concedes, "but it made me feel good" (59). Thus occurs a significant moment in the history of nature writing: committing an illegal act against the government transforms the work that tells of it into a truly subversive, revolutionary genre.

It is as if Abbey anticipates Marx's conclusion that "the machine's sudden entrance into the garden presents a problem that ultimately belongs not to art but to politics" (365). Uprooting the stakes of the surveyors signals Abbey's realization that cultural criticism obligates the critic to go beyond mere words, to engage in political activism—even rebellion. This is the credo of Earth First!, a radical environmentalist group inspired by Abbey's words and deeds. Since its inception in 1980, the group (which now has more than 10,000 members) has spiked trees to prevent logging of old growth forests in the Pacific Northwest and sabotaged machinery to halt road construction in potential wilderness areas. Abbey himself joined with some members in March 1981 in a startling bit of environmental theatre to fulfill, at least symbolically, his greatest fantasy: the deconstruction of Glen Canyon Dam. By unfurling a 300-foot black plastic tarp down the concrete face of the dam it appeared from a distance that the eco-raiders had succeeded in cracking it (Nash, *Rights* 189–98). Abbey has even gone so far as to contribute a "Foreward!" to Earth First!'s manual *Ecodefense: A Field Guide to Monkey Wrenching,* as well as articles to the organization's newsletter. Together they have advanced the cause of biocentrism and deep ecology (McKibben 177–209).

The vehemence of Abbey's prose and his radical actions have indeed "incited a generation of environmentalists" (Sipchen 25). Abbey may echo Thoreau when he writes that "wilderness is not a luxury but a necessity of the human spirit, and as vital to our lives as water and good bread" (169);

he may call to mind Muir's religious rhetoric when he declares that "the forests and mountains and desert canyons are holier than our churches" (52); and he may recall Leopold's denunciation of our car culture when he scorns Americans on vacation who "roll up incredible mileages on their odometers, rack up state after state in two-week transcontinental motor marathons, [and] knock off one national park after another" (51). But none of these key figures of the conservation movement openly advocated and practiced illegal acts against the state to protect the wilderness. It is impossible to imagine calm, gentle, rational Leopold engaged in radical acts; and Muir, for all his rage over the damming of Hetch Hetchy, never suggested violent opposition in protest. Only Thoreau, in the white heat generated over the issue of slavery prior to the Civil War, committed civil disobedience and the illegal act of harboring a fugitive slave (Harding 315). Only Thoreau called for war against the state by letting one's life "be a counter friction to stop the machine" ("Resistance to Civil Government" 73–74).

In all but his most recent work Abbey is systematically careful not to suggest that intentional violence to humans be done in order to defend wilderness. But in *Hayduke Lives!* an accomplice of the Monkey Wrench Gang shoots and kills an armed guard who defends the GEM (Giant Earth Mover), a mega-machine which threatens to obliterate the canyon country of southern Utah. This event confirms the opinion of Paul Bryant, who feels that Abbey is more radical in his fiction than in his essays (37–39); and it suggests that near the end of his life Abbey was more radical than he had been about the means by which wilderness is to be defended.[4]

▪ ▪ ▪ What, in sum, is Abbey's eco-vision? His philosophy is not so much refined as merely repeated in subsequent works, and so *Desert Solitaire* stands as an accurate statement of his views. His consistent criticism of science and technology misapplied places him squarely in the Thoreauvian tradition of antimodernism. His own lifestyle of plain living and high thinking, the preference for conscientious over conspicuous consumption, also links him to the tradition of the simple life (Shi 3–7). And his celebration of solitude and careful, prolonged, meditative engagement with the wild place him in the long-standing and distinguished line of nature writing, associated in particular with those writers who developed "an intimate acquaintance with one cherished spot on earth" (Brooks 141). Like Thoreau at Walden, Muir in Yosemite, and Leopold in the sand counties of southern Wisconsin, Abbey succeeded in creating one more sacred place in American culture, continuing the "American apotheosis of pastoral retreat" begun by *Walden* (Buell 189). When making a pilgrimage to Arches National Park in 1978 I noticed a number of tributes to Abbey. Backpackers scrawled messages such as "Hayduke Lives!" on a blackboard at one trailhead, perfect strangers greeted each other with nicknames from Abbey's works, and yes, deep in the bowels of the canyon-lands, prospective monkey-wrenchers plotted the downfall of the machine in the garden. If the turn of the century was the era of the "Back to Nature" cult, the 1960s and '70s marked the emergence of a "Back to the Wilderness" movement, and—thanks to *Desert Solitaire*—Arches became one of its meccas.

The fact that Abbey popularized a relatively unknown portion of America's wilderness poses a problem, however. "If Abbey's books only convinced readers that the desert was worth seeing," Patricia Limerick suggests, "he would encourage a flood of automobile tourists, compounding problems of overcrowding and use" (161). Then one of the reasons the desert appealed to Abbey, its solitude, might be destroyed by his very effort at celebrating—and in effect selling—the place. The wilderness would have to be managed to control the number of visitors, which could very well destroy or significantly reduce the freedom it represented. That is, if Abbey was correct in his missionary-like certainty that he knew best what kind of outdoor recreation Americans should experience.

To the charges of elitism and causing overcrowding of wilderness Abbey, I believe, had two responses. First, if wilderness visitation did indeed increase—and he most certainly hoped it would, such was one of the aims of his twenty books—then the solution was to create more wilderness. Less than two percent of America consists of official wilderness, Abbey points out; surely we could afford to preserve yet more. Second, to the charge of elitism he pleaded guilty. As a secular prophet of the modern religion of environmentalism he believed that he stood for time-honored American values produced in response to the frontier: independence, self-reliance, self-sufficiency. His task, as he saw it, was that of a moralist out to convert the American public. Joseph Sax describes the essence of this preservationist message:

> Though he knows that he is a member of a minority, [the nature writer] believes he speaks for values that are majoritarian. He is, in fact, a prophet for a kind of secular religion. You would like to emulate the pioneer explorers, he says to the public; you would like independently to raft down the wild Colorado as John Wesley Powell did a century ago. You would like to go it alone in

> the mountain wilderness as John Muir did. Indeed that is why you are stirred by the images of the great national parks and why you support the establishment of public wilderness. But you are vulnerable; you allow entrepreneurs to coddle you and manage you. And you are fearful; you are afraid to get out of your recreational vehicle or your car and plunge into the woods on your own. Moreover you want to deceive yourself; you would like to believe that you are striking out into the wilderness, but you insist that the wilderness be tamed before you enter it. So, says the secular prophet, follow me and I will show you how to become the sort of person you really want to be. Put aside for a while the plastic alligators of the amusement park, and I will show you that nature, taken on its own terms, has something to say that you will be glad to hear. (15)

Following Abbey's death in March 1989 a flurry of obituaries appeared, many placing him in the same exalted ranks of the conservation movement as Thoreau, Muir, and Leopold. "Can Edward Abbey be compared to them?" Edward Hoagland asked, then answered in the affirmative in one of many tributes (45). Abbey, I think, bears closest resemblance to Thoreau. Both were cantankerous, contradictory, great defenders of individual freedom and vociferous critics of the state. In an introduction to *Walden* Abbey confessed that "Thoreau's mind has been haunting mine for most of my life," an acknowledgment, long in coming, that the many critical comparisons drawn between him and Thoreau were not, after all, that far-fetched. In paraphrasing the conclusion of Emerson's eulogy to Thoreau he then crafted his own best self-tribute: "Wherever there are deer and hawks, wherever there is liberty and danger, wherever there is wilderness, wherever there is a living river, Henry Thoreau will find his eternal home" (13, 48).

NOTES

1. In introductions to other of his works Abbey issues the same disclaimer. See *The Journey Home: Some Words in Defense of the American West* xi; and *Abbey's Road: Take the Other* xviii–xxi.

2. It should be noted that Abbey was once a hunter but, like Thoreau and Muir, gave up the sport. See *Cactus Country* 113–17; "Fire Lookout: Numa Ridge" 50–53; "The Right to Arms," *Abbey's Road* 130–32; "Gather at the River," *Beyond the Wall: Essays from the Outside* 173; and "Blood Sport," *One Life at a Time, Please* 33–40.

3. See for example *Slickrock* (1971; Salt Lake City: Gibbs M. Smith, 1987) 64–69; and "The Damnation of a Canyon," *Beyond the Wall* 95–103.

4. I disagree with Ann Ronald who claims that "anyone who finds in Abbey's world a prescription for violence misreads his books completely" ("Edward Abbey" 7). In *Desert Solitaire, The Journey Home, The Monkey Wrench Gang,* and subsequent works, Abbey endorses violence *against machines;* and, as I have noted in *Hayduke Lives!* appears to endorse *violence to humans* who threaten the wilderness. It is also significant that Abbey was a regular contributor to the newsletter of Earth First!, a group which has done violence to machines on numerous occasions.

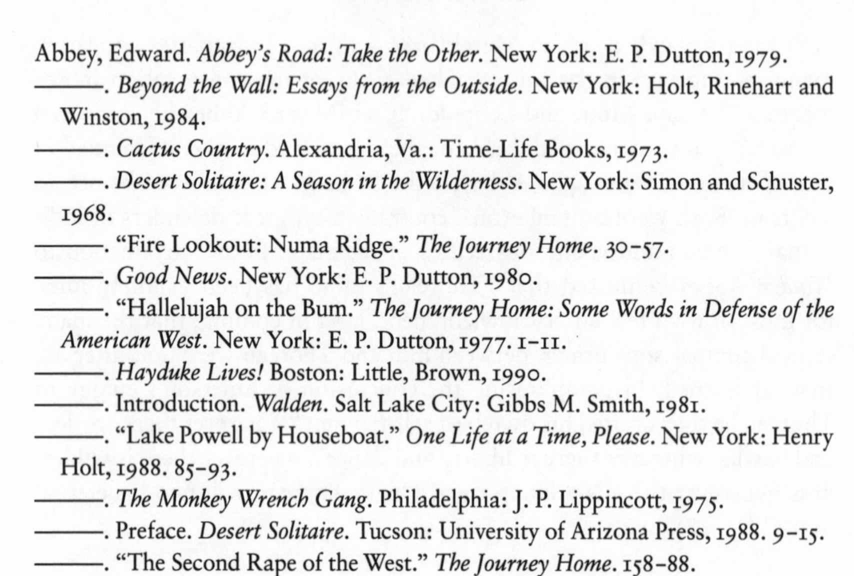

WORKS CITED

Abbey, Edward. *Abbey's Road: Take the Other.* New York: E. P. Dutton, 1979.

———. *Beyond the Wall: Essays from the Outside.* New York: Holt, Rinehart and Winston, 1984.

———. *Cactus Country.* Alexandria, Va.: Time-Life Books, 1973.

———. *Desert Solitaire: A Season in the Wilderness.* New York: Simon and Schuster, 1968.

———. "Fire Lookout: Numa Ridge." *The Journey Home.* 30–57.

———. *Good News.* New York: E. P. Dutton, 1980.

———. "Hallelujah on the Bum." *The Journey Home: Some Words in Defense of the American West.* New York: E. P. Dutton, 1977. 1–11.

———. *Hayduke Lives!* Boston: Little, Brown, 1990.

———. Introduction. *Walden.* Salt Lake City: Gibbs M. Smith, 1981.

———. "Lake Powell by Houseboat." *One Life at a Time, Please.* New York: Henry Holt, 1988. 85–93.

———. *The Monkey Wrench Gang.* Philadelphia: J. P. Lippincott, 1975.

———. Preface. *Desert Solitaire.* Tucson: University of Arizona Press, 1988. 9–15.

———. "The Second Rape of the West." *The Journey Home.* 158–88.

Austin, Mary. *The Land of Little Rain.* 1903. Albuquerque: University of New Mexico Press, 1974.

Berry, Wendell. "A Few Words in Favor of Edward Abbey." *Resist Much, Obey Little: Some Notes on Edward Abbey.* Ed. James Hepworth and Gregory McNamee. Salt Lake City: Dream Garden Press, 1985. 9–19.

Brooks, Paul. *Speaking for Nature: How Literary Naturalists from Henry Thoreau to Rachel Carson Have Shaped America.* San Francisco: Sierra Club Books, 1980.

Bryant, Paul. "Edward Abbey and Environmental Quixoticism." *Western American Literature* 24.1 (May 1989): 37–43.

Buell, Lawrence. "The Thoreauvian Pilgrimage: The Structure of an American Cult." *American Literature* 61.2 (May 1989): 175–99.

Cohen, Michael. *The Pathless Way: John Muir and American Wilderness.* Madison: University of Wisconsin Press, 1984.

Devall, Bill, and George Sessions. *Deep Ecology: Living As If Nature Mattered.* Salt Lake City: Gibbs M. Smith, 1985.

Harding, Walter. *The Days of Henry Thoreau.* New York: Dover, 1982.

Hoagland, Edward. "Standing Tough in the Desert." *New York Times Book Review* (7 May 1989): 44–45.

Krutch, Joseph Wood. *The Desert Year.* New York: Penguin, 1952.

Lawrence, D. H. *Studies in Classic American Literature.* New York: Penguin, 1961.

Leopold, Aldo. *A Sand County Almanac with Sketches Here and There.* New York: Oxford University Press, 1949.

Limerick, Patricia. *Desert Passages: Encounters with the American Deserts.* Albuquerque: University of New Mexico Press, 1985.

Lyon, Thomas J., ed. *This Incomperable Lande: A Book of American Nature Writing.* Boston: Houghton Mifflin, 1989.

McKibben, Bill. *The End of Nature.* New York: Random House, 1989.

Marx, Leo. *The Machine in the Garden: Technology and the Pastoral Ideal in America.* New York: Oxford University Press, 1964.

Muir, John. *John of the Mountains: The Unpublished Journals of John Muir.* Ed. Linnie Marsh Wolfe. Madison: University of Wisconsin Press, 1979.

Nash, Roderick. *The Rights of Nature: A History of Environmental Ethics.* Madison: University of Wisconsin Press, 1989.

———. *Wilderness and the American Mind.* Third Edition. New Haven: Yale University Press, 1982.

Paul, Sherman. "From Lookout to Ashram: The Way of Gary Snyder." *Repossessing and Renewing: Essays in the Green American Tradition.* Baton Rouge: Louisiana State University Press. 1976. 195–235.

Powell, J. W. *The Exploration of the Colorado River and Its Canyons.* 1875. New York: Dover, 1961.

Ronald, Ann. "Edward Abbey." *Fifty Western Writers: A Bibliographical Sourcebook.* Ed. Fred Erisman and Richard Etulain. Westport, Conn.: Greenwood Press, 1982. 3–12.

———. *The New West of Edward Abbey.* Albuquerque: University of New Mexico Press, 1982.

Runte, Alfred. *National Parks: The American Experience.* Second Edition. Lincoln: University of Nebraska Press, 1987.

Sax, Joseph. *Mountains without Handrails: Reflections on the National Parks.* Ann Arbor: University of Michigan Press, 1980.

Sayre, Robert F. "The Proper Study: Autobiography in American Studies." *The American Autobiography: A Collection of Critical Essays.* Ed. Albert F. Stone. Englewood Cliffs, N.J.: Prentice-Hall, 1981. 11–30.

Shi, David. *The Simple Life: Plain Living and High Thinking in American Culture.* New York: Oxford University Press, 1985.

Sipchen, Bob. "A Resurgence of Life in Writer's Death." *San Francisco Chronicle* (23 May 1989): 4.

Stegner, Wallace. *Beyond the Hundredth Meridian: John Wesley Powell and the Second Opening of the West*. Boston: Houghton Mifflin, 1954.

Thoreau, Henry David. *The Illustrated Walden*. Princeton: Princeton University Press, 1973.

———. "Natural History of Massachusetts." *The Natural History Essays*. Ed. Robert Sattlemeyer. Salt Lake City: Gibbs M. Smith, 1980. 1–29.

———. "Resistance to Civil Government." *Reform Papers*. Ed. Wendell Glick. Princeton: Princeton University Press, 1973. 63–90.

———. "Walking." *Natural History Essays*. 93–136.

Van Dyke, John C. *The Desert*. Salt Lake City: Gibbs M. Smith, 1980.

VERA L. NORWOOD

Heroines of Nature

■■■

FOUR WOMEN RESPOND TO THE AMERICAN LANDSCAPE

Rachel Carson was a heroine to many women of the 1950s and '60s who were only beginning to realize that women could make significant contributions to our understanding of the American environment. While Carson's achievements in writing about ecology still shine with a quality few women or men have achieved, her work can also be studied as part of a continuing tradition of women's natural history literature. This paper considers four texts by four women nature writers: Isabella Bird, Mary Austin, Rachel Carson and Annie Dillard. Each represents a stage in the development of women's responses to the American landscape; taken together the writings form a basis for beginning to address the degree to which women have acted as heroines in preserving the natural environment so central to American culture.[1]

To date, most studies of the American response to nature have focused on the problematic, ambivalent experience of men. Hans Huth and Roderick Nash document men's dominance of American natural history; Annette Kolodny and Richard Slotkin demonstrate that the myth of the masculine hero conquering the virginal landscape is a primary source of male ambivalence. Masculine culture in America characteristically sees wilderness as a place for defining virility, for playing out aggressive, adventure-seeking, sometimes violent impulses. Survival in a hostile natural environment is an ego-gratifying achievement and feeds the achievement-oriented male psyche, enabling men to return to civilization and improve their culture. Thus, nature is preserved because it is useful to culture. Men's ambivalence to the destruction of nature stems from this sense of the potential loss of a useful setting for a specific, and important, cultural drama. These environmental fantasies are not merely a function of the settlement process but continue into the twentieth century in metaphoric language of conservationists, preservationists and ecologists. As Roderick Nash describes the "new environmentalism" of the 1960s and '70s, the same fantasies recur: wilderness preservation is justified by the American need for an untamed environment in which we can play "pioneering" roles, renew "civilized man," and develop "self-sufficiency."

Women's responses to nature have been given attention only very recently. Work by Kolodny and others reveals that cultural stereotypes as well as physical hardships excluded many women from willing participation in the discovery of the wild American landscape, thus providing some explanation of the earlier scholarly neglect of women's experience in nature. In the typical frontier scenario women either avoided wilderness or were forced to venture onto the frontier by more adventuresome husbands. Women were thought to be more comfortable in rural, cultivated nature—in civilized gardens. Women's experiences in nature became problematic only when they were forced by men to acknowledge wilderness as an aspect of the environment; they were not perceived to experience any of the ambivalence to settlement of the frontier landscape that men did and do.[2] Lacking such ambivalence, women then might not be expected to be leaders of the late-nineteenth and twentieth century movements to conserve and preserve aspects of the wilderness, of the uncultivated, the uncivilized landscape.

Paradoxically, women's separation from pristine nature can be traced to the belief that woman is to man as nature is to culture. As Sherry Ortner posits in her essay on the subject, the issue is not a belief that women *are* nature but that they are closer to nature than men. Using Simone de Beauvoir, Ortner argues that woman's physiology, social roles and psychic structure combine to place her in a position perceived to be nearer to nature than man.[3] Although Ortner has been criticized legitimately for her attempt to defend her thesis as universally true, her conclusions as to its results remain unchallenged if one limits them to Western traditions.[4] Ortner concludes that the results of woman's perceived relative closeness to nature are a greater restriction on her activities and a "narrow and generally more conservative set of attitudes and views than men."[5]

Ortner's thesis is supported not only by historians of eighteenth and nineteenth century American women's experience, but has been documented by scholars of the scientific revolution and Enlightenment periods of the sixteenth and seventeenth centuries in Europe. Of particular interest is a fine essay by Maurice and Jean Bloch on the reluctance of French Enlightenment *philosophes* to accord women the same "natural" freedoms, including access to an untamed environment, they so passionately argued for men.[6] That these proscriptions against women's mobility in nature continued into nineteenth century America is borne out by Kolodny and Slotkin as well as Julie Jeffrey and Lillian Schlissel. That they continue into the twentieth century is evidenced by the difficulties many modern and contemporary women have found in making their voices heard in conservation organizations, in being accepted in "male" fields such as geology, and in being "permitted" access to such wilderness areas as the Himalayas.[7]

Given such documented, deep-seated bias against women moving freely into unsettled landscapes, how does one account for the women, such as those discussed herein, who opt to adventure forth and/or who support conservation movements? Are they merely exceptions to the rule? In *The Death of Nature,* Carolyn Merchant implies that such is the case when she notes that the women's movement and the ecology movement of the 1960s erupted around the same rejection of beliefs that have dominated Western culture since the scientific revolution: "Both the women's movement and the ecology movement are sharply critical of the costs of competition, aggression, and domination arising from the market economy's modus operandi in nature and society."[8] While Merchant's thesis may be an accurate portrayal of the goals of radical feminism (and radical ecology), there exists in both movements a broad spectrum of values that make such a conjunction problematic. For example, many of the issues raised by one group of feminists in the 1960s and '70s had as much to do with women's aspirations to participate in and contribute to the "market economy" as they had to do with a critique of the dominant beliefs of that society. Further, some radical feminists are now arguing against analyses that might imply women's "natural" propensity to protect the environment.[9]

While much thought has been given either to proving that women are carriers of culture resistant to nature or to proving the reverse, that women are defenders of nature against culture, very little has been said about women's ambivalent response to the nature/culture debate. This paper looks at four women who freely choose to seek out wild nature and defend it, thus defying the traditions limiting women access to and appreciation of the natural environment, but who also conclude their explorations in a state of ambivalence, thus complicating the models that assume either a total acceptance or total rejection by women of the undeveloped natural environment. Although one cannot state that these four, whose writings span a period of a hundred years, are representative of all European or American women's responses to the American environment, each of their books discussed here has had a significant readership and continues to be read in the present. Thus, each can be seen to be challenging Western cultural assumptions about women's appropriate response to nature.

In the following consideration of women as nature writers I will be exploring several questions. What comparisons arise from a study of the women as a group? What historical changes does their work reveal as we move from the late-nineteenth to the late-twentieth century? How do they describe, place value upon, or interact with the variety of environments covered—from Isabella Bird's mountains, to Mary Austin's deserts, to Rachel Carson's oceans, and Annie Dillard's creek? A study from these perspectives should provide both a feeling for the developing tradition of women's nature writing and a beginning hypothesis about the differences between masculine and feminine environmental ethics.

ISABELLA BIRD

Isabella Bird was born in 1831 in England. She had travelled the world, including visits in London and the United States, before making her celebrated journey to the Rocky Mountains in the fall and winter of 1873. As Daniel Boorstin and others have pointed out, she was not an explorer, yet she earned the respect of geographers of her time and is one of the few Victorian women travellers whose works continue to be read today.[10]

A Lady's Life in the Rocky Mountains is a series of letters Bird wrote to her sister during her visit. The series was initially published in *Leisure Hour* (an English weekly) in 1878 and by 1882 was in its seventh edition. It was a widely read, popular look at a woman's experience in the American Western wilderness. That people would find Bird's journey intriguing was clear even during her travels. She describes her notoriety thusly: "the newspapers, with their intolerable personality, have made me and my riding exploits so notorious, that travellers speak courteously to me when they meet me on the prairie, doubtless wishing to see what sort of monster I am."[11] While she was certainly not the only woman in the territory at the time (there were increasing settler families), nor was she the only female tourist (though she notes that she is not at all like the other women tourists who are too taken with themselves to appreciate the place), she was one of the most articulate, observant women who came West, sharing the same goals as many male nature lovers—to experience the place.[12] She provides an excellent beginning point in understanding how women respond to nature in America.

The first quality one notices in Bird's letters is her total determination to experience the wilderness on her own terms. The letters chronicle her emancipation from the category of female tourist to solitary traveller, from someone viewing the West out of train windows to someone on horseback able to blaze trails through rough terrain.[13] She loves the mountains, and upon seeing Long's Peak for the first time, feels she must go there. The journey is difficult, and for a time she is at the mercy of an incompetent guide, but she resolves to reach Estes Park "come what might" (p. 63).

Her efforts are tinged with a certain ascetic quality. She seeks in wilderness not only a denial of the weakness of self; the magnificent vista reached becomes a reward for the preceding purifying self-denial. She usually takes the longer, more difficult or dangerous route; her tour of the Rockies could have been done by train, but she chooses the rougher ride and the unmarked trails. This means that she quite often feels like one who "goes to sea without a compass." She is courageous also in her choice of seasons. Arriving in the Rockies just prior to winter and spending a part of the winter in isolated Estes Park, she notes that no other women tourists will appear before May (p. 240). Yet she occasionally has second thoughts. Once, after a particularly arduous escapade, she comes upon the train and reports: "I saw the toy car of the Rio Grande Railroad whirl past, all cushioned and warm, and rather wished I were in it, and not out among the snow on the bleak hillside" (p. 142).

At bottom this determination to visit the Rockies in such an uncomfortable fashion is prompted by her need for religious solitude. She constantly attempts to get far enough away from cities and settlements so that she can experience nature alone. Many of the early letters, prior to her arrival in Estes Park, lament her inability to escape from a variety of protectors and escorts, and reveal frustration at being so close to wilderness and yet unable to find privacy in it.[14] Bird discovers herself in nature, comes to a better understanding of her place in the world, while seeking a transcendant experience in nature that will take her beyond her self and into contemplation of God.[15] The letters are seeded with religious references and metaphors. Estes Park is the best place to understand religious works. There, when the "last glory of the afterglow has faded, with no books but a Bible and a prayer-book" she finds a "temple not made with hands" (p. 114). The tradition which inspires her teaches the need to simplify one's life in order to focus on higher questions.

In part, the landscape Bird values as a religious experience is conjoined with what she finds esthetically satisfying. She seems quite cognizant of the changing values attached to landscapes in Europe between the eighteenth and nineteenth centuries. For example, she makes a point of disparaging scenery that "imitates" art and cautions her readers against assuming that Estes Park implies "park palings well-lichened, a lodge with curtsying women, fallow deer, and a Queen Anne mansion" (pp. 103–6)—all qualities of "natural" landscapes valued in the eighteenth century. Being an educated woman of her age, she glories in the romantic vistas that imply moral improvement in the beholder: "Nature, glorious, unapproachable, inimitable . . . raises one's thought reverently upwards to her Creator and ours. Grandeur and sublimity, not softness, are the features of Estes Park" (p. 106).[16]

Perhaps one reason Isabella Bird's letters were so popular both in her day and the present, is that, try as she might, she is never totally successful in her search for the grand, awe-inspiring vista or the meditative setting. She wages a constant, sometimes distracted, sometimes humorous, battle with the world to reach this meditative place and state of mind; often it is nature herself which intrudes.[17] For example, insects are constantly a problem. At one point Bird, desiring solitude, takes a stroll with a book (*Imitation of Christ*) up a canyon. She naps, is wakened by a snake and finds herself "covered with black flies. The air was full of a busy, noisy din of insects, and snakes, locusts, wasps, flies, and grasshoppers were all rioting in the torrid heat. Would the sublime philosophy of Thomas a Kempis, I wondered, have given way under this?" (pp. 49–50). Such experiences are reported continually as she weaves a tale whose warp is educated, religious and meditative and weft experiental, materialistic and charged with a sense of the ironic.

Just as the irritating aspects of the biophysical world distract her, so she abhors the development of the natural landscape by American entrepreneurs. As an urbanite travelling through the wilderness, she seeks and finds for herself experiences that improve her character, but she does not find any like improvement in those Americans participating in the frontier adventures of commodity development in the West. She deplores the destruction miners are wreaking on the geological and biological landscape (p. 193).[18] Describing the settlers' lives she says they are "hard, unloving, unlovely, unrelieved, unbeautified, grinding . . ." (p. 50).[19]

She is careful to separate herself and her role as traveller from that of frontier women. Her account of an encounter with a family moving west by wagon train is a case in point. She notes that the family has been travelling four months and has lost a child and several oxen:

> They were rather out of heart. Owing to their long isolation and the monotony of the march they had lost count of events, and seemed like people of another planet. They wanted me to join them, but their rate of travel was too slow, so we parted with mutual expressions of good will, and as their white tilt went 'hull down' in the distance on the lonely prairie sea, I felt sadder than I often feel on taking leave of old acquaintances (pp. 136–37).

While Bird is sympathetic to the trials of settlement and presents a vision filled with terrors particular to women,[20] she moves more lightly, more quickly across the landscape, hoping to make as little impression on the place as possible.

In contrast, she is much taken with the lives of the solitary mountain men who do not try to change the landscape but merely to blend in with it. Her concluding letter notes that it is the company of these men she will miss the most: "never again shall I hear that strange talk of Nature and her ways which is the speech of those who live with her and her alone" (p. 244). It is, however, just such a man, Mountain Jim, who points up the inherent conflicts in her role as Victorian Englishwoman and wilderness explorer. With the exception of her relation with Mountain Jim, Bird is able to clearly delineate her conflicting roles in her travels. Her manner of horseback riding offers a most vivid glimpse of how she separates her spheres of action. In the wilds, Isabella Bird rides astride her horse, but when she comes near settlements she switches to side-saddle—willingly maintaining her role as a cultivated lady.

While the "mission" of the Victorian woman in general may have been to "civilize" men, it is not, however, hers. She does not go West to civilize the land—that she sometimes does so is not out of choice. Bird's response to her courtship by Mountain Jim expresses the priority of her search for wilderness over her civilizing function. Jim contains for Bird the same conflicting pulls between wild nature and civilized culture she experiences in the landscape of the West. He is a mountain man—rough, violent and dangerous, in many ways reminiscent of a bear she once met in the woods. He also knows the wilds, how to live in them and appreciate their beauty. With his aid Bird climbs Estes Peak. Jim is also, at times, a gentleman. He has golden curls, dresses well and writes poetry. He treats her as a lady, with respect. The conflict arises in the different values each places on the other. Jim sees Isabella as his civilizing angel—one who can return him fully to culture. Much as she regrets his violent, destructive character, it is the "natural" man, the wilderness in Jim, that Bird finds attractive. When she rejects his proposal, she rejects the "mission" to civilize the man just as she rejects the "mission" to civilize the place.

Did Isabella Bird's return to England, her rejection of Mountain Jim's offer, imply a need to return to "civilization" because the wilderness proved too threatening?[21] While Bird senses the dilemma a Victorian woman's presence in the wilderness raises, neither she nor Mountain Jim can marry and maintain their allegiance to wilderness. She feels that the journey's end for the settlers' wives can result neither in the comforts of wild nature nor the comforts of Victorian domesticity, but sadly in a loss of both. Rather than become a part of the weary drama of changing the frontier into a settled land, she returns to England in order to prepare to explore other frontiers. In a preface to *A Lady's Life* written seven years after the first publication of the book, Bird warns off other wilderness lovers noting that "the framehouse is replacing the log cabin, and . . . the footprints of elk and bighorn may be sought for in vain on the dewy slopes of Estes Park" (p. 5). In this she was wrong; the wildlife survived and does today because a national park now virtually surrounds Estes Park. But Bird foresees what was indeed the usual result of the drama; she refuses to become part of it. As an Englishwoman and a city-dweller she can avoid it, so she does not grapple with alternative solutions to America's response to the unsettled landscape. Bird changes only her definitions of beautiful landscape in her encounters with the wilderness; she does not feel a need to adapt her culturally determined definitions of good and evil, civilized and uncivilized to the requirements of the terrain. Thus, she can find inspiration in the mountains while rejecting as annoyances both classes of creatures and classes of people engaged in creating life on that landscape.

MARY AUSTIN

Mary Austin, supremely concerned with relationships between the geologic and biophysical landscape (including, in the latter, humans) seeks to resolve the conflict between nature and culture—to find a means of valuing all aspects of nature—by overcoming hierarchical traditions in Western culture that imply the desert is wasteland, snakes are evil and man controls nature.

Austin is an American writing about a landscape that is her home. She was eighteen when her family took up dry land farming in the San Joaquin Valley in 1886; most of the rest of her life was spent in the Southwest. The tourist experience is only a minor part of Austin's concern, where for Bird that sense of being a foreigner in an exotic land is constantly stressed. While Bird dismisses the settlers and the native populations as equally problematic, Austin finds them very important to her audience's understanding of how one can live in this difficult landscape. *The Land of Little Rain,* Austin's most famous book, in many ways rebuts Bird's dismissal both of American culture (native and imported) and of the possibility for responsible, civilized, life in the wilderness landscape.[22]

While Isabella Bird is continually on the watch for the magnificent vista, the thundering herd, or the grand sunset and often finds the details of nature a trial to be borne, Austin values all life in the desert, and attempts to show how each small piece is integral to that larger whole. *The Land of Little Rain* provides vibrant descriptions, achieved only by patient observation, of the interacting physical and biological landscape of the desert Southwest. One of the early essays in the book, "Water Trails of the Ceriso," is remarkable for its loving description of the wildlife of the desert and its chronicle of the dependence of animals on the scarce water.[23] As Bird gradually realizes, one comes to a different aesthetic in rugged wilderness than in hospitable gardens. For Bird, beauty can be found in mountain terrain, for Austin in the desolate colors of the desert. Austin explains why people come to dwell "in the loneliest land that ever came out of God's hands": "The rainbow hills, the tender bluish mists have the lotus charm. They trick the sense of time, so that once inhabiting there you always mean to go away without quite realizing that you have not done it."[24]

Rather than critiquing the desert for its lack of qualities that are common in England or the American East for that matter, Austin explores those differences with a sense of wonder at the adaptations they require:

"There are hints to be had here of the way in which a land forces new habits on its dwellers. The quick increase of suns at the end of spring sometimes overtakes the birds in their nesting and effects a reversal of the ordinary manner of incubation. It becomes necessary to keep eggs cool rather than warm" (p. 9). Many of these observations come from the soul of one who lives in this place and who has to understand what personal adaptations are required. Thus Austin begins at a point of acceptance Bird never reached.

Like Bird, she subjects herself to the hardest route, the worst weather—but the object of her search is often quite different. For example, Austin describes the desert wind in terms initially reminiscent of the negative experiences humans have in it: "There is no looking ahead in such a wind, and the bite of the small sharp sand on exposed skin is keener than any insect sting" (p. 158). The description evokes the very human perception of nature as challenge; the normal response in such winds is to seek shelter, but Austin goes out: "It is hot, dry, fretful work, but by going along the ground with the wind behind, one may come upon strange things in its tumultuous privacy. . . . I like the smother of sound among the dunes, and finding small coiled snakes in open places . . ." (p. 159). Austin values the challenges of nature not for the magnificent views overcoming them provides, but in themselves, for the effect they produce and the interactions they reveal. In this context a snake then becomes as wonderful a sight as the herds of elk Bird discovered in Estes Park.

Although Bird values wilderness as a place of freedom from civilization, she never doubts that civilization will overtake the wilds. She does not see the possibility of a relationship, other than that based on challenge, between man and nature. Austin does, and what concerns her in *The Land of Little Rain* is the emergence of mechanistic definitions of nature and culture supporting the assumption that humans can and should impose their will on the world with no repercussions. Her ambivalence to the settlement of the desert is thus expressed in a concern for the misrepresentations of nature, particularly wilderness nature, that her Anglo, Western culture brought to the desert. In other words, she is not as concerned that the desert landscape will disappear as she is that people will misunderstand the adaptations in their lives that it requires. She writes a great deal about people who are successful at living in the desert, on its terms, finding examples in independent prospectors, American Indians and Hispanic communities.

While Bird sees enough in America to grasp the destruction the Anglo invasion brings to the native cultures, she is never close enough to the American Indians she observes to have any sense of how they live. She also responds most strongly only to people with an educational background and culture similar to her own. Mary Austin takes a totally different approach, valuing both the Indian and Hispanic for their alternate approach to the development of the American landscape—natural and cultural. Her sense of the American Indian's graceful adaptations to nature is at the core of this response. Describing "Shoshone Land" Austin comments that "the manner of the country makes the usage of life there, and the land will not be lived in except in its own fashion. The Shoshones live like their trees, with great spaces between . . ." (p. 59). Furthermore, they make the Southwest their home, meaning for Austin that home is inseparable from the country surrounding it. It is not possible to build a home that looks like a Shoshone's anywhere but in the Southwest. The surrounding landscape, not the architecture, gives weight to the word "home": "Not the weathered hut is his home, but the land, the winds, the hill front, the stream. These he cannot duplicate in any furbisher's shop as you live within doors, who, if your purse allows, may have the same home in Sitka and Samarcand" (p. 108).[25]

Austin responds similarly to Hispanic settlements. The *Land of Little Rain* concludes with a celebration of the virtues of life in El Pueblo de Las Uvas—"The Little Town of the Grapevines." What impresses her most is her perception of a slow tempo, a relaxed life unfilled with the ambitious, industrious motion of Anglos: "Come away, you who are obsessed with your own importance in the scheme of things, and have nothing you did not sweat for, come away by the brown valley and full-bosomed hills, to the even-breathing days, to the kindliness, earthiness, ease of El Pueblo de Las Uvas" (p. 171).

Excepting the solitary prospector, Austin provides only one example of Anglo community in the desert—Jimville, a dying mining town "about three days from anywhere in particular" (p. 70). Jimville both reveals the problems of the Anglo approach to nature and provides hope for adaptation of that culture to the landscape. At one time it was a successful mining town, reeking of industry and ambition. But the boom failed and the society that is left is a survivor in a very organic sense: "You could not think of Jimville as anything more than a survival, like the herb-eating, bony-cased old tortoise that pokes cheerfully about those borders some thousands of years beyond his proper epoch" (p. 70).

Austin's account of Jimville expresses her ambivalence to Anglo settlement: ambition, industry, development, progress, simply do not apply to the desert. Jimville is a successful adaptation to the desert *because* it failed. The people who remain have adapted to the rhythms of the land. This is not to imply that they no longer engage in mining but that they do so on the land's terms: "They develop prospects and grow rich, develop others and grow poor, but never embittered . . . at Jimville they understand the language of the hills" (p. 77). Jimville evinces the enforced humility of frontier settlements—due to their tenuousness—that makes Isabella Bird so uncomfortable. The ugly, unadorned settlements and dwellings that are such a torment to Bird's sensibilities become, in this context, doors to nature rather than obstructions in its path.

Mary Austin knows that her culture requires a certain defeat of pride before it can accept the requirements of life in the wilderness. At bottom she espouses a humility before nature that entails rejecting the burgeoning scientific and technological approaches to the wilderness. She likes the Jimville approach to mining because it is not "educated." She learns more about herbs from local, native women than from her own scientific training. She chides her culture for following "on a very careless usage, speaking of wild creatures as if they were bound by some such limitations as hampers clockwork" (p. 19).[26] Nature and culture are interactive processes: human culture is affected by the landscape as well as effecting change on it. Austin teaches her culture how best to respond in an interactive rather than an hierarchical mode.

Both Austin and Bird envision a nature, most specifically an undomesticated nature, that is skewed toward the ideal. One in her travels and the other in her ever increasing centering on one spot search for the perfect fit between a dream of a place and its actual experience. While each is honest enough to describe the death and destruction both in nature and upon nature they witness in passing, it is to this ideal their writing points. Although Austin seems less disturbed than Bird by the "peopling" of this land, she hints at the coming destruction of the wilderness in *Land of Little Rain* as she ruefully notes that "there is an economy of nature, but with it all there is not sufficient account taken of the works of men. There is no scavenger that eats tin cans, and no wild thing leaves a like disfigurement on the forest floor" (p. 40). Austin's comment, made in passing in a book written in 1903, makes a fine introduction to the work of Rachel Carson.

RACHEL CARSON

Rachel Carson is best remembered for her indictment of the life-destroying potential of pesticides in her classic *Silent Spring*. But Carson was an established and well-respected naturalist before *Silent Spring* was published. Her study of the oceans—*The Sea Around Us*—published in 1951, earned her the John Burroughs Medal and the National Book Award. The book was so popular that it was difficult to keep in stock, and was ultimately made into a film (which was itself an Oscar winner). Many readers were surprised that a woman could write such a comprehensive, "scientific" book. Carson received fan mail assuming that she was male, or implying that, if she were a woman, she must be a very old woman to know so much about the ocean. (She was in her early forties at the time.)[27]

While *The Sea Around Us* is not exclusively about American waters, its impetus was time Carson spent at the Marine Biological Laboratory at Woods Hole, Massachusetts, where she says she was literally surrounded by the ocean: "I could see the racing tidal currents pouring through the 'Hole' or watch the waves breaking at Nobsha Point after a storm, and there I first became really aware of the unseen ocean currents."[28] Carson echoes Mary Austin's concern that one does not understand a people until one has lived in the place from which they spring. In her acceptance speech for the National Book Award for *The Sea Around Us*, she explains why a scientific book such as hers, which has little to say directly about human life, was so popular: "The materials of science are the materials of life itself. Science is part of the reality of living; it is the what, the how and the why of everything in our experience. It is impossible to understand man without understanding his environment and the forces that have molded him physically and mentally."[29]

Carson recognizes an organic, interactive connection between humans and the rest of the biosphere. There is, however, a major difference in Carson's definition of knowledge and Austin's. Mary Austin, skeptical of the burgeoning science of her time, presents it as potentially another aspect of her Anglo culture that separates humans from nature rather than joining them together. Scientific method can violate the organic, interactive terms of the human/nature environment; its developing importance in her culture was one of the causes of her ambivalence to Anglo intrusion into the desert landscape. Carson, writing forty years later, committed to a life of science, was concerned not with whether we should accept the knowledge science brings, but how best to use it. The difference between her vision of scientific ethics and her perception of her society's lack of such ethics forms her ambivalent response to increased human involvement with the undeveloped sea, for Carson saw the ocean as the womb of life, the perfect place to begin to understand the forces that have molded human life.

The Sea Around Us opens with grand vistas of nature—the geologic events leading to the creation of earth and ocean. The coda for the section "Mother Sea" looks to origins: "Fish, amphibian, and reptile, warm-blooded bird and mammals—each of us carries in our veins a salty stream in which the elements sodium, potassium, and calcium are combined in almost the same proportions as sea water."[30] The core of our being is determined by the ocean for each generation comes from the sea again: "each of us begins his individual life in a miniature ocean within his mother's womb, and in the stages of his embryonic development repeats the stages by which his race evolved, from gill-breathing inhabitants of a water world to creatures able to live on land" (p. 14).

For Carson adaptation—change caused by pressures in the environment—is interactive and ecological. As Austin notes the pressures desert terrain puts on plant life, so Carson notes similar demands on sea life. But Carson extends the work of earlier naturalists like Austin by a new sense of the value of all aspects of nature. While Bird marvels only at "glorious" vistas and thundering wildlife and Austin gives the scavengers and snakes of the world a certain charm, Carson, benefitting from advances in research, offers a whole new pantheon of heroic creatures—"hordes of small carnivores" in plankton the human eye has difficulty seeing at all (p. 19). Their worth stems not only from their importance in the food chain; they are described so as to give a sense of their strength. Carson gives plankton a value beyond its use as a food source for other creatures; plankton contains in itself those beautiful adaptations and interactions that are appreciated among larger species.[31]

Throughout *The Sea Around Us* Carson points out humankind's inability to live in terms of the grand natural cycles science has enabled us intellectually, at least, to know. Science reveals events we cannot experience but only know. Thus, in describing how a newly created island develops plant and animal life, she first acknowledges the typical human response to the time scale such population takes: "To wonder impatiently why man is not a constant witness of such arrivals is to fail to understand the majestic pace of the process" (p. 90).

The incongruity between our urge to discover and our inability fully to comprehend the nature of the discovery shapes Carson's ambivalent response to man's presence on a wilderness landscape—the ocean. But, Carson is as much a twentieth century scientist as Bird is a nineteenth century traveler. Much of *The Sea Around Us* details the discoveries new scientific technology has made possible.

Yet, *The Sea Around Us* also reveals a deep concern with the hubris attached to discovery and with the historical inability of people to take the long view of their actions in respect to nature. "The Birth of an Island" documents the results of such hubris through a chronicle of human destruction of island ecosystems. Often the havoc is done simply because we attempt to "improve" on nature by importing new species. Carson is not hopeful about the results of our exploratory urges, our need to use knowledge to change the world.

Her lament echoes similar concerns of Austin and Bird over destruction of wild landscapes, but she defines the causes with far more precision and concern than either earlier writer could. Both Bird and Austin take solace in escape—one to other exotic lands, the other to a "rosy mist of reminiscence." Both engage in idealized descriptions of nature. Carson does not, finding enough wonder in the actual experience.

For example, Carson is more overt than Bird and Austin in her handling of the destructive qualities of nature. While Bird does not appreciate "soft" nature, loving instead the untamed, neither is she able to meld such experiences as her visit by a bear or attack by insects into her vision of a sublime world. Austin makes the unpleasant aspects of nature—from scavengers to violent storms—useful, helpful and even beautiful. Carson is more conscious of the paradox; she occasionally hints at beauty interwoven in violent aspects of nature in descriptions such as a close study of the sea surface, but she does not apologize. A beautiful shower of fish, which initially seems a sight given by an artist, is actually so much dinner for larger fish below and gulls above (p. 17).

In the early 1950s, when Carson finished *The Sea Around Us,* she was optimistic about the use science could make of nature while still respecting the final priority of natural processes over human manipulation. The book evinces some ambivalence to human attempts to change natural cycles, because they seem doomed to failure and can have negative consequences, but the negative consequences do not threaten the continuance of natural life cycles. Ten years later, at work on *Silent Spring,* Carson was no longer as sanguine about the ability of the environment to protect itself from human interference. She had begun to understand the destructive impact civilization had on the environment, and was presented with a dilemma: The growth of civilization destroys the environment, but only through increased knowledge (a product of civilization) can destruction be stopped.

Growth in science and technology led to the use of the ocean as a dump for radioactive wastes. The choice of the ocean as dump was based on the belief that it was "inviolate, beyond man's ability to despoil" (p. xi, 1961 ed.). Carson now realized that radioactive waste can have disastrous impacts both on ocean life and life on land. Carson wanted both to use the ocean—to settle it—and to maintain a proper respect for the environment that gave us life. She became ambivalent about settlement when she recognized the human potential for destruction of life.

Where Mary Austin took solace in a mystery that seemed to protect the world, an unexplainable organic rhythm that made human works look small and gave the wild environment priority, Rachel Carson, living in the atomic age, had no such solace. In describing her loss of faith and using it to explain her earlier optimism about the growth of knowledge Carson says:

> It was pleasant to believe . . . that much of Nature was forever beyond the tampering reach of man: he might level the forests and cloud the streams, but the clouds and the rain and the wind were God's. . . . It was comforting to suppose that the stream of life would flow on through time in whatever course that God had appointed for it—without interference by one of the drops of the stream, man. And to suppose that, however the physical environment might mold life, that life could never assume the power . . . to destroy the physical world.[32]

Her humbling prophecy of the future of life reverberates back through American culture to the Puritans' fear of God's potential abandonment and banishment into a "howling wilderness" void of life.[33] In 1960 the choice between garden and desert was as live an issue as it had been in 1660—wilderness continued as both threat and promise.

ANNIE DILLARD

The biblical echo Carson voiced in *The Sea Around Us* is used quite consciously by the last woman discussed here; the choice remains alive in the 1980s as well. Annie Dillard's *Pilgrim at Tinker Creek* begins with a classic vision of uncertainty about the American landscape—are we in Eden or the desert? The book opens with a story of Dillard's "old fighting tom" cat, who would jump "through the open window by my bed in the middle of the night and land on my chest . . . And some mornings I'd wake in daylight to find my body covered with paw prints in blood . . . the sign on my body could have been an emblem or a stain, the keys to the kingdom or the work of Cain. I never knew."[34] She provides a contemporary voice speaking the doubts and confusions about ethical responsibility to God in the natural environment that the Puritans brought with them to "wild" America.

Dillard's primary concern is her individual, personal relationship to God and nature. This focus gives her work a different character from the more socially oriented writings of Bird, Austin, and Carson: "I must start somewhere, so I try to deal with . . . Tinker Creek . . . and let those who dare worry about the birthrate and population explosion among solar systems" (p. 131).

Pilgrim at Tinker Creek is so engrossing in its approach to nature that one critic has described Dillard as bringing to her work "an artist's eye, a scientist's curiosity, a metaphysician's mind, all woven together in what might be called, essentially, a theologian's quest."[35] Her book contains intentions toward nature that existed separately in all three of the previous writers. Following Bird, Dillard sees nature as a religious door; following Carson, she brings all her knowledge, training and sense of historical event to bear on her experience in nature; following Mary Austin she centers on one place, feeling that all the rest of the world can be understood in terms of this place—Tinker Creek.

Like the earlier writers, Dillard is a master of natural description. She has lived in her place and come to know it intimately as Austin knew her desert. She wants one to know everything about Tinker Creek, how it appears at various seasons, various times of day, the animal and human life that live on it, and its position in terms of the rest of the globe.

She is interested in any piece of information or advance in understanding that better describes the particular environment and she is equally taken with the gaps in knowledge that continue the mystery. Reminiscent of Carson's examination of the creatures in plankton is Dillard's essay on "Intricacy." Beginning with a general description of her goldfish Ellery, stressing how ordinary he is (p. 126), she moves into a description of Ellery's circulatory system, explaining how she learned about it by looking at an etherized goldfish tail under a microscope: "The red blood cells in the goldfish's tail streamed and coursed through narrow channels. . . . They never wavered or slowed or ceased flowing, like the creek itself; they streamed readily around, up and on, one by one, more, and more, without end" (p. 127). Through her description she connects the small world of Ellery's circulation with the larger universe. She then does the same thing with the water plant elodea, concluding with a short lesson on the chemical similarities between Ellery's blood and elodea chlorophyll commenting that "it is, then, a small world there in the goldfish bowl, and a very large one" (p. 129). She goes on into metaphors of art:

> We go down landscape after mobile, sculpture after collage, down to molecular structures like a mob dance in Breughel, down to atoms airy and balanced as a canvas by Klee, down to atomic particles, the heart of the matter, as spirited and wild as any El Greco saints. . . . The creator, I would add, churns out the intricate texture of least works that is the world with a spendthrift genius and an extravagance of care (p. 130).

The knowledge of the molecular structure of Ellery's tail opens nature for her in the same way scientific knowledge did for Carson, to larger and larger circles of meaning.

As Rachel Carson points out, the more we know, the less sure we are of our knowledge and the more we want to know. Her world, and Austin's, are based on the hope that there is a fit between natural demands and adaptations to those demands: circumstances change and organic forms change to meet them. The problem is to understand the fit. Yet the mysteries, the unanswered questions, seem to expand. Carson wants to move toward solving pieces of the mystery. Dillard is content with the quality of natural mystery itself—its ultimate unsolvability.

Her concentration on the metaphysical heart of the issue leads her to find the concept of a fit most problematic. Using Werner Heisenberg's Principle of Indeterminacy as a base point Dillard asserts that we will never know why nature operates as she does: "nature is a fan dancer born with a fan; you can wrestle her down, throw her on stage and grapple with her for the fan with all your might, but it will never quit her grip. She comes that way; the fan is attached" (p. 207). For Dillard, one of the great mysteries of nature is that everything does not seem to fit together, does not fall neatly into place:

> The point . . . is not that it fits together like clock work—for it doesn't, particularly, not even inside the fishbowl—but that it flows so freely wild, like

the creek, that it surges in such a free . . . tangle. Freedom is the world's water and weather, the world's nourishment freely given, its soil and sap: and the creator loves pizazz (p. 140).

Pilgrim at Tinker Creek is a meditation upon the beauty and horror of and in creation. In this it is akin to Bird. Occasionally Dillard experiences nature as a door to the eternal; the best experience for this being the vision of a flaming tree (p. 35). An epiphany of destruction is watching a frog sucked to death by a giant water bug: "He was a very small frog with wide, dull eyes. And just as I looked at him, he slowly crumpled and began to sag. The spirit vanished from his eyes as if snuffed . . . it was a monstrous and terrifying thing" (p. 7).

Even more appalling is the vision of the two strands meeting. The bulk of *Pilgrim at Tinker Creek* is Dillard's attempts somehow to reconcile the images of beauty and horror: humans and their civilization are really the only true holders of moral beauty in the world; or the terror itself contains beauty if we only look correctly; or in contradiction, beauty does not exist. She concludes that beauty exists in spite of the horror and terror of the great bulk of the natural world and that it is finally found equally in the grand and the simple—both in "the fissures between mountains. . . . the wind lances through" (p. 276) and in a maple key, falling to "the wind of the spirit where it listeth, lighting and raising up, and easing down" (p. 275).

Dillard is a much more self-conscious writer than any of the other three, perhaps the effect of life in a self-conscious age. Understanding that the Principle of Indeterminacy reveals how impossible it is to separate subject and object she chooses to place her personal voice at the forefront of her work.[36] Also motivating this choice is Dillard's conception of the artist/writer, which is different from Carson's. Dillard is not in the business of losing herself in nature (however much she may enjoy the occasions when she does so); she interacts both positively and negatively with nature. She once described the process of writing *Tinker Creek,* from 1,103 note cards, working in a library carrell: "You're writing consciously, off hundreds of index cards, often distorting the literal truth to achieve an artistic one."[37] That is something Carson tried not to do.

As Austin did, she finds in the American Indian culture a way of responding to nature that seems close to what she seeks. Much of what she says about the Eskimo has to do with the hunt and how it parallels her own hunt in nature, particularly in the concentration with which they stalk

(p. 185). She is also taken with their understanding of the cruelties of nature and even their participation therein. At one point, Dillard describes the way Eskimo women and children once used live birds to entrap other birds to make bird-skin shirts. She goes on to comment: "I doubt that they make birdskin shirts anymore. . . . They do not do many of the old things at all any more, except in my mind, where they hunt and stitch well, with an animal skill, in silhouette always against white oceans of ice" (p. 187).[38]

Dillard dismisses the artifacts of Anglo-European culture. Early in the journal she is walking to the creek and must go around some steers:

> They are all bred beef: beef heart, beef hide, beef hocks. They're a human product like rayon. They're like a field of shoes. They have cast-iron shanks and tongues like foam insoles. You can't see through to their brains as you can with other animals; they have beef fat behind their eyes, beef stew (p. 4).

They are domesticated nature, not the experience she seeks.

Finally Dillard distorts the reality of the contemporary American landscape in order to challenge the hubris that would place culture as a construct above nature. Just as Rachel Carson's jeremiad argues for the continued presence of wilderness—in its potential for return through the destruction of humanity—so Dillard makes a case for the priority of nature. But she rejects the duality between nature and culture. No matter what we create as humans, it will reflect back to nature—there is no escape, only acceptance.[39] Our tame world, our controlled, created garden is only a momentarily calm surface; if we look closely, everything opens back to nature. Even that which we create is but a mirror of nature and as such provides apt reflections of natural processes.

Dillard's journal is really a time machine—a modern, well-educated woman arrives on the shores of America in the seventeenth century. The question is whether the wilderness is Eden or the desert, whether God intends to visit her with milk and honey or howling beasts and hordes of locusts, whether she can march through the world at her ease or must fight for survival. Dillard's answer is both. The benefit she has over her seventeenth century ancestors, her knowledge of three centuries of trying, shows her the futility of attempts to turn the wilderness into a garden and the possibility that the garden will yield to wilderness at any moment.[40]

In such knowledge is freedom from the agonies of doubt about what God expected or expects in "setting us down here." Dillard's book concludes in a delicious celebration and an invitation:

> There is always an enormous temptation in all of life to diddle around making itsy-bitsy friends and meals and journeys for itsy-bitsy years on end . . . I won't have it. The world is wilder than that in all directions, more dangerous and bitter, more extravagant and bright. We are making hay when we should be making whoopee; we are raising tomatoes when we should be raising Cain, or Lazarus (p. 276).

With this comment Dillard frees women from safe, cultivated gardens, playing out their burden of guilt for destroying Eden. Her statement of freedom only reflects, however, the choices of her three predecessors to leave the garden and venture forth into the wilderness.

The issue is freedom. At the core of the restrictions on women's movement into wilderness is the masculine fear of "the other." Women are more likely to express this "otherness" in an untame environment than when they are controlled, restricted by cultural bounds.[41] Much of the recent scholarly work by Western historians on women's responses to the frontier is basically a validation of women's internalization of this view. Believing it was dangerous for women to trespass in the wilds, they were fearful of the experience. Once settled on the frontier, they proceeded to "civilize" the environment with a single-minded energy. Yet the diaries and journals of the pioneers (male or female) reveal little about the next stage in America's definition of nature—the stage that began to value the untouched environment and the people who lived closest to it.[42]

There is evidence suggesting that women's voices in that next stage, in the conservation and preservation debates, were limited by continuing social restraints. As Roderick Nash notes, much of the "cult of wilderness" contained a message specifically for the male psyche—that civilization emasculated and wilderness returned virility.[43] The taboos against women's participation in any but civilized nature continue into the twentieth century. Women nature writers have been described as filling only secondary roles; they seem mostly to have written for children (fulfilling their roles as mediators between nature and culture) or helped organize the Audubon clubs in order to raise other women's consciousness about the destructive effects of wearing bird feathers in their hats.[44] They were thus limited to roles as followers, carriers of culture, not themselves offering the lead in new understandings of either scientific ecology or environmental ethics. This study of four women nature writers indicates that there has been another female voice, one which critiques the dominant culture as well as functioning within it, by calling into question the basic language of challenge in which even the proponents of wilderness seem often snared.

Finally, the question of women's voice must be addressed: are women saying something different than men? This sense of a different experience has been the impetus for much of the research on women's experience as pioneers. This was the question that began this paper: what is women's response to the development of the American wilderness? Do these nature writers phrase their ambivalence to growth in terms similar to their male colleagues? Based on the four books discussed herein, there is one striking difference between men's and women's sense of their responsibility to the environment.

Feminine culture characteristically defines nature in a much more "immanent" fashion. Nature is: before culture there was nature, after culture there will continue to be nature. Their cultural drama is not one of successful challenge, nature overcome, but of full recognition, nature comprehended. Until Annie Dillard, their ambivalence to the progress of culture grew out of the fear that development can destroy the opportunity for recognition. Dillard's security is her educated guess that human culture is but one aspect of nature, as much a part of the ecology as her pet goldfish. All four, however, are concerned not with action on the environment, but with understanding how nature (particularly wilderness) acts on them. That such understanding might better human culture is, for them, a peripheral issue.

Rachel Carson's heroism began this paper and can also fittingly conclude it. In the early 1950s two best-selling books about the ocean were written: Carson's *The Sea Around Us* and Thor Heyerdahl's *Kon-Tiki*. Heyerdahl presents a classic tale of adventure and heroism on the high seas—a tale of challenge, virility, and dominance of the environment. It is the traditional hero's journey. Carson, simultaneously, provides the heroine's drama in an equally classic tale of immersion of self into nature—a tale filled not with dominance but humility, that forfeits the individual voice so that nature can speak. We know a great deal about the heroism of the first voice, but very little about the equally heroic acts of the second.

NOTES

1. No comprehensive study of women nature writers has yet been done, although several authors have provided discussions in other contexts. Anne La Bastille's

Women and Wilderness (San Francisco: Sierra Club Books, 1980) describes women's response to American wilderness, focusing on a series of interviews with women who lived in the wilds (as scientists, explorers or solitaries) but did not necessarily write about nature. Paul Brooks's *Speaking for Nature: How Literary Naturalists from Henry Thoreau to Rachel Carson Have Shaped America* (Boston: Houghton Mifflin, 1980) offers a chapter, "Birds and Women," that considers nineteenth century women who wrote about birds, mostly for juvenile audiences. Brooks's text also includes discussions of Mary Austin and Rachel Carson, but he makes no attempt to consider the women as a group.

2. Roderick Nash, *Wilderness and the American Mind* (New Haven: Yale University Press, 1967, 3rd ed. 1982). Hans Huth, *Nature and the American* (Lincoln: University of Nebraska Press, 1973). Richard Slotkin, *Regeneration Through Violence: The Mythology of the American Frontier* (Middletown, Conn.: Wesleyan University Press, 1973). Annette Kolodny, *The Lay of the Land* (Chapel Hill: University of North Carolina Press, 1975). Wayne Hanley, *Natural History in America: From Mark Catesby to Rachel Carson* (New York: Quadrangle, 1977). For discussions of the underlying cultural taboos to the frontier women's response to wilderness see Julie Roy Jeffreys's *Frontier Women: The Trans-Mississippi West, 1840–1880* (New York: Hill and Wang, 1979), Lillian Schlissel's *Women's Diaries of the Westward Journey* (New York: Schocken Books, 1982), and two essays by Annette Kolodny, " 'To Render Home a Paradise,' Women and the New World Landscape," in *Women's Language and Style*, ed. Douglass Buttruff and Edward Epstein, *Studies in Contemporary Language, No. 1* (Akron: University of Akron, 1978); "Turning the Lens on 'The Panther Captivity': An Exercise in Feminist Practical Criticism," *Critical Inquiry* (Winter 1981): pp. 329–45. Kolodny's forthcoming book explores the ways in which women use their own fantasies of landscape as garden to acculturate themselves to new frontiers. Kolodny's text offers one of the first analyses of women's ambivalence to the environmental destruction wrought by settlement. *The Land Before Her* (Chapel Hill: University of North Carolina Press, 1984).

3. Sherry B. Ortner, "Is Female to Male as Nature Is to Culture?," in *Women, Culture and Society*, ed. Michelle Rosaldo and Louise Lamphere (Stanford: Stanford University Press, 1974), p. 73.

4. *Nature, Culture and Gender*, ed. Carol P. MacCormack and Marilyn Strathern (Cambridge: Cambridge University Press, 1980).

5. Ortner, p. 85.

6. Maurice Bloch and Jean Bloch, "Women and the Dialectics of Nature in Eighteenth-Century French Thought," in *Nature, Culture and Gender*, pp. 25–42. Carolyn Merchant's *The Death of Nature: Women, Ecology and the Scientific Revolution* (San Francisco: Harper and Row, 1980) is an examination of the conjunction of increased repression of women with the coming of the scientific revolution. Merchant shows that the arguments for restrictions of women's roles were based in

great part on fears of their closeness to "wild" nature (see Chapter 5: "Nature as Disorder: Women as Witches," pp. 127–49).

7. Bastille, *Women and Wilderness*. See also Arlene Blum's story of the societal blocks to her assault on Annapurna in *Annapurna: A Woman's Place* (San Francisco: Sierra Club Books, 1980).

8. Merchant, *Death of Nature,* p. xvi. In a recent essay, Merchant offers an analysis of political "realities" that, in practice, have separated the two movements. "Earthcare," *Environment* (June 1981), pp. 6–40.

9. For an analysis of the complexities of feminism in the 1970s see Sarah J. Stage, "Women," *American Quarterly* 35 (Spring/Summer 1983), 169–90. Michele Rosaldo offers one of the best examples of the changing constructs through which men's and women's lives need to be analyzed in "The Use and Abuse of Anthropology: Reflections on Feminism and Cross-Cultural Understanding," *Signs: Journal of Women in Culture and Society* 5, No. 3 (1980), 389–417.

10. See Daniel Boorstin's introduction to the 1960 edition of *A Lady's Life in the Rocky Mountains* (Norman: University of Oklahoma Press), p. xviii. A fine study of these travelers is Dorothy Middleton's *Victorian Lady Travellers* (New York: E. P. Dutton, 1965).

11. *A Lady's Life in the Rocky Mountains,* p. 235.

12. Pat Barr, *A Curious Life for a Lady* (Garden City, New York: Doubleday and Co., 1970), p. 15. Dorothy Middleton feels that Bird's need to travel was kindled by the housebound life of Victorian women and was an urge acted upon by a surprising number of women of her time, p. 6.

13. Middleton notes that Bird and her contemporary trekkers sought solitude and were reluctant to have traveling companions.

14. Boorstin notes this frustration but does not connect it with her determination to seek the hardest route, LL, p. xxii.

15. The best study of religious and romantic background in America is Roderick Nash's *Wilderness and the American Mind*. See Chapter 3: "The Romantic Wilderness," pp. 44–66.

16. For a summary of the changing esthetic values of landscape from the eighteenth to nineteenth centuries see Edward Relph, *Rational Landscapes and Humanistic Geography* (London: Barnes and Noble Books, 1981), pp. 22–41. In keeping, however, with the general tendency to deny women's serious participation in the development of landscape meaning, Relph mentions women only once in this section, commenting that "common late-nineteenth century attitudes . . . understood landscape as an object for casual contemplation and the development of sentimental associations, something to be indulged in by daughters of the nouveaux riche," p. 41. One questions whether such a statement adequately summarizes the regard in which Isabella Bird was held by her contemporaries.

17. Nash deals extensively with this ambivalent response to nature: "On the one

hand it is inhospitable, alien, mysterious and threatening; on the other, beautiful, friendly, and capable of elevating and delighting the beholder. Involved, too, in this second conception is the value of wild country as a sanctuary in which those in need of consolation can find respite from the pressures of civilization," p. 4.

18. Pat Barr adds another dimension to Bird's preservationist stance in noting that Bird was not much interested in the adventure of "Opening the West. . . . She took little satisfaction in seeing an iron track tame a hitherto inaccessible pass," p. 80.

19. Middleton notes that her interest in people diminished even further in her later travels: "Only the sky and hills never failed her," p. 44.

20. Lillian Schlissel's *Women of the Westward Journey* is especially helpful in delineating the isolation, loss and fear of death of family that overwhelmed many women on the overland trails.

21. Bird's biographer sees her choice not to marry Jim to be part of an ultimate need to return to the "civilization" of Victorian England, Barr, p. 90.

22. For background in Austin's life see her autobiography, *Earth Horizon* (New York: Houghton-Mifflin Co., 1932), her letters, *Literary America: 1903–1934: The Mary Austin Letters,* ed. T. M. Pearce, Contributions in Women's Studies, No. 5 (London: Greenwood Press, 1979) and Pearce's biography, *Mary Hunter Austin* (New York: Twayne Publishers, Inc., 1965). In Pearce's mind Austin's "greatest gift was that of interpreting the land in outline and meaning. . . ." p. 128.

23. Austin seemed a little ahead of her time in proposing a theory about the relationship between all the parts of nature which was similar to Aldo Leopold's later vision of a "land ethic." Like Leopold, she believed in the rural farm and the small community. She was also fearful of the changes that industrialization and specialization could bring to such delicate balances between man and land, as she had witnessed some of this destruction in her time following shepherds in Southern California. For her record of that time see *The Flock* (New York: Houghton-Mifflin, 1906).

24. Mary Austin, *The Land of Little Rain* (Albuquerque: University of New Mexico Press, Orig. publ. 1903, rep. 1974), p. 11.

25. Austin, however, understands that any human life in the landscape leads to disruption and pollution, and she includes American Indian cultures in this recognition. See her comments on the Paiutes in LLR, p. 97. She feels, nonetheless, that American Indians do live more lightly on the landscape than any other people.

26. It is important to realize that Austin was a mystic, and had, in fact, experienced something of a religious conversion in nature while a child. She further believed in animism, both in the sense of there being a sentience in all natural objects and in the sense of the continued presence in the world of the spirits of the dead. See Pearce, *Mary Hunter Austin.*

27. Paul Brooks's biography of Rachel Carson provides background informa-

tion on her life; Brooks is, however, primarily interested in describing Carson as a writer. Brooks reprints some letters to Carson, from which the information on readers' reactions to a woman science writer is taken. *The House of Life: Rachel Carson at Work* (Boston: Houghton Mifflin, 1972), p. 132.

28. Ibid., pp. 110–111.

29. Ibid., p. 25. Not only did Mary Austin's concern for the pollution of the natural environment presage Carson's work, she also saw a need for just this kind of humanistic writer who could present the findings of science to a general readership. See her essay "Science for the Unscientific," *The Bookman*, 55, No. 6 (August 1922), 5.

30. Rachel Carson, *The Sea Around Us* (New York: Oxford University Press, 1951), pp. 13–14.

31. Both Bird and Austin had some training in natural history. When in England, Bird read much, attended lectures and generally tried to stay current. Mary Austin studied science in college and clearly used her training in her writing. But neither pursued formal advanced training nor worked as professionals in the field, which Carson did. It is interesting to note that Rachel Carson entered college with the intention of becoming a writer and only changed her career goal after studying with a woman biology professor.

32. Brooks, *House of Life*, p. 10. Apparently this facet of Carson's belief system was not unusual to scientists trained in her generation. See Hanley, p. 329.

33. Sacvan Bercovitch's study of the importance of the religious symbols of Puritanism to the development of the American response to the landscape provides an excellent background to this choice. Bercovitch contends that a specifically American form of the jeremiad, incorporating a future of both promise and condemnation "was based on a continuing sense of crisis: The American Puritan Jeremiad made anxiety end as well as means. Crisis was the social norm it sought to inculcate. The very concept of errand, after all, implied a state of unfulfillment." Further, Bercovitch contends that the Puritans, and succeeding generations of Americans, believed in themselves as God's chosen people, inhabiting a landscape predestined in biblical prophecy. Thus the urgency of the concern for the meaning of the landscape. Carson's threat of destruction is a contemporary jeremiad form. *The American Jeremiad* (Madison: University of Wisconsin Press, 1978).

34. Annie Dillard, *Pilgrim at Tinker Creek* (New York: Bantam, 1975), p. 111.

35. Mike Major, "Pilgrim of the Absolute," *America*, 138 (May 6, 1978), 363.

36. Eudora Welty finds this self-absorption somewhat limiting, but it fits the traditional search for solitude found even in the Victorian lady travellers. See Welty's review of *Tinker Creek* in the *New York Times Book Review*, Mar. 24, 1974, pp. 4–5. Her further evaluation that Dillard is a much better nature writer than she is metaphysician is, however, quite valid. Significant portions of *Tinker Creek* sink from the weight of Dillard's speculations on the "larger" themes to which a contemplation of nature leads.

37. Major, 363.

38. This connection of naturalism and hunting is not unusual. Many have noted that the initial urges to preserve and protect nature were integrally linked to the wish to hunt the very animals being protected. See especially Donald Fleming's discussion of Theodore Roosevelt in *Roots of the New Conservation Movement,* Perspectives in American History, 6 (Cambridge: Harvard University Press, 1972), p. 17.

39. In a review of *Pilgrim,* Eleanor Wymard posits that Dillard is not so much a transcendentalist as she is an existentialist. For Wymard this means that "Living with nature . . . provides Dillard neither escape from life, nor therapy to return to life, nor programs designed to improve the status quo." Although I would agree with Wymard's contention of Dillard's slippery refusal to be "moral," she is very consciously providing a method for living, one based on a lack of duality between nature and culture. She is emphatically stating an ethic in this text. "A New Existential Voice," *Commonwealth,* October 24, 1975, pp. 495–96.

40. This is a more complex feminine image and voice than that proposed for Dillard by David Lavery. Lavery, trying to show how Dillard responds as a woman to nature, falls into the trap of looking at only the "Madonna" image, the supportive mother image, forgetting that women as well as men participate in and understand destruction. Thus, in his conclusion, he does not really allow Dillard the self-conscious vision she finally offers. David L. Lavery, "Noticer: The Visionary Art of Annie Dillard," *Massachusetts Review,* 21 (1980), 255–70.

41. A good study of the taboo against white women's presence in the wilderness (with the concurrent assumption of American Indian women's "savage" state in the wilds) is Dawn Lander's "Eve Among the Indians" in *The Authority of Experience: Essays in Feminist Criticism,* ed. Arlyn Diamond and Lee R. Edwards (Amherst: University of Massachusetts Press, 1977), pp. 194–211. Carolyn Merchant explores the fifteenth and sixteenth century fear of the "dark side" of woman and its concomitant suppression of women into culturally acceptable roles in her discussion of witches, *Death of Nature,* pp. 128–48.

42. Nash sets the date for the beginning of the change in attitude in the middle decades of the nineteenth century, a time when "wilderness was recognized as a cultural and moral resource and a basis for national self-esteem," WAM, p. 68. He further sees the popularization of this attitude evidenced in 1874: "When congress . . . appropriated $10,000 for a painting of the Grand Canyon to hang in the Senate Lobby, the American Wilderness received official endorsement as a subject for national pride," (p. 83). Historians of the overland trail period, who have done the majority of the work on women's response to undomesticated nature, usually end their studies around 1880.

43. See Nash's quotes from Muir's works: "a little pure wilderness is the one great present want, both of men and sheep" and "civilized man chokes his soul as the heathen Chinese their feet," pp. 127–28.

44. Brooks, *Speaking for Nature,* 165–80. Brooks is to be credited with documenting women's participation in the history of nature writing in America and with his sympathetic evaluations of their contributions. He leaves unexamined, however, the possibility of any difference between the reasons for men's and women's valuations of the natural world.

SCOTT SLOVIC

Nature Writing and Environmental Psychology

■ ■ ■

THE INTERIORITY OF OUTDOOR EXPERIENCE

I only went out for a walk, and finally concluded to stay out till sundown, for going out, I found, was really going in.—John Muir, Journal (1913)

Wilderness is above all an opportunity to heighten one's awareness, to locate the self against the nonself. It is a springboard for introspection. And the greatest words, those which illumine life as it is centrally lived and felt, intensify that process.—Bruce Berger, *The Telling Distance: Conversations with the American Desert* (1990)

Sharon Cameron has suggested that "to write about nature is to write about how the mind sees nature, and sometimes about how the mind sees itself" (44). I believe this statement holds true not only for Henry David Thoreau, to whom Cameron is referring specifically in her book *Writing Nature: Henry Thoreau's Journal* (1985), but also for many of Thoreau's followers in the tradition of American nature writing. Such writers as Annie Dillard, Edward Abbey, Wendell Berry, and Barry Lopez are not merely, or even primarily, analysts of nature or appreciators of nature—rather, they are students of the human mind, literary psychologists. And their chief preoccupation, I would argue, is with the psychological phenomenon of "awareness." Thoreau writes in the second chapter of *Walden* (1854) that "We must learn to reawaken and keep ourselves awake" (90). But in order to achieve heightened attentiveness to our place in the natural world—attentiveness to our very existence—we must understand something about the workings of the mind.

Nature writers are constantly probing, traumatizing, thrilling, and soothing their own minds—and by extension those of their readers—in quest not only of consciousness itself, but of an *understanding* of consciousness. Their descriptions of this exalted mental condition tend to be variable and elusive, their terminologies more suggestive than definitive. Thoreau himself (drawing upon classical sources and daily cycles for his imagery) favors the notion of "awakening"; Dillard and Abbey use the word "awareness" to describe this state, though for Dillard such activities as "seeing" and "stalking" are also metaphors for stimulated consciousness; Berry, at least in his major essay "The Long-Legged House" (1969), emphasizes "watchfulness" as a condition of profound alertness; and for Lopez, two complementary modes of "understanding" natural places, the "mathematical" and especially the "particularized" (or experiential), serve as keys to mental elevation.

Both nature and writing (the former being an external presence, the latter a process of verbalizing personal experience) demand and contribute to an author's awareness of self and non-self. By confronting "face to face" the separate realm of nature, by becoming aware of its "otherness," the writer implicitly becomes more deeply aware of his or her own dimensions, limitations of form and understanding, and processes of grappling with the unknown. Many literary naturalists imitate the notebooks of scientific naturalists, the logbooks of explorers, or even the journals of nonscientific travelers in order to entrench themselves in the specific moment of experience. The verbalization of observations and reactions makes one much more acutely aware than would a more passive assimilation of experience. As Annie Dillard bluntly puts it in describing one of her two principal modes of awareness, "Seeing is of course very much a matter of verbalization. Unless I call my attention to what passes before my eyes, I simply won't see it" (*Pilgrim,* 30).

Giles Gunn writes that "Modern man tends to view the encounter with 'otherness' . . . as a mode of access to possibilities of change and development within the self and the self's relation to whatever is experienced as 'other.' " We associate "reality," he continues, "with the process by which we respond to [other worlds'] imagined incursions from 'beyond' and then attempt to readjust and redefine ourselves as a consequence" (*Interpretation of Otherness,* 188). The facile sense of harmony, even identity, with one's surroundings (a condition often ascribed to rhapsodic nature writing) would fail to produce self-awareness of any depth or vividness. It is only by testing the boundaries of self against an outside medium (such as nature) that many nature writers manage to realize who *they* are and what's what in the world.

Most nature writers, from Thoreau to the present, walk a fine line (or, more accurately, *vacillate*) between rhapsody and detachment, between aesthetic celebration and scientific explanation. And the effort to achieve an equilibrium, a suitable balance of proximity to and distance from nature, results in the prized tension of awareness. "This oscillating movement between man and his natural doubles is," according to Alain Robbe-Grillet, "that of an active consciousness concerned to understand itself, to reform itself" ("Nature, Humanism, Tragedy," 69). Geoffrey Hartman, in commenting on Wordsworth, uses different terms to say something similar: "The element of obscurity, related to nature's self-concealment, is necessary to the soul's capacity for growth, for it vexes the latter toward self-dependence" ("Romance of Nature," 291). In other words, the very mysteriousness of nature contributes to the independence and, presumably, the self-awareness of the observer. This dialectical tension between correspondence and otherness is especially noticeable with Thoreau, Dillard, and Abbey—these writers vacillate constantly between the two extreme perspectives. Berry and Lopez, however, do not vacillate so dramatically. Their sense of correspondence with the natural world in general or with particular landscapes does fluctuate, sometimes seeming secure and other times tenuous, but for the most part these two writers assume an initial disjunction (that of a native son newly returned from "exile" in Berry's case, and that of a traveler in exotic territory in Lopez's) which is gradually, through persistent care and attentiveness, resolved. The result, for Berry, is a process of ever-increasing "watchfulness"; for Lopez, one of deepening respect and understanding.

For all of these contemporary American nature writers, the prototypical literary investigation of the relationship between nature and the mind is Thoreau's Journal (*The Journal of Henry D. Thoreau,* hereafter referred to and cited as Thoreau's Journal). The Journal, far from being a less artful and therefore less interesting subject for scholars than the works published during Thoreau's lifetime, is actually an example of nature writing at its purest, no conscious attempt having been made to obscure and mystify the writer's intense connection or disconnection with his natural surroundings. In the published works the temporal element tends to be muted (by extensive philosophical digressions in his 1849 *A Week on the*

Concord and Merrimack Rivers and by the somewhat concealed seasonal movement in *Walden,* for instance) and the authorial self often dissolves into multiple personae. The Journal, on the other hand, generally presents consistent temporal and spatial locations; we receive almost daily entries from a consistent narrator and it's usually clear exactly where Thoreau was and what he did or thought while he was there. The Journal gives us the sense throughout of Thoreau's actual presence in the natural world, something we encounter only intermittently in the published works, even in the many essays organized according to the excursion format. And not only is the author's proximity to nature more consistent and concrete in the Journal, but there is also a more explicit *testing* of the boundaries of self against the "other world" of nature.

One of the major "issues" of the text, which covers more than twenty years of Thoreau's life (1837–1861), is whether there is, in Emersonian terms, a "correspondence" between the inner self and the outer world, between the mind and nature. This is a question that Thoreau never answers finally—and thus results the rich tension of identity forging. The Journal, an almost daily record of observations (predominantly measurements of seasonal transformations), shows the author's efforts to line up his internal rhythms with those of external nature. There are times when Thoreau takes pleasure in the apparent identity of his own fluctuating moods and the "moods" of the passing seasons. At other times, though, it is nature's very *otherness* which fascinates and delights him: "I love Nature partly because she is not man, but a retreat from him" (4.445). The idea of nature as distinct from man gives the cranky author more than mere refuge from the annoyances and trivialities of the human world. This understanding, which comes from constant and thorough observation of natural phenomena, helps Thoreau both to enlarge his minute self by anchoring it in nature and, conversely, to become more deeply conscious of his human boundaries. Along these lines, in his 1986 study William Rossi provides an illuminating discussion of Coleridge's theory of "polarity" in the context of Thoreau's frequent opposition of civilization and wildness. Rossi suggests that the very independence of the two realms (and, on a smaller scale, the individual human observer and the specific natural phenomenon) creates a vital tension that binds the poles together ("Laboratory of the Artist," 57–103). Virtually all nature writers in Thoreau's wake perpetuate his combined fascination with inner consciousness and external nature, but I have chosen to focus my comments in this essay on Dillard, Abbey, Berry, and Lopez because they represent with particular clarity modern variations of Thoreau's two opposing modes of response to nature: disjunction and conjunction.

For the purposes of the writer at the time of the actual observation (or of the journal-writing, which may, in Thoreau's case, often have occurred back at his desk), the journal is simply the most expedient way to keep a record, to protect observations from the foibles of memory. But even more importantly, as Dillard suggests in the quotation I gave above, putting things into language helps people see better; and this can happen either at the moment of confrontation or in retrospect while sitting at a desk hours later. Of course, it is possible to record observations without strictly keeping track of chronology, but for the nature writer the omission of time-of-day and time-of-year would betoken a vital lapse of awareness. Nature changes so dramatically between noon and midnight, summer and winter, and sometimes even minute by minute, that the observer fails to grasp the larger meaning of phenomena if he or she overlooks the temporal aspect. Also, by making regular entries, the writer establishes a consistent routine of inspection; the condition of awareness thus becomes more lasting, and is not consigned to occasional moments of epiphany alone. For the reader, the journal form in nature writing (either the private journal or the various kinds of modified journals and anecdotal essays) produces a vicarious experience of the author's constant process of inspecting and interpreting nature, and heightens the reader's awareness of the author's presence in nature.

My interest in the way nature writers both study the phenomenon of environmental consciousness and attempt to stimulate this heightened awareness among their readers has led me to consult some of the scientific literature on environmental perception. Stephen and Rachel Kaplan—most recently the authors of *The Experience of Nature: A Psychological Perspective* (1989)—edited an earlier collection of essays called *Humanscape: Environments for People* (1982), which I have found particularly useful. In his introductory essay, Stephen Kaplan cites William James's seminal definition of the perceptual process: "Perception is of probable and definite things" (31). "By 'probable,'" Kaplan writes, "[James] meant that we tend to perceive what is likely, what is familiar, even when the stimulus is in fact not familiar. By 'definite' he meant that we tend to perceive clearly, even when the stimulus is vague, blurred, or otherwise ambiguous" (32). In other words, rather than attending fully and freshly to each new experience when we look at the world, we tend to rely upon previously stored information—what Kaplan and others refer to as "internal representations" (33). Although we may generally feel certainty when we perceive external reality, we are actually making what Kaplan calls "best guesses" (32) and *not* perceiving everything thoroughly, in detail. The reasons for this perceptual process are, of course, understandable. Often we don't have the time for thorough inspection—when we round a bend in the mountains and glimpse a large gray object, it is useful to decide quickly whether we have seen a dozing grizzly or a mere boulder. What especially interests me, though, is the implication that even when we feel certain we *know* our natural environment, we probably do not—we may not even have really looked at it.

It seems to me that Annie Dillard and Edward Abbey, in their efforts to stimulate our attentiveness to nature and to the foibles of our own minds, our delusions of certainty, take pains to invoke and then upend precisely the system of perception which Kaplan, echoing James, describes. Later in the *Humanscape* volume, William R. Catton, in an article entitled "The Quest for Uncertainty," suggests that "one important type of motivation underlying the recreational use of wilderness by the average devotee may be the mystery it holds for him" (114). The excitement of mountain climbing, he explains, "is not in reaching the summit but in carrying on the task in the face of doubt as to whether the summit will be reached or will prove unattainable" (113). With a similar sense of the grippingness of uncertainty, Dillard and Abbey tend to place special emphasis on the startling, sometimes even desperate, *un*predictability of the natural world. They capitalize in their essays on the harsh and chilling features of the landscapes they love, recounting with particular avidness experiences in which perception has not been probable and definite. The emotional result is disgust, horror, annoyance, surprise, and almost always (at least in retrospect) satisfaction with the intensity of the experience.

Critics have traditionally been thrown off track by the flashy catchwords of Dillard's *Pilgrim at Tinker Creek*—specifically, the language drawn from either religion or natural science—and by their own desires and expectations. Think of the book's title, for instance: *Pilgrim at Tinker Creek*. This in itself indicates the usual poles of critical response. Many readers approach the book expecting (and frequently *finding*) a "pilgrim," a person making a quest for spiritual knowledge or fulfilling a spiritual commitment through meditation on wonders of divinely mysterious origin. Others dwell upon the *final* words of the title, "Tinker Creek," suggestive of a natural place. They expect to read meditations on nature or on man/nature interaction, and these readers are often put off by what they perceive as the work's anthropocentrism. Hayden Carruth, in an early review, deplores Dillard's abstractness and her failure to attend "to life on this planet at this moment, its hazards and misdirections," referring to Wendell Berry's writing as more responsible and "historically . . . relevant" than Dillard's (640). And still other readers combine the two "poles" of the title and label Dillard a "visionary naturalist," though not always a successful one (Lavery, 270).

But Dillard is not now and never has been precisely a religious mystic *or* an environmentalist. She calls herself an "anchorite" on the second page of *Pilgrim* and a "nun" in her next book of prose, *Holy the Firm,* which appeared in 1977 and in which one of the few characters other than Dillard herself is an accident-scarred—"Her face is slaughtered now" (41)—girl named "Julie Norwich." But despite her beguiling hints and suggestions Dillard is not a latter-day Julian of Norwich. Nor is she Rachel Carson's literary "daughter," alerting the nation to the urgent problems of the environment. She is, I would say, a kind of hybrid—if we were to push this hypothetical lineage to absurdity—of Thoreau and William James. The "wake-up call" of Thoreau's chapter "Where I Lived, and What I Lived For" (*Walden*) reverberates throughout her works, as does the process of psychological experimentation demonstrated in the Journal, the alternating closeness to and estrangement from nature. Dillard is—and here I believe I deviate, at least in emphasis, from previous readers of her early work—a devoted student of the human mind, of its processes of awakening, its daily, hourly, and even momentary fluctuations of awareness. And in this way she is much like William James, an investigator of the varieties of human consciousness. However, whereas James dwelled upon the varieties of *religious* experience, Dillard's emphasis (especially in *Pilgrim*—less so in her recent work) is on the varieties of *natural experience*—or, more precisely, on the experience of both heightened and dulled awareness of nature.

This is not to discount entirely the important religious and natural historical currents in her work. But I do think the *central* focus of her writing has always been the psychology of awareness. Even *Living by Fiction* (1982), with its concern for how writers working in various fictional and nonfictional genres experience "the raw universe" (145) and transform this experience into literature, is, to a great degree, psychological. In *Pilgrim* and *An American Childhood* (1987), Dillard displays with particular vividness her habit of provoking insight and wonderment by estranging herself from ordinary scenes and events. Fecundity and death, the opposing processes of nature so prominent in *Pilgrim,* are probably the most fundamental and therefore common processes in the natural world. Yet Dillard, in her dream-like observations of a giant water bug sucking the life out of a frog and the reproduction of a mantis ("I have seen the mantis's abdomen dribbling out eggs in wet bubbles like tapioca pudding glued to a thorn," *Pilgrim,* 167), uses unexpected language to transform the quotidian into the cataclysmic, thus snapping herself alert to the world and to her own thought processes. It is the verbalizing process, as she herself notes in the chapter of *Pilgrim* called "Seeing," which makes her a more conscious, meticulous observer of the commonplace, an observer able to appreciate the strangeness (the "otherness") of the world. Through her encounters with nature and her use of language, she awakens to her own participation in and distance from the organic world and to the dimensions of her own mind.

Readers of *Pilgrim at Tinker Creek* usually have the impression of the author's palpable proximity to nature, and her intimate knowledge of it. But the book is actually a study of Dillard's *disconnection* with the little patch of Virginia countryside near Tinker Creek, full of awareness-prompting misperceptions, occasions when the author recalls expecting to see one thing and then encountering another. Every little thing surprises Dillard—awakens her. For her, being awake is not a steady condition or even an evolutionary process, but a repeated event. One key example of this awakening process—which few readers are likely to forget—appears at the very outset of the book. Dillard recalls how she once walked beside the creek with growing confidence—indeed complacency—in her ability to perceive the landscape: "I learned to recognize, slowing down, the difference in texture of the light reflected from mudbank, water, grass, or frog" (5). The sense of a *certain* environment, it soon becomes clear, is evidence of the viewer's unawareness. Eventually she saw a frog that didn't jump when she neared it, and she writes that as she stared, "lost" and "dumbstruck,"

> he slowly crumpled and began to sag. The spirit vanished from his eyes as if snuffed. His skin emptied and drooped; his very skull seemed to settle and collapse like a kicked tent. He was shrinking before my eyes like a deflating football. I watched the taut, glistening skin on his shoulders ruck, and rumple, and fall. Soon, part of his skin, formless as a pricked balloon, lay in floating folds like bright scum on top of the water: it was a monstrous and terrifying thing. I gaped bewildered, appalled. (5–6)

However, this "monstrous and terrifying thing," every bit as much as the glorious "tree with lights on it" (33) which she later encounters, is just what Dillard seeks in her explorations of nature. It is a stimulant of awareness, much as her highly animated language stimulates the engagement of her readers through surprise and exaggeration. Dillard's own alertness to nature is erratic, sometimes seriously flawed. In an essay called "Dancing With Nature," Don Mitchell points out that Dillard's knowledge of praying mantises was less than adequate when she wrote *Pilgrim at Tinker Creek*. Merely passing along a misconception (typically a grotesque one) that she received from the nineteenth-century French entomologist Henri Fabre rather than something she glimpsed with her own eyes, Dillard sustains, in Mitchell's words, "a hundred-year-old libel on praying mantises" by suggesting that females "devour their male sex partners" ("Dancing," 195–96). This misconception inspired some of the most memorable prose in Dillard's book—yet I would imagine that even Mitchell's rebuttal would be, for her, an occasion of celebration, a surprising disruption of the world flattened into predictability.

Edward Abbey, like Dillard, has often found his work co-opted by readers who need his voice for purposes other than his own. In his tongue-in-cheek Introduction to *Abbey's Road* (1979), Abbey claims to recall an incident which occurred after he gave a reading "at some country campus in Virginia." When a student accused him of not looking "right," not fitting the image of "a wilderness writer. An environmental writer," Abbey supposedly responded with the following indignant self-definition: "I am an artist, sir, . . . a creator of fictions" (xxi–xxii). But this poor student is certainly not alone in his failure to sort out Abbey's intriguingly overlapping literary personalities. The critics, too, have often been baffled, either ignoring his work altogether or confining it to rather predictable and inadequate labels. Much of Abbey's writing, both his fiction and his nonfiction, defies easy categorization—like George Washington Hayduke, the green-beret-turned-ecoterrorist in *The Monkey Wrench Gang*, Abbey's 1975 novel, the writer's own language feints one way, dodges capture, hides out until the coast is clear, then parades itself once again before carrying out yet another daring escape.

Desert Solitaire, his most famous work of nonfiction, exists for many readers as pure rhapsody—indeed, as an elegy for the lost (or, at least, fast-disappearing) pristinity of the Canyon country in Utah. *The Monkey Wrench Gang*, on the other hand, is usually read as a straightforward call-to-arms for environmentalists, and such radical preservationist groups as

Earth First! have even claimed it as their Bible. But neither description is really adequate. Ann Ronald encompasses part of the truth when she explains, in *The New West of Edward Abbey* (1982), how he uses "his sense of humor to pronounce a sobering message" in the latter work (200). I would push this explanation one step further by suggesting that Abbey's abundant humor—which typically takes the form of puns—is merely one aspect of his broader devotion to the aesthetics of language. I believe that Abbey's true project, his essential consciousness-raising effort, hinges upon the conflation of pure aesthetics and volatile moral issues (such as the sacredness of the wilderness, the inviolability of private property, and the appropriate use of public lands). "I write in a deliberately outrageous and provocative manner," Abbey once told Judy Nolte Lensink in an interview, "because I like to startle people. I hope to wake up people. I have no desire to simply soothe or please" (Trimble, *Words from the Land,* 27). This tension between aesthetics and morality is evident throughout Abbey's work, but it is particularly noticeable in *Desert Solitaire* and *The Monkey Wrench Gang,* the latter of which I consider the *Lolita* of the environmental movement. Just as Nabokov's 1955 novel *Lolita,* ideally, throws its readers into a richly conflicted state of disdain, pity, admiring sympathy, and aesthetic pleasure, Abbey's novel heightens our attentiveness to issues of the environment (while providing little explicit dogma) by presenting *disturbing* extremes of both preservation and development in a literary context aimed to *please.* Obviously, *The Monkey Wrench Gang* is a novel, and hardly a journal-like one at that. But I believe it demonstrates a bold extension of the exploration of human awareness which Abbey began in *Desert Solitaire,* a more direct echo of Thoreau's own psychological journal.

The multiple layers of *The Monkey Wrench Gang,* although present throughout the work, are particularly evident in a scene midway through the narrative. While lying with his lover Bonnie near a campfire, Hayduke (alias "Rudolf the Red") is awakened by raindrops falling on his face. " 'What's the matter, Rudolf?' " Bonnie asks.

> "It's raining."
> "You're nuts. It's not raining. Go to sleep."
> "It is. I felt it."
> She poked her head out of the hood of the bag. "Dark all right . . . but it's not raining."
> "Well it was a minute ago. I know it was."
> "You were dreaming."

> "Am I Rudolf the Red or ain't I?"
> "So?"
> "Well goddammit, Rudolf the Red knows rain, dear."
> "Say that again?" (282–83)

End of scene. On one level, of course, this dialogue fits into the larger context of the narrative: the two characters are out in the wilderness and it starts to rain. But the main purpose of this scene is simply to set up the reindeer pun, which Hayduke supposedly utters unconsciously but which Bonnie, in her half-sleep, catches. Is Abbey merely having fun with language here? Is this why the novelist intrudes elsewhere with more or less explicit references to himself? In one scene, for instance, a ranger named "Edwin P. Abbot Jr." (190) inspects a box of Bonnie's belongings and finds, among other things, a "personally autographed extremely valuable first-edition copy of *Desert Solipsism*" (196), an allusive echo of Abbey's original title ("Desert Solecism") for the work which became *Desert Solitaire*. It seems that Abbey had a great deal of fun in writing this novel, but I don't think this is the only reason for the work's many conspicuous aesthetic games and extravagances. All of this, I believe, is related to Abbey's exploration of the way our minds work, and his discovery that we frequently become alert to things (including ourselves) not through harmony, but through opposition, even antagonism.

The epistemologist Michael Polanyi suggests in his essay "The Structure of Consciousness" (1965) that there are "*two levels of awareness:* the lower one for the clues, the parts or other subsidiary elements and the higher one for the focally apprehended comprehensive entity to which these elements point." He goes on to explain that "The way we know a comprehensive entity by relying on our awareness of its parts for attending to its whole is the way we are aware of our body for attending to an external event. We may say therefore that we know a comprehensive entity by *interiorizing* its parts or by making ourselves *dwell in them* . . ." (214). The strain of trying to interiorize disparate elements—such as the self and nature or, perhaps, the divergent moral and aesthetic strata of a novel such as *The Monkey Wrench Gang*—vaults us to higher levels of awareness.

There is a sudden shift in mood and language when we turn to consider the final two writers, Wendell Berry and Barry Lopez, whom I have selected for this overview because they contrast so vividly with the more flamboyant and whimsical modern nature writers. Whereas Dillard and Abbey tend to emphasize disjunction and unpredictability in their efforts to prompt awareness, Berry and Lopez take the opposite approach, mirroring the correspondential swing of Thoreau's mental pendulum. For Dillard and Abbey, the most effective stimulus of intense alertness is change, surprise, the disruption of the facile certainty implied by the Jamesian concept of perception. But Berry and Lopez assume ignorance or limited awareness to begin with, then proceed to enact a gradual and almost linear progression, a continual deepening of awareness. What most people merely *perceive* as "probable and definite" in the external world, these two writers attempt to make ever more solid, ever more certain. Neither of these writers ever claims to have achieved a fully developed consciousness, an unsurpassable plateau of awareness. Like Thoreau, they emphasize the *ongoing process* of mental growth, but they deviate from the dazzling erraticness of Thoreau's other heirs, Dillard and Abbey, in their steady and (perhaps to some readers) tediously persistent movement toward the world.

In "The Long-Legged House," the lengthy essay which is my primary example of Berry's "watchfulness," the author presents the history of his attachment to his native place along the Kentucky River, showing "how a person can come to belong to a place" (145). It was only after contemplating Andrew Marvell's poetry about man's place in nature that Berry began "that summer of [his] marriage the surprisingly long and difficult labor of *seeing* the country [he] had been born in and had lived [his] life in until then" (141). Thus Berry's work implies the need to move beyond complacent acceptance of our "internal representations" of the places where we live or visit, the need to see things consciously, to become *aware*—and it indicates also the role of literature in inspiring and guiding "awakening" (to use Thoreau's word) of its readers. The essay sweeps through many years of Berry's life, recounting the history of the place where he eventually, after years as a wandering academic, came to live and re-vitalize his roots. Berry also digresses from direct discussion of this place, known as "the Camp," in order to reflect abstractly on connections between the self and the natural world, on ways of coming to know intimately a specific natural place. The place, he says, will reveal its secrets to the human observer, but it takes prolonged contact: "The only condition is your being there and being *watchful*" (169—my emphasis).

This necessary watchfulness is enhanced by the process of writing. At the point in the history when Berry and his wife have returned to the Camp and he has vowed to become (as he later puts it) "intimate and familiar" with the place (161), he recalls that he began writing "a sort of journal, keeping account of what [he] saw" (146). Immediately after he mentions this, the style of the essay, too, changes—it becomes much more detailed and concrete, the pace of the narrative slowing to allow the presentation of specific natural observations, examples of how "the details rise up out of the whole and become visible" to the patient observer (161). What is interesting to me about this process of observation is that Berry associates it explicitly with the act of writing, a connection manifested even in the way the prose of the essay changes, becomes more journal-like and immediate, at the point in the history when the author is finally making contact with the place. The result of this increasing intimacy with the Camp and the nearby river landscape, despite the deepening sense of attachment, is an awareness that the man belongs to the place without the place belonging to the man. So there remains a disjunction between man and his most familiar natural place—the separation lessens, but is never erased entirely. This awareness does not mitigate the author's feeling of attachment, but it does result in the distinctive humility of Berry's work, in the frequent reminders that people are part of a vast world.

Although Berry narrates this process of return and re-connection most thoroughly and explicitly in "The Long-Legged House," he also meditates compellingly on exile, homecoming, and belonging to a place in such works as "Notes from an Absence and a Return" (a 1970 essay/journal which tersely parallels "The Long-Legged House"), the Odysseus section in *The Unsettling of America* (1977), and "The Making of a Marginal Farm" (1980). In the latter essay, Berry makes an important distinction between writing about a place from afar, treating it merely as "subject matter," and actually living on the land that is, in turn, on his mind. "In coming home and settling on this place," he writes,

> I began to *live* in my subject, and to learn that living in one's subject is not at all the same as "having" a subject. To live in the place that is one's subject is to pass through the surface. The simplifications of distance and mere observation are thus destroyed. . . . One's relation to one's subject ceases to be merely emotional or esthetical, or even merely critical, and becomes problematical, practical, and responsible as well. Because it must. It is like marrying your sweetheart. (*Recollected Essays*, 337)

Although, for Berry, awareness or watchfulness is indeed an exalted state of mind, it is not an innocently blissful one. "The Long-Legged House" tends to emphasize the difficulty of achieving watchfulness and the pleasure of paying attention to the subtleties of place once one's mind begins to get in shape. However, "The Making of a Marginal Farm," written a decade later, admits that paying attention can reveal horrors as well as delights. In this essay Berry is particularly attuned to the problem of erosion, a problem so severe along the steep slopes of the lower Kentucky River Valley that "It cannot be remedied in human time; to build five or six feet of soil takes perhaps fifty or sixty thousand years. This loss, once imagined, is potent with despair. If a people in adding a hundred and fifty years to itself subtracts fifty thousand years from its land, what is there to hope?" (335). Despite this expression of despair and futility, Berry's life and literary work are both processes of reclamation, rehabilitation. To write about a problem is not necessarily to produce a solution, but the kindling of consciousness—one's own and one's reader's—is a first step, an essential first step.

One of the important issues in contemporary nature writing is how this literature translates into concrete changes in readers' attitudes toward the environment, and into more environmentally sound behavior. Some scholars—such as Cheryll Burgess [Glotfelty], the author of a paper entitled "Toward an Ecological Literary Criticism" which was delivered at the 1989 meeting of the Western Literature Association—argue that it is the responsibility of critics and teachers to point out the environmental implications of literary texts, to engage in "ecocriticism." At a panel called "Building a Constituency for Wilderness," which took place during the 2nd North American Interdisciplinary Wilderness Conference in February 1990, such writers and editors as Michael Cohen, Stephen Trimble, and Gibbs Smith contemplated more specifically the likely audience for nature writing and the possible effects—or lack thereof—which this writing might have. Are nature writers "preaching to the choir," or do their voices reach out even to the unaware and uncommitted? With the 1990 Earth Day celebration now more than five years behind us, it is clear that the Thoreauvian process of awakening is not merely a timeless private quest, but a timely—even urgent—requirement if we are to prevent or at least retard the further destruction of our planet. But how can nature writers lead the way in this awakening, this "conversion process"?

This is, of course, the problem Barry Lopez presents movingly in the prologue to *Arctic Dreams:* "If we are to devise an enlightened plan for human activity in the Arctic, we need a more particularized understanding of the land itself—not a more refined mathematical knowledge, but a deeper understanding of its nature, as if it were, itself, another sort of civilization we had to reach some agreement with" (11). The book itself consists of nine chapters, which could be said to represent such academic categories as anthropology, geology, biology, history, and aesthetics. Much of this material, however elegantly worded, is discursive—that is, non-narrative. And this alone would not be enough to achieve the special understanding Lopez seeks for himself and his readers. But what he does is to crystallize all of his scholarly passages around vivid kernels of personal experience, demonstrating his own profound engagement with the place and soliciting his readers' imaginative engagement, the first step toward active concern.

In his 1988 interview with Kay Bonetti, Lopez explained that "The sorts of stories that I'm attracted to in a nonfiction way are those that try to bring some of the remote areas closer for the reader by establishing some kind of intimacy with the place, but also by drawing on the work of archeologists and historians and biologists" (59). This description explains the approach in much of his work, not only in *Arctic Dreams*—his process of venturing to exotic, seldom-experienced landscapes (including terrain, flora, fauna, and human inhabitants), and reporting back to his North American readers in a detailed, respectful mode of storytelling calculated to regenerate his audience's concern not only for the specific subject of the narrative, but for their own immediate surroundings. "The goal of the writer, finally," Lopez asserted at the Fourth Sino-American Writers Conference (also in 1988), "is to nourish the reader's awareness of the world" ("Chinese Garland," 41).

The chapters in *Arctic Dreams* are frequently aloof, informative, and coolly prophetic, but then Lopez suddenly presents a pulsing human heart amidst the frozen landscape, pushing understanding beyond the merely mathematical, the intellectual. The personal anecdotes do not show the author melting easily into the landscape, despite intimating his reverence for its beauty and the inspiring abundance of Arctic life—rather, the emphasis tends to be, for instance, on the author's insecurity, his vulnerability, as he stands on the edge of an ice floe which could without warning break adrift or be shattered by the predatory battering of a submerged polar bear. Insecurity, alienation, even gawking wonderment (at the appearance of icebergs, for instance)—yet there is also a sense of deep respect for the place, an awareness of the simultaneous fragility and power of the landscape and its inhabitants. Lopez achieves his thorough understanding of the Arctic by coupling academic research with personal experience of its otherness, of its separate, inhuman reality. He makes use of the personal anecdote to recreate the "experiential moment" and thus guide his audience through a vicarious conversion.

The purpose of Lopez's writing, a goal he hopes to extend to his readers, is to develop an "intimacy" with the landscape which does not interfere with attentiveness (by causing excessive comfort and ease), but rather fuels it, deepens it. When asked by Kenneth Margolis how he served the community, Lopez responded that "There has always been this function in society of people who go 'outside.' . . . [I]f you come face to face with the other you can come home and see the dimensions of the familiar that make you love it" ("Paying Attention," 53). The writer who goes "outside" in order to help himself and his audience understand both the exotic and the familiar forces his readers to draw upon their "capacity for metaphor," to associate their own landscapes with the writer's, their language and conceptual patterns with those of the story. Lopez's own multi-disciplinary approach, as he suggests in his public dialogue with E. O. Wilson (published as part of Edward Lueders's *Writing Natural History: Dialogues with Authors,* 1989), has profoundly impressed him with the idea that people "all see the world in a different way": "And I lament sometimes," he says,

> that there are those who lack a capacity for metaphor. They don't talk to each other, and so they don't have the benefit of each other's insights. Or they get stuck in their own metaphor, if you will, as a reality and don't see that they can help each other in this inquiry that binds people like ourselves together. So this issue arises for me: what do we know? how do we know? how do we organize our knowledge? (14–15)

In *Arctic Dreams,* Lopez "organizes" his own knowledge about the Arctic in a way designed to prompt his readers' vicarious engagement with the place, relying upon a multiplicity of eye-opening metaphors and alternative modes of perception/conception. Much like Thoreau, who demonstrates a constant shuffling of perspectives in both *Walden* and his private Journal, Lopez interweaves the perspectives of various disciplines, cultures, and physical vantage points in an attempt to make us conscious of the constraints of static perspectives. I would say that both Berry and Lopez attempt in their work to demonstrate and explain the process of achieving "intimacy" with the landscape, but while Berry (to adapt his metaphor) establishes a monogamous relationship with one particular place and peels away layer after layer of surface appearance in coming to know this place, Lopez travels to remote places throughout the world and then returns to Oregon to write about them. However, just as Thoreau dreamed of world travel before deciding it was enough to become "Expert in home-cosmography" (*Walden,* 320), Lopez has told recent interviewers, "I'd be happy for the rest of my life to just try to elucidate what it is that is North America" (Aton, 4).

My goal here has been to offer a quick overview of the purposes and processes of "paying attention" in American nature writing since Thoreau. By beginning with a discussion of Thoreau's Journal, I have tried to demonstrate the two principal relationships between the human mind and the natural world—"correspondence" and "otherness"—which the more recent writers have continued to investigate. Thoreau's Journal marks the obvious beginning point of this psychological tradition in American nature writing because it records the author's sustained empirical scrutiny of his own internal responses to the world. The more recent works which I consider in this essay differ in important ways from Thoreau's Journal—I have not traveled to Tucson to read Edward Abbey's Journal, nor have I bothered Barry Lopez for a peek at his (though he told Bonetti that he has kept one as a way to "make sense—daily sense—out of [his] life" since the age of nineteen—68). Instead, I have tried to focus on what I consider to be the primary investigatory genres of each author: Dillard's lyrical, elaborately structured collections of nonfiction essays; Abbey's aestheticized prose in *Desert Solitaire* and, more exaggeratedly, in his fiction; Berry's individual essays of exile and return; and Lopez's psychological essays in *Arctic Dreams* and self-reflective interview performances (he has participated in so many interviews in recent years that perhaps it would be reasonable to regard "the interview" as one of his chief modes of communication).

Although I recognize that several of these writers have political agendas, I prefer to view them all as *epistemologists,* as students of the human mind, rather than as *activists* in any concrete sense of the term. Contemporary nature writers tend to resist openly espousing one particular attitude toward nature, their goal being instead the empirical study of their own psychological responses to the world—or, in other words, objective scrutiny of subjective experience. And yet, having said this, I would be remiss not to admit that there is, in the very concern for the human process of becoming alert to the nonhuman environment, an implicit belief that we need this awareness. Thoreau, although he has served well as the posthumous spokesman for numerous environmental organizations, seems to have been motivated in his musings about nature by an ingenuously philosophical impulse—a desire to know the "truth" about the world and himself. However, it is no coincidence that Dillard, Abbey, Berry, and Lopez have produced their works during or just after the surge of environmental consciousness which occurred during the 1960s and 1970s. These writers, although they may be elusive, nondirective, and even anti-ideological (as is the case with Dillard and Abbey, at least), are hardly as neutral as Thoreau. They may hedge in their pronouncement of why they and their readers ought to be more aware (not just of the environment, but of existence in general), but their advocacy of heightened attentiveness is difficult to miss. However, in Wendell Berry's work, and similarly in Barry Lopez's writings during the 1980s, there is a new sense of timeliness, of urgency—a sense that awareness is not a mental game, but a condition which helps us to act responsibly and respectfully.

Lopez himself has boldly proposed that nature writing might "provide the foundation for a reorganization of American political thought" (*Antaeus*, 297). Ray Gonzalez gave his 1990 interview with Lopez the title "Landscapes of the Interior: The Literature of Hope"—and this captures precisely my own approach to these five important nature writers in this essay. Nature writing is a "literature of hope" in its assumption that the elevation of consciousness may lead to wholesome political change, but this literature is also concerned, and perhaps primarily so, with interior landscapes, with the mind itself.

NOTE

A slightly different version of this essay appeared as the introduction to my book *Seeking Awareness in American Nature Writing: Henry Thoreau, Annie Dillard, Edward Abbey, Wendell Berry, and Barry Lopez* (1992). It is reprinted here with the permission of the University of Utah Press.

WORKS CITED

Abbey, Edward. *Desert Solitaire: A Season in the Wilderness*. New York: Ballantine, 1968.

———. *The Monkey Wrench Gang*. New York: Avon, 1975.

Aton, James Martin. "An Interview with Barry Lopez." *Western American Literature* 21.1 (May 1986): 3–17.

Berry, Wendell. "The Long-Legged House." *The Long-Legged House*. New York: Audubon/Ballantine, 1969.

———. "The Making of a Marginal Farm." *Recollected Essays 1965–1980*. San Francisco: North Point, 1981.

———. "Notes from an Absence and a Return." *A Continuous Harmony: Essays Cultural and Agricultural*. New York: Harcourt, Brace, Jovanovich, 1972.

———. *The Unsettling of America: Culture & Agriculture*. New York: Avon, 1977.

Bonetti, Kay. "An Interview with Barry Lopez." *The Missouri Review* 11.3 (1988): 57–77.

Cameron, Sharon. *Writing Nature: Henry Thoreau's Journal*. Oxford and New York: Oxford University Press, 1985.

Carruth, Hayden. "Attractions and Dangers of Nostalgia." *The Virginia Quarterly Review* 50.4 (Autumn 1974): 637–40.

Catton, William R. "The Quest for Uncertainty." *Humanscape: Environments for People*. 1978. Ed. Stephen Kaplan and Rachel Kaplan. Ann Arbor, Mich.: Ulrich's, 1982.

Deemer, Charles. "Up the Creek." *The New Leader*, 24 June 1974: 18–20.

Dillard, Annie. *An American Childhood*. New York: Harper & Row, 1987.

———. *Holy the Firm*. New York: Harper & Row, 1977.

———. *Living by Fiction*. New York: Harper & Row, 1982.

———. *Pilgrim at Tinker Creek*. 1974. New York: Harper & Row, 1988.

[Glotfelty], Cheryll Burgess. "Toward an Ecological Literary Criticism." Presented at the annual meeting of the Western American Literature Association. Coeur d'Alene, Idaho, 11–14 October, 1989.

Gonzalez, Ray. "Landscapes of the Interior: The Literature of Hope. An Interview with Barry Lopez." *The Bloomsbury Review* January/February 1990: 8, 9, 29.

Gunn, Giles. *The Interpretation of Otherness: Literature, Religion, and the American Imagination*. New York: Oxford University Press, 1979.

Hartman, Geoffrey H. "The Romance of Nature and the Negative Way." *Romanticism and Consciousness: Essays in Criticism*. Ed. Harold Bloom. New York: Norton, 1970.

James, William. *Psychology: Briefer Course*. 1892. Cambridge and London: Harvard University Press, 1984.

———. *Varieties of Religious Experience*. 1902. New York: Macmillan, 1961.

Kaplan, Stephen. "Perception of an Uncertain Environment." *Humanscape: Environments for People*. 1978. Ed. Stephen Kaplan and Rachel Kaplan. Ann Arbor, Mich.: Ulrich's, 1982.

Lavery, David L. "Noticer: The Visionary Art of Annie Dillard." *The Massachusetts Review* 21.2 (Summer 1980).

Lopez, Barry. *Arctic Dreams: Imagination and Desire in a Northern Landscape*. New York: Bantam, 1986.

———. "Natural History: An Annotated Booklist." *Antaeus* 57 (Autumn 1986): 295–97.

Lopez, Barry, Charles Wright, and Maxine Hong Kingston. "A Chinese Garland." *The North American Review* 273.3 (September 1988): 38–42.

Lueders, Edward. *Writing Natural History: Dialogues with Authors*. Salt Lake City: University of Utah Press, 1989.

Margolis, Kenneth. "Paying Attention: An Interview with Barry Lopez." *Orion Nature Quarterly* 9.3 (Summer 1990): 50–53.

Mitchell, Don. "Dancing with Nature." *The Bread Loaf Anthology of Contemporary American Essays*. Ed. Robert Pack and Jay Parini. Hanover and London: University Press of New England, 1989.

Nabokov, Vladimir. *Lolita*. 1955. New York: Berkeley, 1977.

O'Connell, Nicholas. "Barry Lopez." *At the Field's End: Interviews with 20 Pacific Northwest Writers*. Seattle: Madrona, 1987.

Polanyi, Michael. "The Structure of Consciousness." *Knowing and Being*. Ed. Marjorie Grene. Chicago: University of Chicago Press, 1969.

Robbe-Grillet, Alain. "Nature, Humanism, Tragedy." *For a New Novel: Essays on Fiction*. Trans. Richard Howard. 1958. Evanston: Northwestern University Press, 1965.

Ronald, Ann. *The New West of Edward Abbey*. Reno and Las Vegas: University of Nevada Press, 1982.

Rossi, William John. *"Laboratory of the Artist": Henry Thoreau's Literary and Scientific Use of the Journal, 1848–1854*. Ph.D. Diss. University of Minnesota, 1986.

Thoreau, Henry David. *The Journal of Henry D. Thoreau*. Ed. Bradford Torrey and Francis H. Allen. Vols. 1–14. Boston: Houghton Mifflin, 1906.

———. *Walden*. 1854. Princeton: Princeton University Press, 1971.

Trimble, Stephen. *Words from the Land: Encounters with Natural History Writing*. Salt Lake City: Gibbs M. Smith, 1988.

MICHAEL J. MCDOWELL

The Bakhtinian Road to Ecological Insight

■ ■ ■

From Thoreau onward, American literature has had a minority tradition of landscape writing[1] that has countered the values of progress, development, and improvement celebrated by a dominant tradition. These marginalized writings have become increasingly important to us because, as Philip Slater says in *The Pursuit of Loneliness,* alternatives that are antithetical to dominant emphases of a social system function as "a kind of hedge against social change" (Slater 110–11). These alternative values in the margin often rescue the dominant culture in difficult times.[2] Today, a growing number of landscape writers offer essays, poems, and fictions that represent the human relationship to the natural landscape in ways that are often antithetical to our culture's usual emphases.[3]

One of the major shifts in our scientific world view in the twentieth century has been to recognize the importance of systems and relationships in the phenomenal world. We've begun to realize that an entity is largely created and undergoes change by its interaction with other entities; nothing has an unchangeable essence that it can maintain in isolation, and no one can change in isolation merely through the effort of a transcendental ego. As Katherine Hayles (*Chaos Bound*) and others have pointed out, the twentieth century has seen the hope for absolute, discrete facts disappear, to be replaced by Einstein's theory of relativity, by quantum mechanics, by Heisenberg's uncertainty principle, by chaos theory, and by such sciences as ecology. More recently, many have celebrated the rise of a holistic world view that is more compatible with the ecological discoveries of the past thirty years than Cartesian dualism is. But literary studies have been slow to abandon the nineteenth-century certainty of approaches to literature such as New Criticism offers, with its close analysis of a work of art as an object in itself; and many recent postmodernist critical theories become so caught up in analyses of language that the physical world, if not denied outright, often is ignored or dismissed as relatively unimportant.

History, philosophy, anthropology, and other "soft" disciplines have long provided a ground upon which a critic can stand, like Archimedes, to lift the world of literature. But other "hard" disciplines have not been very well incorporated into literary studies, partly because of the difficulties involved in acquiring adequate grounding in the sciences to follow multidisciplinary arguments. However, the Russian philosopher and literary critic Mikhail Bakhtin has incorporated into his literary theories much of the thinking about systems and relationships long ago embraced by the hard sciences. Consequently, his work provides an ideal starting point for an ecological analysis of landscape writing.

Bakhtin's theories might be seen as the literary equivalent of ecology, the science of relationships. The ideal form to represent reality, according to Bakhtin, is a dialogical form, one in which multiple voices or points of view interact. Monological forms, in contrast, encourage the singular speaking subject to suppress whatever doesn't fit his or her ideology. In discussing this theory of dialogics, Bakhtin names authorial speech, the speeches of narrators, inserted genres, and the speech of characters as means the writer employs to achieve an interplay of social voices and a variety of relationships among them. The effect is a kind of dialogue among differing points of view, which gives value to a variety of socio-ideological positions. Beginning with the idea that all entities in the great web of nature deserve recognition and a voice, an ecological literary criticism might explore how authors have represented the interaction of both the human and nonhuman voices in the landscape.

Of course, a few problems soon become apparent in an application of dialogics to landscape writing. The most obvious is that, at least on a literal level, trees and stones and squirrels don't talk, much less write and publish their responses to the many things we say about them. Every literary attempt to listen to voices in the landscape or to "read the book of nature" is necessarily anthropocentric. It's our language, after all, that we're using, and we inevitably put our values into the representation. But there are varying degrees of egoism, and in applying Bakhtin to landscape writing I have generally chosen writers who at least try to dissolve their egos and to enter the private worlds of different entities in the landscape.[4]

Even after having suppressed their egos and achieved some sort of union with nature, however, landscape writers remain open to the charge, as Harold Fromm puts it, of trying "to sneak a look through the back door of the universe so quickly that one's observations would escape the indeterminacy principle and one would see things as they really are in their unseen selves" (Fromm 44). But these writers avoid giving that impression of invisibility by forthrightly projecting themselves or their characters into the landscape as they describe. Through this self-reflexive stance they reject the duplicity, most familiar now in nature calendars and public television's nature specials, that leads viewers to believe that an extreme close-up or telephoto shot with no humans in sight is the "real" nature. Objectivity, as Fromm rightly implies, is an illusion. We are beginning to recognize that Ruskin's "pathetic fallacy," the crediting of natural objects with human qualities, is not merely a Romantic indulgence, but an inevitable component of human perception; it is something to acknowledge and celebrate, not to condemn.

Another problem in applying dialogics to landscape writing is the marked absence of human society in much of the writing. In the absence of characters, it might be thought that the application of a theory developed to explain nineteenth-century novels would become a questionable enterprise. Yet, Bakhtin would say, wherever there is a human voice, there's evidence of other human beings because we are each a result of our interaction with others. A newly discovered Kaspar Hauser has no human voice; language is necessarily a social construct. The language we write carries evidence of social values, which are capable of analysis. In addition, by turning their backs upon human society, landscape writers often enable the nonhuman elements of an ecosystem to take on the qualities of a society, with hierarchies, differing values, and lively interplay. Ants might wage Homeric battles, as in Thoreau's battle of the ants passage in *Walden,* or hummingbird and fly might try to right the balance of things, as in Leslie Silko's *Ceremony.* In any case, the language associated with the particular element of the landscape may be analyzed to understand better the writer's perception of the mountains' or of animals' relationships with other parts of the landscape and with humans.

And writers also associate human characters with elements of the landscape, as when in his 1928 narrative poem *Cawdor* Jeffers makes the fifty-year-old Cawdor part of the ground, with nerves running from all over the land back to him, and makes Fera, his wife, a kind of wild, untamable animal. Writers of nonfictional landscape writing may associate different elements of the landscape with people who have written or spoken about a specific aspect of the landscape. These "real-life" characters may, for instance, have written about a waterway or, as is the case with George McCauslin in Thoreau's *The Maine Woods,* have spent their lives in felling trees. These characters, once incorporated into the text, then give a voice to an element of the landscape, or to a particular perception of an element of the landscape.

Despite these problems, an application of dialogics to landscape literature can open up a text to enable an analysis of ecological relationships among all the landscape's components, including humans.

Dialogics helps first by placing an emphasis on contradictory voices, rather than focusing mainly upon the authoritative monologic voice of the narrator. We begin to hear characters and elements of the landscape that have been marginalized. Our attention is directed to the differences in the kind of language associated with specific characters or elements of the landscape. These "character zones" or "speech zones" give each character or element an autonomous voice distinct from the narrator's and the other characters'. We can analyze the interplay of these different languages for an understanding of the values associated with the characters and elements and for a sense of how characters and elements of the landscape influence each other.

A dialogical analysis of landscape literature emphasizes contradictory voices in part by exploring its intertextuality. Just as an utterance within a text answers other utterances within the text, so too the text answers other texts within its genre (Hirschkop and Shepherd 42–43; Morson 132). For Bakhtin, all meaning is determined by the context of an utterance. That context includes all earlier texts as well as the great multiplicity of contemporary voices and even those of the future, for "great works continue to live in the distant future. In the process of their posthumous life they are enriched with new meanings," Bakhtin says (*Speech* 4). Such an approach is fitting for ecologically oriented literature, for it leads to the discovery of connections between a literary work and its past, present, and future environments. Thoreau in particular knowingly acknowledges, answers, and builds upon many earlier and contemporaneous texts; he weaves into his narrative a variety of facts and anecdotes from his reading. Sometimes intertextuality in landscape writing leads to direct rebuttal, following the pattern Thomas Jefferson sets in *Notes on the State of Virginia,* in which

Jefferson not only answers the questions of François Barbé-Marbois, but also disputes the assertions of the Count de Buffon's *Natural History* as to the size of animals in the New World. Similarly, subsequent landscape writers such as Thoreau, Jeffers, and Silko all find fault with earlier or contemporary explanations of the landscape.

This intertextual quality of dialogism is one aspect of Bakhtin's larger idea of alterity. For Bakhtin as for Darwin, every creature defines itself and in a real sense becomes a "self" mentally, spiritually, and physically by its interaction with other beings and things. "Without contraries is no progression," William Blake tells us, and Bakhtin applies the lesson with delight. Critics have often pointed out that the countryside of the pastoral tradition cannot exist without the city or court as a counterpoint. But with Bakhtin, the contrasts don't stop there; the number of interactions between entities is infinite, which enables a "polyphony" of interacting voices within any given text.

Related to dialogical analyses of intertextuality is the analysis of the play of genres within a text. For Bakhtin, genre is always collective, indicating social forces at work. Style, in contrast, is always individual, and of far less importance. A recognition of genres is important in discussing landscape writing because, as a human social construct, a genre dictates to a great extent how reality is perceived in a text, and landscape writing tends to incorporate a variety of genres. Bakhtin sees the history of literature as the struggle between the novel and other already-existing genres. The result of this struggle is the "novelization" of other genres:

> They become more free and flexible, their language renews itself by incorporating extraliterary heteroglossia and the "novelistic" layers of literary language, they become dialogized, permeated with laughter, irony, humor, elements of self-parody and finally—this is the most important thing—the novel inserts into these other genres an indeterminacy, a certain semantic openendedness, a living contact with unfinished, still-evolving contemporary reality (the openended present). (*Dialogic* 7)

Landscape writing is permanently embroiled in this struggle. Typically a speaking voice goes out to encounter the landscape and all its elements, an "on the road" pattern popular from at least the *Odyssey* onward. Landscape writing, though, like the novel, refuses to solidify as a genre the way Bakhtin says the epic did. Thomas Lyon struggles to provide a taxonomy of landscape writing in his anthology *This Incomperable Lande*, and almost in frustration warns that "the types I have listed tend to intergrade, and with great frequency" (Lyon 3).

The "open-endedness" which Bakhtin mentions is a value that landscape writing demonstrates probably even more than the novels Bakhtin discusses. Also translated as "incompletedness," "inconclusiveness," "non-completion," "unfinalizability," "unfinalized nature," "unfinalizedness," and "unfinishedness," this quality of *nezavershennost'* indicates the writer's willingness to leave the door open to continuing dialogue; it's the writer's refusal to have the final say and achieve closure (Hirschkop and Shepherd 193). Closure or "finalization," while often aesthetically pleasing, implies that the author's view is complete and true, and nothing more remains to be said. The tentativeness and the willingness to be taught by the ways of the natural world, two qualities typical to landscape writing, combine with this "open-endedness" to suggest not only a sense of the writer's humility but also an ethical stance that recognizes that no individual and no era have a monopoly on truth.

Particularly useful to a dialogical analysis of landscape writing is Bakhtin's concept of the *chronotope,* a twentieth-century neologism combining *chronos* (time) and *topos* (place) and which Bakhtin defines as "the intrinsic connectedness of temporal and spatial relationships that are artistically expressed in literature." For Bakhtin the term, "employed in mathematics, and . . . introduced as part of Einstein's Theory of Relativity," designates a "formally constitutive category of literature." "What counts for us," he says, "is the fact that it expresses the inseparability of space and time (time as the fourth dimension of space)" (*Dialogic* 84).

Unfortunately, in his 175-page essay "Forms of Time and of the Chronotope in the Novel: Notes toward a Historical Poetics" (from which I've taken the above definition) and in other treatments of the chronotope, Bakhtin concerns himself more with the "time" aspect than with the "place" (or as he usually says, "space") aspect; the historical engages him more than the geographical, as the subtitle of his essay might suggest. Yet he sets forth a theory which begins to explore how landscapes are tied to narrative in literature.

American literature needs criticism that attends to just such a Bakhtinian concern with the interconnections of time and place in narrative. Much of contemporary American literature tends to portray the sameness of urban life everywhere in the United States and Canada to establish a bond with the reader; the names of the malls and outlying suburbs may change, but the kinds of experience possible are generic to urban living. Although some writers have championed their own urban milieux, such as Saul Bellow with Chicago or Tom Wolfe with New York, writers often set their novels against an urban environment "we can all relate to," which might be called a deprivileging of "place," an ignoring of the human and natural history of a locale which make it distinct, different, and likely to produce a certain kind of character, a certain kind of plot. Such a devaluing of place leads to an increasingly conformist society whose members move comfortably from urban area to urban area, as their careers dictate. It's also ideal for an approved, "official" literature we can all partake in, a literature that bulldozes local hillsides to make a homogeneous American literature.

We can see the kind of praise such a literature gets in *The Columbia Literary History of the United States,* which despite its diversity of critical views nonetheless insists upon calling regionalism "a diminished thing" to be noted and then dismissed in the pursuit of a national, American, literature (Elliott 761–84). James M. Cox's essay in the *CLHUS* on regionalism describes the tendency best in his discussion of early twentieth-century Midwest literature, which he says is characterized by "its essential noninterest in the land," with F. Scott Fitzgerald as a typical example: "Nature and land hardly exist in Fitzgerald's work, except as stage properties—lawns, trees, and beaches—assuming animation in the syncopated rhythm of a world whose final magic is money" (Elliott 774). In Sinclair Lewis, "nature is nothing more than empty space between towns or a spot one visits on vacation" (Elliott 775). Western American literature, which provides a counterpoint to this ignoring of nature, gets a mention only in the concluding paragraph of Cox's essay, where we learn that "the West . . . is not really a region in my context," and hence undeserving of even having any authors named (Elliott 784). In his criticism of the *CLHUS,* James Maguire argues the importance of the region in literary judgment on two counts, first that "experimental psychologists . . . tell us that memory functions best when it has a strong sense of place," and second that "tastes, ideas, and values are shaped in every individual, at least to some extent, by the places where he or she lives" (Maguire 649–50). Others, such as Neil Evernden, suggest that we are deluding ourselves (and courting insanity) when we speak as if we have no environmental context, which includes not just the landscape as "a collection of physical forms," but as "the evidence of what has occurred there"; in short, story, geography, and self are inextricably bound together (Evernden 19).

Bakhtin's idea of the chronotope encourages us to recover the representation of place in even works of "essential noninterest in the land." The chronotope binds together these elements of story, geography and self, reminding us of the local, vernacular, folk elements of literature, which are rooted in place. They are there if we know to look for them. Bakhtin lists a number of different chronotopes: "The importance of the chronotope of the road in literature is immense," he says; "it is a rare work that does not contain a variation of this motif" (*Dialogic* 98). Bakhtin also mentions the chronotope of the public square (*Dialogic* 161), the chronotope of the entr'acte (*Dialogic* 163), the chronotope of theatrical space (*Dialogic* 163), the chronotope of chivalric romance's "alien, miraculous world" (*Dialogic* 165), the "high road winding through one's native land" chronotope of the picaresque novel (*Dialogic* 165), the intervalic chronotope of the theater (*Dialogic* 166), and the Rabelaisian chronotope (*Dialogic* 167). It's not necessary to go into Bakhtin's particular working out of each of these chronotopes to take advantage of the idea. Bakhtin asks, "What is the significance of all these chronotopes?" and answers:

> They are the organizing centers for the fundamental narrative events of the novel. The chronotope is the place where the knots of narrative are tied and untied. It can be said without qualification that to them belongs the meaning that shapes narrative.
>
> . . . [T]he chronotope makes narrative events concrete, makes them take on flesh, causes blood to flow in their veins. . . . All the novel's abstract elements—philosophical and social generalizations, ideas, analyses of cause and effect—gravitate toward the chronotope and through it take on flesh and blood, permitting the imaging power of art to do its work. (*Dialogic* 250)

If the meaning that shapes narrative is to be found in these concrete junctures of time and place of the chronotope, then an analysis of landscape in narrative becomes not only a key to understanding how we have viewed the relationship of humans and nature, but also a key to understanding at least some of the meanings of a narrative.

Bakhtin recognizes that historically a change occurred in how nature was perceived, from something in which we participate, to *landscape,* which Bakhtin says is "nature conceived as horizon" ("what a man sees"), and *environment* ("the background, the setting"). Picturesque "remnants" of nature became "scenes" or "views," surrounded by "closed verbal landscapes," and what is important to humans "begins to shift to a space that is closed and private" (*Dialogic* 143–44). Then "nature itself ceased to be a living participant in the events of life," Bakhtin says; "it was fragmented into metaphors and comparisons serving to sublimate individual and private affairs and adventures not connected in any real or intrinsic way with nature itself" (*Dialogic* 217). Much writing today continues to view nature solely as a backdrop to the really important things, which are human matters divorced from a nature that remains "out there." Scott Sanders's encounter with a family in the Great Smoky Mountains in "Speaking a Word for Nature" provides a memorable image of how "the modern reader" prefers nature: On a late afternoon in May, with the sky "throbbing with color" and the birds already "settling down for their evening song" and the wind smelling of pines, Sanders leaves his tent and crosses the parking lot of a campground to a cliff to watch the sun set. Near the center of the parking lot, a camping van sits with motor running, air conditioner squealing, and curtains drawn; through a gap in the curtains Sanders can see a family watching a television set that is showing a Tarzan movie (Sanders 658–59).

In contrast to this distant, framed idea of nature at which television excels, Bakhtin presents the idyllic chronotope, which has been "very important in the history of the novel."[5] Bakhtin identifies the idyll as a model for restoring "folkloric time." The relationship of time and space in the idyll he describes as

> an organic fastening-down, a grafting of life and its events to a place, to a familiar territory with all its nooks and crannies, its familiar mountains, valleys, fields, rivers and forests, and one's own home. Idyllic life and its events are inseparable from this concrete, spatial corner of the world. (*Dialogic* 225)

Human life is "conjoined" with the life of nature. The limitations of the idyll have led to its dilution in subsequent literature; it is able to deal only with "a few of life's basic realities" such as "love, birth, death, marriage, labor, food and drink, stages of growth," and other cyclical matters, but not with unrepeatable and trivial everyday events common to realistic fiction. However, elements of the "idyllic complex" continued to influence the novel throughout the nineteenth century, which is as far as Bakhtin carries his analysis.

With the rise of capitalism, Bakhtin says, novelists addressed the problems of how a person must fit into a bourgeois society, a process "connected with a severing of all previous ties with the idyllic" (*Dialogic* 234). Now, Bakhtin seems to be saying, we can see how those ties persisted, in attenuated, sublimated forms of the idyllic chronotope, perhaps, but there all the same. It's time to look again. Some of the best recent essays on the relationship of time and space in narrative have done just that, usually by way of Native American storytelling traditions. Barry Lopez's "Landscape and Narrative" in *Crossing Open Ground,* Gary Snyder's "Good, Wild, Sacred" in *The Practice of the Wild,* and Keith Basso's " 'Stalking with Stories': Names, Places, and Moral Narratives Among the Western Apaches" all demonstrate ways in which narrative (with a blurred line between fiction and nonfiction) ties itself to place.

Many of the most familiar English and American literary works would be unrecognizable without their landscapes, such as the Wessex of Thomas Hardy, the Midlands of D. H. Lawrence, the prairies of Willa Cather, or the Big Sur coast of Robinson Jeffers. To illustrate the importance of recognizing the connection of landscape to narrative, Bakhtin quotes Goethe's experience in Sicily:

> Now that my mind is stored with images of all these coasts and promontories, gulfs and bays, islands and headlands, rocky cliffs, fields, flower gardens, tended trees, festooned vines, mountains wreathed in clouds, eternally serene plains, and the all-encircling sea with its ever-changing colours and moods, for the first time the *Odyssey* has become a living truth to me. (Goethe, *Italian Journey;* quoted in *Speech* 48)

Bakhtin's theory of the "carnivalesque," most fully developed in *Rabelais and His World,* brings our attention back from the landscape to our bodies and our interactions with others. According to Bakhtin, every utterance is a "contradiction-ridden, tension-filled unity of two embattled tendencies in the life of language" (*Dialogic* 272). One tendency unifies and centralizes, producing artistic prose genres, which help to achieve cultural, national, and political centralization. Bakhtin uses the carnival of the Middle Ages and Renaissance as an example of an opposing tendency to decentralize, to challenge the established order with its official, approved forms. Lower genres such as parody, folk-sayings, the picaresque, and anecdotes fulfill this function. Here there is no "language center," but an interplay or collision of voices from differing sociolinguistic points of view, a situation which Bakhtin calls "heteroglossia."

It is this "carnivalistic" tendency to talk back to the monologic voice of officialdom that leads such landscape writers as Thoreau, Jeffers, and Silko to a pluralistic, diverse, and hence potentially more accurate representation of a natural landscape. There is no particular agenda of the sort that can be discerned in earlier, more monologic landscape writing, such as the promotion of colonial settlement in William Wood's *New England's Prospects* or the dehumanization of real Indians in Francis Parkman's *The Oregon Trail*. Rather, these more recent writers usually try to divest themselves as much as possible of human preconceptions and enter the natural world almost as though they were animal participants; the animal participants often have almost equal representation with the narrators. Their hope, it appears, is to allow the landscape to enter them in order to be expressed through their writing. In describing the similar experience of farmers, Yi-Fu Tuan says, "The entry of nature is no mere metaphor. Muscles and scars bear witness to the physical intimacy of the contact." The small farmer or peasant's way of knowing nature comes through the need to gain a living, leading French workers to say with aching bodies that "their trades have entered into them" (Tuan 96–97). Bakhtin in his discussions of the carnivalesque champions this nonintellectual, bodily way of knowing the world. It is a way to resist the abstract, intellectual, official reality that a social hierarchy always creates for its own ends.

Ultimately, though, the unofficial, folkloric, bodily reality is still the bodily reality of humans, not of other creatures. Animals' perceptions and hence their realities are different. Jacob von Uexküll's essay "A Stroll through the Worlds of Animals and Men" describes the "bubbles" (*Umwelten*) that each species inhabits to make the point that the world is a different place to each species' sensory organs. A dog knows the world through its nose more than through its eyes, and a human is incapable of knowing the minute distinctions of smell that enable a dog to retrieve one thrown stick out of a heap of seemingly identical sticks. Similarly, a tick's world, in which "a day" might consist of the seventeen years between times of sensing the heat of a potential source of warm blood, remains all but inconceivable to us. Yet, if we recognize that each animal creates its own *Umwelt*, then we can try to imitate its *Umwelt* by confining our sensory perceptions to those of the animal, and imagining the perceptions of those senses in which we're deficient.

Much of Bakhtin's thinking on the carnival parallels John Brinckerhoff Jackson's distinction between the "official" and the "vernacular" in his analysis of landscape in *Discovering the Vernacular Landscape*. Jackson's vernacular landscape is a folk landscape, attuned to the contours of the land and serving local needs. The official landscape, imposed upon the land without concern for local differences, is the only one we're usually able to see intellectually. Jackson encourages the effort to recognize the vernacular landscape as well; this is the landscape that is usually destroyed unwittingly by outside developers and economic forces. The good, locally knowledgeable farmer, such as Wendell Berry, who fights the officially blessed high-tech machine of agribusiness is rare. In many businesses engaged in the extraction of natural resources, it's the locals who destroy the landscape; the very people who might best know the landscape are the ones to overfish the rivers, overlog the forests, poison the soil, and pollute the water. In such books as *The Unsettling of America* and *Home Economics,* Berry explains the situation by lamenting that the locals have often become the pawns of university-sponsored agribusiness thinking, and that locals seldom are knowledgeable in the "vernacular landscape" as J. B. Jackson describes it. In the simplistic "jobs versus environment" arguments, immediate, short-term economic needs usually prevail over the long-term economic and environmental good. Apparently at odds with this extraction-oriented "official landscape" is another more romantic official landscape now increasingly forced upon the local experience, even at the expense of the local economy: It is a nostalgic landscape of national forests still filled with trees, undammed wild and scenic rivers, unplowed national grasslands, and ungrazed and undrilled federal wildlife refuges, all of it nearly peopleless, as the majority of Americans have liked to think the land was before Euro-American settlement.

Although the popular media may portray most Americans as striving to live the officially sanctioned life of well-paying jobs and surfeit of material goods, vestiges of truly "folk" vernaculars remain for Euro-Americans to turn to. The old ways of appropriate, tenable human integration into the landscape, wherever they have been preserved, become the material to study, to write about, to know. This is the direction in which Bakhtin points us, and contemporary landscape writers are often there ahead of us.

PRACTICAL ECOCRITICISM

In "Toward an Ecological Literary Criticism," Cheryll Burgess [Glotfelty] uses Elaine Showalter's model of the stages through which feminist criticism has progressed to describe analogous phases through which ecological literary criticism has been moving. Although we should probably be wary about the notion that we have moved beyond the earlier stages to finer and superior criticism (for the kinds of literary criticism described as earlier stages remain important and continue to be done), Burgess [Glotfelty] presents a very accurate and useful typology of ecological literary criticism. She suggests first an "images of nature in canonical literature" kind of criticism, which raises our consciousness of stereotypes, distortions, and omissions of the representations of nature in literature. The second kind of criticism rediscovers or recognizes the tradition of nature writing in both neglected and celebrated writers; biographical criticism plays a strong role at this stage. The third kind of criticism Burgess [Glotfelty] suggests is theory, which would include discussions of deep ecology, ecofeminism, and ecological poetics. Much good work has been done and much remains to be done on this theoretical level, particularly recognizing points of agreement and disagreement with other current literary theory. I would add as a fourth kind of ecological literary criticism the practical application of theoretical ecological concepts to specific literary works, which in comparison to the earlier stages remains a wide open terrain with few clearly marked paths. What follows is an explanation of what I've been avoiding and what I've been attempting as a Bakhtinian practical ecocriticism.

The first great temptation is to use the analysis of an ecologically conscious writer's work as a springboard for leaping into discussions of pressing environmental issues. Valuable as such discussions are for encouraging social activism, they play no role in most of my ecological literary criticism.

A related scholarly activity, playing ecopolice, I likewise avoid. Joseph Meeker might be credited with introducing many environmentally minded critics to the possibilities of merging literary and environmental interests by asking, "From the unforgiving perspective of evolution and natural selection, does literature contribute more to our survival than it does to our extinction?" (Meeker 25). Meeker's explorations are illuminating and sound, but applying the question to specific literary works can result in something of a witchhunt. Such an application can be done well, as in Carl Bredahl's analysis in *New Ground* of "the Westering imagination" of Mark Twain, James Fenimore Cooper, Francis Parkman, and Lewis Garrard (Bredahl 29–48). But I move in another direction suggested by Meeker's imperative, "Literary form must be reconciled if possible with the forms and structures of nature as they are defined by ecological scientists, for both are related to human perceptions of beauty and balance" (Meeker 25). Such writers as Henry David Thoreau, Robinson Jeffers, Barry Lopez, Annie

Dillard, and Leslie Silko seem to agree with Meeker's view, and their work merits an analysis of how they have achieved their naturally sympathetic literary forms.

Some ecologically minded literary critics also roundly condemn Western civilization for its oppression of nature and all other forms of "the other." They often find answers in Eastern thought or the religious attitudes of primitive peoples. Agreeable as these alternatives are, we remain Westerners, and participants in a tradition that has absorbed many contradictory elements. While admiring the best of primitive and Eastern attitudes toward the natural world, we will do better to recognize the valuable cosmic insights that have been overlooked in our own tradition (what Meeker calls "the minority report" of Western civilization [Meeker 34]). Thoreau's understanding of Buddhism underlies much of his critique of American relationships to nature; Native American tradition underlies much of Silko's writing. Such currents of non-Western thought flowing into and influencing the mainstream of Western tradition need analysis.[6] Gary Snyder says he had to qualify his admiration for the Eastern religions' gentle treatment of the land when he realized that he never heard songbirds in Japan because they had all been eaten long ago. With that comment in mind, I choose an ecocritical path that attempts a radical critique of dominant Western attitudes, but not a wholesale rejection in favor of a stereotyped and polarized alternative system.

Another tendency in criticism of landscape and nature writing is to discover eternal themes and recurring characters in the literature. While an understanding of the integration of natural cycles and rhythms in literature is important, as perhaps Northrop Frye's *Anatomy of Criticism* most convincingly demonstrates, I avoid the myth and symbol school of criticism as much as I can because of the leveling and homogenizing effect of such usually ahistorical approaches. Richard Poirier, R. W. B. Lewis, Richard Chase, Leslie Fiedler, and others writing in similar veins, insightful as they are, inevitably leave out writing that doesn't fit their models. Similarly, Joseph Campbell's totalizing system is a good starting point for understanding literature of unfamiliar cultures, but more value and interest for me lie in differences, not similarities.

With these various types of environmentally oriented criticism put aside, we can look at questions which might be of greater concern to an application of ecological literary criticism. One concern is stylistic: What does the way a writer uses metaphors reveal about his or her representation of landscape? George Lakoff and Mark Johnson's *Metaphors We Live By* provides the rationale and the method for a fundamental analysis of the implications of the metaphors to be found in writing. Annette Kolodny's *The Lay of the Land* provides one of the best models for analysis of metaphors specifically related to landscape. In part, ecological literary criticism might attempt to expand Kolodny's discussion to consider metaphors in addition to her dominant metaphor of land as female body and explorer as rapist, molester, or lover.

A second concern is to analyze how each writer has modified existing genres and modes such as pastoralism to incorporate perhaps more accurately than in the past an understanding of the complex relationships within nature. Many ecologically oriented critics single out pastoralism as an object upon which to vent their wrath because of its benign, simplified, citified view of the natural world. And on the other hand, some ecological critics such as Joan Weatherly point to pastoral literature as "an ageless form of environmental literature" and the repository of ideas about humankind's place in nature (Weatherly 73). As Barbara Currier Bell has pointed out, thinking about humans in the landscape has tended toward polarization, as do most academic schemata. Meanwhile, landscape writers have often tried to break out of the prisonhouse of genre and hybridize new forms, new genres, and new modes. Yet criticism has been slow to follow their progress. "We readily accept that humanists can and should have new license for catalogues regarding, say, images of women, utopian visions, or 'the hero,'" Bell says. "Why not equally flexible attention to views of humanity in nature? What is needed is a freer heuristic 'anatomy' of the views . . ." (Bell 249). Particularly with poetry we can follow the lead of Glen Love and consider how post-Darwinian landscape writers' new assumptions have created a "new pastoralism" with fewer of the objectionable features of earlier traditional pastoral writers (Love 206–7). And, with prose forms, we can accept Bell's challenge to address the pluralism of landscape writing. The beauty and strength of the novel, Bakhtin says, is its ability to absorb many other genres. And so it is with landscape writing, as Silko's *Ceremony* and *Storyteller* demonstrate especially well. My ecological literary criticism has been investigating the consequences of such blendings of genres.

A third concern in the practical application of ecological criticism is the methods landscape writers have used to enable a dialogical interplay of voices and values in contradiction to each other and to each writer's own views. This concern follows from my thesis that the best landscape writers suppress their egos and give voices to the many elements of a landscape by using techniques that Bakhtin identifies and praises in his discussions of nineteenth-century novels. The predominant techniques discussed earlier include the use of character zones, intertextuality, inserted genres, chronotopes, "open-endedness," and carnivalization. An important assumption I make is that environment creates a character or characters, so that the study of the environment with which a character interacts will reveal much about the character.

An exploration of the dialogic voices in a landscape leads naturally to an analysis of the values a writer has recognized as inherent in a landscape, rather than imposed upon it. Most of the early European "discoverers" and later explorers of the American landscape found what they expected to find: Asians, or a howling wilderness, or an abundance of natural resources waiting for exploitation. A few, such as William Bartram or John James Audubon,[7] try to describe what they actually encountered, rather than what they expected to encounter. We've recognized, though, that objective perception and description are impossible. Every human attempt to know the phenomenal world is filtered through a human value system. What we can do is analyze the values that a particular writer has allowed to adhere to his or her descriptions and narrations. A *paysage moralisé* or other commission of the pathetic fallacy is not necessarily a bad thing; at least it recognizes an integral relationship between value and landscape. As Susan Griffin illustrates in *Woman and Nature: The Roaring Inside Her*, impersonal, seemingly objective representations of reality are usually the product of our dominant ideology, whose greatest success is its invisibility as an ideology. Columbus in the journal of his first voyage, for instance, quickly passes over the Bahamian landscape by describing it rather unimaginatively as "big," "very flat," and "green," while he "was attentive and labored to find out if there was any gold," and he "saw that some of them [Arawak Indians] wore a little piece hung in a hole that they have in their noses . . ." (Columbus 71). Columbus's factual report tends to represent the landscape and its inhabitants primarily as potential bearers of gold or as servants. Such a perception of the New World as a set of objects to serve the European newcomers has persisted for half a millennium, and has fitted comfortably with an exploitative relationship between humans and nature.

An analysis of the values a writer recognizes in a landscape might begin by looking at the roles which the narrator or point-of-view character plays in the landscape. Purely visual and journalistically objective descriptions of the landscape deny the truth of our nonstop bodily interaction with our environment. A human is not only a brain; our senses are continually influencing our intellectual processes. A self-reflexive stance in which the narrator admits his or her presence and participation in the landscape produces a very different narrative and suggests a closer understanding of the elements of the landscape.

Writers dealing with landscape tend to emphasize their sense of place and to create narratives that are so geographically rooted, that so link narrative and landscape, that the environment plays a role as important as the roles of the characters and narrator. Richard Poirier's discussion of the two environments of *Huckleberry Finn,* raft and shore, illustrates how thoroughly geographical place can determine the possible ideologies available to a character (Poirier 15–16, 193ff). Unlike much of American literature with its restless rootlessness, the work of landscape writers recognizes the geographical as well as the social context of actions as a major determiner of the significance of a narrative. We hear the defensive tone in their presentations of their own or their characters' commitment to place, as in Thoreau's "I have traveled a good deal in Concord," or in Jeffers's characterization of people like Cawdor as "people / Who are toad-stools of one place" (*Collected Poetry* 1: 448). My criticism has tried to focus on the ways in which these writers use place to establish meaning.

A final concern of practical ecocriticism might be to assess the limits of each writer's view, not necessarily in condemnation but with a recognition of the importance of "a blank spot on the map." For every text, as Bakhtin unfailingly tells us, is a dialogue open for further comments from other points of view. There is no conclusion.

NOTES

1. I've favored the term *landscape writing* in this essay because other, older terms such as *nature writing* carry connotations I'd like to avoid. Nature writers have traditionally been marginalized in literary studies as those who ignore humans (and hence probably ignore "the humanities") and deal instead with wild plants and creatures. Whereas in popular usage *nature* is "out there" somewhere, *landscape* is unavoidable; it's all around us and under our feet. The term *landscape,* I hope, suggests inevitable interaction and mutual influencing of humans and the nonhuman

world in ways the term *nature* doesn't. John Brinckerhoff Jackson's discussion of the etymology of the word *landscape* in his essay "The Word Itself" presents many of the connotations I'm hoping to convey (in *Discovering the Vernacular Landscape* [New Haven: Yale University Press, 1984] 1–8.)

2. For a vivid biological illustration of this idea, see Wendell Berry's discussion of the use of wild potato strains to rejuvenate blighted varieties among Andean farmers in Peru, recounted in an essay entitled "Margins," in *The Unsettling of America* (1977; Reprint, San Francisco: Sierra Club, 1986) 175–79.

3. It might fairly well be argued that our mainstream culture is in the midst of a paradigm shift akin to the sort Thomas Kuhn describes in *The Structure of Scientific Revolutions:*

> In these and other ways besides, normal science repeatedly goes astray. And when it does—when, that is, the profession can no longer evade anomalies that subvert the existing tradition of scientific practice—then begin the extraordinary investigations that lead the profession at last to a new set of commitments, a new basis for the practice of science. . . . [W]e shall deal repeatedly with the major turning points in scientific development associated with the names of Copernicus, Newton, Lavoisier, and Einstein. . . . Each of them necessitated the community's rejection of one time-honored scientific theory in favor of another incompatible with it. . . . And each transformed the scientific imagination in ways that we shall ultimately need to describe as a transformation of the world within which scientific work was done. ([Chicago: University of Chicago Press, 1970] 6).

4. I take the fact of an independent physical reality as undeniable, not purely a construction of language, although we certainly do create in our minds (and literature) a reality that parallels physical reality. These interior landscapes vary in their similarity to the exterior landscapes that initiate them.

For an interesting analysis of the points of conflict between poststructuralist thought and environmental thought, see chapter 6, "The Post-structuralist Attack on Humanism," and chapter 7, "Methods of Inquiry," of David Copland Morris's 1984 dissertation, "Literature and Environment: The Inhumanist Perspective and the Poetry of Robinson Jeffers," University of Washington.

5. Though we should remember that the idyll as Bakhtin discusses it descends from the Greek pastoral, which all would agree is a convention that constructs an artificial landscape, defined mainly in opposition to city or court life. In Bakhtin's discussion, it is principally the perspective rather than the content of idyllic life that is artificial.

6. Especially if we are ever to get away from what Paul Lauter calls "the Great River theory" of American literature, in which "the writing of men like Emerson, Thoreau, Hawthorne, Melville, James, Eliot, Hemingway, Faulkner, and Bellow constitute the mainstream" and "writers of color, most women writers, 'regional'

or 'ethnic' writers . . . might . . . be assimilated into the mainstream, though probably they would continue to serve as tributaries, interesting and often sparkling but, finally, less important" ("The Literatures of America," in *Redefining American Literary History*, ed. A. LaVonne Brown Ruoff and Jerry W. Ward Jr. [New York: MLA, 1990] 9). I agree with Lauter that what is considered mainstream is often what is endorsed by those holding power in a culture, not what is shared and felt by a majority of the heterogeneous population.

7. William Bartram, *Travels Through North and South Carolina, Georgia, East and West Florida, the Cherokee Country, the Extensive Territories of the Muscogulges, or Creek Confederacy, and the Country of the Chactaws* (Philadelphia: James and Johnson, 1791; reprint, as *Travels of William Bartram*, ed. Mark Van Doren, New York: Dover, 1955); John James Audubon, *Ornithological Biography* (Edinburgh, 1831–39).

WORKS CITED

Audubon, John James. *Ornithological Biography*. Edinburgh, 1831–39.

Bakhtin, M. M. *The Dialogic Imagination: Four Essays*. Ed. Michael Holquist. Trans. Caryl Emerson and Michael Holquist. Slavic Ser. 1. Austin: University of Texas Press, 1981.

———. *Rabelais and His World*. Trans. Hélène Iswolsky. Bloomington: Indiana University Press, 1984.

———. *Speech Genres and Other Late Essays*. Ed. Caryl Emerson and Michael Holquist. Trans. Vern W. McGee. Austin: University of Texas Press, 1986.

Bartram, William. *Travels Through North and South Carolina, Georgia, East and West Florida, the Cherokee Country, the Extensive Territories of the Muscogulges, or Creek Confederacy, and the Country of the Chactaws*. Philadelphia: James and Johnson, 1791. Reprint, as *Travels of William Bartram*, ed. Mark Van Doren, New York: Dover, 1955.

Basso, Keith H. " 'Stalking with Stories': Names, Places, and Moral Narratives among the Western Apaches." In *On Nature: Nature, Landscape, and Natural History*, ed. Daniel Halpern. San Francisco: North Point Press, 1987. 95–116.

Bell, Barbara Currier. "Humanity in Nature: Toward a Fresh Approach." *Environmental Ethics* 3 (1981): 245–57.

Berry, Wendell. *Home Economics: Fourteen Essays*. San Francisco: North Point Press, 1987.

———. *The Unsettling of America: Culture and Agriculture*. 1977. Reprint, San Francisco: Sierra Club, 1986.

Bredahl, A. Carl, Jr. *New Ground: Western American Narrative and the Literary Canon*. Chapel Hill: University of North Carolina Press, 1989.

Columbus, Christopher. *The* Diario *of Christopher Columbus's First Voyage to America, 1492–1493*. Abstracted by Fray Bartolomé de las Casas. Trans. Oliver Dunn and James E. Kelley Jr. Norman: University of Oklahoma Press, 1989.

Elliott, Emory, et al., eds., *Columbia Literary History of the United States*. New York: Columbia University Press, 1988.

Evernden, Neil. "Beyond Ecology: Self, Place, and the Pathetic Fallacy." *North American Review* 263.4 (1978): 16–20.

Fromm, Harold. "Aldo Leopold: Aesthetic 'Anthropocentrist.'" *ISLE: Interdisciplinary Studies in Literature and Environment* 1.1 (Spring 1993): 43–49.

Frye, Northrop. *Anatomy of Criticism: Four Essays*. Princeton, N.J.: Princeton University Press, 1957.

[Glotfelty], Cheryll Burgess. "Toward an Ecological Literary Criticism." Western Literature Association 24th Annual Meeting, Coeur d'Alene, Idaho, 13 October 1989.

Griffin, Susan. *Woman and Nature: The Roaring inside Her*. New York: Harper, 1978.

Hayles, N. Katherine. *Chaos Bound: Orderly Disorder in Contemporary Literature and Science*. Ithaca: Cornell University Press, 1990.

Hirschkop, Ken, and David Shepherd, eds. *Bakhtin and Cultural Theory*. Manchester, U.K.: Manchester University Press, 1989.

Jackson, John Brinckerhoff. *Discovering the Vernacular Landscape*. New Haven: Yale University Press, 1984.

Jeffers, Robinson. *The Collected Poetry of Robinson Jeffers*. Ed. Tim Hunt. 3 vols. to date. Stanford, Calif.: Stanford University Press, 1988–.

Jefferson, Thomas. *Notes on the State of Virginia*. London, 1785.

Kolodny, Annette. *The Lay of the Land: Metaphor as Experience and History in American Life and Letters*. Chapel Hill: University of North Carolina Press, 1975.

Kuhn, Thomas S. *The Structure of Scientific Revolutions*. 2d ed., enlarged. Chicago: University of Chicago Press, 1970.

Lakoff, George, and Mark Johnson. *Metaphors We Live By*. Chicago: University of Chicago Press, 1980.

Lauter, Paul. "The Literatures of America: A Comparative Discipline." In *Redefining American Literary History*, ed. A. LaVonne Brown Ruoff and Jerry W. Ward Jr. New York: MLA, 1990. 9–34.

Lopez, Barry. *Crossing Open Ground*. New York: Vintage-Random, 1989.

Love, Glen. "Revaluing Nature: Toward an Ecological Criticism." *Western American Literature* 25 (1990): 201–15.

Lyon, Thomas J., ed. *This Incomperable Lande: A Book of American Nature Writing*. Boston: Houghton Mifflin, 1989.

Maguire, James H. "The Canon and the 'Diminished Thing.'" *American Literature* 60 (1988): 645–52.

Meeker, Joseph W. *The Comedy of Survival: In Search of an Environmental Ethic.* 1974. Reprint, Los Angeles: Guild of Tutors, 1980.
Morris, David Copland. "Literature and Environment: The Inhumanist Perspective and the Poetry of Robinson Jeffers." Diss. University of Washington, 1984.
Morson, Gary Saul, ed. *Bakhtin: Essays and Dialogues on His Work.* Chicago: University of Chicago Press, 1986.
Parkman, Francis. *The Oregon Trail.* New York, 1849.
Poirier, Richard. *A World Elsewhere: The Place of Style in American Literature.* New York: Galaxy-Oxford University Press, 1966.
Sanders, Scott Russell. "Speaking a Word for Nature." *Michigan Quarterly Review* 26 (1987): 648–62.
Silko, Leslie Marmon. *Ceremony.* 1977. Reprint, New York: Viking Penguin, 1986.
———. *Storyteller.* New York: Arcade-Little, Brown, 1981.
Slater, Philip. *The Pursuit of Loneliness: American Culture at the Breaking Point.* Boston: Beacon, 1970.
Snyder, Gary. *The Practice of the Wild.* San Francisco: North Point Press, 1990.
Thoreau, Henry D. *The Maine Woods.* Ed. Joseph J. Moldenhauer. 1864. Reprint, Princeton, N.J.: Princeton University Press, 1972.
———. *Walden.* Ed. J. Lyndon Shanley. 1854. Reprint, Princeton, N.J.: Princeton University Press, 1971.
Tuan, Yi-Fu. *Topophilia: A Study of Environmental Perceptions, Attitudes, and Values.* 1974. Reprint, New York: Columbia University Press, 1990.
Uexküll, Jakob von. "A Stroll Through the Worlds of Animals and Men: A Picture Book of Invisible Worlds." In *Instinctive Behavior,* trans. and ed. Claire H. Schiller. 1934. Reprint, New York: International Universities Press, 1957. 5–80.
Weatherly, Joan. "Pastoral: An Ageless Form of Environmental Literature." In *Teaching Environmental Literature: Materials, Methods, Resources,* ed. Frederick O. Waage. New York: MLA, 1985. 73–76.
Wood, William. *New England's Prospect.* Ed. Alden T. Vaughan. The Commonwealth Series. 1634. Reprint, Amherst: University of Massachusetts Press, 1977.

RECOMMENDED READING

■ ■ ■

Thanks to several recent bibliographical recovery projects, newcomers to the field of ecological literary studies face a different challenge than did students ten years ago. A decade ago, a person interested in the connections between literature and environment scarcely knew how to locate a single book on this subject. Today, scholars entering this field may find themselves bedazzled by an embarrassment of riches. Where to begin?

In an effort to create a list of recommended books that does not too strongly reflect our own biases, we polled the 150 subscribers to the electronic-mail network of the Association for the Study of Literature and Environment (ASLE). We asked these electronically capable ecocritics what dozen titles they deemed essential reading for someone new to this field. Certain titles were repeated so often that something like a canon emerged. The fifteen most frequently recommended books share, as one recommender put it, "depth of vision, breadth of intellect, and eloquence of style." These books are listed below, with annotations.

To our surprise, however, in addition to the consensus selections, each responder seemed to have his or her personal favorite book, a book of utmost importance to the responder, but cited by no one else. Because of the vehemence of these recommendations, we decided to list those titles in a bibliography of "Also Recommended" books. Thus, the first fifteen titles below constitute the preeminent books in the field, while the subsequent forty-seven books have been strongly endorsed by at least one scholar. We would like to thank subscribers to the ASLE e-mail network for their help in compiling this bibliography.

TOP FIFTEEN CHOICES

Bate, Jonathan. *Romantic Ecology: Wordsworth and the Environmental Tradition.* New York: Routledge, 1991.

Discusses William Wordsworth as the first ecological poet, arguing that Wordsworth's politics were neither Left nor Right, but, rather, were "green." Contends that Wordsworth's ecological vision influenced later environmental writers and remains relevant today. Bate historicizes ecology and considers the implications of romanticism and pastoralism for the 1990s, also treating John Clare, John Ruskin, Samuel Coleridge, and William Hazlitt.

Buell, Lawrence. *The Environmental Imagination: Thoreau, Nature Writing, and the Formation of American Culture.* Cambridge: Harvard University Press, 1995.

An ambitious study of environmental perception and the place of nature in the history of Western thought, using Henry Thoreau as the reference point for an inquiry into the American environmental imagination, arguing that the environmental crisis has precipitated a crisis of the imagination and that we must find better ways of imaging nature and humanity's relation to it. Buell is theoretically engaging as he rethinks our assumptions about representation, reference, metaphor, characterization, personae, and canonicity. Examines literary nonfiction from St. John de Crèvecoeur and William Bartram to the present, including discussion of William Cullen Bryant, Susan Fenimore Cooper, Ralph Waldo Emerson, Charles Darwin, John Burroughs, John Muir, Mary Austin, Aldo Leopold, Rachel Carson, Annie Dillard, Edward Abbey, Wendell Berry, and Leslie Silko. A monumental work.

Cohen, Michael P. *The Pathless Way: John Muir and American Wilderness.* Madison: University of Wisconsin Press, 1984.

Traces John Muir's "spiritual journey" by following the evolution of Muir's thinking as expressed in his writing. Cohen poses fundamental philosophical and ethical questions directly to Muir, such as "What is the right relationship between Man and Nature, Civilization and Wilderness?," finding answers as Muir worked them out in writing. Makes connections between Muir's thought and the ideas animating the counterculture of the 1960s and '70s. An important early peregrination in ecological philosophy.

Ehrenfeld, David. *The Arrogance of Humanism.* New York: Oxford University Press, 1978.

A provocative book by a professor of biology, documenting the "failure of humanism" as "the dominant religion of our time" and as a guiding philosophy of life. Argues that the pervasive faith in reason and human power have led us into a mistaken belief in human omnipotence and a naive assumption that all problems are soluble by people. Wide-ranging literary references, from Lucretius to Charles Dickens to Isaac Asimov. Redemptively misanthropic.

Elder, John. *Imagining the Earth: Poetry and the Vision of Nature.* Urbana: University of Illinois Press, 1985.

A fine study of contemporary American nature poetry and its precursors, tracing a common pattern of "imaginative passage from estrangement to transformation and reintegration," thus enacting a circuit of healing that makes possible a more balanced culture. Detailed, thematic readings of William Wordsworth, T. S. Eliot, Robinson Jeffers, Gary Snyder, Wendell Berry, Robert Pack, Denise Levertov, William Everson, A. R. Ammons, Annie Dillard, and Peter Matthiessen; informed by Zen Buddhism and Alfred North Whitehead's philosophy of organism.

Evernden, Neil. *The Social Creation of Nature*. Baltimore: Johns Hopkins University Press, 1992.

Examines the changing concept of "nature" in Western understanding of the last five centuries, outlining the ways that the concept has been used to "naturalize" social policies of control and domination, with attention devoted to the medieval period, the Italian Renaissance (especially Leonardo da Vinci), the seventeenth-century empiricism, and contemporary environmental discourse. Employs the work of Roland Barthes, Edith Cobb, Richard Jeffries, Carl Jung, C. S. Lewis, Maurice Merleau-Ponty, and Richard Rorty. Concludes that "nature" must be liberated from its conceptual imprisonment so as to let "wildness" be.

Harrison, Robert Pogue. *Forests: The Shadow of Civilization*. Chicago: University of Chicago Press, 1992.

A history of forests in the cultural imagination of the West. Shows how powerful institutions such as religion, law, family, and city established themselves in opposition to the forest, an area that paradoxically has been seen as both profane and sacred, lawless and just, gloomy and enlightening. Argues that deforestation is the loss not merely of ecosystems but of cultural memory, myths and symbols. Treats a capacious selection of texts, including Gilgamesh, Greek mythology, Ovid, Aristotle, Zarathustra, medieval chivalric romances, Dante, Boccaccio, Ariosto, Shakespeare, Descartes, Le Roy, Rousseau, Conrad, Wordsworth, the brothers Grimm, Baudelaire, Leopardi, Constable, Thoreau, John Clare, Frank Lloyd Wright, and Andrea Zanzotto.

Kolodny, Annette. *The Lay of the Land: Metaphor as Experience and History in American Life and Letters*. Chapel Hill: University of North Carolina Press, 1975.

Surveys male-authored American literature from early exploration narratives to the present, discovering a pervasive metaphor of "land-as-woman," a linguistic construction that reveals much about our fantasies of gratification, and provides psychosexual clues to historic patterns of domination and exploitation of the land. Argues that if we are to change our treatment of the land, we must change the language that we use to describe it. Discusses documents of exploration and colonization as well as later works by Freneau, Crèvecoeur, Irving, Audubon, Cooper, Simms, Fitzgerald, and Faulkner. A pioneering ecofeminist study of American literature.

Marx, Leo. *The Machine in the Garden: Technology and the Pastoral Ideal in America*. New York: Oxford University Press, 1964.

A classic study of American pastoralism, demonstrating that in American "high" literary culture, the theme of withdrawal from society into an idealized landscape is transformed by the intrusion of a machine (representing technology, industrialization, and economic progress)—"noise clashing through harmony"—thereby creating a complex literary form that expresses fundamental tensions in the American experience. Analyzes Shakespeare's *Tempest* as "An American Fable," followed by readings of Robert Beverley, Crèvecoeur, Jefferson, Carlyle, Emerson, Thoreau, Hawthorne, Melville, Twain, Adams, and Fitzgerald.

Meeker, Joseph W. *The Comedy of Survival: Studies in Literary Ecology.* New York: Scribner's, 1972.

Regarding human beings as the earth's only "literary creatures," Meeker, who is trained in ethology and in comparative literature, asks, "From the unforgiving perspective of evolution and natural selection, does literature contribute more to our survival than it does to our extinction?" Defines *literary ecology* as "the study of biological themes and relationships which appear in literary works" and as "an attempt to discover what roles have been played by literature in the ecology of the human species." Examines comedy and tragedy, pastoral and the picaresque; provides innovative readings of Shakespeare's *Hamlet* and Dante's *Divine Comedy;* posits some tenets of "ecological esthetics." Bridges the gulf between art and science.

Merchant, Carolyn. *The Death of Nature: Women, Ecology, and the Scientific Revolution.* San Francisco: Harper and Row, 1980.

A historian of science, Merchant documents how the rise of a mechanistic world view during the European scientific revolution taught people to regard nature as inanimate, thus sanctioning unrestrained exploitation of the earth, replacing an earlier organic paradigm which had fostered ethical treatment of a living "Mother Earth." Critically reevaluates the ideas of Francis Bacon, William Harvey, René Descartes, Isaac Newton, G. W. Leibniz, Anne Conway, and Margaret Cavendish.

Nash, Roderick Frazier. *Wilderness and the American Mind.* 3d ed. New Haven: Yale University Press, 1982.

This book, which was cited most frequently in our poll, considers wilderness to be an idea created by civilization—"a perceived rather than an actual condition of the environment"—and studies America's changing attitudes toward wilderness, from the early pioneers' fear of an ungodly wilderness, through the romantics' enthusiasm for the sublimity of wilderness, to the contemporary concern for a vulnerable wilderness. Reviews political speeches and public law and touches upon authors such as Bradford, Mather, Winthrop, Tocqueville, Bartram, Freneau, Irving, Bryant, Cooper, Emerson, Thoreau, Parkman, Muir, Leopold, Faulkner, Stegner, Snyder, Abbey, and McPhee.

Oelschlaeger, Max. *The Idea of Wilderness: From Prehistory to the Age of Ecology.* New Haven: Yale University Press, 1991.

Influenced by Clarence Glacken's *Traces on the Rhodian Shore* and by Roderick Nash's *Wilderness and the American Mind,* philosopher Oelschlaeger undertakes an intellectual history of the idea of wilderness. Unique in its coverage of the Paleolithic and Neolithic periods and challenging in its revisionist readings of well-known writers such as Thoreau, Leopold, and Muir, this book articulates the philosophical positions embodied in literary texts, also analyzing the poetry of Robinson Jeffers and Gary Snyder and, finally, exploring the ecocentric philosophy of Deep Ecology and envisioning a "postmodern hierophany." Philosophers discussed include Bacon, Descartes, Heidegger, Kant, Nietzsche, Spinoza, Ouspensky, Prigogine, Schopenhauer, Whitehead, Naess, and Sessions.

Snyder, Gary. *The Practice of the Wild.* San Francisco: North Point Press, 1990.

Deeply learned in Zen Buddhism, Native American ways, and conservation biology, poet, traveler, and bioregionalist philosopher Gary Snyder here offers nine meditative essays on place, language, freedom, grace, wildness, work, mountains, forests, animals, and culture. These essays, punctuated by stories and poems, reconceptualize words such as *nature, wild, wilderness,* and *grammar,* nudging the reader to move beyond dualistic, linear thinking. Snyder asks us to imagine "a civilization that wildness can endure."

Worster, Donald. *Nature's Economy: A History of Ecological Ideas.* Cambridge: Cambridge University Press, 1977.

A history of the science of ecology, beginning in the eighteenth century (before the word *ecology* was coined), noting how a succession of metaphors rooted in particular times and places have shaped ecological research. Shows how scientific ideas grow out of specific cultural conditions. Key figures who participated in major formative moments in the development of modern ecology include Gilbert White, Carl Linnaeus, Henry David Thoreau, Charles Darwin, Frederic Clements, Aldo Leopold, and Eugene Odum.

ALSO RECOMMENDED

Alcorn, John. *The Nature Novel from Hardy to Lawrence.* New York: Columbia University Press, 1977.

Applewhite, James. *Seas and Inland Journeys: Landscape and Consciousness from Wordsworth to Roethke.* Athens: University of Georgia Press, 1985.

Bachelard, Gaston. *The Poetics of Space.* Trans. Maria Jolas. 1958. Reprint, Boston: Beacon, 1969.

Berman, Morris. *Coming to Our Senses: Body and Spirit in the Hidden History of the West.* New York: Simon and Schuster, 1989.

———. *The Reenchantment of the World.* Ithaca: Cornell University Press, 1981.

Berry, Wendell. *Standing By Words.* San Francisco: North Point Press, 1983.

———. *The Unsettling of America: Culture and Agriculture*. San Francisco: Sierra Club, 1977.

Brooks, Paul. *Speaking for Nature: How Literary Naturalists from Henry Thoreau to Rachel Carson Have Shaped America*. San Francisco: Sierra Club, 1980.

Clough, Wilson O. *The Necessary Earth: Nature and Solitude in American Literature*. Austin: University of Texas Press, 1964.

Devall, Bill, and George Sessions. *Deep Ecology: Living as if Nature Mattered*. Salt Lake City: Gibbs M. Smith, 1985.

Diamond, Irene, and Gloria Feman Orenstein, eds. *Reweaving the World: The Emergence of Ecofeminism*. San Francisco: Sierra Club, 1990.

Dixon, Melvin. *Ride Out the Wilderness: Geography and Identity in Afro-American Literature*. Urbana: University of Illinois Press, 1987.

Ekirch, Arthur A., Jr. *Man and Nature in America*. 1963. Reprint, Lincoln: University of Nebraska Press, 1973.

Elder, John, ed. *American Nature Writers*. New York: Scribner's, 1996.

Evernden, Neil. *The Natural Alien: Humankind and Environment*. Toronto: University of Toronto Press, 1985.

Foerster, Norman. *Nature in American Literature: Studies in the Modern View of Nature*. New York: Russell, 1923.

Fritzell, Peter A. *Nature Writing and America: Essays upon a Cultural Type*. Ames: Iowa State University Press, 1990.

Glacken, Clarence J. *Traces on the Rhodian Shore: Nature and Culture in Western Thought from Ancient Times to the End of the Eighteenth Century*. Berkeley: University of California Press, 1967.

Griffin, Susan. *Woman and Nature: The Roaring inside Her*. New York: Harper, 1978.

Halpern, Daniel, ed. *Antaeus* 57 (Autumn 1986). Reprint, as *On Nature*, San Francisco: North Point Press, 1987.

Huth, Hans. *Nature and the American: Three Centuries of Changing Attitudes*. Lincoln: University of Nebraska Press, 1957.

Hyde, Lewis. *The Gift: Imagination and the Erotic Life of Property*. New York: Vintage, 1979.

Killingsworth, M. Jimmie, and Jacqueline S. Palmer. *Ecospeak: Rhetoric and Environmental Politics in America*. Carbondale: Southern Illinois University Press, 1992.

Kroeber, Karl. *Ecological Literary Criticism: Romantic Imagining and the Biology of Mind*. New York: Columbia University Press, 1994.

Lawson-Peebles, Robert. *Landscape and Written Expression in Revolutionary America: The World Turned Upside Down*. Cambridge: Cambridge University Press, 1988.

Lyon, Thomas J., ed. *This Incomperable Lande: A Book of American Nature Writing*. Boston: Houghton Mifflin, 1989.

Miller, Perry. *Nature's Nation*. Cambridge: Harvard University Press, 1967.

Mitchell, Lee Clark. *Witnesses to a Vanishing America: The Nineteenth-Century Response*. Princeton: Princeton University Press, 1981.

Murphy, Patrick D. *Liturature, Nature, and Other: Ecofeminist Critiques*. Albany: SUNY Press, 1995.

Nash, Roderick Frazier. *The Rights of Nature: A History of Environmental Ethics*. Madison: University of Wisconsin Press, 1989.

Nicolson, Marjorie Hope. *Mountain Gloom and Mountain Glory: The Development of the Aesthetics of the Infinite*. Ithaca, N.Y.: Cornell University Press, 1959.

Norwood, Vera. *Made from This Earth: American Women and Nature*. Chapel Hill: University of North Carolina Press, 1993.

Norwood, Vera, and Janice Monk, eds. *The Desert Is No Lady: Southwestern Landscapes in Women's Writing and Art*. New Haven: Yale University Press, 1987.

O'Grady, John P. *Pilgrims to the Wild: Everett Ruess, Henry David Thoreau, John Muir, Clarence King, Mary Austin*. Salt Lake City: University of Utah Press, 1993.

Paul, Sherman. *For Love of the World: Essays on Nature Writers*. Iowa City: University of Iowa Press, 1992.

Regis, Pamela. *Describing Early America: Bartram, Jefferson, Crevecoeur and the Rhetoric of Natural History*. DeKalb: Northern Illinois University Press, 1992.

Ryden, Kent C. *Mapping the Invisible Landscape: Folklore, Writing, and the Sense of Place*. Iowa City: University of Iowa Press, 1993.

Schama, Simon. *Landscape and Memory*. New York: Knopf, 1995.

Shepard, Paul. *Man in the Landscape: A Historic View of the Esthetics of Nature*. New York: Ballantine, 1967.

Slovic, Scott. *Seeking Awareness in American Nature Writing: Henry Thoreau, Annie Dillard, Edward Abbey, Wendell Berry, Barry Lopez*. Salt Lake City: University of Utah Press, 1992.

Smith, Henry Nash. *Virgin Land: The American West as Symbol and Myth*. New York: Vintage, 1950.

Stegner, Wallace. *Where the Bluebird Sings to the Lemonade Springs: Living and Writing in the West*. New York: Random House, 1992.

Thacker, Robert. *The Great Prairie Fact and Literary Imagination*. Albuquerque: University of New Mexico Press, 1989.

Tichi, Cecelia. *New World, New Earth: Environmental Reform in American Literature from the Puritans through Whitman*. New Haven: Yale University Press, 1979.

Tuan, Yi-Fu. *Space and Place: The Perspective of Experience*. Minneapolis: University of Minnesota Press, 1977.

Turner, Frederick. *Spirit of Place: The Making of an American Literary Landscape*. San Francisco: Sierra Club, 1989.

Watts, Alan W. *Nature, Man and Woman*. 1958. Reprint, New York: Vintage, 1991.

PERIODICALS AND PROFESSIONAL ORGANIZATIONS

■ ■ ■

PERIODICALS

American Nature Writing Newsletter. Ed. Scott Slovic. English Department, University of Nevada, Reno, Nevada 89557-0031.

Amicus Journal. Ed. Francesca Lyman. Natural Resources Defense Council, Inc. 40 West 20th Street, New York, New York 10011.

Earth Ethics: Evolving Values for an Earth Community. Ed. Thomas S. Barrett and Sara Ebenreck. Center for Respect of Life and Environment, 2100 L Street, NW, Washington, D.C. 20037.

Ecologist. MIT Press Journals, 55 Hayward Street, Cambridge, Massachusetts 02142.

Environmental Ethics. Ed. Eugene Hargrove. Environmental Philosophy, Inc., Chestnut Hall, Suite 14, 1926 Chestnut Street, University of North Texas, Denton, Texas 76203-6496.

Environmental History Review. (Formerly *Environmental Review*.) Ed. Hal Rothman. Arlene J. McKenna, managing editor, Center for Technology Studies, New Jersey Institute of Technology, Newark, New Jersey 07102.

ISLE: Interdisciplinary Studies in Literature and Environment. Ed. Scott Slovic. English Department, University of Nevada, Reno, Nevada, 89557-0031.

North American Review. Ed. Robley Wilson. University of Northern Iowa, Cedar Falls, Iowa 50614-0516.

Orion: People and Nature. Ed. George K. Russell. Myrin Institute, Inc., 136 E. 64th Street, New York, New York 10021.

Terra Nova: Nature and Culture. Ed. David Rothenberg. Department of Social Science and Policy Studies, New Jersey Institute of Technology, University Heights, Newark, New Jersey 07102.

The Trumpeter. Ed. Alan R. Drengson. LightStar Press, P.O. Box 5853, Stn B, Victoria, B.C., Canada V8R 6S8.

Western American Literature. Ed. Thomas J. Lyon. English Department, Utah State University, Logan, Utah 84322-3200.

Wild Earth. Ed. John Davis and Dave Foreman. P.O. Box 492, Canton, New York 13617.

Writing Nature. Ed. J. Parker Huber, 35 Western Avenue, Brattleboro, Vermont 05301.

PROFESSIONAL ORGANIZATIONS

The Association for the Study of Literature and Environment (ASLE) publishes *The American Nature Writing Newsletter;* the journal *ISLE: Interdisciplinary Studies in Literature and Environment;* an annual, annotated bibliography of scholarship; an annual membership directory, which includes members' research areas; and the *Handbook on Graduate Study in Literature and Environment*. Among its activities, ASLE manages a syllabus exchange, coordinates a graduate mentoring program, organizes panels at national conferences, and holds biennial conferences and special symposia. The address of ASLE's Home Page on the World-Wide Web is http:// faraday.clas.virginia.edu/~djp2n /asle.html. In addition, ASLE maintains an e-mail discussion group on literature and environment. To subscribe, send a message to Majordomo@unr.edu. The text of the message should read, "subscribe asle." For membership information on ASLE, please write to Cheryll Glotfelty, English Department, University of Nevada, Reno, Nevada 89557-0031.

CONTRIBUTORS

■ ■ ■

PAULA GUNN ALLEN, MFA, Ph.D., Laguna Pueblo/Sioux (American Indian), is professor of English at the University of California, Los Angeles. She has published a novel, several collections of poetry, one of essays, and one of American Indian myths and legends concerning Native American goddesses. She has edited a collection of critical essays and course designs for teaching American Indian literature as well as three fiction anthologies devoted to the works of American Indian writers. Her most recent publications are *The Voice of the Turtle, American Indian Literature 1900–1970,* and *The Song of the Turtle, American Indian Literature 1974–1994,* a two-volume set published in 1994 and 1995, respectively.

MICHAEL BRANCH is assistant professor of English at the University of Nevada, Reno, where he also teaches environmental studies. He is vice president of the Association for the Study of Literature and Environment (ASLE), assistant editor of *ISLE: Interdisciplinary Studies in Literature and Environment,* and book review editor of *The American Nature Writing Newsletter.* He has published articles and reviews on ecocriticism and natural history writing, and is currently co-editing a collection of nature writing from Virginia's Blue Ridge Mountains and Shenandoah Valley.

ALISON BYERLY is assistant professor of English at Middlebury College, where she teaches an English/Environmental Studies course, "Visions of Nature." In addition to publishing articles in the field of Victorian fiction, she has contributed essays on Lewis Thomas and artist-naturalist Cathy Johnson to *American Nature Writers,* edited by John Elder (Scribners, 1996). She is currently completing a book manuscript entitled "Realism at Risk: Aesthetics and Representation in Nineteenth-Century Fiction."

SUEELLEN CAMPBELL grew up in Colorado and lives now in Fort Collins, where she teaches literary theory, environmental literature, twentieth-century fiction, and miscellaneous other subjects at Colorado State University. In recent years her main interests have been in nonfiction wilderness narrative and in the intersection of critical theory and nature writing. Her essays have appeared in *American Literary History, North Dakota Quarterly, Western American Literature,* and *Environmental Review.*

CYNTHIA DEITERING teaches writing and literature at Indiana University–Purdue University at Fort Wayne. Previously, she taught writing in the University of Michigan's English Composition Board. She completed her doctoral work at State University of New York at Binghamton. The essay in this book is a section of her dissertation, "The Postnatural Novel: American Revisions of Nature, Home, and the Body in Fiction since 1980."

NEIL EVERNDEN was born in Vancouver, Canada and was educated principally at the University of Alberta, where he did research in mammalian ecology and in ecological aesthetics. Since joining the Faculty of Environmental Studies at York University he has concentrated on "environmental thought" in general, and more specifically on the human apprehension of the wild "other" and on the social constitution of natural entities. He is the author of *The Natural Alien: Humankind and Environment* and of *The Social Creation of Nature.*

HAROLD FROMM is a visiting professor of English at the University of Illinois at Chicago. Besides a book on Bernard Shaw and his recent book, *Academic Capitalism and Literary Value* (University of Georgia Press, 1991), he has written on literature, critical theory, and ecology for the *Yale Review, Georgia Review, Massachusetts Review,* and *ISLE,* and his literary writings appear widely. In recent years he has been a regular contributor to the *Hudson Review.*

CHERYLL GLOTFELTY is associate professor of literature and the environment at the University of Nevada, Reno. She is co-founder and associate editor of *ISLE: Interdisciplinary Studies in Literature and Environment;* co-founder, past president, and co-president of the Association for the Study of Literature and Environment; and co-founder and associate editor of *The American Nature Writing Newsletter.* Her essays on ecocriticism and on women and nature have appeared in *ISLE, Western American Literature, Weber Studies,* and several international and interdisciplinary anthologies and reference works.

WILLIAM HOWARTH is professor of English at Princeton University, where he teaches courses in environmental literature and history. His books include *Nature in American Life, The John McPhee Reader, Thoreau in the Mountains, The Book of Concord, Traveling the Trans-Canada,* and *Mountaineering in the Sierra Nevada.*

ANNETTE KOLODNY's studies of the cultural mythology of the United States frontiers, *The Lay of the Land: Metaphor as Experience and History in American Life and Letters* (1975) and *The Land before Her: Fantasy and Experience of the American Frontiers, 1630–1860,* were among the earliest explorations of what has come to be known as ecocriticism, and they helped frame the developing inquiry of ecofeminism. Her many journal articles have concentrated on both the theory and practice of feminist literary criticism and the reconceptualization of literary history. Dr. Kolodny has served on the faculty at Yale, the University of New Hampshire, the University of British Columbia in Canada, the University of Maryland, and Rensselaer Polytechnic Institute; from 1988 to 1993, she was Dean of the Faculty of Humanities at the University of Arizona. She is currently working on a book that intertwines personal and scholarly essays titled "Dancing Through the Minefield."

URSULA K. LE GUIN writes both poetry and prose, and in various modes, including realistic fiction, science fiction, fantasy, young children's books, books for young adults, screenplays, essays, verbal texts for musicians, and voicetexts for performance or recording. By 1994 she had published more than eighty short stories (many collected in six volumes of stories), two collections of essays, ten books for children, several volumes of poetry, and sixteen novels. Among the honors her writing has received are a National Book Award, five Hugo and four Nebula awards, the Kafka Award, a Pushcart Prize, and the Howard Vursell Award of the American Academy of Arts and Letters.

GLEN A. LOVE is a professor of English at the University of Oregon. He is the author of *New Americans: The Westerner and the Modern Experience in the American Novel* (1982) and numerous articles and reviews on American literature and western American literature. He has also edited, with Oregon colleague Edwin R. Bingham, *Northwest Perspectives* (1979), a book of essays on the literature and culture of the Pacific Northwest. He has recently completed an anthology of short fiction from Oregon and a book on Sinclair Lewis's *Babbitt.* He has a long-standing interest in the pastoral and the relationship between literature and the environment.

THOMAS J. LYON has taught at Utah State University since 1964, and edited the journal *Western American Literature* since 1974. He has edited *A Literary History of the American West* (1987), *This Incomperable Lande: A Book of American Nature Writing* (1989), and *On Nature's Terms* (1992); and he co-edited with Terry Tempest Williams *Great and Peculiar Beauty: A Utah Centennial Reader* (1995).

CHRISTOPHER MANES is an author, attorney, and Ph.D. candidate in Medieval Literature at the University of Oregon. His book on the radical environmental movement, *Green Rage,* was nominated for a *Los Angeles Times* book award. His articles have appeared in *Los Angeles Magazine, Lears, Orion,* Houghton Mifflin's *Encyclopedia of the Environment, Environmental Ethics, Human Ecology Review, English Language Notes,* and numerous anthologies. He is an editorial adviser to *Wild Earth,* a journal of conservation biology. He has a B.A. in English from UCLA, an M.A. in English from the University of Wisconsin, and a law degree from the University of California at Berkeley.

DAVID MAZEL earned his bachelor's and master's degrees at Adams State College in Colorado and is now a doctoral candidate in English at Louisiana State University. His current research, motivated by his experiences in the water politics of the Southwest, examines the discursive interplay of gender, race, and the environment. He has written for a variety of academic and nonacademic publications, and his books include *Arizona Trails: One Hundred Hikes in Canyon and Sierra,* and two edited collections, *Pioneering Ascents* and *Mountaineering Women.*

MICHAEL MCDOWELL teaches composition, creative writing, and American literature at Portland Community College in Portland, Oregon. He completed a Ph.D. at the University of Oregon with a dissertation on environmental attitudes in American literature.

JOSEPH W. MEEKER is a human ecologist with a Ph.D. in comparative literature, and master's and postdoctoral studies in wildlife ecology and comparative animal and human behavior. He has been a ranger in the National Park Service. He produced and hosted the radio series "Minding the Earth," which aired on many National Public Radio stations during the 1980s. He has taught in several universities and is currently a Core Faculty member at the Graduate School of the Union Institute. He is also a research fellow with the "New Story" project at the California Institute of Integral Studies in San Francisco. His books include *Spheres of Life, The Comedy of Survival,* and *Minding the Earth.*

VERA NORWOOD is a professor of American Studies at the University of New Mexico. She and Janice Monk are the coeditors of *The Desert Is No Lady: Southwestern Landscapes in Women's Writing and Art* (1987). Her research on women's contributions to nature study, gardening and landscape architecture, nature art, and nature writing culminated in her recent book *Made from This Earth: American Women and Nature* (1993). Currently, she is working on a study of the contributions of amateur gardeners and garden clubs to wildflower preservation in North America.

DANA PHILLIPS received his Ph.D. at Duke University and has subsequently taught at the University of Pennsylvania and Princeton. In addition to his work on the representation of nature in literature and popular culture, he is interested in natural history and environmental issues, and also specializes in the study of American literature. He has published essays in *Raritan, Arizona Quarterly, Nineteenth-Century Literature,* and *American Literature.*

WILLIAM RUECKERT has taught English and American literature at Russell Sage College, Oberlin College, the University of Illinois at Champaign-Urbana, the University of Rochester, and the State University of New York at Geneseo, from which he retired in 1988. He is the author of a study of Glenway Wescott; three books on Kenneth Burke, most recently *Encounters with Kenneth Burke* (1994); and numerous essays on American criticism and culture. His long essay on Barry Lopez was included in *Earthly Words,* edited by John Cooley (1994).

SCOTT RUSSELL SANDERS is the author of more than a dozen books of fiction and nonfiction, including *Wilderness Plots, The Paradise of Bombs, Secrets of the Universe,* and *Staying Put.* His work has been supported by grants from the National Endowment for the Arts, the Lilly Endowment, and the Guggenheim Foundation. He is especially concerned with understanding our place in nature, the sources of violence, and the character of community. His latest book, *Writing from the Center* (1995), is about the effort to live a gathered life in a scattered world. He teaches at Indiana University, in Bloomington.

DON SCHEESE is an assistant professor of English at Gustavus Adolphus College in St. Peter, Minnesota, where he teaches courses on American literature, nature writing, and environmental history. He has published numerous articles on nature writing and is coeditor (with Sherman Paul) of "Nature Writers/Writing," a special issue of *North Dakota Quarterly* (Spring 1991). His book, *Nature Writing: The Pastoral Impulse in America* (1995), is part of Twayne's new series on literary genres.

LESLIE MARMON SILKO is a novelist from Laguna Pueblo, New Mexico. In 1981 she received a five-year MacArthur Fellowship. Her novels include *Laguna Woman* (1974), *Ceremony* (1977), *Storyteller* (1981), and *Almanac of the Dead* (1991).

SCOTT SLOVIC received his B.A. from Stanford University and completed his M.A. and Ph.D at Brown University. He spent 1986–87 as a Fulbright Research Scholar at the University of Bonn (Germany), and in 1993–94 served as a Visiting Fulbright Senior Lecturer at several universities in Tokyo, Japan. Slovic was a faculty member at Southwest Texas State University from 1990 to 1995 before leaving to join the English Department at the University of Nevada, Reno, in Fall 1995. His publications include *Seeking Awareness in American Nature Writing* (1992), *Being in the World* (1993), *Worldly Words* (1995), *The Culture of Nature* (1995), and a forthcoming volume on Barry Lopez for Twayne's United States Authors Series. Slovic is the founding president of the Association for the Study of Literature and Environment and the editor of *The American Nature Writing Newsletter.*

FREDERICK TURNER is Founders Professor of Arts and Humanities at the University of Texas at Dallas. Educated at Oxford University, he has taught at the University of California at Santa Barbara and at Kenyon College, where he was editor of the *Kenyon Review.* He is the author of over a dozen books of poetry, criticism, and fiction, including *The New World: An Epic Poem; Natural Classicism:*

Essays on Literature and Science; Genesis: An Epic Poem; Rebirth of Value: Meditations on Beauty, Ecology, Religion and Education; Tempest, Flute, and Oz: Essays on the Future; Beauty: The Value of Values; April Wind; and *The Culture of Hope.* He is a regular contributor to *Harper's Magazine* and has been interviewed on two PBS Smithsonian World documentaries.

LYNN WHITE JR. (1907–87), began his teaching career in 1933 at Princeton as an instructor in history. He later taught at Stanford (1937–43), served as president of Mills College (1943–58), and directed the UCLA Center for Medieval and Renaissance Studies (1964–70), finally ending his teaching career as a professor at UCLA in 1974. Best known for his studies of technology in medieval Europe, White won numerous medals, prizes, and awards throughout his lifetime and is regarded by many as the most widely read and influential medievalist of his generation. His most highly acclaimed publication is *Medieval Technology and Social Change* (1962), while his more recent work includes the collection of essays *Machina ex Deo: Essays in the Dynamism of Western Culture* (1968), subsequently reissued as *Dynamo and Virgin Reconsidered* (1978).

INDEX

■ ■ ■